"Growing up with Lindsey's sports commentating has given me many hours of pleasure and understanding about sports and the people who 'play the game.' His book mirrors a wonderful man and career."

—STEVE GARVEY

"Lindsey Nelson, on and off the mike, has been a world class raconteur for years. Now he finally has put those wonderful tales down in print in a captivating book that is as enlightening as it is enthralling—and more than worth the wait."

—W. C. HEINZ
Author of *The Professional*

"Lindsey Nelson, in his broadcasts, has always done a superb job of combining reportorial accuracy with a refreshingly entertaining delivery. I have read *Hello Everybody, I'm Lindsey Nelson*, and I'm happy to report that same reportorial accuracy and entertaining delivery. This book is not only a must for a sports library but a broadcasting library as well."

—JACK BRICKHOUSE
Former Vice-President and Broadcaster, Chicago Cubs

"Lindsey tells delightful stories of the great and near-great, without ever considering himself a member of that rank. Which, of course, he is."

—BLACKIE SHERROD
Columnist, *Dallas Morning News*

"The opportunity to work with Lindsey Nelson for twelve years on the Notre Dame TV network was the best thing that happened to me in my years of broadcasting. Reading *Hello Everybody, I'm Lindsey Nelson* has proved one thought I have always had. It's an honor to know the man. He is truly the voice of college football and the most experienced man in radio/TV sports."

—PAUL HORNUNG

"Lindsey's portrayal of the glory days of the New York Mets is in every detail the way it was. He presents a unique, detailed account of the Mets on the field
off the field—as far off the field as Paris, Casablanca, and the bull
Spain. This is not hearsay reporting. Lindsey was there, and so wa

—JERRY GROTE
Former New York M

"Is the title of this book needed? No longtime sports fan needs an intr
Lindsey Nelson. The smiling face is warm. The familiar voice is excitin
is true, on both counts, about the words he has written between th
His style as a sports journalist is pure vanilla. This book has added
cream to it."

—AL BROWNING
Sports Editor, *Knoxville News-Sentinel*

D0895378

Hello Everybody,
I'm Lindsey Nelson

LINDSEY NELSON

Hello Everybody, I'm Lindsey Nelson

BTB
BEECH TREE BOOKS
WILLIAM MORROW
New York

Copyright © 1985 by Lindsey Nelson

All rights reserved. No part of this book may be reproduced or utilized in any form or by any means, electronic or mechanical, including photocopying, recording or by any information storage and retrieval system, without permission in writing from the Publisher. Inquiries should be addressed to Permissions Department, Beech Tree Books, William Morrow and Company, Inc., 105 Madison Ave., New York, N.Y. 10016.

Library of Congress Cataloging-in-Publication Data

Nelson, Lindsey.
Hello everybody, I'm Lindsey Nelson.

1. Nelson, Lindsey. 2. Sportscasters—United States
—Biography. I. Title.
GV742.42.N45A36 1985 070.4'49796'0924 [B] 85–9070
ISBN 0–688–04186–8

Printed in the United States of America

First Edition

1 2 3 4 5 6 7 8 9 10

BOOK DESIGN BY ROBERT FREESE

BTB

The word "book" is said to derive from *boka*, or beech.
The beech tree has been the patron tree of writers since ancient times and
represents the flowering of literature and knowledge.

For Mickie and Sharon,
to Nancy and Andy

Foreword

A sportcaster meets some interesting people, especially if his life takes him on a side trip to a big war. I have visited with such as Casey Stengel, General George Patton, Red Grange, Ernie Pyle, Tom Seaver, Willie Mays, Bob Hope, the New York Mets, the Chicago Bears, the Fighting Irish of Notre Dame, and the 9th Infantry Division.

As a college student, I was an academic tutor for scholarship athletes, and a "spotter" for network radio announcers, particularly Bill Stern.

I spent five years in the U.S. Army, mostly in North Africa and Europe in World War II. My military career was unspectacular. I was not a combat soldier but I kept turning up in combat zones, where the military effort got precious little help from me. I got a few minor decorations and some trivial court-martials. I have announced the Army-Navy football game thirteen times. That is my most distinguished military achievement.

On television, I have announced twenty-one years of football games for CBS, twelve years for NBC, a game here and there for ABC, and a variety for Mutual and CBS radio. I did the Notre Dame games for thirteen seasons, remaining Protestant all the while. I have done some bowl games, including the Cotton Bowl Classic in Dallas twenty-five times.

I was the "voice" of the miraculous New York Mets for seventeen seasons, the San Francisco Giants for three, and NBC's *Major League Baseball* for five years. In between times, I did a heavyweight boxing championship, the world's bowling championship, the world's bobsled championship, some regular studio shows, some syndicated series, some movie scenes, and some recordings. Otherwise, it's been fairly slow. I did baseball in Japan, football in Canada, and something in Germany.

Unfortunately, a sportscaster can't make a living sitting on his front porch. So I traveled quite a lot, too. But I've been on some assignments when I probably should have been on the front porch—the day Notre Dame and Houston played in the ice storm at the Cotton Bowl, the night the lights went out on Alabama and Boston College in Foxboro, Massachusetts, the cold day when the San Diego Chargers played the Cincinnati Bengals and the windchill factor must have been fifty below.

Anyway, I traveled from Tennessee to Timbuktu, from Brownlow Creek to Bora-Bora, from Moscow to Rio, with a stop or two in Katmandu.

I have witnessed changes. In major league baseball we have seen the small, intimate ball parks of yesterday replaced by the spacious and sweeping arenas of steel that offer more seating comfort and acreage on which the athletes may perform. What we have lost, as a side effect, is the intimacy of the game.

When you sat in the seats of Ebbets Field, you were close enough to the ballplayers to see their facial expressions. They were very real individuals with whom the fan seemed to be closely acquainted. Then the rash of big new ball parks sprang up across the land, and we had a new product. Oh, it's exciting and interesting, but it is different. From a seat midway back in the second deck, the ballplayers look like the figures on the screens of video games. You can see them make their every move, but you aren't close enough to be able to discern how they themselves feel about it. The grimace is not visible. The smile, the human emotion is missing. And most of all, baseball is a *human* game.

For the ballplayers, it is different, too. In discussing the change, Stan Musial has said that in the old parks the players could see who was at the game. From the field, you were close enough to recognize the fans in the stands. You can't do that anymore. For a player, it must be like performing in a vacuum.

It is surely more functional to take your computer-punched ticket, ride the escalator up to your level, and seek out your contoured seat. But I am not sure that it is better than the days when you sat close enough to yell at your favorite or unfavorite ballplayer and be sure that he could hear you.

This narrative has been related with malice toward very few, if any. I have not attempted to settle any old scores, because offhand I couldn't think of any that were pending.

People who live in the world of sports lean mostly toward a life of fun, and that is the life I have attempted to convey. But the lives of us all are touched with sadness, failure, misfortune, and tragedy from time to time. I have made no attempt to ignore these. In various places throughout the book I talk about my friendship with Bob Prince. I'm saddened to say that just before this book went to press, Bob died. His loss will be greatly felt.

A broadcaster's opening "signature line" doesn't always come out as planned. Once I heard myself saying, "Hello Lindsey Nelson, I'm Everybody." And another time I said, "Hello Everybody, I'm CBS." Of course, Mr. Paley is CBS, and don't you ever forget it. Surely I was someone else, but for the moment I just couldn't remember who.

What I always mean to say, and usually do, is "Hello everybody, I'm Lindsey Nelson."

Acknowledgments

I am grateful to so many people whose contributions to the realization of this book have been greater, perhaps, than my own.

I want especially to acknowledge the great value I place on my longtime association with Ralph Mann. It was indeed fortunate for me that more than twenty years ago, I effected an arrangement with Ralph Mann of International Creative Management to represent me. Through all the years, the name of the firm has changed a few times, but never the arrangement. Ralph has been a good and trusted friend who has always been available with advice, encouragement, and assistance on matters personal and professional. Ralph represents some of the biggest names in the entertainment business, and certainly he has had no comparable financial gain from his arrangement with me. I have not been altogether kidding when I have told people that Ralph represents me "for batting practice." He is out there making million-dollar deals right and left, and then when he needs a little change of pace, he can handle me. In any case, it was a fortunate day for me when I met up with Ralph Mann.

One may discover, too, that one needs help and assistance in associated matters of business, investments, taxes, pension plans, and the like. And it was another fortunate day when I became associated with Harvey LaKind and International Artists and Athletes Management, Ltd. I have leaned heavily on Harvey. I have not been one of the big money makers in the trade, but he has helped me to retain a proper portion of that which I have earned.

I must recognize the ceaseless support of my friend Willie Morris, who persisted even during our moments at the bar at Bobby Van's popular pub in Bridgehampton, Long Island, in declaring that there was a book to be written, based on the experiences we were even then discussing and recounting.

My long friendship with W. C. (Bill) Heinz pushed me toward this project, as he was generous during his earlier years as a developing author in sharing some of his convictions about the craft of writing, convictions that led him to the creation of some of the purest prose that I have ever read.

There was encouragement from friends such as Roy Wilder, Jr., Jack Whitaker, Paul Hornung, Jim Silman, Larry Cavolina, Ric LaCivita, Scott Hunter, and a great many more. And I am particularly grateful for the support and friendship of Perry Smith for more than thirty years.

Most of all, I am grateful to Jane Meara, who skillfully edited the final product but who, more than that, conceived the idea, convinced me of its worth, and saw it through to a conclusion. In more than two years of work on this book, when I have been stalled or lost, she has hurriedly come to my aid with guidance, encouragement, suggestions, and a smile.

And I am grateful for the help of copy editor Amy Edelman.

Although I have made my living largely by the spoken word, I was attracted to the written word. I wanted to write a book, and not just have my ideas expressed by a collaborating professional colleague.

For better or worse, I wrote this book—every word of it.

Contents

Foreword 7

Acknowledgments 11

1. Ninety Seconds in Stuttgart 15
2. Discovering Sports 23
3. Meeting the Major 37
4. Into Announcing 49
5. Rolling to the Rose Bowl 59
6. You're in the Army Now 71
7. The Way to War 79
8. Old Blood 'n' Guts 85
9. Crossing Paths with Ernie Pyle 93
10. Those Who Compose 107
11. Back Home Again 121
12. My Break into Broadcasting 135
13. Now the Networks 145
14. Me to NBC 163
15. College Football 179
16. Galloping Ghost of the Illini 217
17. Baseball in the Big Apple 229

18. Sports on Television 243
19. Meet the Mets 263
20. Fascinating Football 285
21. The Rocky Road to Glory 307
22. In the Booth 327
23. "Ball One, Strike One, First and Ten" 339
24. Shake Down the Thunder 355
25. Menorca in the Mediterranean 361
26. Mets Win Again 373
27. End of My Life with the Mets 379
28. Open Your Golden Gate 387
29. Commuting to Japan 399
30. Back in the Classroom 409
31. And the Beat Goes On 415
Index 423

CHAPTER 1

Ninety Seconds in Stuttgart

I was certainly in strange circumstances. It is rare for an American sportscaster to find himself just outside Stuttgart, West Germany, waiting for a cue, or waiting for a bus, or waiting for anything.

I realized that this had once been a military barracks of the German army. The day was Sunday, and on Saturday night I had gone for dinner with a half-dozen guys to a crowded restaurant in town. There was singing and loud talk and laughter and beer drinking.

At the hotel, I had wanted to exchange some American money for German marks. The hotel clerk said that the cashier was not on duty and he could not make the exchange. "After all," he said arrogantly, "who wants American money?"

Well, I thought, there was a time when the whole world did. And I thought that American money had done a lot to establish the flourishing economy that West Germany now enjoyed. And I thought that if circumstances were a bit different I might want to punch that particular arrogant West German in his puffy nose. But I didn't. Because I realized that while my army had beaten his army soundly in two big wars, back to back, in an individual rematch I was likely to lose, and I do not favor losing.

This was now a recreation hall and part of VII Corps Headquarters, United States Army in Europe. And I was waiting for a cue to start a telecast that would be carried back to the United States, live by satellite.

This had nothing to do with the army or with war. It had to do with sports—the pregame show for the Super Bowl, the national ritual played that year of 1980 at the Rose Bowl in Pasadena, California, between the Pittsburgh Steelers and the Los Angeles Rams.

As I waited, I vaguely wondered how many times I had been at VII Corps Headquarters, waiting for one thing or another. During World War II, VII Corps had been one of the most efficient and spectacular units of General Omar Bradley's ground forces. The commander had been General J. Lawton Collins—"Lightning Joe," they called him. I had been in the 9th Infantry Division, and much of the time we were part of that Corps. Particularly memorable were those days in the hedgerows of Normandy when the 9th Division, as a part of VII Corps, had cut the peninsula and sealed off the city and port of Cherbourg. When General Bradley wrote his autobiography he made no secret of his admiration for the accomplishments of this particular Corps.

But I was there now for something else. When the cue came along, at any second now, I would be seen and heard via earth-circling satellite back at CBS's Television City in Los Angeles, and then in millions of homes around the world.

I had been sent by CBS to the armed forces base and to Kelley Barracks in Stuttgart to talk to some of the people stationed there and to prove to the rest of the world that interest in this sports event extended all the way to Europe. CBS had apparently figured that it would not take me very long to make the point. They had allotted me ninety seconds.

As a baseball and football announcer, I am a fellow who is accustomed to a little more than ninety seconds a shot. I usually work in blocks of about three hours. There are advantages to that. If you happen to get yourself into an embarrassing situation through some misinformation or misstatement, you have time to work your way quietly out. In a ninety-second insert, you can't afford a fluff or a cough. If you clear your throat, you've blown your show. Even the "Thanks, Brent" and "Now back to Brent" time would be charged to my ninety seconds. Brent Musburger was back in Los Angeles, tying these far-flung segments together.

And there was another thing that got my attention. We were having communications problems. In the television business, that's not unusual. But having communications problems at Shea Stadium in New York is one thing. You can always pick up the commercial phone and call the control room in Manhatten. But if you're in Stuttgart, well, you're out of touch is what you are. And picking up the phone to anywhere is not easy.

We had a mixed crew that we might have picked up at the United Nations but didn't. Our producer was an American who presently resided in London and sometimes sounded British. Our director was from Manhatten and spoke strictly American. We had two French cameramen who spoke no English at all and could not communicate with the director. And we had a switcher who had been in an automobile accident and presumably lay injured out there on the shoulder of the autobahn somewhere. We didn't really know. All we knew for sure was that he wasn't in the truck. To me it seemed just as well. I had tried to get into the truck and I don't think there was room for the switcher, dead or alive. There surely wasn't room for me.

The recreation hall was packed with servicemen and -women, hoping for the chance to be seen and heard live on television by their friends and neighbors back home. Because of the time difference between Los Angeles and Stuttgart, it was now approaching midnight. I think that some of my people had been drinking German beer—for hours. I wasn't sure that I'd be able to hear the cue when it came. There is something about German beer that makes its consumers talk loud. And, too, our director had casually advised me that so far we hadn't had any real direct communication with the control room in Television City. The producer was trying to get through on the commercial circuit. I somehow conjured up a vision of him standing at the phone booth down on the corner putting German coins into the pay phone.

Then I heard our director say, "One minute!" Okay, somehow, some way we were going to get this baby rolling in about sixty seconds, although the monitor, the little TV set in front of me, was still dark.

Then suddenly I heard a familiar voice. Through the little white button stuck in my ear came the voice of CBS's Sid Kaufman all the way from L.A., saying calmly, "Okay, Lins, the jacket looks just fine, stand by for Brent in thirty seconds." And then I heard Brent Musburger saying something about "Lindsey Nelson is at VII Corps

Headquarters in Stuttgart." And on the little monitor Brent and I were side by side in a split-screen effect. And we were on.

I talked to six servicepeople and then drowned in a sea of noise and soldiers as I threw it back to Brent. We had taken ninety seconds. And we had orchestrated my disappearance into the crowd and the noises at the finish. My work was done.

We went outside into the dark German night to get a breath of air. Actually, I had been out there a half-dozen times in the past hour. I kept slipping out the side door, walking out into the snow for a little ways, and rehearsing my opening lines aloud. I do not like for my opening line to be a surprise, especially to me. Now, we stood around and congratulated each other in the manner of television performers everywhere. Los Angeles had been very pleased, somebody said. Why wouldn't they be pleased? What could they complain about? We had done our ninety seconds without a bobble. The eighty thousand dollars the network had invested in that little insert was spent, for better or for worse. And now we went over to watch the live telecast of the football game.

The Pittsburgh Steelers won.

As I sat there that night watching that international football telecast, it occurred to me that all of this—Stuttgart, the Super Bowl, VII Corps, and television—was somewhat removed from Tennessee, where I had begun this busy life.

I got started in Pulaski, Tennessee. Maybe you've heard the country music song, sometimes presented on the Grand Ole Opry, that goes, "Giles County, Pulaski Post Office, in the state of Tennessee." Well, for better or worse, that's me.

Actually, I wasn't born right in Pulaski. That's the county seat where the courthouse is located. So that's where my birth records are, I think.

I was really born in Campbellsville, which is not close enough to be considered a suburb of Pulaski. It's out there in the county. We used to say that Campbellsville had two streets—High Street and Low Street. And you must admit that that is sound municipal planning. You weren't likely to take a wrong turn or lose your way or get hung up in the rush-hour traffic. When I was small, as I recall it, there were several stores, a blacksmith's shop, and a bank.

Actually, I wasn't born right in Campbellsville, either. My birthplace was a cabin on the side of a rather steep hill in the community of Brownlow Creek. The most prominent terrain feature was the creek. Though you wouldn't be likely to drown in it; you wouldn't get too damp if you lay down in it.

I never met Brownlow. Maybe he had gone by the time I came along. My paternal grandfather owned a little rocky acreage up there, which is where my parents were living in that low-rent cabin.

Abraham Lincoln got a lot of mileage, and some votes, out of having inherited the human characteristics of sturdiness and simple honesty, presumably from having been born in a log cabin. Alas, my cabin was not log. And it was neither sturdy nor particularly honest.

I remember only a very few things about life in Brownlow Creek. I recall stumbling around out there in the tobacco patch with the farmhands who were working beneath the scorching summer sun. I was the water boy.

And I remember the cow dung. I was about six years old. My family had moved, but I was back for a visit. I have always remembered the cow dung from that one summer's afternoon. You see, we were transporting this truckload of cattle from the barn to the railway siding. They were packed in there pretty tightly in the back of that truck. And they were not accustomed to riding. All that bouncing around and jostling up against each other apparently made them nervous. It wasn't long before the bed of that truck was filled to a depth of several inches with fresh, steamy cow dung. That was all right. We farmers could handle that.

But then came time for us to back the truck up to the siding to unload the cattle. I was dressed that day in a brand-new set of coveralls, a one-piece outfit of which I was extremely proud. I had been advised by my elders to stand well out of the way during the unloading process, and I had chosen a position beside the cab of the truck at the far end of the truck bed. My location was faulty.

When the cows would make the transition from the truck to the lower platform, they would scramble to keep their balance. They would scrape their hooves deep into that cow dung. And when they moved, they kicked it backward in great quantities. When the first cow made her move, I was covered from head to foot with fresh cow dung. It was in my hair, and my eyes, and all over my new coveralls. That incident did a lot to diminish my interest in life on the farm and was contributory to my inquiry about other paths of endeavor. Whatever else I have done occurred partially, at least, because of that losing battle with the cow dung. That's the way life is, I guess—win some, lose some. I was learning something every day.

When I was about four, my parents moved the family to Columbia, Tennessee, a small town about forty miles south of Nashville. And that would be my home until I went away to college.

Much of our sports information came from the sports pages of the Nashville newspapers that arrived by train from the capital city. But one of the biggest days in our family life was the day that Daddy came home to announce that he had purchased a radio. We had seen some radios. There were a few in town, not many. Sometimes you had to put on headphones to hear. This cut down on the mass audience but increased the feeling of self-importance for the owner, who had the headphones. He listened and then was our sole source of information. He was the fount from which all knowledge flowed. We liked it better with the radio spreading the information all around the room.

The radio itself was an Arbiphone. I haven't run into a lot of people since then who confess to having had Arbiphones, so I guess maybe Atwater Kent was a bigger seller, and perhaps RCA and Philco. The bulk of the set consisted of a wooden chest about a foot deep and about three feet long. There were three dials with graduated markings, and in order to tune in a particular station you had to have all three dials at a particular spot. Since there were no published listings available anywhere, we were advised to keep a pencil and paper near the set. When you spun those dials around, if you heard a particular station you would write down the position of the dials. That's how you determined how and where you might hear something. For some reason, I seemed to get Denver a lot. It was not an altogether reliable system. But it was all we had.

The speaker itself was about two feet high and was shaped like a large question mark. It sat atop the chest with the dials. There was a volume control and a lot of squealing sounds.

The radio and the speaker had been delivered in a large cardboard box. The movers had been careful in removing the set and its carton had remained undamaged. To me, this became an important part of our new life. I discovered that I could conceal my small body inside that cardboard box, and I could close the top so that I was completely hidden. And then I punched several holes in the box to provide air and to allow my voice to be heard as though from the radio. I would climb into the box and impersonate the announcers on the real radio.

"Hello everybody," I would say, "this is Lindsey Nelson." Sometimes, if he was trying to listen to something on the set, Daddy would say, "Shut up and get out of the box." Neither of us suspected that I was beginning a career, and that to me the most important part of our first radio would be the box it came in. I suppose I was fortunate that this story was not generally known at the time I was broadcasting for the losing Mets in New York. Some of those disappointed, dissatisfied, and dejected fans would doubtless have suggested in the strongest Brooklynese that I "get back inna box!"

The realization of the very existence of radio had a tremendous impression on me. I remember the night we gathered in the living room of our home to listen to Graham McNamee's broadcast of the 1927 heavyweight championship fight between Jack Dempsey and Gene Tunney at Soldier Field in Chicago. We had read all about the buildup. We knew that this was a rematch, and that Tunney had won a decision in Philadelphia the year before. And we knew that millions of dollars had been wagered on the outcome. A million dollars was an indefinable sum of money, far beyond our comprehension. It was surely a lot more than any of us would ever see. We knew that tickets to the fight were impossible to obtain and that the police were posted to keep drifters without tickets from coming to the vicinity of Soldier Field down near the lakefront in Chicago. And we were pulling for Jack Dempsey. We had read that Tunney had studied Shakespeare and we knew that no Shakespearean scholar could beat our man. Of course, we were wrong there.

In describing his position, I remember Graham McNamee saying he was so close to the ring that he could reach out and touch the canvas with his hand.

"Golly," I said, "can you imagine having a seat that close!"

I spent a lot of time in front of that radio. And on Saturday afternoons, I loved the football broadcasts. We would hear Graham McNamee and Ted Husing doing the big games from up East. We didn't know much about Yale and Harvard and Army, but we heard their football games. We heard a lot of the Columbia University games, and I didn't understand then that it was mostly because Columbia played its home games at Baker Field in New York City, and broadcasts from there did not require the network to go to the expense of traveling a crew.

Some of those inflections inflicted on us by the announcers were as strange to me as my southern accent would have been to them.

Speaking of a rules infraction, they would inform us that "Yale has been 'peen-a-lized.' " I didn't understand that long *e.* But I listened.

The biggest broadcasts of the year were those of the World Series. The whole town took on a sort of carnival atmosphere. All the games were afternoon games. There was no problem with time zones—all of major league baseball was played in only two time zones, the Eastern and the Central. There were reports of teams taking a "western trip." That meant they were going to Cincinnati, Chicago, and St. Louis.

Stores around our town would keep a running score-by-innings on the show window. White liquid chalk was used to mark the score on the glass.

It was the only time of the year at school that we were permitted to go into the auditorium during recess or a non–class period to listen to the World Series. One year, I had an afternoon history class in a room that was near the auditorium. Since this was before the days of air conditioning and since it was still quite warm in Tennessee at World Series time, all windows were wide open. I discovered that by concentrating and listening intently, I could hear the World Series broadcast as I sat in history class. One day our teacher, who was not a big sports fan, was deep into an emotional dissertation about Julius Caesar. I was deep into hearing a description of Lou Gehrig who had just doubled to the right-field corner. Discerning my inattention, the teacher, with reference to the deeds of the mighty Caesar, asked, "Now, Lindsey, who was that?" I was so deep into my baseball trance that I blurted out, "Gehrig—doubled to right."

CHAPTER 2

Discovering Sports

I had an older brother, James, and an older sister, Mary Sue, but the central figure in our household was our mother. I was not really that close to my father, simply because I did not see him that much. He worked hard at the task of supporting his family, and he worked at the trade of a "traveling man." He sold monuments. At least, that was what I used to say he did when people would ask. When they asked him, he would say truthfully that he sold tombstones. I somehow thought "monuments" was a little more dignified. In any case, I was strong in my moral support of that project because my daily bread came from the sale of those rocks. (Later I would discover another father who made his living working with monuments—as a stonecutter, actually. His son was named Thomas Wolfe.)

In the hot southern summertime, Daddy would usually take each of us children on the road with him for a week. It was a sort of a contribution to general continuing education. There was careful prior instruction in avoiding items on the restaurant menu with big numbers beside them. There was also some geographical exploration, and perhaps some practice in driving the automobile. We never heard of the term "driver education."

But we were seeing the world. And I discovered that I had an early attraction to the faraway places with the strange-sounding names. We went to Decatur and Russellville, Alabama. We went to Clarksville and Murfreesboro, Tennessee. And once we went all the way to Hopkinsville, Kentucky.

It was there, in those long hot hours spent waiting in the car, that I pursued what was becoming an intense interest. I read *Baseball Magazine, The Sporting News,* and all the sports pages until I could almost repeat them by rote. At one extended stop, I committed the long poem "Casey at the Bat" to faultless memory. I have repeated it since then at sports gatherings in large and sometimes flamboyant ballrooms from the Waldorf-Astoria in New York to the Fontainebleau in Miami to the Fairmont in San Francisco. Sometimes as I am getting ready to deliver this baseball standard I reflect that I learned it while my dad was listening to some son's mother tell him about the dying days of her firstborn.

Once sprung from the dreary confines of those surroundings, my dad was inclined to drink quite a lot. I don't blame him. I wouldn't have lasted twenty minutes at that business. He was extremely sensitive, which made him successful at his trade but also left him open to all wounds that the touch of sorrow brings.

But while Dad was out there doing his Willy Loman with the survivors, my mother was keeping our household together. Different families have different customs, of course, and for some reason we never called her "Mom." We certainly did not call her "Mommy." To us, she was "Mother," with an attitude of respect and fear akin to that in which we supposed Queen Elizabeth was held. There was no minority opinion in our house. It was an absolute monarchy. You could plead your case, but when the decision came down from Mother, that was just about it.

She did find time to take a strong interest in the activities of all her children. My older brother, whom we called "James" and never "Jim," was into all the sports. He played football, baseball, and basketball, and I was generally hanging around him soaking up all the knowledge of these things that I could.

I not only was the youngest of the three children in the family, I also showed early signs of being the runt. I didn't grow very much. But I watched a lot, listened intently, and showed an early inclination to offer a spoken opinion, whether invited or not.

Mother had to operate the house on a fixed and somewhat austere budget. And I suppose it was fortunate that she was an accomplished seamstress. She used that talent to supplement the family coffers. We didn't say, "Mother is a seamstress." In the vernacular of the day, we said, "She takes in sewing." And when she took in sewing, she made a few extra bucks. When I was in the very first grade of my grammar school she decided to spend a few of those hard-earned bucks by enrolling me for special instruction in what was known as "Expression."

Our school did not take an announced interest in public speaking. But there was a teacher available who specialized in this field. For a dollar or two, students whose parents thought they could benefit from special instruction in public speaking could be enrolled.

I was doing all right in reading and writing and arithmetic, but I really warmed up to this "Expression." I jumped immediately in there to learn whatever I could about proper posture on the dais, emphatic delivery, proper breathing, pregnant pauses (although heaven knows we never called them that), and speechmaking in general. I was seven years old and sailing.

Very shortly I was on the public circuit. I had developed a humorous routine or two that lasted for ten or fifteen minutes, and I could reel them off without hesitation. That got me nonpaying engagements at a number of county schools and at the Kiwanis, the Lions, and the Rotary. I was a program filler. My standard uniform was a blouse that buttoned on the wrong side because it had been handmade by my left-handed mother, knickerbockers that buckled above the knee, long stockings held up by elastic garters that sometimes choked off the circulation, and shoes that lasted a long time after they were worn out. I learned the early art of folding the cardboard to fit into the sole of the shoe. This covered the hole in the shoe most effectively in dry weather.

One night I made a scheduled appearance in the white waiting room of the L&N Railway depot. (This was as opposed to the "Negro waiting room." There were carefully marked distinctions.)

The principal speaker was the pastor of the First Methodist Church. I was the warm-up speaker. At age seven, I delivered the fluff to set up the minister. He followed with the message. This particular night he departed from the scriptures and spoke of "teamwork." He pointed out that teamwork was required for success in any field. He said, with some enthusiasm, that even the great Red Grange of Illinois could not succeed without those teammates blocking for him.

I was interested. I had never heard of Red Grange and I didn't know what he did. So I asked. And I was told that he was a great ball-carrying football player at the University of Illinois, maybe the greatest runner who had ever played. I decided to remember that. Funny name—"Red Grange"!

My brother and most of the boys on my block worked at one time or another as carriers for *The Daily Herald,* which was our local daily newspaper. One did not rise rapidly in the newspaper trade. You started probably as a substitute carrier, then progressed to regular carrier on a route that served the lowest-income sections of town, where collections were apt to be slow if not impossible. Resident dangers were the inordinate number of vicious dogs, none of which was ever on a leash, and gangs of slightly older boys who thought that harassment and possible physical dismemberment of the carrier would break up the boredom of their day. As time wore on, more attractive routes became available. The cream of the crop was West Seventh Street, where on Christmas morning the clients might throw in a tip of as much as fifty cents. That was real money, considering that the weekly pay was probably a dollar and a half.

The Daily Herald did not employ any sportswriters as such, but they had people who doubled at reporting sports and handling other jobs. I took careful note of the manner in which this worked. It seemed to me that the editor was pleased to get accounts of the sporting events from any source. And I was also aware that at the local high school they had informal "class" basketball teams. The freshmen would play the sophomores. And it was one of these games that I decided to report. It was virgin territory. None of these games had ever been covered. Often when the game had been concluded, they were not real sure who had won. I thought I would be able to handle this assignment without too much pressure. I was eleven years old at the time and had not yet mastered the typewriter. Besides that, I did not have a typewriter or access to one. So I folded back a sheet of my lined tablet paper, and with a lead pencil I carefully inscribed, "By Lindsey Nelson." Then I wrote about the basketball game, and I dropped my piece off on the editor's desk, choosing a time when he was not present. I felt certain that he did not know me by name. And I did not want him to see me and get the impression that he had a midget sportswriter. It worked just as I had hoped. My piece made the paper, and I had a by-line at age eleven. And I soon began to cover the games at Columbia Military Academy, where the football, basketball, and baseball coach was named Red Sanders.

As the grammer-school years passed, I was less in demand as a speaker around the county. I had reached the awkward age, and I wasn't "cute" anymore. And if I wasn't small and cute, my appearances weren't nearly as effective.

But I was turning more toward sportswriting, anyway. I followed all sports avidly. I particularly followed the Vanderbilt Commodores in nearby Nashville. And I followed the baseball fortunes of the Nashville Vols in the Southern League. It seemed to me that new worlds were opening up all around me.

When I was in the fifth grade of the Andrews Elementary School, I sat in the rear of the room with a friend named Albert Fisher Oakes. He was an athlete. He played all the sports. And he knew a lot of things that I didn't know. He taught me, for instance, that "Vanderbilt" did not have a *u* in it.

He also told me something more valuable. He said that at the high-school football games, which were played in Pillow Park on the banks of the Duck River, the ticket takers retired at halftime and went to watch the game themselves. If we waited until halftime, he said, we could get in free. That was about what we could afford. So I went with Albert Fisher Oakes to see my first football game. It was to become a habit. During my lifetime I have seen a lot of football games.

We played pickup games of all sorts. Sometimes we would start playing baseball at eight o'clock in the morning and we would play right through until dark, maybe two or three games. We would try to impersonate our favorites among the Vols, or maybe a major league star we had never seen. I remember one day when I took over at first base and screamed, "Looka me, I'm Lou Gehrig." I really wasn't anything like Lou Gehrig. In fact, nobody had ever told me that he was left-handed. I read he was from "Columbia" and thought he was one of us.

But I did begin to study the game. I read everything I could read about baseball. I listened to my elders when they talked about the game. The Shamrock billiard parlor was a center for baseball discussions because the baseball dressing room was upstairs. Youngsters under sixteen were not permitted to avail themselves of the poolroom on the theory that there was the possibility of their becoming tainted with the habit of gambling. But since I was handy for errand running of all sorts, I was not expelled. And I listened to all the talk about baseball plus occasional talk of sex. I learned about the hit-and-run and the squeeze. I listened to pitchers talking about how to throw an "out," an "in," and a "drop." On the field, I also learned that I couldn't hit any of these. If I did make contact, I drove it not very far with not much power. But I could handle the glove. I played first base and I learned the hard way how to handle the short hop. It was harder for me to handle the half-hop. For my continuing efforts, I got hit by the ball in the mouth, on the nose, in the eye. But I had to keep trying and I had to master the art of fielding. If I didn't, I just couldn't play, because I surely wasn't learning anything about hitting the curve ball. I did not know then what I know now—that the curve ball has sent more budding ballplayers into what Casey Stengel called "some other line of work" than any other single aspect of the game.

But I persisted and I made the American Legion team. I suppose that the highlight of my career as our first baseman came the day the coach and manager, Morgan Farris, called my home to say he would not be able to make our game that day against Franklin, Tennessee, scheduled that afternoon at Pillow Park. He said he was appointing me to take his place. I was fifteen years old, but I would manage the team that afternoon. That would make me a playing manager, and in American Legion baseball that is unusual. In later years, when I would do some work to promote American Legion baseball nationally, I would mention occasionally that I had been a playing manager. The national authorities were aghast. The idea of a fifteen-year-old running a team in their competition was not exactly the kind of adult supervision they advertised.

I can vividly recall the instructions that the coach gave me over the phone that morning. He gave me the batting order for the first six men. Then, in deference to my elevated management position, I thought, he said, "You can bat yourself, the catcher, and the pitcher in any order you want."

Well, the painful fact is that he had frequently batted me ninth. It was that continuing problem I had with the breaking pitch. The catcher and the pitcher were both better hitters than I. But they weren't the manager. That day I batted seventh.

I did learn some other things. I became an accomplished bunter. I could make contact, no matter what the pitch. Our coach chose his strategy accordingly. An onlooker might have thought it strange to see the sign he flashed with the bases loaded, two men out, and me at bat. He flashed the bunt sign. With me at the plate, that was our only chance.

In later years, I saw a lot of major leaguers who couldn't bunt as well as I could. They didn't want to bunt. I saw them lose some games because they couldn't bunt.

I played on the high-school baseball team with about the same proficiency. But I was learning to love that game of baseball.

Then we got some lights at Pillow Park, and we formed a city softball league. Although I was a junior in high school at the time, I was named to manage one of the teams and I learned some very valuable lessons. I went out and signed as many outstanding players as I could, and I learned that is not necessarily good.

I soon discovered that I had some very unhappy players on the bench. I couldn't play everybody every day. But they all thought they should be playing. In later years, when I would see major league managers inserting bench players for no apparent reason, I knew what they were doing. You've got to try to keep them happy if you want them to remain productive. That means you must see somehow that they play—all of them, sometime.

And I also began to suspect that there is not as much direct cause and effect in the game of baseball as the reporters like to think and as they report. By that I mean that there is not a direct reason for everything that happens on the baseball field. There is a lot of happenstance out there. Some games are won in spite of the managerial moves instead of because of them.

When Walter Alston had managed the Dodgers, in Brooklyn and Los Angeles, for nineteen years, he brought his troops to Shea Stadium in New York one night. I was doing a radio pregame show and I interviewed Walter. I said to him, "In managing a major league team, how important is the batting order? You always hear that the leadoff man should have a good eye and good speed, and that the second batter should be able to hit behind the runner and be adept at taking pitches, and that the number-three man should be a power hitter."

Walter reflected silently for a moment, and then he said, "As far as I can tell, the batting order is of no importance at all. After the first time around, you don't know where you'll be starting in the order for any particular inning."

That seemed to confirm my belief that maybe the game wasn't as scientific as sometimes supposed. I then said, "In the nineteen years that you've managed in the major leagues, what is the biggest thing that you've learned?"

And he said, "I've learned that you just put 'em out there every day and some very strange things happen."

They certainly do. And Walter put 'em out there for twenty-three years and made the Hall of Fame in Cooperstown, New York.

I would finish out my high-school years as the starting first baseman with a lucky glove and an impotent bat. But I would also develop an ardent interest in the game that would last a lifetime. I knew a great deal about the history and romance of major league baseball before I ever saw a game.

Meanwhile, my personal football career was not progressing very satisfactorily. We played pickup games a good deal of the time. Some of them we played on the paved street. We had a lot of skinned knees and knuckles and elbows and a lot of ripped pants. We lost considerable blood, and we didn't portray much finesse. We leaned heavily on the long forward pass. And our conception of the rules was not specific. While the ball was in the air on one of those long "bombs" there was nothing you could possibly do to an opponent that would be considered against the rules. Oh, I suppose that's an exaggeration. Knives and guns were frowned upon. But any damage that could be accomplished without concealed weapons was within the scope of the rules.

At other times, we played on fields that did not provide a very smooth surface. There seemed to be a lot of rocks and gravel.

We didn't know about what are now referred to in sophisticated football circles as the "skilled positions." But we did understand without instruction that them that was throwing the ball and them that was catching it had better jobs than them that was blocking and tackling. And those good positions went to the first players to arrive. I shall never forget the day that I was extremely late and I was designated to play tackle. I was about a one-hundred-pound tackle, which might be all right if you've got seventy-five-pound running backs. But ours were a little heavier. On the first play, somebody knocked me down and stepped on my ear. It began to bleed a lot, mostly at the place where it had been torn away from my head.

On the next play, somebody stepped in my face and my nose started to bleed. I began to have a new appreciation of the risks run by the people who play tackle. And I also determined that in my own particular case, I would not be playing tackle anymore. I would be playing end, halfback, or checkers. The whole American Red Cross did not have enough blood for me to continue at that very unskilled position.

One of my favorite games was basketball. It seemed to me that here was a game where there was a place for the little man. It wasn't *much* of a place but if he had some speed and could handle and pass the ball, there *was* a place for him.

In high school, though, my basketball career had taken a turn for the worse. I wasn't a bad shooter, with a two-hand set shot. Everybody used a two-hand set shot. If you dared to throw the ball up there with one hand, you would likely be sent home and perhaps dismissed in disgrace. Everybody knew that you couldn't shoot a basketball with one hand. You might just as well try to catch a fly ball in a baseball game with one hand. Either effort was comparable to an attempt to fly on one wing.

But I was short on other skills, and I reached an arrangement that suited both me and the coach. I was appointed official scorer, since I was also the newspaper sportswriter. I was given a uniform and I made the trips. I would engage in the pregame warm-ups. I was a whiz in the drills. I would also participate in the warm-ups before the start of the second half. But whenever hostilities began, I retired to the scorer's table. Each team was required to provide a scorer, in the interest of impartiality, and I was ours. Naturally, the scorer could not leave his post. I never played a second in a game. But as a reporter, I certainly occupied a privileged position.

I also learned that not a great many people understood the rules of basketball, and strong among those who misunderstood were the coaches and players. That led me into an early career of basketball officiating. In those days, there was only one official per game. He ran the show. And I worked both girls' games and boys' games.

When the coaches at our school discovered that they had a budding basketball official in their midst they put me to work. Otherwise, the coaches had to officiate their own scrimmages and they preferred not to do that.

I remember an early girls' scrimmage when a particular running center came to my attention. She kept bumping into opposing players and I kept calling fouls, and soon she was ejected from the game. Her name was Mickie Lambert, and in succeeding years she got even with me. She married me. And we were together for twenty-six years, until her death did us part.

I was officiating a game in the industrial-mill league one night that had a direct bearing on the course of my career as a basketball official. The games between teams representing the various mills of the area were not terribly well supervised. Some of the participants were inclined toward taking matters into their own callused hands from time to time. There was frequent disagreement with the opinions of the official—in this case, me.

I made one call that met with the particular disfavor of a large visiting player. This was a fellow who had not shaved or combed his hair in some time now, and he looked threatening before they even got off the bus. On the court, he was menacing. And right now, he seemed to be menacing me. His intent became even more clear when he reached into the elastic top of his jock and withdrew a switch-blade knife. It was at that precise moment that I began to reevaluate the role of basketball officiating in my future life. Suddenly it had lost some of its appeal. In that split second while he was examining his weapon, I carefully removed the whistle cord from around my neck. I laid it gently on that hardwood floor and I went hastily home. I knew then that my future held safer things for me, like global wars.

Throughout my high-school years, my skills as a participating athlete were seeking their natural level, which was low. Truthfully, worse than that. My football future was the first to declare itself. I became the treasurer of the Athletic Association, handling financial arrangements. I was also a student manager, in charge of a lot of things, ranging from the washing of the socks and jocks to diagramming the plays on squares of cardboard.

I was also pressed into service as an official timer at the games, learning shortly before the first kickoff how to operate the stopwatch. I had not previously seen one or been aware that there existed a timepiece that could be halted by the pressing of a button. I was intrigued to know time could be stopped in full flight.

I was even more intrigued to learn that official time in a football game was stopped when a forward pass struck the ground incomplete, and did not commence again until the ball was snapped on the succeeding play. Nobody had ever told me that. I thought the game began at two P.M. and quit at four. My knowledge and understanding of football was broadening.

In those years I was also a fan of big-band music. I spent a lot of hours in front of the radio, spinning those dials to bring in the sounds afforded us by the likes of Jan Garber, Glen Gray, Guy Lombardo, Kay Kyser, Art Kassell and, from Nashville, Francis Craig.

We had a talented musician in our midst named Jimmy Lynn. He was a pianist and put together a little dance band called "Jimmy Lynn and His Columbians."

I did some of the vocals and I fronted the band with the baton. We played college sorority dances, roadhouses, nightclubs, and specials.

I either waved that baton or sat out front in my neatly pressed white trousers and dark jacket, waiting for the bridge following the instrumental chorus, which was my cue to make my way suavely over to the stand microphone.

In those high-school years, I was getting some things going that would shape my future direction. I had taken strongly to sportswriting.

There were three newspapers in Nashville—the *Morning Tennessean,* the *Evening Tennessean,* and the *Banner.* The papers were delivered to Columbia by train and were then home-delivered by carriers. At our home, economics did not allow us to subscribe to more than one paper a day, and our family had chosen *The Daily Herald* so that we could keep abreast of all the local news. Anything happening in Nashville seemed too far away to affect us much anyway. But I soon devised other means of gaining access. The filling station and the poolroom subscribed to the papers. So I became a steady visitor to both. I read stories written by Freddie Russell, Blinkey Horn, Raymond Johnson, Will Grimsley, Tom Anderson, and Red O'Donnell. And I read wire stories by Grantland Rice, Henry McLemore, and Davis J. Walsh.

And now I was covering all the local games for the local paper. This required that I arise early in the morning, go to the paper and do my work, and then get on to school in time for assembly.

It was along in there, too, that I discovered there was more than just fun and games in the sports business. There was big money in there, too.

When I covered an organizational meeting of our softball league, I was interested to learn that they would require two umpires for every game and that these officials would be paid fifty cents per game. Simultaneously, I discovered that I was no longer interested in being an unpaid manager. I was interested in being a paid umpire. So I put on the blue shirt and prospered.

I also discovered that the local mill baseball team did not have an official scorer. If they had no official scorer, they had no way of getting the box score into the local paper. The box score contained all the names, and that is what they wanted in the paper. Since I already had a newspaper connection, I was employed as the official scorer at what seemed to be my going rate of fifty cents per game. I was completely happy with this arrangement. I didn't think a fellow really needed to ever make more than about a half a buck a day for work like this.

I was beginning to take on a little local stature as a sports figure, but my range was not unbounded. The Chicago Bears came to Nashville to play an exhibition game, and their big draw was running back Red Grange. I surely did want to see Red Grange but all the half-a-bucks I had managed to hang on to would not provide transportation, food, and admission. So Red Grange would have to wait until another day.

I did make it to Old Hickory, Tennessee, to the DuPont High School gym to see the New York Celtics, the barnstorming professional basketball team starring Joe Lapchick, Dutch Dehnert, Davy Banks, Nat Hickey, Pete Barry, and others.

The price of admission was twenty-five cents, which was within my budget. And after the game, I waited almost two hours to get Joe Lapchick's autograph. We were lined up outside the gym waiting for the Celtics to shower and dress. Although it took a lot of time, Joe Lapchick was very patient, and I figured he must be a nice guy. I liked him.

And there was the day that the New York Yankees came to Nashville to play an exhibition game at the home of the Vols, Sulphur Dell. It was a strange name for a ball park, and that was fitting because it was a very strange ball park. At a point just behind first base, the terrain took a sharp turn skyward. It went almost straight up, making it precarious for an outfielder to station himself there. About halfway up, there was a little level spot for the right fielder to occupy. But he had a lot of irrevocable decisions. If the ball came his way, he had to determine right away whether his first step would be up or down. Once committed, there was no turning back. Outfielders frequently tumbled, in a style described locally as "ass over teakettle," with resulting damage to their dignity. For this reason, the New York Yankees did not favor the idea of their treasured right fielder, Mr. Babe Ruth, occupying that geographical position. In other years, Ruth had been switched to left field. But this time, the Babe had said, "I want to play the dump." And so, he was out there, thin ankles and all, rolling around that treacherous real estate and seemingly having a ball.

During batting practice I somehow managed to get out onto the field and I went from one Yankee to another, getting autographs on a baseball from Babe Ruth, Lou Gehrig, Tony Lazzeri, Ben Chapman, Red Rolfe, and Bill Dickey. I have seen a few thousand major league games since then, but I still prize that baseball and the vivid memory of my conversations with Ruth and Gehrig and Dickey. The experience there at Sulphur Dell that Sunday afternoon has been mine to treasure for all my life.

CHAPTER 3

Meeting the Major

By the time I finished high school, I knew where my future lay. I was knee-deep into sports, one way or another. I had acquired a store of historical and practical sports information. I had become a dedicated fan of college football and major league baseball. And I followed minor league baseball, which was more accessible.

When I graduated from high school, I was the runner-up and alternate for the alumni scholarship which would provide financial aid for college. On the form I was asked to list the first two colleges of my choice. I wrote down Vanderbilt and Middle Tennessee. I didn't get the scholarship and I didn't get to either of those schools.

I really didn't see how I was going to any school. You may have read that in 1936 the nation was coming out of the Depression. In our town, we had not noticed that we were coming out. I sent away for some college catalogues, but when I would turn to the section on financial arrangements I would run into a wall of discouragement. I didn't find any that I could afford. This was not surprising because the simple fact was that I was stony broke. I don't mean "short of funds" or "a little light." I mean stony broke. I did the only remaining thing possible and adopted a public posture of having found college attendance undesirable. People would ask where I was going to college, and I would say, "I'm not gonna waste my time at no old college." Freely translated, that meant, "There ain't no way I can afford to go to college. I am stony broke."

While I waited around, I was mostly hoping, like Micawber, that something would turn up. My financial status did now seem to be on the brink of alteration, because I had gone to work at *The Daily Herald* for a negotiated salary of nine dollars per week. This was for a six-day week and figured out easily at a dollar and a half per day. My duties included those of circulation manager, sportswriter, copy reader, and sometimes chauffeur to the publisher. He was a very learned fellow who had declined to learn to operate an automobile. Presumably, in the early stages of the car in this country he had considered it a passing fad. In 1937 he still wasn't sure. The job of chauffeur guaranteed a certain amount of health-giving physical exercise since this unreliable vehicle conked out from time to time for a variety of reasons, requiring long hikes in search of fuel, water, assistance, or all of the above.

But many of my friends were making plans for college. So to be fashionable I began to explore the slim possibility of going to the University of Tennessee in Knoxville. And I thought about Louisiana State University because I was attracted to their ROTC uniforms.

I did not know exactly where Knoxville was. I had certainly never been there. I could not recall ever having actually wished to be there. I knew it was somewhere east, maybe northeast. A lot of places were northeast—Kingsport, Washington, New York, Boston. I had never been to any of those.

On inquiry, I determined that, surprisingly, tuition fees were not very high at the University of Tennessee for state residents. And I had begun to build up my financial resources beyond my expectations. The dollar and a half a day at the newspaper and the half-buck for umpiring the softball games at night were adding up. With money like that rolling in, I now suspected that I might be able to handle the initial expenses. I had a friend and high-school classmate named Frank Thomas, Jr., who had been offered a basketball scholarship at Tennessee, and he was about to enroll. Not only that, his father was going to drive him to Knoxville and offered me transportation without charge. That was right in line with my budget. So I packed my bag and went away with Frank in his father's car to Knoxville, Tennessee.

We had a friend who was a Sigma Nu, and he offered us free

lodging for the night at the Sigma Nu House on West Hill Avenue. As I pulled the bunk-bed covers up under my chin there that first night away from home, I happily reflected on the fact that I was really sailing. I had made the trip and was safe in bed, and so far I had not been forced to dip into my meager savings. I did not then savor the realization that by choosing Knoxville and the University of Tennessee, I had made one of the major decisions that would influence the rest of my life. But sometimes I would still think longingly of LSU and those uniforms.

Next day, I made two important discoveries. I found a drugstore there on Henley Street just beyond the Church Street Methodist Church, where a ten-cent breakfast included one large sweet roll and a large cup of coffee. And I discovered that the Church Street Methodist Church was nowhere near Church Street, which interested me. I was starting my education by learning that you can't believe everything, even in church.

Without mishap and in rapid succession, I enrolled, located a room in which to live, and witnessed a football game in which Tennessee defeated Wake Forest. I sat in the student section and remained comparatively quiet, as befits a freshman. I was rushed by the Sigma Nus, the ATOs, and the Sigma Chis. Social expenses had no place in my plans, however, and I respectfully declined membership feelers.

I paid close attention to the sports programs. I went to all the football and basketball games. Student tickets were inexpensive. I listened to all the broadcasts on radio and I read all the sports pages. Tennessee did not have a very good year on the football field. They lost three and tied one. The coach, Major Robert R. Neyland, reckoned that as a disaster. He did not like to lose. He had not had much experience at losing.

At Christmastime in 1937, I went home to Columbia, where I properly celebrated New Year's Eve with friends and family. It would be a long time before I would spend New Year's Eve at home again. I would be at bowl games or wars.

Both my sister and my brother were working, and they were generous in my support with a surprise check in the mail from time to time.

When I got back to the Knoxville campus to start classes in the winter quarter, I discovered the presence of another bustling activity—football practice. There were no NCAA restrictions then. You could practice anytime. And Tennessee had begun on January 9. Sports publicist Jones Ramsey used to say that the University of Texas had two major sports, football and spring football. That's about what Tennessee had under Bob Neyland.

Teams now sometimes go to big postseason bowl games and come back with a check for a million dollars with a record like 6-3-1, the record that Neyland's Vols had in 1937, but the major figured the time had come for a complete overhaul. He knew that the one thing he must do was beat Alabama, coached by arch rival Frank Thomas (no relation to my Columbia classmate). And the Neyland-Thomas rivalry went even deeper than Tennessee vs. Alabama. Neyland had been an outstanding end at West Point. (He had been at Army that afternoon in 1913 when Gus Dorais and Knute Rockne of Notre Dame combined to popularize the little-used forward pass for an upset victory that made the little school in Indiana a headline football name, "the Fighting Irish of Notre Dame." He had been busy walking off a "slug," a disciplinary cadet penalty.) Thomas was a native of East Chicago and a quarterback for Coach Rockne at Notre Dame. Neyland vs. Thomas was Army vs. Notre Dame.

As a freshman I had aspirations of being a sportswriter, and I was constantly on the athletic scene. I had also discovered radio, and there were two stations in Knoxville. That got my attention. WNOX had a weekly amateur night, so I entered myself, singing an Eddie Cantor-type version of "Ma, She's Making Eyes at Me." The lyrics didn't have a lot of depth, but I walked off with the first prize of five cash dollars.

I also spent a lot of time at the Varsity Inn on West Cumberland Avenue, where the training table was located. There was a piano in the living room where a big tackle named Bob Fulton could usually be found before dinner, pounding out the popular songs of the day—immortal numbers like "Moon Over Miami," "In My Little Red Book," "Red Sails in the Sunset," and "A Sailboat in the Moonlight." Bob didn't know a note of music and neither did I. We were a perfect team. We appeared on the amateur hour, won, and got a weekly show of our own called *Campus Parade.* The station paid us nothing, which was about what the show was worth. But it certainly gave us some social clout we had previously been without. We could invite aspiring co-eds for guest shots on our show.

Meanwhile, Major Neyland had the Vols out there working hard every day for Alabama. That would not be the opener. Fact was, it would be the fourth game. But Neyland knew what the key to his success was. The key was to beat Alabama, for whom he had the greatest respect. When a Vol freshman would have a good day and observers would tend to go overboard about his potential ("He's gonna be the best we've ever had"), Neyland would smile the faintest trace of a wry smile and say, "Well, you never can really tell about a football player until after he's played against Alabama."

Since I had invited myself onto the football scene, I was close to most of the players and was privy to privileged information. Except I didn't really realize that it was so privileged. I was also trying to make a buck on the side as a stringer for the Knoxville *Journal.* My contact there was a writer named Tom Anderson who was new in town. But Major Neyland had learned all that he wanted to know about Anderson. He had learned that Anderson had once played football at Alabama, and that was all the paranoid Major needed. He wanted no part of him.

Meanwhile, I had made it a point to become acquainted with Anderson. He was a talented writer, perhaps the most talented sportswriter I ever knew. I had studied the little picture that ran at the top of his column carefully. And I walked into the city room of the paper one day, searched out a fellow who matched that picture, and introduced myself. It was the start of a lifelong friendship, and over the years we engaged in some of the most bizarre escapades imaginable. While they were intended to be in fun, they led to occasional disciplinary actions by family and employers and, on at least one memorable occasion, to jail—for disturbing the peace.

Now, since Anderson through his Alabama heritage was denied a natural channel of information as a reporter, I decided to step in and fill the void. The idea was all right. It was just that my timing was bad. I chose the dinner hour to call the Tennessee coach at home and query him about his football practice. You may have heard about the fools who rush in. I was prominent among them.

Our society had not yet forced all college football coaches to have unlisted telephone numbers, so I simply looked in the phone book and dialed the number. I got the maid, to whom I identified myself, more or less correctly, as a sportswriter, and asked to speak to the major. When he got on the phone he was cordial enough, if unenthusiastic, until I asked, "Who are you running on that Alabama practice team?"

There was a brief silence, then a bellowed "What?" And that was followed by a loud "click" and the termination of the only press interview I ever had with a man I was to know for twenty-five years.

You see, he had a practice team running plays from Alabama's box formation every day. My friends among the players talked about being on the Alabama practice team. But obviously that knowledge was not for public consumption.

At the squad meeting the next day, Major Neyland let it be known that he wanted Nelson to report to him, whoever Nelson was. He had determined that I was more of a student than a sportswriter. Everywhere I went on campus, members of the football squad, with slight smiles playing on their faces, said, "The major wants to see you." Everyone seemed pretty sure that an invitation to see the major was a likely introduction to the guillotine. And the invitation was a command.

I was not anxious for my career to end before it began, so I decided to handle the case through diplomatic channels without actually coming face to face with the sovereign himself. So, in the alcove doorway of Fred Brown's Toggery, which carried clothes far too expensive for me to consider, I approached the captain of the team, a handsome All-American end named Bowden Wyatt. He agreed to take my message to the major, who promptly sent a message back by Wyatt that he wanted to see NELSON and NOW!

That's how I came to be standing in front of his desk, in the office located on the second floor of the weather-boarded old structure known familiarly as the AA, for Athletic Association.

And the first words ever spoken directly to me by Major Neyland were: "Nelson, I'm gonna hang you by the balls!"

Major Robert Reese Neyland (West Point '16) surely got my complete attention, because I knew his reputation as a man of his word. I had no doubt that he meant what he said and I contemplated a rather painful process. But presently he softened his approach somewhat. It was just that he didn't want careless information spread around, he said. True, he was pointing for Alabama, but he felt that for Alabama to know that for certain would be to give aid and comfort to the enemy. It wasn't that he really had any cause to doubt my personal loyalty to the cause of the Orange and White, although he wanted me to know that I was somewhat suspect because of my association with Tom Anderson, who had not only played football at the University of Alabama but, worse still, had even been born in Alabama.

Damaging information can get passed around innocently, he said. There was the time in the early thirties, he recalled, when Tennessee was getting ready to play Vanderbilt. On Wednesday of the game week, the major was walking down Knoxville's main thoroughfare,

Gay Street. Cars had rumble seats then, little caboose affairs located where the trunk should be. A young fellow stood up in the rumble seat of a passing car and yelled to Major Neyland, "Look out for a short kickoff on Saturday." And sure enough, Vandy tried it, but Tennessee was ready.

The point was, the major said, that he still didn't know who his benefactor was. But somebody had spread some valuable Vanderbilt information around and he didn't want that to happen to the Volunteers.

I had wanted somehow to get to know Major Neyland, and I had certainly accomplished that. There was thereafter no doubt in his mind as to who I was. He was not exactly an admirer, but he was an acquaintance.

Neyland grew up in Greenville, Texas, at the turn of the century, when the West was a way of life. An appointment to West Point was a golden opportunity, but it wasn't easy to come by. Neyland attended Burleson Junior College and Texas A&M for a year each before his appointment came through from Congressman Sam Rayburn—an opportunity for life in the East, an education, a profession.

In the fall of 1912 he took the train to New York, then up the Hudson to the West Point station. He walked up the steep hill to the academy, which was to shape his future life.

Neyland was a scholar and an all-round athlete. He played on the football team with a young cadet named Dwight Eisenhower until a knee injury ended Ike's football career.

Neyland became a star pitcher for and captain of the baseball team. His career record at the academy was 35–5, twenty consecutive victories, and pro offers from the New York Giants, the Boston Red Sox, the Detroit Tigers, and the Philadelphia Athletics. But Neyland was headed for a career in the military.

His left fielder on that West Point baseball team was Omar Bradley. And in those days, the corps was small. Intimate friendships were formed for a lifetime.

Neyland also became heavyweight boxing champion of the academy, and in his senior year received the saber, symbolic of his being considered the best athlete in the senior class. In fact, he shared it with Bill Britton, who would become a Neyland aide at Tennessee.

Neyland chose the Corps of Engineers, graduated in the class of 1916, and was assigned to duty along the Mexican border, building bridges, dredging rivers. And then he went to France.

Neyland returned to West Point from 1921 to 1924, initially as an aide to the superintendent, General Douglas MacArthur. And as a labor of love, he worked as an assistant football coach. When General Pershing, chief of staff, hustled MacArthur out to the Philippines before his normal tour as superintendent ended, Neyland remained at the academy.

By 1925 Neyland was married, a captain, and he had settled into the sometimes humdrum life that a professional soldier knows in peacetime. The army of those days permitted a certain mixture of civilian employment with army duty, so Neyland began to look around for work as a football coach. There was a job open at Iowa and one at Tennessee. He was recommended to Tennessee by the Army head coach, Colonel John McEwan, and the Centre College coach, Charlie Moran, who had coached Neyland in baseball at Texas A&M. He was ordered to the University of Tennessee as an ROTC instructor, and he was paid seven hundred dollars to serve as an assistant football coach. Following that 1925 season, Head Coach M. B. Banks was relieved, and Neyland became the head coach.

He was also working out of the district engineer's office and was assigned to the army engineering project of making the Tennessee River navigable, the beginning of a plan that became the Tennessee Valley Authority.

Three days after Neyland took over as head coach, practices were closed to the public for the first time ever, and the Neyland dynasty was under way. For a lifetime, he was to have that paranoia about spies prowling the adjacent premises with the mission of stealing his secrets.

During his first seven seasons as head coach, Neyland's Tennessee teams lost only twice in a span of sixty-eight games—once to Vanderbilt and once to Alabama.

By 1928 he had recruited what were called "The Flaming Sophomores," with names like Bobby Dodd, Gene McEver, Buddy Hackman, and Fritz Brandt. They beat Wallace Wade's famed Alabama Crimson Tide 15–13. And only a tie with Kentucky marred an otherwise perfect slate that season. Tennessee was on the national football map to stay.

The Neyland system was getting established, and it never really changed. The emphasis was on defense and the kicking game. "In a closely fought game," he said, "the winner seldom wins—instead the loser usually loses. Football is a game of mistakes, and the team that commits the fewest number wins."

Neyland was a disciplinarian. On the field he usually had a whistle around his neck and a baseball cap on his head. When he blew that whistle, it meant "Everybody behind me."

When his players went on to become head coaches themselves, as so very many did, they all went out and bought whistles and caps.

There was no doubt of his domination over his players for life. When Murray Warmath (Minnesota) and Bowden Wyatt (Arkansas) had become nationally famous head coaches in their own right, they waited outside the Tennessee dressing room after a bowl game one day. Wyatt was smoking a cigar. When he saw Neyland coming, he looked frantically for a way to get rid of that cigar. Warmath began to laugh. "What are you doing?" he said. "That old man hasn't got any control over you. You're a grown man and a head coach."

Wyatt said, "I know that, and you know that, but I'm not sure he knows that."

By the time I stood there in front of Neyland's desk in that winter of 1938, he was about to begin one of the most spectacular three-year stretches in the history of intercollegiate football.

He was working on a defense designed to stop Alabama, the opponent he knew he must beat. And as an engineer he realized that he should leave as little to chance as possible. He used to say that when you build a bridge you want to be as certain as you can that it is constructed to bear the stress and strain to which it will be subjected. Guessing and hoping are not good enough. Unchallenged principles of mathematics and engineering are what you want. And he attempted to build a football defense the same way. He realized that there would always be the human element. But he wanted to eliminate the variables as much as possible.

From the opening of the 1938 season and continuing for three years, he did not lose a regular-season game. And that defense, which shut out Alabama in 1938, went through one stretch of seventeen consecutive games in which it did not give up a single point—not a touchdown, not a field goal, not a safety. Some elements of that famous Neyland defense, sometimes called the "loose-tackle Tennessee," survive in the game today.

During my undergraduate years in college, I realized that I would have to arrange for a little income in some manner. On the basis of my experience with *The Daily Herald* in my hometown, I considered myself a somewhat accomplished and veteran newsman. I had also worked as a stringer and "space writer" for the Nashville papers. A space writer is somebody who gets paid by the column inch. The more you write, the more you get paid. It is apt to lead one into what may become a lifelong habit of being a little wordy. But at the end of the month, when you have pasted up all your clippings end to end and measured the lot with a yardstick, you're not looking for literature or the Pulitzer. You're looking for volume in inches. Fifteen cents per inch is not to be regarded lightly. Not by a fellow who doesn't have fifteen cents.

Since my work as a stringer for the *Journal* was irregular, I was reasonably sure that the other daily paper in town, the *News-Sentinel,* might just be waiting for me to take over their sports department, and I marched into the office of Editor George Carmack to proclaim my availability. Under my arm I had a scrapbook of my clippings, which I presented for his inspection. I waited anxiously for his endorsement of my singular talents as he perused the clips. When he had finished, he said something that I shall never ever forget. He said, "Well, it wouldn't be as though you were starting entirely from scratch."

From scratch!

What did he mean? Here he was with an opportunity to employ young Ernest Hemingway and he was talking about "from scratch."

The job he gave me wasn't from scratch maybe, but it was just about as close to scratch as you're gonna get. George Carmack employed me as the "morgue clerk."

Let me hasten to explain that the job had nothing to do with newly arrived corpses. There is a department at the paper where pictures, clippings, and such are filed. When a current story demands a little research or support, one digs into the "morgue." The morgue clerk handles the details of filing and maintaining this department. That was me.

My immediate superior was a delightful lady named Gertrude Penland, who was secretary to the editor. She gave me excellent guidance in a number of areas, and my tenure as the morgue clerk was one of value as an educational experience. I was given a card file and a rollaway typewriter table that was situated in a space near the entrance to the editor's office. I was trampled daily by all the visitors who came to see the boss, plus the general staff of the newspaper, who were pretty constantly in motion in my area.

There is no morgue clerk at the paper anymore. The position has been upgraded by title and is now known as "librarian."

I was settled nicely into a steady income of $3.20 per week, and when the softball season began I presented my credentials as an umpire and was signed on to work night games at a dollar a game.

And on Sunday afternoons we would always gather around the radio and listen to the big-band music of Guy Lombardo and His Royal Canadians. We never missed Guy Lombardo. To us, he represented the big time.

This was what has become known since as the big-band era, and one of the big bands that came to the University of Tennessee was that of Tommy Dorsey. One afternoon a softball game was arranged between members of that band and a group of UT fraternity boys, mostly SAEs. They played on what was then a vacant lot next to the northwest end of the stadium. My friend Frank Thomas pitched for the frat boys, and at one crucial point in the contest he struck out a skinny vocalist with a lot of hair named Frank Sinatra. Some members of the band looked as though that might have been their first fresh air in weeks. The surgeon general had not yet given us his warning about the dangers of cigarettes, and big bands did their work mostly in dark, smoke-filled rooms.

I was rolling in newly acquired wealth. And Bruck's beer sold for only ten cents a bottle, and a pack of Circle City brew was four for a quarter. This was a college boy's delight. You couldn't live much better than this.

CHAPTER 4

Into Announcing

Enrollment in ROTC at Tennessee was mandatory. I didn't mind that. In fact, I liked it. But our uniforms were not nearly as attractive as those at LSU. Our uniforms were not as attractive as those in the Salvation Army or the department of sanitation.

And we didn't have much space in which to drill. Our close-order instruction was accomplished on a paved street. But I discovered that even under those circumstances, I was attracted to the military life.

After the basic aptitude tests in various areas at the start of my freshman year, I had been placed in an advanced English course taught by Dr. Roscoe E. Parker. He was occupied mostly with upper-class and graduate courses, but handled this group of freshmen for exercise, I suppose. The last week of the spring quarter he called me in to inquire about my future plans. He wanted me to know, he said, that his assistant, a graduate student, was going off to Oxford University, and for the coming year he would have a job open on his staff for a reader.

I felt a lot like I did the day they handed me that stopwatch for the first time in high school. I had never heard of *reader.* I scuffed my feet and looked out the window, hoping for some enlightenment. Dr. Parker was properly perceptive. "As my reader, you would grade my essay papers, monitor an occasional quiz, keep the grade book, and tidy up the office," he said. And when he mentioned that the handsome stipend would be fifteen dollars per month, Dr. Roscoe E. Parker had a brand-new reader named Lindsey Nelson.

Coming up, then, would be a year of some development for me at the University of Tennessee. First of all, I was assigned to a bed in a room in Humes Hall, where the scholarship athletes lived. And I was assigned to room with Joe Black Hayes, who had been captain of the football team and was now a graduate coach. I was getting into the daily life of a major college football team. I was at practice every day, and I was learning some things about this game. I have not found anyone who could teach it better or more convincingly than Bob Neyland. I watched and I listened and I learned.

At one of the early games, I heard the public-address announcer make a few errors of identification. He was a fellow named Jack Joyner, from Sharon, Pennsylvania. He had a beautiful voice with a Pennsylvania sharpness that seemed to cut right through our somewhat softer Tennessee accents. But it really doesn't matter how impressively you say it if, in the end, you've got the wrong information.

I came upon Jack outside the campus hangout on the Ellis & Ernest corner one night. And I suggested to him that I could advance the efficiency of the public-address operation by serving as a spotter. He said he could offer no payment and that he was already firmly committed to a faulty spotter for the remainder of the year. He also said that there was no room for me to sit in the small booth, but that I could stand in the back if I wished.

I pondered his offer and evaluated it. Let's see—he had offered me no money and no seat, but standing room in the rear from which, if I had long arms, I could assist with the spotting. But it was the best offer I had. And I heartily accepted. A fellow starts his career where he can.

As the 1938 football season wore on, my skills as a spotter were finely honed. By the time we reached the final game of the season against Vanderbilt in Nashville, I figured I was ready for the big time. So I wrote a letter to Jack Harris of radio station WSM in Nashville. Jack was the broadcaster of the Vanderbilt games. When I was growing up in Columbia, he had been the first football broadcaster I ever listened to on a regular basis. (Jack later became a distinguished broadcast executive, and reminiscing about his sports days would say, "I was not as good as Husing but better than Stern.") I outlined my very special qualifications and offered my services as a spotter. The going rate in those days was five dollars. And I got a return letter from Jack saying that he would be glad to have me work with him.

When I got to the stadium, however, I discovered that Jim Britt would be broadcasting the game for NBC. He needed a spotter and Jack Harris had traded me to them. I was in the national-network business, but the pay was still the same—five dollars.

During the season, the Vols had gone undefeated and untied and were invited to the Orange Bowl in Miami, Florida, to play Oklahoma. With a couple of friends, I drove from Columbia to Miami. We were carefully budgeted, and located a room at a hotel in Miami where the price was one dollar per night for each of us. Ted Husing was there to broadcast the game for CBS and I had a chance to meet him and watch him prepare for his broadcast. His regular spotter was Jimmy Dolan. I was assigned to serve as a spotter for the print media in the press box. The pay was a "Thank you very much." Print reporters did not throw money around carelessly, then or now. But I was happy just to be on the fringe of media coverage of football.

As I've mentioned, the big early-season game in the South was undoubtedly that between Tennessee and Alabama. Both teams scheduled comparatively soft opposition leading up to the big game. In 1939 Tennessee preceded Alabama with North Carolina State, Sewanee, and Chattanooga. Alabama played Howard, Fordham, and Mercer. In those days, Fordham was first-rate (Neyland had been offered the head coach's job there) and Alabama had squeaked by to a 7–6 victory. That brought the Vols and the Tide into the game undefeated and untied. The winner would likely go to a major bowl. While Tennessee had won and gone to the Orange Bowl the season before, the season before that, Alabama had been at the Rose Bowl.

This was building to what was easily the biggest game that I had ever seen. That was not exactly a monumental distinction. Up to that point, some of the best games I had ever personally seen had been between Columbia High and Mount Pleasant.

First came the announcement that the game would be broadcast by Bill Stern of NBC. And then the announcement that the game would also be broadcast by Ted Husing of CBS. This was before the era of analysts and color men. A football broadcaster worked alone. He did it all. After I got to the networks some years later, I learned that there was a very good reason why Stern and Husing worked alone. If he monopolized the microphone, the announcer was not building future competition for his job. The top play-by-play men of that day intended to remain the top play-by-play men. And they didn't want any pretenders to the throne throwing their names around on the air for the audience to know and perhaps love. It was a sound practice for survival.

By this time, I had taken on additional duties for Jack Joyner, the director of sports publicity. The Vols had not previously had such a staffer. Not many schools in the South did. Ted Mann was working for Wallace Wade and Eddie Cameron at Duke, and Rea Schuessler was working for Frank Thomas at Alabama, but Rea was a student. The previous year, when the Vols were moving toward their bowl bid, they got a lot of requests from the national media for stories, information, and pictures. So, they had made Jack Joyner the publicity man. He had been a campus salesman for Balfour jewelry and a public-address announcer. And, having served faithfully as a spotter, I was now legman for the new publicity chief. Being an English major, I was also instructed to proofread the publicity releases for possible, even likely, errors in grammar and punctuation. The pay was invisible.

The fact is that Jack had a most difficult job because Major Neyland was not the easiest product to market. The major really didn't want any publicity. If the truth be known, he didn't even want spectators. He would have preferred to lock the gates and play the game in private. He thought that paying fans were an intrusion. In later years, I once accused him. I said, "If you could get away with it, you'd bar all spectators." He said, "You're damned right I would." To Neyland, a football game was far too important a thing to be threatened by the presence of outsiders.

But that week of the 1939 Tennessee-Alabama game, it seemed that we were all about to be involved one way or another. It was an early sellout. There were no tickets. The national press was coming. Grantland Rice, the dean of sportswriters, arrived from New York by train. As a gag, Ted Husing arranged for Rice to be met by a porter with a wheelchair. Rice, a native of Tennessee and ever the Southern gentleman, made no serious protest, but he was clearly not very much amused, either.

Henry McLemore was along from United Press, and Scripps-Howard columnist Joe Williams, Francis Wallace from *The Saturday Evening Post,* and Harry Grayson of NEA, the Scripps-Howard feature service.

It was big time, all right, and I figured this might be the moment for me to take my spotting skills to the networks again.

I proposed to Jack Joyner that just maybe he should recommend me to Bill Stern of NBC, who had requested that a spotter be assigned. Ted Husing still had Jimmy Dolan. Stern picked up spotters from each team. Of course, a lot of people wanted to be the spotter for Bill Stern, and Jack chose a friend named Carl McFall. I returned to my position as the spotter in the PA booth. Maybe I would get another shot somewhere down the pike. After all, I had come a long way. I now was allowed to squeeze into a seat on the bench in the booth next to Jack. That was considerable advancement from my standing start of the year before.

It was plain to see, also, that a man of my talents could not be kept under a bushel forever, and I got my break several weeks later at the Vanderbilt game in Knoxville. Jack Harris was coming to town to do the game for WSM and he wrote to inquire if I would be available. Since he had traded me away to NBC the year before, I had never actually worked for Jack.

Of course, I first had to get my release from Jack Joyner. I explained my case carefully and he was understanding. I explained mostly that Harris was offering five dollars for the day's work, which was that much more than I was getting from Joyner. He was very understanding about the five dollars. He understood anything above fifty cents. He was said to be able to fold a silver dollar. So with his blessing, I went away to work for WSM on the 1939 broadcast of the Tennessee vs. Vanderbilt game in Knoxville. And that is where one of those unpredictable factors entered the scene and perhaps changed my entire life and profession. It was a matter of plumbing.

Not a great deal of attention had been paid to facilities for the media representatives at Shields-Watkins Field. There surely had been no exorbitant expenditures on their behalf. The press box was a dinky little coop on the rim of the west stands. And when radio had come along, a few booths had been stacked on top of the press box. There was no ready access. In order to get to the booth, an announcer had to climb a ladder. He was in ever-present danger of being spilled off onto Fifteenth Street below. Even after he arrived on top and was making his way precariously to his place of work, there was only a shaky railing consisting of one two-by-four with vertical supports to keep him topside. Needless to say, there were no restroom facilities. Plumbing had not reached that vicinity, and the nearest comfort station was situated beneath the stands far below. A trip for that necessary purpose required a battle through thousands of fans, some of whom sometimes showed early signs of public drunkenness and belligerence. A fellow just didn't want to get down there in the midst of those people unless he absolutely had to. There was always the chance that if somebody recognized him, he might get punched in the nose for something he had written or said. Fans were somewhat provincial.

None of this was on my mind, however, as I took my duty station at the elbow of announcer Jack Harris, and prepared to assist him with my incomparable expertise. It might be good to point out that Tennessee used a single-wing offense with a direct snap from center to tailback or fullback. Following the path of the ball was not difficult.

In order to exhibit my total familiarity with the job, I left the moment the gun sounded to end the first half, and started for the ladder. The statistics were kept in the press box, and the idea was that if I could beat the crowd to the ladder, I could get a copy of the stats and return before the traffic jammed up. It worked out just as I had planned and I returned in a somewhat triumphant mood to hand the statistics to Harris. I thought he would be pleased, but instead he looked pained. His eyes seemed to bulge as he handed the sheet back to me and said, "You do 'em." With that, he was up and scrambling in the direction of the ladder and the restroom. Jack had clearly been called by nature, leaving a vacancy for me to make my debut in the football-broadcasting business on a fifty-thousand-watt, clear-channel station. I moved over in front of the microphone and announced the halftime statistics. It was my "on air" start in a business that I have since pursued the length and breadth of this land and around the world. By such chance incidents is life directed. Just a little thing like Jack Harris sitting there in the coffee shop of the Farragut Hotel on Gay Street in Knoxville, Tennessee, that November morning and asking for a second cup of coffee. As a result, he made an unscheduled halftime dash to the men's room and I became a sports announcer. If he had declined that second cup, I might have been an insurance salesman or a short-order cook.

The very next week, the Vols were going to Lexington, Kentucky, to play the Wildcats. Tennessee was rolling now. They were undefeated, untied, and unscored on. Bill Stern was coming with his NBC microphone to Lexington to broadcast the game, because NBC also did the Rose Bowl game at season's end and it looked as though the Vols might be invited to Pasadena. When Stern asked Jack Joyner for a spotter, Jack nominated me. There were some quickly arranged details. The fee was five dollars and I would pay all of my own expenses.

There had been another pertinent development back there at the start of my sophomore year. I had properly taken up my duties as Dr. Parker's reader, which meant that I was reading and grading a lot of English papers. I was also being sought out to lend assistance to an occasional athlete on projects in freshman English. One day I was approached by Assistant Coach John Barnhill. The usual varsity coaching staff in those days consisted of three men—a head coach, a line coach, and an end coach. Among them they distributed all the other duties, such as recruiting, eligibility, scholarships, training table, and so on. Barnhill was the line coach and he was also handling eligibility. He wanted to know if I would be interested in tutoring some of the scholarship athletes who were deficient in English. That was most of them.

Barney proposed that the Athletic Association would pay the usual going rate for tutorial services, which was one dollar per hour.

I thought I had a better idea. The Athletic Association was controlling room assignments in the stadium dormitory that was under construction. As soon as rooms were completed, we were moving athletes out of Humes Hall. It wasn't so much that we were anxious to get them into the new rooms, although sometimes we did move folks in before the windowpanes were installed. It was just that old Humes Hall looked for all the world as though it might collapse at any moment.

Most of my friends among the athletes ate at the training table. On rare occasions they slipped me a pint of milk or a piece of toast. I proposed to Barney that I be permitted to live in the stadium dormitory and to eat at the training table. In return, I would expect no money and would tutor the athletes religiously, and besides that I would be handy. Barney thought it was an accommodating arrangement and we struck a bargain. I was assured room and board for three years.

It was easily the most fortuitous arrangement of my young life thus far. In these circumstances, I was in a position to learn a great deal about the game of football. I would be living in it. And as a spotter, I was learning something about broadcasting. I was learning a trade. And I was also making a firm stand against my old adversary—starvation—with the permission to dine at the training table. Life was clearly on the upswing.

And there was another developing benefit. Coach Neyland continued to send a great many men into the coaching field. A lot of them became head coaches at major colleges right across the country: Herman Hickman at Yale, Murray Warmath at Minnesota, Phil Dickens at Indiana, Beattie Feathers at North Carolina State, Quinn Decker at The Citadel, Bobby Dodd at Georgia Tech, Bob Woodruff at Baylor and Florida, Jim Myers at Texas A&M, Billy Meek at SMU, Bowden Wyatt at Wyoming, Arkansas, and then Tennessee, Clay Stapleton at Iowa State, Dewitt Weaver at Texas Tech, Ray Graves at Florida, Billy Barnes at UCLA, and more.

When I later began my career of announcing games nationally, I was able to get privileged information from many of them before a major telecast. I had either graded their papers, tutored them, or met them at Tennessee. The "Tennessee connection" was of great value. And friendships that had been formed earlier paid valuable dividends in the early days of television, when announcers were discovering for the first time that their information had to be right. This wasn't radio, where you might be able to get away with fairy tales. This was television, where the viewer at home could see better than the announcer on top of the press box.

I tried to pay attention at all times. One day after football practice, along about midseason, I listened as Major Neyland was interviewed by the head of the Knoxville bureau of the Associated Press, a young man from Harlan, Kentucky, named Don Whitehead. Neyland was reluctant to be quoted at all, and Whitehead was explaining the difficult position in which that stance left him. "Joe Williams [Scripps-Howard sports editor in New York] can write that Tennessee has a great defensive team and the point is valid because Joe Williams is an acknowledged expert," Whitehead said. "But I can't get by with an opinion that is just my opinion. I've got to have your opinion."

The major was unbending. "I am not yet ready to say that this is a great football team," he said. "I am of the opinion that up to now it may be as good a defensive team as I've had."

Major Neyland was not exactly going out on a limb. That was 1939, and that season the Tennessee Volunteers went undefeated, untied, and unscored on—something that no major college football team in America has done since.

We finished the season—we Vols—with a victory over Auburn, and the night after the game I went with some of the boys to the Tennessee theater downtown, where all the first-run pictures played.

We often went to the Tennessee because the sympathetic management admitted scholarship athletes without charge. And I had come to consider myself a scholarship athlete in all such circumstances. I was rarely excluded, and if there seemed to be a move in that direction I feigned deafness and proceeded. You'd be surprised how far a fellow can go if he just keeps going. As they say in the military, faint heart ne'er screwed the cook.

When we came out of the theater onto Gay Street near midnight, there was a carnival scene. People were literally dancing in the street and we soon joined them. The Sunday newspapers were out and they proclaimed in screaming black headlines that Tennessee was going to the Rose Bowl.

We bought the papers, went to the stadium dormitory, and sat up until well past dawn. Most of us had never been west of the Mississippi. Most of us had only dreamed of going to California. We had followed the publicity about the Rose Bowl through the years. We knew there were trips to the movie studios. Hollywood was heaven. That's where all the movie stars worked. We might even see Lana Turner. Can you imagine seeing Lana Turner? She might even say "hi," and if she did I might faint. How was I going to get all the way to Pasadena and the Rose Bowl? I really didn't know, but when they teed up the old pigskin, I'd be there. You could bet on that.

CHAPTER 5

Rolling to the Rose Bowl

Plans had been completed with the railway company for advancing the Volunteers by train across the country with appropriate stops, and I had inspected those plans carefully. There seemed to be no provisions that would allow Lindsey Nelson to make that trip. On shorter hauls, I had stowed away underneath the equipment and made it to places like Baton Rouge and Lexington. But, hell, this was all the way across this broad country. A fellow could starve to death trying to survive beneath those duffel bags all the way to Pasadena, California. Providence was going to have to take a hand. And Providence did.

All things come to he who sits in the publicity office and waits. And I was sitting right there, rather forlornly, when a friend named Billy King burst exuberantly into the room. Billy was a football player who had played at Compton Junior College in California and was now redshirted. He had been sitting in the campus hangout—Ellis & Ernest drugstore—when a stranger had come in to say that he was a bricklayer from Sevierville who had just purchased a new automobile a few days ago. And even as we spoke, his car was being serviced at Skeets Brandau's filling station across the street. When the car was ready he was going to drive to California to visit his parents. And he would surely like some company on this long trip. Well, right off he had Billy. And now he had me. And he added Bob Broome and several others, and we were off to the land of the wizards in sunny Southern California.

Although we drove Cole Porter-style (night and day), we had not suspected that there was so much real estate between Knoxville and Pasadena.

Our sight-seeing tour took us all the way to San Diego and then up the coast to Los Angeles and the campus of the University of Southern California. We realized we were about to lose our transportation because our man's parents lived on up the coast, and so we tried to see all we could before he took his wheels northward. We milled aimlessly around the student center, until by chance we met a kindly fellow who offered to point out things of interest and answer our considerable number of questions. He said that his name was Dean Cromwell. And that's how we met one of the most famous track-and-field coaches of all time.

Our next stop was the Los Angeles Memorial Coliseum. It was easily the biggest stadium we had ever seen, and we imagined that it must be the largest in the whole world. Playfully, we romped up and down the steps in the aisles, from top to bottom. Boy, this was some stadium!

But if you were up there in the top row, way back there, how could you really see the football game? We didn't know then. The answer is—you can't.

We then proceeded to the railway station at Alhambra where the train bearing the Vols would make its arrival. The welcoming party had already gathered. There were some movie stars there, including Florence Rice, the daughter of sportswriter Grantland Rice. She would be a sort of hostess for the Tennesseans. And suddenly here came the Volunteers pouring off the train. There was a band playing, and there was lots of screaming and yelling and laughing, and flashbulbs were going off. And now the buses were loaded and headed for the Huntington Hotel in Pasadena.

I sought out my man Jack Joyner, who now would be in constant demand. And because of his busy schedule, Major Neyland had authorized Joyner to rent an automobile. In recognition of the fact that we had hit the big time, Jack made it a convertible. This was a strong concession for the major. Spending money in the interest of publicity was counter to the fundamental tenets of his soul.

Jack had what I considered some great news when he told me that Bill Stern had called from New York to Knoxville before they left to confirm that I would be his spotter for the Rose Bowl broadcast. And for this biggest of bowl games, coast to coast, the fee had gone up from five to twenty-five dollars. I was now on my way to great wealth.

But since great wealth had not quite struck me as yet, I was more pressingly in need of quarters for the night. This was going to require some ingenuity. Providence had delivered me to Pasadena, but I had the feeling that Providence was leaving me on my own there.

Tom Anderson, that sportswriter for the Knoxville *Journal,* was now a good friend, and I noticed on the rooming list that he was occupying a twin-bed room with Wirt Gammon of *The Chattanooga Times.* That looked like my best bet for lodging. I inquired as to the availability of a corner portion of the thick rug where I might lay my weary body. They were agreeable and I resided there with them. Somehow I overlooked the formality of informing the registration desk of our little arrangement.

Since hours and behavior patterns were somewhat staggered, occasionally I would ease up onto the mattress of one bed or the other for a few hours of more comfortable rest.

The Rose Bowl trip just continued to be one revelation after another for me. Like the day that famed director Clarence Brown, who was an alumnus of Tennessee, invited the entire group to motor up to his lavish layout for an afternoon and evening of entertainment. He had asked a few of the cowboys to drop by and entertain—fellows like Tom Mix, Gene Autry, Roy Rogers, Leo Carrillo, Ken Maynard, and Monte Montana. They went through their paces in the spacious estate. Aviator Paul Mantz did some stunt flying. And our host had asked Edgar Bergen to entertain on the patio. Lana Turner, Laraine Day, and Ann Rutherford circulated among the guests, as did Oliver Hardy, Jack Oakie, and Gail Patrick. Mistakenly thinking that I was one of the football players, an impression that I did nothing to discourage, Miss Turner had autographed a slip of paper on which she had written, "To Lindsey—Do it for me, Lana Turner."

The note itself did not specify what it was that Miss Turner wanted me to do for her. But in the succeeding years that I spent in the army, I carried that note in my wallet. And on social occasions, when I would pull this trophy from my pocket and display it for the drooling troops to see, it got lots of attention and enhanced my stock.

Meanwhile, as we cavorted on the Hollywood social scene, the socks-and-jocks brigade was practicing daily at Brookside Park, not far removed from the Rose Bowl itself.

Major Neyland, like many people of accomplishment, had a variety of personality traits seemingly in direct conflict with others. While he himself was a master psychologist who worked to instill confidence in his players, he was still paranoid about the presence of spies. He felt threatened at every turn. Back in Knoxville, he had envisioned foreign agents crouching behind the brush on Cherokee Bluff across the Tennessee River from his practice field. He frequently dispatched guards, particularly Gus Manning, to search the barren spot. Manning duly reported that they found no football spies charting formations. On Cherokee Bluff, all they found was a well-undressed couple engaged in a sensuous session of outdoor afternoon sex. They could not have had less interest in football.

Now the major was having recurrences even in that far-off promised land of California. He looked off into the towering San Gabriel Mountains, which radio announcer Graham McNamee had once mistakenly identified as the Sierra Madre range, and Neyland thought he saw spies. The major called Billy King and me to his side there at Brookside Park. He handed Billy the keys to his rented car and explained that he had left his army field glasses on the dresser in his room at the Huntington Hotel. He wanted us to fetch the glasses, and we did. The major spent the next hour training the powerful glasses on the distant mountainous terrain. But he never found anything that he could identify definitely as a Southern Cal spy. He did not, in fact, even discover any outdoor afternoon lovers. We didn't know that afternoon lovers in Southern California do not necessarily seek seclusion.

Jack Joyner came to me with the exciting word that he had been in touch with Bill Stern, who would be broadcasting his regular network *Colgate Sportsreel* show from network studios at Sunset and Vine, and he had invited Jack and me to meet him at his hotel, the Hollywood Roosevelt. Then we would go to the studios nearby, and after the show Bill would drive to Pasadena and check into the Huntington Hotel to be near the Rose Bowl.

Bill packed a small overnight bag, which he carried to the car as we proceeded to the NBC studios. At the front door, we were met by a uniformed page who said, "Right this way, Mr. Stern, your studio is ready." We walked three abreast down a wide corridor to a brightly lit studio. In the center of the room there was a rectangular table with a green felt surface. And there was a boom microphone suspended over the center of the table. To one side of the room there was a glass partition through which one could see a good many lights and dials and several busy people. This, we were told, was the control room, where the engineers and the director operated. There was another booth we could see into. We were told that this was the clients' booth. If representatives of the sponsor happened to be present, they occupied this privileged place. On this particular night, however, Mr. Colgate and all his kin were apparently celebrating the Christmas season at home, for all was bare.

There were a good many chairs off to one side, and Jack and I were invited to make ourselves at home. We were the entire studio audience. Pretty soon, the night's featured guest came in. He was Elmer Layden, once one of the famed "Four Horsemen" of the great 1924 backfield, and then head coach of the Fighting Irish of Notre Dame.

I didn't miss much that went on there that night. This was a rare opportunity for me to see how a network radio show operated, and I intended to learn all about it I could. The entire show was scripted. All the questions and answers had been written. Bill and Elmer did a rehearsal. The director in the control room had a stopwatch suspended on a chain around his neck. He kept pointing his finger at Bill to indicate that he should begin a certain segment. He was keeping time and writing down the figures on a pad he held.

There was a male quartet that sang an opening and closing commercial ditty. I couldn't catch all the words, but there was a lot in there about shave cream, and about Colgate and Bill Stern. At dramatic points in the narration, at the cue from the director still in the control room, the quartet would hum, as a sort of background, moodsetting sound. This was a bit uptown from the way I heard the sports news reported at home.

When we arrived back at the Huntington, I went up to Bill's room as we went over details of the football game, checking out positions, pronunciations, and probable strategy. I noted that Tennessee's big star, George Cafego, had a knee injury and would probably start just as a sort of a reward for outstanding past service. But he would probably be replaced early by Johnny Butler or Buist Warren. Bill said that he had already visited Southern Cal, and the Trojans' top tailback, Grenny Lansdell, was injured and it was likely that the position would be manned most of the afternoon by Amby Schindler or maybe Doyle Nave.

Bill said, with the starters at tailback ailing on both teams, it was fortunate that they were so well backed up. The backups played most of the game.

Next morning I met Bill for breakfast in the Huntington dining room. It was a big day, and I remember everything that happened. I remember that he ordered Grape-nuts. I had never heard of Grape-nuts, and I wondered if you had to hull 'em, like walnuts. Or I thought that maybe in a swanky place like this, they would be served already shelled. When they came, in a bowl with sugar and cream, they hardly looked like nuts at all.

Then Bill decided that he and I would watch a little of the Tournament of Roses Parade. We drove to a lot where a spot had been reserved for Bill. And then we walked in front of the bleacherlike grandstand sections along the street to seats in the reviewing stand. As we walked down the street that morning, before the parade itself had reached this section of the route, people politely applauded Bill Stern. He smiled and waved. I hope it was not apparent to them that I was quietly acknowledging their plaudits and fantasizing that they were applauding me.

We couldn't stay for much of the parade because Bill said we couldn't afford to take the chance of getting caught in the game traffic. Pretty soon, we walked back to the car and drove on down to the Rose Bowl parking lot. Bill explained to the attendant that we would prefer to park as near the press box entrance as possible because he was an amputee and long walks were difficult.

The broadcast booth was one of the worst I have ever seen. To begin with, it was small. And it was way down toward one end of the field. When they played at the other end, identifications would be difficult.

Also, people sitting in the top row of seats could stand up and almost block the view of the announcers in the booth. Just now, the fans were flocking to the booth to ask for Bill Stern's autograph. Bill had been through this before. "It will continue," he said, "until the first movie star shows up and then they will quickly abandon us." About that time, Gary Cooper came in to take his seat in the stands and we never had any more requests for autographs.

The color announcer was Ken Carpenter. NBC thought that an event of this stature should have two announcers. Bill surely did not want another football announcer in there. But he thought Carpenter was just right. He was primarily a commercial announcer, best known for his work on the Bing Crosby show. When he came into the booth, he didn't have any notes or papers. He had a program in his hand that he referred to now and again. I got the idea that he might be checking the cover to be sure of the correct name of the event. Other than that, Ken Carpenter's remarks were all ad-lib and as smooth as silk in that mellow voice. He wasn't saying anything, but it certainly sounded good. I thought I should be able to learn something from that performance, but I wasn't sure what it was.

The spotter's boards that Bill used were primitive. They were two pieces of soft wood, cut into boards about one foot by six inches, and there were a lot of thumbtacks. Bill wrote the lineups down by position on pieces of white cardboard that were then thumbtacked to the soft wooden boards. The lineups were written in pencil, and when there was a change, the spotter rubbed out a name with an eraser and replaced it by writing in another. The outcome was a disappointment. Southern Cal won 14–0. At the end of the game, Bill enthusiastically declared that the season was over. Presuming that he, then, would have no further use for the spotter's boards, I asked if I might have them. He said I might. And when I eventually did my first broadcast of a football game, I had not yet had wide experience. But my boards had. They had been in the Rose Bowl.

I suppose that the practical high point came as we walked away from the Rose Bowl and Bill Stern handed me a twenty-dollar bill and a five. The idea of getting paid twenty-five dollars for spotting a football game was overwhelming. It also came just in time, since my shallow funds had been almost completely exhausted. My brother, James, had sent me a check that got me through the Christmas holidays in California, but we show-biz folk run through money with abandon. I had quickly spent the money my sister, Mary Sue, had given me.

But now I was pumped up. I had twenty-five dollars. I would need it because I was thousands of miles away from home with no prospects for transportation. Unfortunately it did not appear that my bricklaying friend from Sevierville, who had delivered me westward, would be returning. And worse still, Mr. Anderson was about to check out of the Huntington Hotel, and that would instantly cut off my source of food, not to mention shelter.

Billy King suggested that we take a public transport "red car" (trolley car) from Pasadena into Los Angeles and move our base to the Biltmore Hotel. But the football folk were leaving there in droves, too, heading for the railway station. Fortunately, we came upon a Tennessee student who had driven to California for the game in his somewhat reliable automobile, and he offered to sign us on as passengers. He reckoned that our share of the expenses would be seventeen dollars each. Billy had raised a few bucks somewhere and was covered. I was about to expend the major portion of NBC's payment for my scintillating performance at the Rose Bowl. I knew it was scintillating, because Bill Stern sent me a note in which he said, "You are my idea of the best spotter in the U.S." This was plainly my field.

It was required at the university that you take two years of ROTC training. And then you could elect to take advanced ROTC for two more years. At the end of that time, if all had gone well, you would be commissioned a second lieutenant in the infantry. But that was not the most inviting inducement. What was was the fact that the government sent a small check every three months, and that was sufficient to cover minor social expenses. Naturally I had been busily engaged in the work of the ROTC.

One summer, I was ordered to Fort McClellan, Alabama, for six weeks of advanced ROTC training. And it was while I was there at Fort McClellan honing up my skills at defending my country, that I got a letter from Bill Stern of NBC. He said that they would be broadcasting the College All-Star game to be played at Soldier Field in Chicago in August, and that if I planned to be in the neighborhood he would certainly be glad to have me as a spotter on the broadcast. Since I had practically worn out the note from Bill designating me as "my idea of the best spotter in the U.S.," I thought I was in need of some new credits and made plans to go to Chicago. I did notice that nobody was yet offering to pay the expenses of the spotter, and I wished that the Knoxville *Journal*'s Tom Anderson were planning on covering the game. But he wasn't, and I was not acquainted with anyone in Chicago in whose hotel room I might borrow a little space.

I had been there during the World's Fair—the Century of Progress Exposition—in 1933, but about all I remembered about that was Sally Rand and her fan dance. I still remember Sally Rand and her fan dance. I expect that I will always remember Sally Rand and her fan dance. You see, she had these big, soft fans that she moved from one portion of her healthy body to another. As far as I could tell, she was not wearing anything at all beneath the fans. Hundreds of anxious males, somewhat like myself, gathered for each performance, hoping that Sally, in some manner, would fail to get the proper fan to the proper place at the proper time. As far as I know, she never did. But for me it was memorable because I had discovered puberty and Sally Rand at about the same time.

But memories of Sally Rand were not going to get me to Chicago. So when I had completed my military obligation for the summer, I returned to my hometown in Tennessee and set about the task of raising funds. It wasn't easy and I didn't raise much. My principal backer was a classmate named Porter Wiley who put up fifteen dollars. But as the lyrics of a later popular song proclaimed, "I had my fare, and just a trifle to spare." I settled into a seat on the Greyhound, bound for Chicago. I was armed with a letter from a Charles Fredericks of the *Chicago Tribune* sports staff. Presumably that would get me into the practice facilities at Dyche Stadium on the campus of Northwestern University.

As I slept peaceably on the big bus roaring through nocturnal Indiana, I did not realize that there had been another development. The NBC Radio Network had canceled the proposed broadcast of the game. Almost all sports broadcasts in those days were "sustaining," meaning without sponsors. It would be no financial loss to the network. And the programming department had opted to carry a political speech by Vice-President Henry Wallace.

Bill Stern had thoughtfully sent me a note, explaining that NBC would not be carrying the game and that he would likely be seeing me in Knoxville sometime in the fall. But since I had not received Bill's note before leaving Tennessee, when I finally arrived at Hinman House, Northwestern University, and dragged my lone piece of luggage, an overpacked Gladstone bag, inside the door, Mr. Fredericks informed me that I was in quest of a mission that had already been scratched. He told me about NBC's cancellation, which seemed to leave me stranded and unemployed, broke, and in a strange city. Other than that, things were just swell.

Mr. Fredericks said that I was welcome to watch practice, so I went out to the field. Coach Eddie Anderson of Iowa was the head coach of the All-Stars. Frank Carideo, the legendary Notre Damer, was one of his assistants. Nile Kinnick, who had been a star on Anderson's Iowa team the season before, was one of the players. They were installing the Notre Dame offense. I stayed until everybody headed for the showers, and I headed for the El.

Night was coming on, and it was time for me to appraise my situation. It appeared initially to be not too promising. I was capitalized at a total of fifty cents. I was an accomplished hitchhiker, and I decided that this would be my means of transportation. But nighttime is not suited to the best results in hitchhiking, so I thought that I would wait until what the military calls "first light." I had learned that at Fort McClellan.

That brought up the question of where I would spend the night, and my budget would not allow expenditure of any funds whatsoever in that direction.

My midtown strolling had borne me out upon Michigan Avenue, where I discovered Grant Park. As the hours wore on, it seemed to me that there were others in Chicago also in my general financial state, because already some of them were stretching out for the night on the soft grass of the park.

I went into a cafeteria and purchased two small sweet rolls for ten cents and then bought a copy of the thick *Chicago Tribune.* I was not all that knowledgeable about Colonel McCormick's editorial attitudes in the *Trib.* I was not in quest of information or entertainment. I was interested in girth. It was best suited among the papers on the newsrack for being spread out as protection against the dampness of the grass, where I proposed to sleep.

And that is how I spent that night in Chicago, among the drunks and perverts in the park. The most that could be said for it was that it was inexpensive. (In later years, I would come back to Chicago to broadcast the College All-Star game, and I would get a somewhat small room at the Conrad Hilton Hotel because of my tardy arrival. A friend said, "You didn't get much of a room, did you?" And I said, "No, but it's better than that park over there, and I've slept there, too!")

Next morning, I made another slight expenditure for bus fare to take me as far south as the city bus route would go. We old hitchhikers know that you can't just start out in the middle of Michigan Avenue, or State Street, or Lake Shore Drive. You've got to get out there where the long travelers are running. My first hitch took me all the way to Kokomo, Indiana, in my frustrating return trip home. I had not seen the All-Star game.

That summer I was in Nashville, spending the night at the James Robertson Hotel. And the new Vanderbilt head football coach, Red Sanders, came by for a visit.

"You don't know my line coach, do you?" he asked.

I said, "I don't know him, but I know who he is."

"Well, he has some reports that I should have and I asked him to bring them to me here," Sanders said.

About this time, there was a knock on the door, and I opened it to discover a tall, raw-boned, handsome fellow in tan slacks and tan shoes and a white short-sleeved shirt. He stuck out his hand and said, "I'm Paul Bryant." And that is how I first became acquainted with Bear Bryant, who became a legend among football coaches. We were friends for forty years. (Incidentally, Bryant had not been Sanders's first choice. That had been Murray Warmath, then an assistant at Mississippi State and later longtime head coach at Minnesota.)

During the football season of my senior year, I graduated from the spotter's job in the public-address booth. The Tennessee games were being broadcast by an announcer named Lowell Blanchard, and he engaged me as both spotter and general assistant. "General assistant" meant that on rare occasions he would ask me for an opinion on the air. And I would be permitted to say a few words, very few. But that seemed to me to be a step in the right direction.

Neyland's football team kept right on winning and went through a third consecutive regular season undefeated and untied. Then they lost to Boston College in the Sugar Bowl, and on the NBC broadcast I served as spotter for announcer Fort Pearson. Abe Schecter, a legendary special-events and news executive from NBC, was in town and he sat in on the production meetings. I was widening my circle of acquaintances in the broadcasting business.

With graduation approaching now, I was turning my interest toward other areas. In Europe, war was spreading out in all directions. Adolf Hitler had turned his legions loose on the unsuspecting, and it looked as though he might take over the whole world.

I assumed that we ROTC folk would somewhere, sometime, be invited to block his path, and that prospect intrigued but did not entice me. I noticed that most of the people who had attempted to block his path so far had come to a cruel end, and I did not favor the prospect. I began to pay more attention in ROTC classes. When I commanded the "point" in our attack on Hudson Field, I imagined that there really were German soldiers firing down from the heights of the football practice field, and I was not overjoyed at the security of my position.

CHAPTER 6

You're in the Army Now

In January 1941, Major Bob Neyland was ordered back to active duty. There seemed to be little doubt where all of us were headed. It seemed to us that only the dramatic voice of Winston Churchill, the prime minister of Great Britain, stood between us and the advancing Germans.

In ROTC classes, it was made quite clear that we would be well advised to pay a little closer attention than perhaps we had in the past. When we graduated, we would be commissioned second lieutenants in the army. And our instructor, a Captain Walter Sherfey, who had served in World War I, said, "You had better learn all you can because this summer when you are an infantry platoon commander you can't come crying to me when there are fifty-three soldiers calling you 'Daddy.' "

I wasn't all that thrilled by that prospect, and I also was not thrilled at the prospect of having to cross an Atlantic Ocean that was fairly well controlled by German submarines. This was of real concern to me. I had an abiding fear of being on a ship that was sunk by a German sub in the mid-Atlantic. A lot were. I had had a general fear of water that I think I inherited from my sainted mother.

She had carefully explained to me the great danger and ever-present possibility of my drowning in the rivers and streams of Tennessee, and I had taken her warnings perhaps a little too much to heart.

I remember sitting in the Riviera theater on Gay Street in Knoxville watching a movie starring Robert Young. There was a battle scene where they suspended hostilities on the battlefield for a moment while he and the German officer shared a cigarette. I remember thinking, "Yeah, but no matter what happens now, he got safely across the Atlantic." I was pretty sure that there was a big old ship-sinking submarine out there just waiting for me.

Shortly after I graduated with a bachelor's degree in English, I received army orders instructing me to report to Camp Forrest in Tullahoma, Tennessee, for the beginning of active duty as a second lieutenant, and thence to the 9th Infantry Division at Fort Bragg, North Carolina. Early August was the designated date.

Since I had a couple of summer months to spare, I went back to my home in Columbia, Tennessee, and went to work once again for *The Daily Herald.*

When I had been employed there in the summer before I entered college, I had made $9 a week. But in the four years since then, I had obtained a college education, I had worked for national radio networks, I had traveled to Hollywood and Chicago, I had obviously grown in stature and experience in several directions. This was properly taken into account. At the paper, I would now be something akin to city editor, I would write sports, and I would handle wire copy. My salary accordingly advanced from $9 to $15 a week. I was on stilts. And I also knew that in my immediate future lay that military land of opportunity where second lieutenants drew a stated stipend of $143.50 per month. Make way for the wealthy!

When I reported to Fort Bragg, North Carolina, I was ordered to the 9th Infantry Division, and thence to Company C of the 47th Infantry Regiment. This was in the summer of 1941, and there were some folks around there who would become pretty famous before the war was finished. The division commander was Major General Jacob L. Devers. Jakie Devers became commanding general of an army group and later of all U.S. Army Ground Forces.

The 47th Infantry Regiment, to which I reported, was commanded by Colonel Alexander M. (Sandy) Patch, who became commanding general of the U.S. Seventh Army, the assault force in the invasion of southern France.

The 34th Field Artillery Battalion was commanded by a young West Pointer named William C. Westmoreland who, during a later war, would be the U.S. Army Chief of Staff. His battalion executive officer was Otto Kerner, later the governor of Illinois.

And then, in considerable contrast, there was me.

I wish to make it very clear here that I stayed with the 9th Division until the end of the war in Europe. And I wish to make it clearer that I was never a combat soldier. Most of my years in the service were spent in the capacity of staff officer, assigned to a variety of sometimes unusual duties. But I was associated with some of the great combat soldiers in the war because the 9th Infantry Division was one of the greatest fighting units the U.S. Army ever put in the field.

That was all a long time ago, but I have discovered that the pride of a soldier is enduring. Even at this late date, when I hear a mention of the 9th Division, my chest pops out and I smile at the feeling that comes with memories of soldiers, living and dead, who fought proudly for their country.

Somewhere in those early army days, the military seemed to be beginning to feel that I was not going to be the greatest platoon leader of our time. The only thing I seemed to have in common with Sergeant Alvin York was the fact that we were both Tennesseans. And then there was the incident of the forty-eight hours that I spent, with and without platoon, wandering through the wastes of the Fort Bragg reservation in search of some and any other part of the army.

So it was really no surprise when I got word that the regimental commander wanted to see me. When I reported, he explained that there was a new directive from the First Army headquarters of General Hugh Drum saying that all units down to and including regiment must have public-relations officers. There was no amplification, no explanation, no details. You had to have a public-relations officer. That was all.

The colonel stared at the directive and then he stared at me.

"Do you know what a public-relations officer does?" he asked.

"No, sir," I said, "I've never heard of a public-relations officer."

"Don't you even have an idea of what he might do?" asked the colonel.

"No, sir. I wouldn't have any idea."

"Well, neither do I," he said. "But we've got to have one, it says here. Do you want to be the public-relations officer?"

"Yes, sir," I said, "I want the job."

And that is how I became a public-relations officer and quit being a platoon leader. I was fortunate, I think. Later on, one side or the other just shot incompetent platoon leaders like me.

I had just completed the transfer of my gear up to regimental headquarters when our adjutant, Captain Sam Sauer, received an interesting note from a former associate stationed at Camp Croft, South Carolina. The note said that we were being favored with a batch of recruits who had just completed basic training, and among them was Private E. J. Kahn, Jr.

Captain Sauer, a native of New York State and a graduate of West Point, was already aware of Private Kahn's considerable literary ability. He was an avid reader of *The New Yorker,* on whose editorial staff Kahn had worked for several years. And because I was now the public-relations officer, the adjutant said he'd put our new man on special duty with me. I thought that was all right, although I had not yet figured out exactly what, if anything, the public-relations officer was expected to do. Whatever it was, I supposed that I could do it better with an assistant.

I recall that I was seated calmly there at my desk at regimental headquarters bright and early one morning when Private Kahn reported. Now I had a staff.

Division headquarters was having the same kind of time that we were. Actually they had more men than we who did not know what the public-relations section did. But the assistant division commander was Brigadier General Forrest Harding, and when General Harding heard that we had E. J. Kahn, Jr., of *The New Yorker,* he had him transferred immediately to division headquarters. Whereupon Private Kahn packed up his things, shook hands, promised to write often, and went away to division headquarters across the street.

A few days later, I got a call from Private Kahn. He had found a friend at division, he said, in Corporal Danny Herr, formerly of the New York *Daily News.* Herr was another of our growing fraternity of public-relations men who didn't know what to do. Sometimes they assigned him to the duty of ticket taker at the movie theater.

Oddly, though, Herr had been promoted. There was no table of organization for public relations, no position vacancies, thus no promotions. But they liked Danny at division. And they had hunted everywhere for some paper promotion they could give him. In the process, they discovered that the latrine orderly, the keeper of the bathroom, rated a corporal. So they made Danny Herr a corporal, giving him the latrine orderly's promotion.

Kahn said that he and Danny Herr wanted to talk to me. They had a public-relations section but they didn't have a public-relations officer.

"Do you want to be our officer up here?" Kahn asked.

I didn't know. I wasn't unhappy where I was, but I supposed I wouldn't mind moving. But I wanted to know what they did in public relations at division.

"Same thing we did at regiment," said Kahn. "Same thing exactly, only there's more of us to do it. But we don't have a commander. We don't have an officer. You want to come up here?"

"In case I do," I said, "how am I going to do it? Who's going to get me transferred?"

"We are," said Herr. "We know the general. We'll get you transferred."

And they did. A week later, I got orders transferring me officially to 9th Division headquarters, those orders having been issued at the insistence of a buck private and a latrine corporal.

So I packed up and went across the road, too. I stayed with 9th Division headquarters in the United States and overseas until the end of the war.

It was in November 1941 that I got a note from a friend and former classmate, Jimmy Coleman, of St. Albans, West Virginia, who had played football at Tennessee. He was writing to tell me about a proposed reunion in Washington at an upcoming football game. The Redskins would be playing the Philadelphia Eagles, and we had mutual friends on both teams. Also Fritz Brandt, a former Tennessee great as a teammate of Bobby Dodd, had indicated that he would join us at the game. Coleman thought that if I would come to Washington, we could have a reunion with Ed Cifers of the Redskins and with Bob Suffridge, Burr West, and Sam Bartholomew of the Eagles. The game would be played at Griffith Stadium in Washington on a Sunday afternoon the first week in December. I have never managed to forget the exact date of that game.

On Saturday, I took the train from Fayetteville, North Carolina, to Washington, arriving near midnight.

When that crowded train pulled into Union Station in Washington, I was lost in a sea of disembarking passengers. I followed them out into the rotunda of that station and then I made my way underneath those stone arches at the front entrance. Outside, a scene was opening up to me that thrilled me right down to the tips of my toes. As I edged toward Massachusetts Avenue in front of Union Station, I walked between massive stone columns, and as I looked straight ahead, in a direct line-of-sight up Delaware Avenue, I saw, for the first time in my life, the Capitol of the United States.

Next morning, I took a taxi to Griffith Stadium and was standing in front of the box office, just about to purchase a ticket, when I heard a familiar voice say, "Don't buy that ticket. Keep your money."

I looked around. It was Bob Suffridge, former all-American at Tennessee. The Eagles were just getting off the bus.

"Come on with us," said Suffridge. "Take off your army hat and come on."

I was well aware that complimentary tickets in the National Football League of those times were extremely scarce. They needed all the paid admissions they could muster. And I knew, too, that taking off my army hat would not quite complete the disguise, since I also wore an army mackinaw, pinks, and army shoes. But Suffridge dragged me right up to the gate where a uniformed employee was checking the ballplayers through.

"This is our recruiting officer," said Suffridge. "He recruits for the Eagles, came with us from Philly."

By this time he had shoved me through the gate, and the gateman was scratching his head and saying, "Just a moment," as we disappeared inside.

"I'll see you after the ball game," I said, heading for the stands.

"Oh, no, no, no," said Suffridge. "Come on into the dressing room. I want to talk to you."

Inside the locker room, a man outfitted smartly in a brown topcoat and a brown hat stared at me as though he were about to have me bodily removed. I wouldn't have blamed him because I had a feeling that I certainly didn't belong in the dressing room of the Philadelphia Eagles.

As Suffridge came over to where I waited, I pointed to the man in brown. "I don't think he likes me very much," I whispered.

"Oh, him. Don't mind him," said Suffridge, turning to the man. "Coach, this is Lieutenant Nelson. Lindsey, this is Greasy Neale."

No wonder the man was staring at me. He was the head coach, getting ready to deliver his pregame instructions.

I tried to get out again, but Suff wouldn't listen. Moments later, I found myself trotting in the midst of a stampede of human flesh down the runway, through the dugout, and onto the turf, as thousands cheered.

A chilled wind blew across the grass of Griffith Stadium as the football fans settled into their places that afternoon.

On the field, Tommy Thompson of the Eagles and Sammy Baugh of the Redskins loosened up their arms. Kicker Augie Leo booted a few practice field goals. On the Eagles bench, Coach Greasy Neale pulled his heavy topcoat more closely about him.

On the rooftop, public-address announcer Frank Blair (who would later gain television fame as the newsman on the morning *Today Show* on NBC-TV) looked over his notes. In the stands, a young naval officer named John F. Kennedy made himself comfortable.

Seated on the Eagles bench, I watched and waited.

None of us there at Griffith Stadium, none of us in the nation's capital, none of us in the Washington area or anywhere else would ever forget that afternoon.

It was December 7, 1941—Pearl Harbor day.

As the game progressed, we suspected that something unusual was happening somewhere, but we didn't know what. Frank Blair kept calling for various members of the military establishment to report to their stations.

On the Eagle bench we asked each other what might be happening. No one knew. Frank Blair has since written that he went to George Preston Marshall, the owner of the Redskins, for instructions, and then announced that the Japanese had bombed Pearl Harbor. Let me say simply that if he did we did not hear him. I know it sounds strange to say that somebody announced the start of World War II on a loudspeaker and that I, sitting there on the bench in the uniform of an army second lieutenant, didn't hear it. But that was the way it was. I saw the kickoff of the football game and missed the kickoff of the war.

Harry Thayer, the general manager of the Eagles, was on that bench, too. At one point, Coach Neale said, "Harry, see if you can find out what's going on."

What was going on, of course, was that the Japanese had successfully completed their carrier-based raid on Pearl Harbor and destroyed our Pacific Fleet. But all of this was not immediately clear to us. The game itself was uninterrupted. Suffridge put on a spectacular performance, but the Redskins won by a score of 20 to 14. Even as we went postgame right out of the dressing room through the crowds to a waiting taxi, mostly we heard wild rumors. Some screaming fans said that enemy soldiers had landed in San Diego.

We went directly to Ed Cifers's apartment. Then we went to a preplanned season-ending party the Eagles had at the Willard Hotel. Suffridge was still telling people that I was the Eagles' recruiting officer. But I wasn't having any trouble getting around now. The mood had changed abruptly in that short time. My army uniform was my pass to anywhere. As I walked back through Union Station, a man rushed up, slapped me on the back, and said, "Give 'em hell, Lieutenant."

I realized then that I now had permanent employment. This would be a steady job, perhaps the last I'd ever have.

CHAPTER 7

The Way to War

By the end of the year, the country was thoroughly unsettled because of the war. For instance, the Rose Bowl football game was not played in the Rose Bowl. It was played at Duke Stadium in Durham, North Carolina, which was considered somewhat less vulnerable to possible Japanese air attack. The teams were Duke and Oregon State. The NBC broadcasters were Bill Stern and Harry Wismer. And I took a few days' leave to sit in on the proceedings as an observer and guest of Stern.

In early 1942, public-relations life went on at Fort Bragg. One afternoon the phone rang and it was my boss, the G-2 colonel, calling. He said he had a newspaperman in his office and wanted me to come right up and take the visitor off his hands. I grabbed my cap and departed for the G-2 office. G-2, by the way, is the staff designation for Intelligence, an obvious misnomer in the case of both the colonel and me. And public relations was now a subsection of G-2, handling publicity, correspondents, and the like.

As I drew near, I could see that this was no ordinary newspaperman standing there outside that door. He didn't have the harassed look of a man who had spent years under the unbending yoke of a city editor. I figured he might possibly be a foreign agent posing as a newspaperman.

The G-2 colonel had been keeping the guest company until I arrived, and he had become bored with the job. He wanted to get back to something important, like looking at the pictures in *Life* magazine. He did that a lot.

As I came within range, he pointed offhandedly toward what the clothiers might have called a "short-stout" man, or possibly just "stout," and said, "This is Mr.—what did you say your name was?"

The stranger swallowed and said rather softly and overdistinctly, "Anderson, Maxwell Anderson."

"He's Mr. Anderson, a newspaperman. See what he wants," said the colonel, disappearing out the side door and removing himself from this ghastly intrusion to his routine.

So there I stood with this Maxwell Anderson. Sure seemed as though I had heard that name somewhere before. The colonel hadn't heard it, though, so he couldn't be very prominent. Maybe he was a sportswriter. I knew some sportswriters. Maybe he was from Montgomery or Tallahassee.

I said, brightly, "What paper do you work for, Mr. Anderson?"

He didn't answer right away. He seemed to swallow again, more slowly this time, before saying in a rather deliberate tone, "I don't work for any paper. I'm Maxwell Anderson."

This time I awakened. This was no sportswriter. And this was no pedestrian newspaperman. This was an author, a very famous author. I had studied him at the University of Tennessee. This was the fellow who had been coauthor of *What Price Glory?,* and had written such things as *Elizabeth the Queen, Mary of Scotland, Winterset, High Tor,* and *Knickerbocker Holiday.*

As we talked now, he said he was gathering material for a new presentation, which would turn out to be *The Eve of St. Mark.* He wanted to see some of our soldiers as they worked at their training. I knew that we had a battery of artillery firing out on Gruber Road and I suggested we drive out and see them. About this time, the G-2 colonel came roaring back. Somebody had explained to him that Maxwell Anderson was a man of considerable stature, so the colonel now said, "Why don't you take my sedan? Take my car and drive Mr. Anderson out to Gruber Road."

That was the first time I'd ever seen the inside of an army sedan. Infantry soldiers don't see the inside of a lot of cars. But we rolled along until we came to the artillery pieces, parked the car, got out, and approached the firing positions.

A Lieutenant Brown was in command. He explained to Mr. Anderson how they fired the pieces in battery. "Just like this, see?"

There was a loud roar, a lot of smoke, and the two men stood shading their eyes and peering out over the tops of the trees toward which the artillery pieces were pointed. I peered, too, since it seemed fashionable. And I didn't see a thing except a small sparrow. Again, they fired. The lieutenant and the author peered. I looked and still didn't see a thing.

"Oh, I see," said Anderson, "hmmm." And he nodded his head affirmatively.

The artillery men took a break, and the lieutenant turned to Anderson. "Did you read Westbrook Pegler this morning?" I had heard of Westbrook Pegler. He *was* a newspaperman, a columnist.

"I certainly did read him this morning," said Anderson. "He's clever, isn't he?"

And presently we were back in the comfort of the sedan headed for downtown Fayetteville. As we drove, Anderson said, "You know, I certainly feel better after talking to that young man."

I had not heard Brown say anything of very special note, unless Anderson was conducting a reader survey for Westbrook Pegler, which I doubted. But the big man was lost in meditation. Either that, or about to drop off. I'll admit that my conversation was not calculated to keep him long awake.

The biggest hotel in Fayetteville was the Prince Charles. In fact, it was the only one you'd give any sort of rating. I was sure that Maxwell Anderson would be staying there. That's where all the newspapermen stayed. I instructed the driver to pull up at the Prince Charles.

"Oh, no." Mr. Anderson smiled. "I'm not staying here, I'm at the LaFayette." That was farther down the street, a little establishment that reputedly housed transient vermin in addition to paying guests.

As he got out of the car, he waxed philosophical for a moment. "You know," he said, "when you're out like this, you don't expect the comforts of home and you most assuredly don't find them."

With that he disappeared behind the swinging doors of the LaFayette.

I had not had the heart to tell one of America's most famous playwrights that he was living in a well-patronized North Carolina whorehouse. Maybe he thought it was a convention of Avon ladies.

Anyway, wars do make strange bedfellows.

Maxwell Anderson next day went to the Field Artillery replacement center, evidently fascinated by artillery pieces and the men who fire them. There he met a young soldier named Marion Hargrove, formerly of the Charlotte *News.* He had been working on a manuscript for a book about soldier life. Maxwell Anderson liked what he read, appended an introduction, and they called it *See Here, Private Hargrove.* It sold a lot of copies, was made into a movie, and made Private Hargrove famous. Maxwell Anderson was already famous, everywhere except in the office of the 9th Division's G-2.

Even during these times when we did not have famous visitors, life was not dull in Fayetteville. We were training to fight the Germans and in the meanwhile we sometimes fought among ourselves. Some enterprising promoter constructed a vast beverage dispensary that was appropriately named the "Town Pump." Because of local statutes, the Town Pump was not licensed to sell anything stronger than beer. But the equipment always gave promise of better things. There were a couple of circular bars, garish jukeboxes, plush red-leather upholstered banquettes, highly polished floors, and lots of frosted plate glass. It was a popular rendezvous place.

The 9th Division had been at Fort Bragg for a long while. The 9th had a sort of proprietary attitude. And then the 82nd Airborne Division came into Bragg. The paratroopers wore highly polished boots, creased trousers, lacquered helmet liners, and a smug look. They had been given to understand that they were extremely tough, and most of them believed it. A lot of them really were. But the 9th and the 82nd were just never very happy together.

If you are a dogface infantry soldier in town on a Saturday-night pass and you come across your girl in the company of a slick paratrooper who makes more money than you do, it may irritate you, especially if he is wearing a lacquered helmet liner.

So it was one Saturday night, and the Town Pump was jammed with soldiers and their gals, plus soldiers and the wives of other soldiers who had gone off to war. Somebody from the 82nd said something uncomplimentary to somebody from the 9th and all hell broke loose.

It was one of the bitterest pitched battles of the entire war. And I happened to see it real well. I was in one of those leather banquettes up front when it started. But suddenly there were exits where exits had never been before. Many were leaving through that frosted plate glass. The proprietor ran into the street yelling for the police. Soldiers were throwing beer glasses, pretzels, and fists. Women were screaming and scratching and pulling hair.

One lady left just ahead of me, tossed through the enlarged window, and lay a little stunned out in the debris. An enterprising soldier asked for her phone number.

The local police could not make a dent in these proceedings and returned equipped with tear-gas grenades. In time, the riot was brought under control, and a good portion of the army was impounded in the local jail. A number of company commanders missed church services the next morning as they went downtown to bail their soldiers out.

A couple of years later, when the 9th Division cut the Cotentin Peninsula in France to seal off the port of Cherbourg, a patriotic merchant in Fayetteville put a sign in his window: HURRAH FOR THE 9TH DIVISION. THEY FOUGHT ALL THE WAY FROM THE TOWN PUMP TO CHERBOURG.

CHAPTER 8

Old Blood 'n' Guts

One hot late-summer afternoon the entire division was assembled on the sandy parade ground. We had not been told what the occasion was, but we were accustomed to such things by this time. Since a speaker's scaffold had been erected at one end of the quadrangle, we assumed that there would be a speaker.

We had been standing there only about an hour, packed closely together under that hot Carolina sun, when we heard the wail of sirens indicating either a raid, a fire, or the approach of dignitaries.

All eyes were on the army sedan that pulled up near the speaker's platform. We noticed that the nurses from the dental clinic across the street had come out on their porch to hear this military address.

The speaker was introduced as "the man who will be in command of our Task Force, an officer who has never asked anyone to do anything he wouldn't do himself."

He was already doing things that most of us would never do. He was wearing cavalry boots and riding breeches. He carried a baton or a riding crop, whichever. And he was adorned with decorations.

I wondered where he'd been while I was standing up to my ankles in hot sand with perspiration pouring down my face. I noted that he had come from the direction of the air-conditioned officers' club.

The speech was pretty much to the point. He told us that we were going to be terribly tough in combat. He told us that in a high, squeaky voice. And he made it sound inviting.

"We'll rape their women and pillage their towns and run the pusillanimous sons of bitches into the sea," he screamed.

He was using a public-address system that spread his words around the cantonment area. With those first few declarations, the nurses scampered back inside, and a few chaplains began to make little marks in the sand with the toes of their army brogans.

There was considerable repetition in the remarks and we kept getting back to "those pusillanimous sons of bitches." That phrase impressed me, that and the part about raping their women and pillaging their towns.

Our commander had said that this was a Major General George S. Patton, Jr.

I had never heard of him before, but I heard of him quite a lot afterward—"Old Blood 'n' Guts."

In the fall of 1942, we went away to North Africa. And I successfully evaded those German submarines in the Atlantic aboard a vessel named the N.S.S. *Slotterdyk,* which would hardly have been worth sinking. The chances were fairly good that it would sink on its own. But we made it safely afloat into the harbor at Casablanca. We had been told that this was a sparkling, glistening, exciting city. Like Rick, the character played by Humphrey Bogart in the film *Casablanca,* we had been misinformed. We spent our first night sleeping in hay on the hillside out by the lighthouse near the Anfa Hotel. A very short time later, the Anfa would be the site of a high-level conference among representatives of the Allies, including Churchill and Roosevelt, at which the unbending policy of "unconditional surrender" was agreed on. A member of the American delegation there was Alger Hiss, later accused of treason.

We had moved our headquarters north, past Rabat to Port Lyautey. And our big thrill of that time came the afternoon we were unexpectedly reviewed by President Roosevelt, riding in a jeep. Because of his physical disability, Roosevelt was not expected to be in the field. His presence there with the troops in North Africa gave us a real lift.

We soon regrouped and moved eastward. By the time we got to Tunisia, General Patton had taken over command of II Corps. So there we were, under Old Blood 'n' Guts, ready to "rape their women and pillage their towns." A surprising order came down saying that we would wear neckties at all times. I thought this was a strange touch.

And that was only the beginning. The meticulous orders from General Patton continued. We received word that shoes would be kept shined, all personnel would be clean-shaven, and sleeves would be kept at full arm's length and buttoned, even in combat. There was no offense worse than wearing the little issue wool cap without the helmet. There were also strict orders against looting of any kind. Molesting of civilians would be punishable by death.

Then late one afternoon, I came bouncing into our command post, which was located near Bou Chebka. I had ridden in a jeep from Tebéssa, and jeep-jockeying over those roads did strange things to the kidneys and bladder. I felt an immediate urge to race for the latrine, and I did.

The North African war, generally, was less organized than the later war in Europe. Our latrine consisted simply of a canvas fly that surrounded a small plot of level ground. Inside was a slit trench for the use of ordinary humans. Exclusively for generals, there was a box that was popularly referred to as the "throne."

The throne was situated just inside the opening to the fly so that you had to pass closely in front of it in order to get to the slit trench where I was impatiently bound.

My mission was becoming more urgent with each hurried step. Then, as I whirled through the opening in the fly, I came face to face with a neat row of three silver stars mounted on a helmet. The stars were on the helmet of the man who adorned the throne at the moment. I came to a skidding halt. I was petrified.

I knew my military courtesy pretty well. I knew whom to salute. In my case it was just about everybody, since I didn't know of anybody that I outranked. But here I really did not know what to do. Nothing I had ever read or studied had told me what to do when one encounters a three-star general in the latrine. I didn't know whether to tie my tie or zip my fly, advance or retreat. And the three-star was giving me no help. He was just sitting there. And I was just standing there. He apparently did not feel inclined to introduce himself, and he surely did not have to. I knew who he was. He was George S. Patton, Jr.

I do not think that Congress had yet authorized the wearing of that third star on his helmet, but it was certainly all right with me, and I had no plans to bring up the subject.

I eased carefully on over to the slit trench and accomplished my mission. He continued just to stare at me and never said a word.

As I left, I again had to pass close by the three-star, who was still motionless. When I had passed, on an irresistible impulse, I turned and tipped my helmet in a bit of a farewell. Once outside, I ran like hell. I did not want to be in the neighborhood when he finally pulled up those trousers and emerged.

Since the war years, at social gatherings people have sometimes said to me, "Did you ever see General Patton during the war?" And I invariably reply, "Oh, yes, we met."

As the Tunisian campaign continued, I found that the climate wasn't entirely conducive to my typing out of doors as I had been doing. The keys on the machine would freeze.

As a result, I moved into a tent being used by the Division G-1, the man in charge of personnel. Each night I would set my portable typewriter over near his little gasoline stove and beat out my copy for the day. Of course, we got to be close friends, the G-1 and I. And I casually observed some of the many duties with which he busied himself. He had to submit daily strength reports, recommendations for promotions and decorations, and handle a lot of administrative work. Then at El Guettar, the first night the Germans made their bed-check aerial call over the olive grove, the colonel was taken violently ill.

General Patton arrived at that command post, and in a voice loud enough for all to hear, said to our General Eddy, "Manton, I want you to get these staff officers out of those holes and out here where they can be shot at."

Our G-1, already anxious, went beserk and was taken away to a field hospital for observation. Since I was already there by the stove, I became his replacement.

I was a little surprised to find that we had as our allies four *tabors* of *Goums,* native Berber tribesmen who were mercenaries and primarily knife-fighters. Some bleeding heart in Washington decided that all our allies had to be as well equipped as we, so we outfitted these very unmechanical people with Thompson submachine guns. They, of course, didn't know how to use them. They did a lot of killing, mostly of each other. And when II Corps instructed me to send them a strength report on the *Goums,* I replied, "I don't know how many *Goums* we've got, and I don't think they know how many we've got. But we've got a hell of a lot less than we had before we gave them those Thompson submachine guns."

When the war in Tunisia ended for us at Bizerte, most of the American army units were pulled back into Algeria for brief rest periods before invading Sicily. Some of the troops went to Oran, some to Algiers. The 1st Division misbehaved so violently on the return trip that two important things resulted. General Terry Allen was eventually relieved as the commander, and the 9th Division, which was following, was sent to an unpopulated spot about fifty miles south of Sidi-bel-Abbès in the direction of the Sahara desert.

There were occasional junkets, maybe up to the port of Oran, adjacent Ain el Turck, or Mers el-Kébir. If you were lucky you might get a mission to Algiers, where you could get a room at the Aletti Hotel and get anything you wanted and some things you didn't at the Sphinx Club.

But mostly we went about our assigned business of resting until the next campaign. That was without a doubt the most unique rest area any outfit ever endured.

It was as hot as seven hundred hells. Without dysentery and allied afflictions even your best friends wouldn't associate with you. You simply had to have them or you didn't belong.

There were flies by the million, and they were the most discourteous I have ever lived with. I was reared in the Southland, where we had plenty of flies. But our flies had absorbed all the old Southern gallantry, culture, and charm. They just swarmed lazily and gently around whatever food happened to be in the house and stayed right there. Our flies knew their proper place.

These Algerian flies were aggressive and loved to live dangerously. If you opened your mouth to say "Yessir" to the general, at least two dozen flies flew in and settled heavily on your tongue.

To pass the time properly, one of our West Point graduates got the idea that we should set up a school of close-order drill. Because of the heat, he conceded that we attend in informal uniform, which consisted of helmet liner, shorts, and high-topped GI shoes. Our little sessions were held on a shadeless plot of ground that was also several inches deep in hot sand.

Each afternoon at four, we gathered for the roll call, formed two ranks, and stood inspection. The West Pointer went down the line. "Pull in your butt! Throw out your chest! Suck in your gut! Pull down your chin!"

I did not really put my heart completely into this activity down there in the Sahara desert, so I feared for the worst one afternoon when a runner said that General Eddy wanted to speak to me.

When I approached, he said, "Nelson, there's a little town down the road named Bedeau." He pointed toward the inner Sahara. "They're having a native celebration there. And there's a post of the French Foreign Legion located in Bedeau. We want to cooperate with these people all we can. So I am detailing you as a liaison officer with the French Foreign Legion. Keep in mind that the Foreign Legion is a proud and ceremonial organization. Their officers will invite you to join in their ceremonial toasts. To refuse to drink with them would be an affront, and I do not wish to hear of you affronting the French Foreign Legion."

Well, I went down there as ordered and reported to the French Foreign Legion. And the general was surely right. They drank a lot of toasts. They toasted everything that moved, and the sunset and the sunrise and France and America. And they drank most of the toasts in eau de vie, a drink once described by correspondent Ernie Pyle as consisting of equal parts of kerosene and barbed wire.

I had been there for several days and I hadn't affronted anybody. But I noticed that my health was failing. So I decided to move on to the Foreign Legion headquarters at Sidi-bel-Abbès for a few days before returning to my division. I now think it was a lifesaving move. But it was a unique experience, and even now when the talk turns to war I do get attention when I speak of my days with the French Foreign Legion.

For instance, there was the night in the 1970s when we were on the turnpike just outside Pittsburgh, driving to dinner. Bob Prince, the legendary Pittsburgh sports announcer, was at the wheel. That was appropriate, since our understanding was that the ride and the dinner check both were to be on him.

Ralph Kiner, onetime home-run king of the Pittsburgh Pirates and one of my partners on the Mets' announcing team, was in the front seat. I was in the rear.

Prince had experienced a little difficulty in locating me and he proceeded to apply the needle. "We thought perhaps you had slipped away and joined the French Foreign Legion," he chortled. "From now on we'll just call you the old Legionnaire."

Very quietly, I said, "I was in the French Foreign Legion." And before Prince could say anything, Kiner said, "As a matter of fact, he was."

Prince pulled the car onto the shoulder of the turnpike and stopped. "You were what?" he said. "You were in the French Foreign Legion?"

And so I sat there on the side of the road outside Pittsburgh and explained to Bob Prince that actually I was not *in* the Foreign Legion, I was *with* the Foreign Legion. There was a technicality involved.

I further explained that at dinner in New York several years ago General Westmoreland mentioned my service with the French Foreign Legion, extolling their virtues as proud professional soldiers. I have forgotten his precise reference to me, but certainly it was not as a proud professional soldier. In any case, after the general's speech and mention of me and the Legion, my stock went up in that company a thousandfold.

I have been in the company of Mr. Prince on numerous occasions since that night. And late in the evening, when the crowds have thinned, the lights have dimmed, the sounds of the night are quiet, and the bartender is sleepy, Bob Prince is likely to mumble, with greatest disdain, "French Foreign Legion!"

I reply with a silent, palm-forward French army salute.

CHAPTER 9

Crossing Paths with Ernie Pyle

After our campaign in Sicily, we moved up to a very crowded England, with our headquarters in the ancient cathedral city of Winchester, sometimes referred to as the Camelot of King Arthur's time, with the Round Table in the Grand Hall and with a prominent statue of King Alfred in the main street.

We learned first that the British Isles were in danger of sinking from the weight of the number of American troops there waiting for the invasion of the continent, which reportedly was coming off sometime soon.

We also learned that we would be quarantined for a period of two weeks while we underwent a strict program of orientation and instruction in proper conduct among the civilized peoples of this area.

Although we were an experienced combat unit, we also underwent instruction at the hands of the British. The brigadier lecturer opened up by saying, "We of the British forces have concluded, on the basis of our experience at Dieppe and other places, that an opposed landing is more difficult than an unopposed landing." Well, maybe we didn't know much, but we had already discovered that it is easier to cross a beach if nobody is shooting at you.

There was no question in those days but that the grandest figure in all the British Isles was Prime Minister Winston Churchill. During earlier, bleaker times he seemed to be the one staunch figure standing between the conquering hordes of Hitler's legions and the free world.

Princess Grace of Monaco once described Churchill as a "page in history," and there is no doubt that he left his mark. And I suppose that none of us knows just when he may be thrown briefly into the presence of a "page in history" and then pass on.

It was about two weeks before D-Day and the invasion of Normandy in 1944, when Churchill and General Dwight D. Eisenhower, the Supreme Commander, came down to the south coast of England to inspect the troops.

We had an aging colonel named Paddy Flint who had wangled a regimental command despite his years. He was considerably older than Eisenhower. And as the dignitaries drove slowly down the road, there stood Paddy at rigid attention, holding a firm salute with his left hand! Eisenhower ordered his driver to stop the car. And the Supreme Commander bounded onto the dusty road, raced over to where the grizzled old soldier stood, and held him in a fond embrace.

"Paddy," said Eisenhower, "you old son of a gun."

Parenthetically, the old son of a gun did not survive the war. He was a combat casualty, and General Patton named the Flint Kaserne, the American barracks, in Bavaria, in his honored memory.

That day, our cavalcade moved on until we reached High Street in ancient Winchester. Despite the protests of the British secret service assigned to protect him, Churchill insisted on alighting and walking through the crowds of people toward the speaker's platform, which was erected in the quadrangle of the barracks once occupied by the storied British infantry regiment, the 60th Rifles.

Who knows, maybe Churchill had some personal thoughts of his own there that afternoon. When young Churchill had first come into the service, his father had insisted that he join the 60th Rifles. Young Winston favored the cavalry. The disagreement at times grew bitter before Winston finally won out. Maybe some thoughts of his father's fondness for this infantry unit, housed in these very barracks, assailed him that day.

In any case, discomfort certainly assailed him. Having arrived, he felt a strong urge and disappeared in the direction of the latrine. As the assembled soldiers waited at parade rest, the prime minister reappeared, being careful to continue buttoning his fly, so the soldiers would have no doubt of the reason for the delay. The soldiers loved it. Here was a man earthy enough for them.

While Churchill and Eisenhower were out inspecting the troops, there were a great many war correspondents based mostly in London who were looking for any sort of stories they could find. It was my job to serve in a liaison capacity and to encourage them to visit and write about the 9th Division.

One who accepted our invitation was Drew Middleton of *The New York Times* (he is still at the *Times* as an expert on military affairs). He was getting ready for the invasion, like the rest of us, and one day he came down to Winchester for a visit with General Eddy.

Drew and his charming wife checked into a small, comfortable hotel in midtown and we went away for dinner at General Eddy's quarters. As the evening wore on, we recalled that the hotel had a posted closing time of eleven P.M. That was customary. At eleven o'clock, the door was locked and that was that. General Eddy thought perhaps we should call the hotel and explain that Mr. and Mrs. Middleton might be a little bit late. When I made the phone call, I explained carefully to the custodian of the hotel that Mr. and Mrs. Middleton were the guests of General Eddy and we would all appreciate a slight relaxation of the rules on their behalf.

The crusty reply gave me the idea that this old gentleman didn't care if Winston Churchill was calling—at eleven o'clock the door would be locked tight until next morning. And when we arrived around midnight, that is precisely what had happened. The premises were surrounded by a stone wall some ten feet high, and we solved the problem only by boosting the distinguished Mr. Middleton and the very tight-skirted Mrs. Middleton over that wall. It was not a dignified operation, but it was effective. The Middletons were thus relieved of the alternative of sleeping in the street, or maybe the cemetery of the adjacent Winchester Cathedral.

One of the most prominent war correspondents in England now was Scripps-Howard reporter Ernie Pyle. He had just come up from Italy.

I first met him one hot afternoon in Sicily when a jeep came swirling into our command post in a cloud of white dust. I knew the fellow in the front seat, General Omar Bradley. I had not yet met the little fellow in the backseat, but I soon did. And Ernie Pyle and I remained close friends until his death.

I knew a few things about Ernie Pyle, not much. I knew that before the war he had written a general-interest column for Scripps-Howard newspapers, the kind of gentle little column that was usually buried somewhere deep inside the paper.

I knew that he was now a war correspondent, and some of the soldiers were getting clippings from back home. And they discovered that Ernie Pyle was telling people back home what this war was like, and doing it better than anybody else. He conveyed the truth, that it wasn't very heroic or very thrilling. It was miserable.

Ernie Pyle was from Indiana, and at the University of Indiana he had been editor of the school paper. He had also been in love with a flame-haired co-ed who was inconsiderate enough to marry someone else. I suppose that if one examined the genius of Ernie Pyle, which was later to bring him international fame, one would discover that his one incomparable gift was his sensitivity. He felt things on the battlefield that were unknown to others. In his senior year in college, the defection of the girl he loved touched that sensitivity and drove him to drop out of school and take a job as a newspaperman. It was about the same as running away to join the Foreign Legion.

Ernie went to work for Scripps-Howard in Washington. Eventually, he settled into an assignment as a roving correspondent—picking his own assignments, going where he pleased, writing what he saw and felt.

The war came and Ernie went to London, where he covered the blitz of London and gained early attention with descriptions like this of the devastation: "These things all went together to make the most hateful, most beautiful single scene I have ever known."

Moving with the war from England to North Africa, then to Sicily, Pyle was developing into the conscience of America. Parents scrambled to read his column, accepting and trusting it as the letter home their son had been too busy to write. No one in the nation had greater credibility than Ernie Pyle. If he made a serious suggestion, it was likely that Congress would act on it. His fame came so quickly that he himself did not suspect the magnitude of his role.

The army men in Washington, however, were well aware of the power of Ernie Pyle. And they suggested that he spend some time with and do some columns about General Omar Bradley. It was quite apparent that Bradley would move ahead of General George Patton, but the army had a problem of public acceptance. Patton was flamboyant, adventuresome, colorful. The public loved him. Bradley was none of these. He was an exceptionally competent general in the field, but not given to doing things that would make the American people love him. He was often thought of as a "schoolteacher" type. So, with a little urging on both sides, Ernie Pyle and Omar Bradley joined forces. It proved to be a mutually beneficial association. Not directly as a result of this alliance, but along the way, Ernie Pyle became the most influential journalist of his time, maybe the greatest columnist ever. And Omar Bradley went down in history as one of the greatest five-star generals in the history of the U.S. Army, beloved as the "GI's general."

From Sicily, correspondent Ernie Pyle had gone on to mainland Italy. And it was there in the Italian mountains that he wrote what may have been the greatest column written by any correspondent in World War II. It was a column that described the reaction to the death of Captain Henry T. Waskow, Company B, 143rd Infantry Regiment, 36th Infantry Division.

Captain Waskow was killed on December 14, 1943, but Ernie's column was not published until January 10, 1944. He was in a period of depression, and doubted his ability to write anything. Having written this column, he decided it wasn't worth sending. He asked fellow correspondent Don Whitehead of the Associated Press to look at it. Don's reaction was instantaneous. Don said, "This may be the best thing that you've ever written."

Others had no difficulty in judging the merit of the piece. When the copy arrived at the Washington *Daily News,* they devoted the entire front page to it. There was no headline, there was no Russian story, there was no weather information, just the text of Ernie's column spread out there all over page 1. By five o'clock in the afternoon you could not buy a copy of the paper in Washington. It was sold out.

Ernie had moved on to England and was in his room at the Dorchester Hotel in London when Don Whitehead called from the AP office on Fleet Street to tell him that the information had just moved on the wire—Ernie had won the Pulitzer Prize. His reaction was typical. He said, "Don, you wouldn't kid me, would you?"

Ernie Pyle, then, was in England in 1944 and so was I, and occasionally we came across each other in those busy times. And we were about to welcome the British spring. There were some sunny days when the weather was almost warm. And we could arrange a brief trip up to Waterloo Station in London, with perhaps a visit to the bar of the Regent Palace, or the Dorchester, or the Mayfair, or the Gros venor House. We could stop at the officers' club at 8 South Audley. And after dark, we could run the obstacle course populated by the female "commandoes" of Piccadilly Circus. Life got very social in the blackout. One could fall in love without ever actually getting a clear look at the object of one's affection. Maybe it was better that way.

But we were never able to forget why we were there. The invasion of the German-held continent would be coming any time now. It was the sort of thing that one did not like to dwell on constantly, however. It could be depressing, even frightening. And that was one of the big reasons why the pubs were doing all the business they could handle. Ours was a beer and booze war. Marijuana, cocaine, and heroin were for later conflicts.

We had nearly approached D-Day when I received word that I would be required to attend a two-day seminar on army public relations to be held in Bristol. And when I arrived, I was a little more than surprised to learn that I would speak to the gathering on the subject "The Public-Relations Officer in Combat." That was to me an intriguing title because I had made every effort up until that time to keep the public-relations officer out of combat.

I did not actually have a lot to say on the subject, partially because General Bradley was in the audience. I did point out that since public-relations officers were not listed in the tables of organization, they were not authorized to draw any equipment and would be obliged to steal anything they got. It helped if you were an accomplished thief.

When we moved to another room, there were not enough seats for all of us and I was required to stand in the back of the room, against the blackboard, between correspondents Ernie Pyle and Clark Lee of INS. Clark Lee had been the glamour correspondent of the early war in the Pacific when he was out there with MacArthur.

Most of the officers in attendance at this seminar were from units that had come directly to the United Kingdom from the United States and had not been in combat and probably never in the field.

Major Jim Quirk was running this program, and he said, "Tonight we are going to take our bedrolls and our pup tents and go out into the woods south of Bristol and show you what it is like to spend a night in the field."

Well, I did not take immediately to this news, because I had been down there in Africa and Sicily sleeping in uncomfortable pup tents for quite a while. And I was really not all that fond of it.

Then I became aware that Ernie Pyle was speaking softly to me without turning his head, so that he would attract no attention. He said, "Captain Nelson, do you plan to spend the night in a pup tent to see what it is like to sleep in the field?"

Without turning my head and also in a soft voice, I said, "No, Mr. Pyle, I rather thought the best hotel in Bristol, England."

Ernie said, "Do you suppose you could make it a twin-bed room?"

Ernie and I understood each other.

The coming of "Overlord," the code name for the invasion of the continent, was no secret. The only question was when. And as June approached, we knew it would be soon.

We did not know where the target areas would be. That was top-secret information. We didn't much care. One beach area looked pretty much like another to us. We were happy enough that the 9th Division, as General Bradley had recently informed us, would be in the buildup rather than the assault wave.

Every effort was being made to confuse the enemy agents. And heaven knows there were plenty of enemy agents around. More than once we had been rousted out of our beds, loaded onto trucks, and driven down to Southampton to the docks. And then we were brought back. It was a feint. I was quartered with a private family at their residence on Links Road in Winchester. Each time we made one of those late-night maneuvers, I took less equipment. It just seemed like an unnecessary bother.

Finally, the day came when we loaded up and were deposited at a restricted area outside Southampton. I had my carbine and little else. I didn't even have a mess kit. This was an area bounded with barbed wire to discourage any who might suddenly wish to volunteer out of the whole idea. We were now instructed in the location of the beaches, and their code names. They would be burned into my consciousness forever—Utah, Omaha, Gold, Juno, and Sword. Maps of the target areas were provided. They were imprinted on rubber so that they could be carried undamaged in the water.

The 4th Division and the 90th Division would be in assault after the drops of the 101st and 82nd Airborne. Our target beach was Utah. The 1st and 29th Divisions would go in at Omaha.

The night before we moved I had trouble sleeping, so for the first time in my young life I asked for and got a sleeping pill. In the predawn hours, when we were roused to start our move, I couldn't awaken—I almost slept through D-Day. We had heard the planes going over with the airborne troops, and as we were trucked to the docks at Southampton we listened for the radio reports. We had great interest in how the assault troops were doing. If they got thrown back, and they might have gotten thrown back, it would affect our future life and continuing good health. General Dwight D. Eisenhower had scribbled out the draft of an apologetic announcement in case he had to withdraw.

The morning of D-Day, June 6, 1944, we were loaded onto ships and stayed in the Channel for the next several days. It was not exactly the quiet kind of spot you'd be likely to choose for a vacation or a family holiday. Finally we were transferred to landing craft. Our vehicles were waterproofed with the motors sealed and the exhaust pipes of the jeeps extending six feet into the air. The jeep could be underwater and still operate if it didn't hit a shell hole in the ocean floor, which would drop the vertical exhaust underwater and stall the vehicle.

I was in a jeep driven by Private Lawrence Cogan of Alexandria, Virginia, along with Major Jack Houston of Compton, California. When our jeep got about halfway across the sand of the beach, it conked out. We did not wait for the automobile club. We proceeded on foot pell-mell in the general direction of Ste.-Mère-Eglise. We were into the hedgerows of Normandy.

I was not really surprised a day or so later to feel someone tugging at my sleeve and to discover that it was Ernie Pyle.

I was trying to drive the tent pegs of my pup tent, using my helmet as a hammer. It was raining. And there stood this little fellow with a raincoat that was too big, a helmet that looked too big, and a very pained expression.

"Have you got a drink of brandy?" he said.

I told him I thought I did and I went back to hammering on the tent pegs.

He tugged at the sleeve a little more insistently this time and said, "Look, I don't want to be a bother. But if you've got it, I want it now. This ain't social, this is medicinal."

* * *

When the 9th Division was one of the units to capture the port city of Cherbourg, including the German military commander General von Schlieben and the naval commander Admiral Hennecke, their surrender was accepted personally by General M. S. Eddy. And I was on the field phone to First Army trying to get some press credit for our General Eddy.

The presence of the 9th Division on the Continent had not yet been released by the censors, so news stories could not mention Eddy. They would have to say, and did, that the surrender was accepted by the corps commander, General Joe Collins.

Ernie sat on the wet grass inside our tent while I ground away at the field phone.

Ernie quietly said, "I'll take care of it."

I was exasperated with the world. "Oh, sure," I said, "you'll take care of it. You'll just wave a magic wand and everything will be just rosy."

He didn't reply, but a week or so later I met Ernie on a road and we stopped for a visit. He said, "I took care of that thing about the general, about General Eddy. In fact, I saved you a carbon."

From his pocket, he withdrew a carbon copy of his column. In his typical gentle style it said, among other things, that Major General Manton S. Eddy was a favorite among war correspondents because they thought he was a mighty good general. It was a matter of weeks before Eddy was given command of XII Corps in George Patton's Third Army and promoted to lieutenant general. When Ernie Pyle offered an opinion, the army brass listened.

Meanwhile, as the war moved toward Paris, Ernie Pyle and I spent a good deal of time together. We talked a lot about things that soldiers talk about when they are a little lonely and a little afraid. Ernie liked to reminisce about the early newspaper days when he didn't know that they had auditors for expense accounts. He thought if you fooled the gal at the cashier's window you were home free. And he remembered the item he submitted, "ice-cream cones—ten dollars."

He wrote about a night we spent in his tent when our conversation was interrupted by a shrill whine overhead. Ernie promptly identified the sound as a rotating band off one of our own shells. He pointed out that they sometimes sounded like a dog howling, nothing to be afraid of. And I conveniently agreed with him. Rotating band, that's what it was. But we later found that it was a foot-square red-hot, jagged piece of steel from a German 240-millimeter shell that had exploded a hundred yards from us. Ernie wrote, "It's wonderful to be a wise guy."

When he reached Paris, Ernie decided that it was time to go home. He said that he had had it.

But when he got home, he discovered that he was more nationally famous than he had ever guessed. He was in demand, all the time. This was the very thing he was trying to escape. He had come back from Cherbourg one day to relate an incident that happened to him there. And it puzzled and bewildered him. He said he had been traveling with a platoon of doughboys, and on the outskirts of the city there was a lull for a moment. He was crouched in a ditch close to a rather young soldier. This boy just didn't seem to understand what this little old man was doing traveling with his platoon.

"Are you a correspondent?" asked the boy.

"Yeah," said Pyle, keeping his head down.

And then, just conversationally, as though he weren't speaking to anyone in particular, the boy said aloud, "Ernie Pyle is the doughboy's friend."

"I'm Ernie Pyle," said the famous correspondent, a little embarrassed.

The boy half-turned, looking right into Ernie's face, and didn't say a word. When he turned back around, he got the signal to move on up toward Cherbourg. And as he moved out, holding his rifle at a high port and crouched over, he was grinning from ear to ear.

Ernie never understood the magnetism he generated among soldiers, and he wasn't sure he could endure the responsibility of it. Now he was finding more of that at home.

Ernie was busy with a wife who had been ill for years. He was making lots of money and wrestling with the burden of fame. In Hollywood, a Pyle-inspired movie called *The Story of GI Joe* was in production. The role of Ernie Pyle was being played by Burgess Meredith. (Ernie thought it should be Walter Brennan.) Ernie arranged for various of his friends among the correspondents to serve as "technical advisers."

I got a letter that said, "Nothing especially notable has happened to me since I saw you last, except that I've collected two honorary degrees, been kissed by Paulette Goddard, had my teeth filled, spent the first Christmas with my wife in five years, managed to keep well-stocked with booze and cigarettes, and turned down at least 2000 requests to speak, write pieces, or just appear on the stage with my prick hanging out."

All of the military services were now competing to have Ernie Pyle with them. He really didn't want to go anywhere. But he didn't feel he had a choice.

He wrote to me: "I'm not complaining but I've had no rest at all during this stay in America. This 'celebrity' business has a lot of advantages, but it isn't all it's cracked up to be. My life is hardly any longer my own. I haven't done anything, such as make speeches or accept invitations, but even saying 'no' takes up 90 percent of your time."

There was no way that Ernie could escape the pressures that were bearing down on him from all sides. And he agreed to go to the Pacific with the Navy. He did not say so publicly, of course, but he wrote me, "If I hold out I'll probably be gone a year, but I'm hoping for a mild case of malaria or some other semilegitimate excuse to come home."

He was not kidding himself. He wrote: "You know I came home from the war damn good and sick of it, and I'm going back still just as sick of it. The old romanticism about getting itchy feet to get back to the front is a myth as far as I'm concerned. The only reason I'm going is that I feel I've got to."

A book of his columns had been put together and published under the title *Brave Men.* He wrote, "The first printing of nearly 700,000 was sold out within a month."

Of course, his big concern had been and was his wife. "My wife, who has been ill most of the time for years, was both very much better and very much worse during my time at home. For five weeks she was in the hospital and even I wasn't allowed to see her. Then she improved miraculously, and was able to come to California with me this last time and take a look around Hollywood. She is now back in Albuquerque in a hospital for the winter, not so much because of a relapse as because of care during convalescence."

Actually, it had been much worse than that. What Ernie did not say was that at one point, Jerry, in a fit of depression, had locked herself in the bathroom and attempted suicide. She had slashed her wrists and her breasts and stabbed herself in the throat repeatedly with a pair of scissors. That is when she was hospitalized, and even Ernie was not allowed to see her.

He remembered my interest in sports when he wrote, "A couple of weeks ago in Pasadena I met a friend of yours named Sweet [Fletcher Sweet] who is publicity man for the Tennessee football team, which was out there for the Rose Bowl game."

It wasn't long before I began to read the Ernie Pyle columns from the Pacific, carried in *The Stars and Stripes.* Somehow, though, they didn't have the Ernie Pyle touch. He wrote: "I sure hated to come back into the war, and it was hell to get started writing again. I still haven't got into the swing of it yet. But I've seen no war at all in the seven weeks I've been out here. Had sworn I was never going on another landing, but looks as though I'll have to if I find any war to write about."

He raised the ire of a lot of Pacific combat veterans by suggesting that their war was not nearly as tough as the one he had left in Europe.

To me, he wrote: "I'm doing the Navy this time and will be with them several months. They live wonderfully. People out here (except the Marines and a few others and the doughboys in the Philippines) have no conception whatever of what our war was like. I have to bite my tongue every now and then to keep from yelling."

While he denied having any real feeling for the war in Europe, there was no doubt that he still felt drawn to it, the moth to the flame.

I got a letter dated "March 1, 1945, Western Pacific." Ernie wrote: "You must have had a bitch of a winter. I didn't even like to think of the boys over there. Surely it can't last very much longer over there. You'll probably beat me home. I suppose I'll be out here a year or more, if I don't get sick. But I do feel homesick for our old gang and the kind of war we knew, bad as it was."

He ended that, the last letter I ever got from him, by reporting, "The new book has already sold nearly 900,000 copies and I'm a rich sonovabitch."

And the final words were "Be good to yourself."

It was not many days after I received that letter that I was in an upstairs room in a German house packing my gear for the move forward. Sergeant Peel came in and said, "I'm sorry to tell you, sir. But we just heard it on the radio. Ernie Pyle is dead."

He had been killed on April 18, 1945, on the little island of Ie Shima by Japanese machine-gun fire. He was forty-four years old.

In casual conversations, people have said to me, "Did you ever see Ernie Pyle during the war?" And I have said, "Oh, yes. We met."

I have been asked by some for an explanation of the basis of the unlikely friendship between Ernie Pyle and me, since he was twenty years the older.

I have an explanation that is valid, at least to me. When one is in a combat zone, there is no future. It does not exist. One who gives a serious thought to it is a fool. And since there is no future, there is no past. Everything that has gone before sort of runs together. All that one has, then, is the present. And the present is ageless. And so was the relationship between Ernie Pyle and me. I never knew him in the United States, before or after the war. We were close friends in a combat zone, where he was in his forties and I was in my twenties, and we were the same age.

CHAPTER 10

Those Who Compose

The great names of world journalism were there in Europe to cover the war and I was afforded a daily opportunity to become acquainted with some of the legendary figures in the field.

One afternoon in Normandy, Clark Lee and I made a trip to VII Corps headquarters. There were dead cattle in every field. They were lying with all four hooves pointed skyward, and they were bloated and smelly. In some of the fields there were battered gliders in which our airborne troops had landed. Silk parachutes were lying all around where supplies and ammunition had been dropped. Signs warned that the roads had been cleared of mines only to the hedges.

When we got to VII Corps headquarters we came upon two more correspondent types. Sitting there in the dust on the side of the road was a grayish, balding man who wore a leather jacket and dark green officer's trousers. He was unshaven and the dust of the countryside had not passed him by. His name was Charles C. Wertenbaker, distinguished correspondent for *Time* and *Life*.

Kneeling beside him was a handsome shorter man, fiddling with the cork in a bottle of wine. He wore a wool cap and paratrooper's pants and jacket. He also had a camera around his neck. I was introduced by Clark Lee. This fellow was Bob Capa, perhaps the most famous combat photographer of all time.

One time these two correspondents and Ernie Pyle invited me to join them for dinner. It was Sunday afternoon and they had made an arrangement with the owner of a small café in Bricquebec to whip up a meal. And so we gathered—Ernie Pyle, Bob Capa, Charles Wertenbaker, and me.

The dinner was a smashing success and even finished with a bang. A lone German plane came strafing down the street, and we scattered before dessert. Capa and I landed in the cellar, which seemed the best place to go. But there was no damage, we finished our meal, and returned safely to 9th Division headquarters.

It was just a simple little dinner for four in Bricquebec, France. Nothing to get excited about, unless one looks at what followed in the lives of those dinner guests I was privileged to join that evening.

Ernie Pyle had already become the most famous journalist covering the war. He quickly became rich and more famous. And he had less than a year to live.

Capa seemed to thrive in an atmosphere of combat, and he had been almost constantly in war, going back to the Spanish Civil War. When World War II ended, he wandered. He tried the Hollywood scene and became involved in a torrid and serious affair with actress Ingrid Bergman. But Hollywood was not for Capa.

He would go back to France, buy a house, write a book. It was a good book, called *Slightly Out of Focus.* But his restlessness would not abate. And so he would go back into combat, this time with the French colonial forces in a place called Vietnam.

I read his obituary notice in the *New York Herald Tribune* as I commuted to work in Manhattan one morning. I hurried off the platform at the first station and was sick. Such was my revulsion to the news that Robert Capa was dead. I had many memories of him, mostly of a handsome man with a crooked grin and a cigarette dangling from his lips.

Charles Christian Wertenbaker would survive the war and write books like *Write Sorrow on the Earth* and *Death of Kings.* He would become disenchanted with the magazine business and move to the south of France. There he would discover that he had cancer. He made the choice not to live as less than a complete man and decided to take his own life. This fearless man, who had dodged and cheated death so many times, now sought it.

He had started a book about his thoughts, his decisions, the experience of approaching the end of his life, the unbearable pain. His wife, Lael, finished the book and it was called *Death of a Man.*

All wars leave memories, and this is just a simple recollection of some fascinating people I knew during a war.

After breaking out of Normandy, the 9th Division moved south of Paris and bypassed that exciting city. But then the unit was held in place for several days while positions in that area were consolidated. War, as we have noted, is a chancy business. One never knows just what the morrow may bring, if anything. And I reckoned this as perhaps my only chance to visit one of the world's most glamorous places. Word reached us that the liberation of the City of Light had begun, and that magnificent city had begun to breathe again. And that is how I happened to be on the road that August afternoon of 1945, headed for the Porte d'Orléans and entrance into the city. I worked my way around to Montmartre and stopped for lunch at the Chez Graf on the Boulevard de Clichy hard by the Moulin Rouge. Then I continued to the Scribe Hotel where press headquarters were being set up. On the landing of the stairway leading from the lobby floor down to the lower level, I met Don Whitehead. He was as enthusiastic as a schoolboy. "Did you hear?" he said. "I got the first story filed out of liberated Paris!"

Paris in those several days after liberation was an experience of a lifetime. Ernie Pyle reportedly looked down on that street scene, the beautiful ladies welcoming the soldiers, and observed, "Anybody who sleeps alone tonight is an exhibitionist."

For me, that was the start of a love affair with Paris that has lasted a lifetime. I have been back dozens of times, again and again, and I have always found Paris more exciting than the last time.

But for the moment we had other things to do. So we moved into Belgium and then into Germany itself.

One cold winter's night, Colonel Westmoreland called me to say that some booklets that I had written were finished and ready to be picked up at the printers back in Paris. He wanted to know how long I thought it would take, after my arrival in Paris, to get the books loaded into the command car and to clear the city. I estimated three days. Westy said that seemed like a reasonable estimate, and the mission was so ordered. This was a sort of an author's reward. We both understood that the actual time required for my mission in the city would run closer to twenty minutes. Westy was giving me a three-day margin for error. He and I suspected that there would likely be several errors, and possibly a catastrophe or two, before I got safely out of town.

I went to the motor pool and was assigned a driver appropriately named Private Paul Jones. Together Private Jones and I set out joyously for the City of Light. Our command post was located in the woods just outside Eupen, Belgium, and we made it to Soissons shortly after dark. We stopped there for dinner. I asked Jones if he wanted to spend the night there or try to make it on into Paris. He said we could make it to Paris in a couple of hours, and away we went.

As we came into the outskirts of Paris, I noticed that many of the cafés had dispensed with the blackout curtains. I could see through the front windows, and inside there were people laughing and talking. I remember that these were the warmest-looking scenes I had come across in a long, long time. I had been in blackout countries for so long that I had forgotten the anticipatory pleasure of standing outside and looking into a crowded café or bar.

We drove on to the Paris motor pool, where Jones found accommodations for the night. And since we were only a few blocks away from the Arc de Triomphe, I told Jones that I would check with him the following morning about the books, and I began to walk.

There was a little slush on the streets, and snow was still falling softly as I arrived at the Arc. I stopped for a moment and gazed at the blue flame flickering there and then started down the Champs-Élysées. There were few pedestrians and no motor traffic on the Champs at all. Right there in the middle of perhaps the world's gayest city, I was strangely lonely as I continued my walk, which eventually bore me over to the Scribe Hotel. I knew that many of my friends among the correspondents were quartered there, and I went immediately to the basement bar. It is good to understand one's friends; I had no trouble guessing their probable location.

I had not been mistaken. When I walked in, there was Maxie Zera, the public-relations officer of the 1st Division, the Big Red One, in the midst of a wandering calypso number. Among his audience were Cy Peterman of the *Philadelphia Inquirer,* Tex O'Reilly of the *New York Herald Tribune,* and Neil Sullivan of *Pathé News,* the popular newsreel. I had found my proper Parisian base.

It seemed that we might be rolling now toward an early end to the war, but one learns that the unlikely should not be a surprise.

I remember when our headquarters was near Aachen and I was

the operational duty officer throughout the night, midnight to daylight. One night there were two reports of contact with the enemy—nothing serious, I guessed. It was the sort of accidental contact one could expect when stationary units opposing each other were sending out periodic patrols.

My relief at daylight was Colonel Westmoreland, the division Chief of Staff. I properly reported to him that we had had scant contact. Of course, I was not aware that Field Marshal von Rundstedt had the whole German Wehrmacht poised for the final big German offensive of the war. It was hardly accidental contact by opposing patrols. It was positioning of field armies.

Anyway, I was off to First Army headquarters, in Spa, Belgium, on a public-relations mission, and I was at the Hotel Portugal, having breakfast with Hal Boyle of the Associated Press. He was ready to leave for his daily tour of the Front, and as Hal went out the front door, I lingered over a second cup of coffee and conversation with other companions. Moments later, Hal came back through that door and headed hurriedly for his room.

"I thought you were going to the Front," I said.

"I did," said Boyle, "it's just down that road."

In fact, it was. This was the start of the German push for the fuel dumps in Spa. The Battle of the Bulge which followed was Germany's last all-out offensive effort. There was surprise and confusion and casualties.

When order was restored, I was sent back for a course of instruction in techniques of education at the University of Paris. This was part of a plan the information and education section had, making it possible for members of the occupation army to receive college credit for instruction.

I was delighted with that experience in Paris and got back to my unit just in time to cross the Rhine.

In March, there was that memorable day when a unit commanded by Lieutenant Karl Timmerman of the 9th Armored Division found a bridge across the Rhine at Remagen still standing. The Germans had tried to blow it up and failed. Now the Americans had troops across that last great natural barrier, the Rhine river. Elements of the 9th Infantry Division went across that night. It was so dark that Colonel Westmoreland lay facedown on the hood of his jeep as it crossed the bridge, and gave voice signals to the driver. I had what

I thought was a preferable idea. I said to my driver, "Let's get the hell out of here." We waited until dawn to make our way across.

I established quarters in the cellar of a bombed-out building on the river's bank. That night a big, good-looking war correspondent kicked his bedroll down the stairs and followed it into my cellar. He pushed his helmet back a little, smiled, and said, "I'm Howard Cowan of the Associated Press. Whitehead told me to come to Remagen and find Nelson."

I said, "Well, you've found him, and he ain't got no immediate plans to leave this cellar."

The Germans began a series of counterattacks in an attempt to reach the bridge and blow it. At German headquarters, Hitler was infuriated. The German artillery was firing one shell every two minutes.

Immediately, American units began the construction of pontoon bridges to handle the heavy traffic across.

On March 8, German planes bombed the bridgehead. That brought more American antiaircraft weapons and personnel into the area, the largest concentration of antiaircraft troops and guns during the war.

On March 12, German rocket troops at Bellendoorn, Holland, fired eleven V-2s at Remagen, the only time in World War II that either of the V-weapons was employed tactically. The nearest thing to a hit came when one rocket landed in the river just three hundred yards from the bridge. The farthest landed twenty-five miles away at Cologne.

One day I was with Howard Cowan in an old building that had been a tavern. Before we heard any warning sound, debris began to scatter. It was our first experience with supersonic weapons.

On March 15, the Germans sent over twenty-one bombers. Sixteen of them were shot down.

By then, the Ludendorff bridge had been closed to traffic, and engineers were employed at the job of strengthening the damaged structure. Two pontoon bridges were now in use.

On March 17, at about three o'clock in the afternoon, there was a crackling sound and the bridge began to tumble into the Rhine. Some two hundred American engineers were on the bridge. Twenty-five of them died, and eighteen bodies were never recovered.

A member of an American unit, which had been relieved and left the bridge about twenty minutes before it collapsed, was a twenty-four-year-old soldier named Warren Spahn. Before coming into the army he had been a pitcher, but had never won a single major league game. Fate that afternoon delivered him safely off the bridge at Remagen. He would win 363 games on his way to the Baseball Hall of Fame as one of the great pitchers of all time.

Those of us on the bridgehead rushed to the pontoon bridges to fish as many floating soldiers out of the water as possible.

In my assigned role of working with war correspondents, I quickly notified the First Army press camp. Two newsmen came immediately, Howard Cowan who had gone back, and a sergeant from *Stars and Stripes,* the army newspaper. His name was Andy Rooney. You may have seen him since on television's *60 Minutes,* or perhaps read one of his several books or columns.

I had frequent contacts with correspondent Hal Boyle. It was my job to come up with ideas for stories and columns, if possible, and to assist war correspondents in getting and filing them. Strictly speaking, I was supposed to make the products of my efforts available to all. But I had learned what every good press agent knows. If you are to get good circulation, you had better arrange for an occasional exclusive to a particular writer. In Washington, it's called a "leak."

Hal Boyle was writing a daily column for AP, and doing that from a combat zone is a fairly strenuous assignment. Frequently, I would do a column and ship it off to Hal. And just as frequently, it would run with minor alterations under the Boyle banner at AP.

I got a message once that said, "Don't hesitate to continue sending me any column ideas you may have and don't hesitate to make 'em exclusive."

It was a mutually satisfactory arrangement. Hal got his authentic columns and my division got the kind of publicity we wanted back home. Good publicity back home builds morale on the battlefield.

And then toward the end of the war, there was the night at the First Army press camp at Weimar, when senior AP correspondent Don Whitehead notified Boyle that he had won the Pulitzer Prize for distinguished correspondence. Ernie Pyle had won a Pulitzer, now Hal Boyle had won one, and Don Whitehead still hadn't. Subsequently Whitehead would take the Pulitzer twice.

After the war, when I was working at NBC in New York, I applied for membership in the Overseas Press Club. Rules then required that active members have served for six consecutive months outside the continental limits of the United States, with their principal occupation as a journalist. I, of course, couldn't meet those requirements, so I applied for an associate membership. The application also required the endorsement of at least two active members.

I looked up one day and there stood Hal Boyle in front of my desk. "You are being endorsed," he said, "by Rel Morin and me. We've both won the Pulitzer Prize. And we're changing your classification to that of active member."

"It sounds good," I said, "but how do you figure that?"

"Well," said Hal, "you were over there three years and the army might have thought that you were supposed to be soldiering but we know that you had the principal occupation of journalist."

"Do you think the membership committee will concur?" I asked.

"Yes," said Hal, "I think they will. I happen to be chairman of the membership committee."

Included in my recommendation was: "We feel that, both professionally and socially, Lindsey would be a real credit to OPC. The only moral defect in his character is a weakness toward trying to fill an inside straight at poker.

"He was a close personal friend of Ernie Pyle and Ernie, if alive, certainly would have wanted to add his signature to this letter."

I was an active member of the Overseas Press Club and served on the reunion committee for twenty years.

Tragic was the day years later when Hal came back from his doctor's office in Manhattan with a little slip of white paper in his hand. On it, the doctor had written the diagnosis of Hal's worsening physical condition.

Boyle went into the AP's sports department and asked, "What did Lou Gehrig die of?"

"Some sort of muscular disease," somebody said.

"I want to know exactly," Hal said.

And so the sports guy called the office of the commissioner of baseball, just down the street, and asked Monte Irvin. Monte looked it up, and repeated it on the phone. The guy in AP sports wrote it down and handed it to Hal Boyle.

"This is what Lou Gehrig died of," he said.

Hal compared it to the paper the doctor had given him. They matched—amyotrophic lateral sclerosis.

In three wars and on innumerable assignments, he had never gotten a scratch. He had survived all of that to die of Lou Gehrig's disease in 1974.

* * *

As the war neared its close, we moved from the vicinity of Kassel toward the Elbe, and came upon a sight that is even now almost indescribable. It was a Nazi slave-labor camp near Nordhausen where the slaves had been employed at an underground V-weapons factory.

There were those great mass graves, some still open with bodies scarcely more than racks of bones piled on each other. Wandering aimlessly around were some survivors, skeletal, with hollow eyes and shaven heads, and those striped pajamalike clothes.

War will acquaint one with death but not with this. It was man's ultimate inhumanity to man, the complete desecration of the human being, the robbery of all dignity.

My stomach revolted and I retched there on the ground that day. And that awful scene burned itself so deeply into my consciousness that I have never ever been able completely to rid myself of it.

And then we looked up one day and we had forward elements on the Elbe River about fifty miles from Berlin. We knew that there were Russians somewhere not very far away on the other side of that river. We did not know that a higher-up decision had been made that we were not going to Berlin, we were not going across the Elbe, we were to wait for the Russians.

For a man in the news business, it was plain to see that this was about to be the biggest story of this war—its close, the finish, the curtain.

So I got into a jeep one afternoon and headed off toward our 60th Infantry Regiment, which had elements near Pratau on the Elbe. When I got there, I talked to the executive officer, who was an old friend from way back in Fort Bragg days.

"Where are the Russians?" I asked.

He pointed in the direction of the river and said firmly, "Right there. They are right there on the other side of that river."

"What's between us and them?"

"Nothing but that river," he said.

"No Germans?"

"No Germans," he said.

There were rumors of a linkup downstream at Torgau between the Russians and the 69th Division. I didn't know whether it was true or not. There were always rumors.

Anyway, I went on into Pratau and when I got out of the jeep I was promptly greeted with a rifle shot that deposited a bullet against the wall just back of me.

And as I ducked and searched, I saw a head sticking out from around a part of the bombed-out bridge. And I began to yell, "Americanski, Americanski," which I hoped would identify me.

About that time, another head popped up from behind the bridge, and I recognized him. He was an old friend, a Major Russ Snelling from Denton, Texas.

He explained to the Russians that I was an American, and was not to be shot. Not right now, anyway. I climbed down to where they were standing on the improvised catwalk, and Snelling said his outfit had hooked up with the Russians the night before and they had been celebrating ever since. He had orders to treat the Russians cordially, he said, and they must had had the same kind of orders. Everybody was toasting everybody else.

Snelling suggested that I come on over and meet his Russians, so I did. I climbed perilously across the bridge and entered the town of Wittenberg on the other side of the river. There I was introduced to the Russian commander, who suggested we drink a toast, to anything. The commander was impressed with this historic occasion. I couldn't get rid of him. He insisted that Snelling and I accompany him everywhere he went.

As best I could make out, he was preparing to make an official and historic Russian crossing of the Elbe, and he wanted us to go with him. Since history was being made, we decided that we might as well make some of it. Besides, I had to get back across that river somehow and if he kept whipping out that vodka, I was going to need assistance in negotiating the shaky bridge.

The Russians were wearing parts of German uniforms, they were carrying German rations, they had some German arms, and they had horse-drawn artillery. They seemed to be living off the land.

A soldier drove a trim little black German sedan down to the water's edge and indicated that this was the commander's car. Meanwhile a photographer arrived, and we were posed with the Russians for pictures. And they were readying a barge to float the car across the Elbe. But they continued to take pictures, pictures of us looking across toward the American lines, and pictures of us solemnly shaking hands. Then they took pictures of us as we stepped onto the barge together, the Russians and the Americans crossing the river in unison.

It was late that night when I finally got back to division headquarters, but I wrote a story about the linkup and filed it down to the press camp. It must have got there in a hurry, because the next morning Chris Cunningham of the United Press and Bill Heinz of the New

York *Sun* were there shaking me awake. They wanted to see some Russians, and they'd heard I knew where some were.

Somewhat against my better judgment and in fear of my continuing good health, I got into their jeep and we headed once more for Pratau. This time we ducked the brass, who had come back to the east bank, and went straight to a house that served as platoon headquarters, commanded by a Russian lieutenant.

These were just the plain Russian soldiers and they were super cordial. We toasted a lot of people and were still at it when the sun went down. Chris and Bill decided we should spend the night with the Russians. I had no choice.

After we had eaten some canned German rations, we gathered around a bright campfire there on the banks of the Elbe River. Somebody produced a balalaika, and they began to sing and dance. We all enjoyed the informal performance.

Presently, the Russians stopped and turned toward us, indicating that it was now our turn to entertain them.

Chris and Bill and I looked at each other with some concern. We had not exactly expected this. In effect, we were being persuaded into a command performance, and we didn't have any particular talent. Since we had no interpreter, we could not explain our predicament. It probably wouldn't have helped. They had entertained us, and they wanted us to entertain them.

We have all heard about the pressure of opening night on Broadway. But Broadway was nothing compared to this. If your show bombs out on the Great White Way, you just go home and rest awhile, and get yourself into another show that you hope will do better.

But we were performing for the Russian army. If we irritated them, it was all over. Approval was requisite to survival.

As we searched somewhat frantically for some suggestion, Bill Heinz volunteered, "I know the words to 'Paper Doll.' " That was a popular song prominent in the repertoire of the Mills Brothers.

I said to Chris, "Do you know 'Paper Doll'?"

He said, "No, but I can hum a lot."

So, very slowly Chris Cunningham, Bill Heinz, and I got to our feet. We were a little stiff and unsteady from all the vodka. But we began our rendition, "I'm gonna buy a paper doll that I can call my own . . ."

We were swaying a little there in the dim light of that campfire.

And we were trying very hard. But we were aware that it had become very quiet. And one by one, the Russians were getting to their feet and making a strong effort to stand at attention.

They had guessed that this might be the American national anthem, and they did not wish to seem disrespectful.

That, then, was a little tableau that recorded history may have missed: Russian and American soldiers standing respectfully if unsteadily at attention, as three pained Americans sang "Paper Doll."

We were happy to escape next morning. Chris and Bill dropped me off at our command post at an early hour. I went straight to bed, instructing the sergeant to awaken me for no purpose whatever.

I could not have been asleep for more than a half hour when I felt myself being shaken awake. I was ready to read that sergeant off when I opened my eyes to discover that this was no sergeant. This was Colonel Westmoreland.

"General Craig is going up to make his official linkup with the Russian forces at Pratau," he said. "I want you in charge of interpreters."

Westy was not aware that I had been primary among those visiting with the Russian forces for several days now. He certainly did not know that I had served in the entertainment section of what amounted to the Russian USO. I had no intention of telling him.

Years later, I was sitting in the living room of my home on the North Shore of Long Island when the phone rang. It was Hal Uplinger from Los Angeles. He was a television producer with whom I had worked a lot, and he was a close friend.

He said, "Where were you at the end of World War II?"

I said I had been on the Elbe about fifty miles from Berlin.

He said, "Were you close to any Russians?"

I told him that I had not only been close, that I had actually been with the Red Army when it crossed the Elbe coming westward.

Then he said, "Have you been watching *The Mike Douglas Show* on television this week?"

He explained that Mike had devoted a portion of the shows to a commemoration of the end of World War II, and he had some historians up from Washington who explained about the linkup and showed some film. "And," said Uplinger, "I said to my wife, 'That's Lindsey, that's Lindsey there with those Russians.' "

I told him that he was right, that it was me, but that I had never seen the film. I discovered the firm on Madison Avenue that had furnished the film, got a copy of it, and took it by CBS. Bill Creasy, a producer and close friend, had some stills blown up from the film and I had them framed on my wall.

Of course, what I really wish I had is a picture of Chris Cunningham, Bill Heinz, and Lindsey Nelson singing "Paper Doll" by the campfire on the banks of the Elbe River while the Russian soldiers stood at rapt, respectful attention.

CHAPTER 11

Back Home Again

The war over, I was transferred in the summer of 1945 down to the 65th Infantry Division situated in Linz, Austria. I lived in the Linzerhof Hotel on the banks of the Danube, and I did some baseball broadcasting with a friend named Charlie Fisher. Let me say here that we had some pretty good baseball players. Our manager was Harry Walker, who would manage the Cardinals, the Pirates, and the Astros. Just one season later, he would be a World Series star. We had a pitching staff consisting of Rex Barney (Dodgers), Ken Heintzelman (Pirates and Phillies), Al Brazle (Cardinals), and Bill Ayers (Giants). We had infielders George Scharein (Phillies) and George Archie (Senators and Browns). Ewell Blackwell (Reds) pitched for the 71st Division team at nearby Augsburg. His teammates there included Johnny Wyrostek (Pirates, Phillies, Reds) and Benny Zientara (Reds).

My baseball pleasures were interrupted one afternoon by one last public-relations matter. I was told that Pierre Laval was flying to Linz to surrender, and that a large press delegation would be coming. It was my assignment to handle them.

Pierre Laval had been premier of France, then a collaborator with Hitler. When Vichy France had fallen, he fled to Germany, then went to Spain, and now he was coming to Austria to give up. He arrived, still wearing the white scarf that was his trademark. In October, he died before a firing squad.

The surrender of Pierre Laval was my last army public-relations assignment. Soon I would head for home to start the fearful transition from soldier to civilian.

That began, I suppose, when we landed in Boston in October 1945. The war was over. The civilian population was anxious to forget all about war, and us, and to get back to the normal comforts.

I remember looking off that ship as we tied up there in Boston and realizing that you didn't see a lot of folks in uniform. The ones who were looked strange, and I was one of those.

I went from Camp Miles Standish by train to Camp Atterbury, Indiana, where I reverted to inactive duty. When I had first landed in Boston, I hurried to the telephone to call my parents in Columbia. They knew I was okay and they knew I was back. But for whatever reason, it seemed to me that I was in no hurry to get home. I went to Louisville, Kentucky, because that's where the next bus was going. At midnight I went to Lexington, because I wouldn't have to check into a hotel room that way, and there weren't any hotel rooms.

From Lexington I went to Knoxville, the scene of my college years. A thousand nights during the war I had dreamed of the day I would get back to Knoxville. On Saturday the Volunteers were playing Villanova in a football game. I stayed for that. It was plain to see that I was in a big stall about going home, but I didn't know why. I didn't examine it too closely. Then I took the bus to Nashville, and had to wait an hour before making a connection with the vehicle that would deliver me to the bus station in Columbia, Tennessee, at midnight. At long last, I was home from the war—almost.

There was a little all-night restaurant, the By-Path, situated in the heart of town, two blocks from the bus station. My luggage consisted of one duffel bag, which contained all my worldly possessions. I swung it over my shoulder and wearily trudged the two blocks. I sat there, unnoticed, unrecognized in this town where I had grown up. I drank one beer and pondered, and then I drank another. And then I got slowly up, shouldered that heavy duffel bag, and started marching toward the home of my parents a mile or so away.

The town was quiet. I didn't meet a single person.

As I crossed the bridge spanning the Duck River, the duffel bag was getting oppressively heavy. I recalled my having left from the Linzerhof in Linz and had a thought—"I have lugged this damned duffel bag all the way from the Danube to the Duck."

My parents' home sat back from the road a ways, and there were a few steps up to the porch, beyond which was the front door. All was dark. There was not a ray of light or any sound. I stood motionless in deep thought.

I knew that when I went through that door, my whole world would change. My life would be completely different. The military life I had been living wasn't all that good, but I had learned how to handle it. I could survive. I didn't know how I would handle the life of a civilian. I just knew that when I went through that door, all the rules would change.

So there in the darkness, I carefully leaned my bag against those steps, I turned around, and I walked back to town. I went into the By-Path and ordered another beer. And I sat and I pondered. There obviously was no way to put it off any longer. The time had come. I wasn't a soldier any longer, and I would have to face up to it.

I got up, settled my overseas cap firmly on my head, and walked again toward home.

This time I made it all the way. My mother and father hugged me and kissed me and cried a little. And so did I. My sister was in the Red Cross in Manila. My brother was in the army, still in Germany.

But I was absolutely right. By the next morning, all the rules had changed.

Like thousands of other young American boys, I was home from the war—and I didn't know what to do.

Back home in Tennessee again, I settled into a great state of inertia. I declined to do anything. I got letters from old friends scattered around the world, inquiring about my postwar plans. And I didn't have any. I was a veteran, and I figured that I would just let the government take care of this old soldier from now on. I saw no real reason for me to do anything ever again. And I was not alone. There were a number of my former high-school classmates who had returned from the war, and many of them felt as I did. We got to where we would go down each day to the Greyhound bus station at the corner of Fifth and Garden to see who was coming back from the army. Each returning veteran was cause for celebration. We did not require much cause. I must now admit that some of them were people I did not recall ever having seen before, but we greeted them all as lifelong close associates, or maybe relatives.

I had four months of terminal leave during which I was continuing to draw full army pay. I saw no reason to alter this life-style.

Even out there in Hawaii with the Associated Press, Don Whitehead got the feeling that just maybe I should make some plans to go to work.

"Come to Hawaii," he wrote. "They are restaffing the newspapers out here and I can get you a job."

Go to Hawaii? I didn't even go to the mailbox.

I did go to Knoxville on occasion, however, and one day I went by the offices of the Knoxville *Journal* to visit my friend Tom Anderson. Tom decided that I not only was going to work, I was going to work now. That was an order. He went in for a conference with Guy Smith, the editor, and came back to tell me that I would be starting on Monday as a city-side reporter at a stipend of thirty-five dollars per week. And that is how I became a member of the sometime-working press. I worked the police beat, hospitals, the courts, and general assignment. I did almost anything until the day they sent me to Newport, Tennessee, to cover the award of a Congressional Medal of Honor to a returning soldier. I was completely compatible with those circumstances and with those people. Before long, I got the feeling that I might get a Congressional Medal of Honor myself. And I got so carried away that I completely overlooked the necessity of getting back to the *Journal* with my story. And instead of getting the Congressional Medal, I got fired.

Now it seemed to me that I needed at least a vacation trip, a change of scene, so I boarded a train that took me away to the nation's capital, which had quieted down somewhat following the war. I spent a few days with Tom Henry who was back at work at *The Washington Star.* "I am now a high-priced copyboy," he complained. "If somebody wants to know something about the military, they have Henry run over and talk to Eisenhower. If they need some information on the Veterans Administration, they have Henry run over and talk to Bradley."

My aimless journey took me next to Baltimore, where I paid a personal visit to one of the shrines about which I had heard so much from soldiers during the war—the Club Oasis. It dealt in strong drink and painted ladies and was everything my soldier buddies had said it was.

Having exhausted my interest in Baltimore, I boarded a train that bore me into Pennsylvania Station in New York City in the darkness of early evening. I did not have a hotel reservation, and it had not occurred to me that there would be a great scarcity of lodging in postwar New York. But there was. I made a few phone calls and discovered that there were just no rooms to be had.

I then enlisted the aid of the only person who seemed available to me—the redcap who was carrying my bag. He said he could get me a room, and away we went in the direction of Eighth Avenue and Thirty-first Street. And there we discovered the Penn Post Hotel.

I doubt that you ever stayed in the Penn Post Hotel on Thirty-first Street in New York City, and if you haven't made it yet, you will be deprived of that experience, because the Penn Post has gone on to that great hotel graveyard in the sky, or wherever it is that old hotels go. Maybe they don't go anywhere. Maybe it's the hotel managers who congregate in that large lobby up yonder. I really don't know where the Penn Post or its manager went, but they certainly aren't on Thirty-first Street anymore.

The Penn Post was not imposing even back then in 1946, but it did have an available room, which made it attractive. One had no trouble getting through the lobby because the hotel did not have a lobby. It had a registration desk about six feet long, snugly situated beneath the stairway. The clerk gave me a rather large key that I would not be likely to carry away. And it admitted me to a second-story room of spartan design and furnishings. The single iron bed was decorated in chipped paint that had formerly been white. The chair and table were bare. The carpet, or portions of it, had apparently been sent out to the cleaners.

I left my bag and scurried away to Bleeck's, a newsmen's hangout in midtown Manhattan. And I met a pair of army friends, Roy Wilder and Howard Cowan. Howard still worked for the Associated Press, and was assigned to daily coverage of some new organization called the United Nations. The prestige of that assignment had landed him in a comfortable hotel in midtown, the Gotham, with twin beds. He graciously offered me the use of one of the beds and I graciously accepted. And I almost forgot completely about the Penn Post. I was purchasing clothes and accessories as the daily need arose.

And then one day I went back to the Penn Post to settle up and check out. There was a padlock on my door and my bag had been moved to the storage room. When I inquired, in some righteous indignation, I was told by the management that if a man did not come back to his room overnight this was standard procedure. The manager said, "We get a lot of suicides among our clientele. So, if a guy don't come back overnight, we figure he ain't coming."

I figured that I wasn't coming back, either.

Instead I went back to Tennessee to examine the state of my affairs. For several months I had been keeping up a correspondence and pretty steady company with Mickie Lambert, whom I had dated in high school. She was now in college at the University of Alabama, and it seemed to me that if she was agreeable, it was my duty to take her away from there and prove to her that there was life after Tuscaloosa. And so we agreed to be wed, and we were.

It was she, then, the practical wife, who again brought up the matter of my getting a job somewhere. She thought it might be a simpler life if I had some income, since my army pay had now run out.

I decided that I would see what I could do about getting my career as a sports announcer started again. First I made a pitch for the job of public-address announcer at the University of Tennessee football games. There were only two applicants, a friend name Tys Terway and me. Admittedly, he was the more experienced. Tys had been a radio announcer for a number of years and had done broadcasting in London during the war years. He got the PA job. I finished second in a field of two.

Next I applied for the public-address job at the Central High School games. Tys Terway and I rode the city bus together out to suburban Fountain City and then walked up the hill to the office at Central High to discuss the public-address assignment. Tys got it. I was second again.

I applied by mail for the public-address job at Knoxville High. I was notified by mail that I had finished second.

That is how I found myself back in my same old part-time role in the broadcast booth with Lowell Blanchard for the Tennessee games. I was a spotter and sometime analyst. But at least I was getting a little time on the air.

In the summer of 1947, when I was working as promotion manager at the Knoxville *News-Sentinel* and was also a leading customer of the Press-Radio Club, there was an interesting development. A friend named Charlie DeVois had come by to have a short beer and to say in passing that there would soon be another radio station in town. It would be WKGN, and he would be the general manager. And he said that I really ought to be in the sports-announcing business, and that if I would provide him with an audition record he could take it to his bosses and see about getting me a job.

He said audition *record* because this was before wire and tape were in general use, and the most common method of recording was on an acetate disc, which was big and unwieldy, not altogether reliable, and totally incapable of being edited.

Well, I had a problem here. Charlie wanted an audition record, and what I really wanted to do was impress him with my prowess as a play-by-play man. This was going to be difficult to do on a record done off a script somewhere in a studio.

I gave it a lot of thought.

Then I borrowed a "home recorder," and gave it a lot more thought. The recorder inscribed the voice on a record, all right, but it just wasn't too clear. Perhaps that was just what I wanted. Like faint copies of hotel bills for expense accounts. Maybe a thin reproduction, a suggestion of performance, would serve my purpose best.

I waited until an afternoon when everyone except me was gone from our little home out on Valley View Road in Knoxville. And I set about doing my audition. I described the scene at the practice field at the University of Tennessee and I began to describe the action, doing the play-by-play of an imaginary scrimmage. Only I didn't say it was imaginary. I explained the obvious lack of noise or sounds of any kind by saying that "we have moved our microphones back from the field in order not to intrude." There was precious little chance of my intruding from Valley View Road, at least five miles distant.

When I had finished, I called Charlie DeVois and he met me on a busy street corner in downtown Knoxville. It was like communists meeting in a pumpkin patch. I surreptitiously delivered my record, in its paper cover, to Charlie. I did not then know it, but my lifelong career in electronic journalism was to be launched in that plain brown wrapper. I was being cautious not to advertise that I was seeking a job, in case it didn't work out.

When Charlie played the audition record, he was impressed. He liked the script and he liked the play-by-play. He proposed that I do a nightly fifteen-minute sports show, and that I do play-by-play of the high-school football games. I thought that was a very good idea.

There was a staff announcer named Jack Britton at the new station, and he would do the color. And so Jack and I showed up for our first play-by-play broadcast of a high-school game at Evans-

Collins Field in Knoxville. I had tried to put together all I had ever learned from the afternoons in the booth with Bill Stern at the Rose Bowl, with Fort Pearson in the Sugar Bowl, and with the writers in the press box at the Orange Bowl. I tried to draw on Stern's sense of drama, and Pearson's professionalism. I had studied the teams and I tried to be exciting and accurate.

When we had finished we got into our automobile and drove to the Press-Radio Club, which we still considered the social center of the working press in downtown Knoxville. When I descended the flight of stairs that led to the club, Charlie was waiting for me. He took me into an exuberant embrace. When I did not seem to respond to his mood, he pulled me aside. And as we stood against the wall, leaning on the war-surplus bunk beds that I had purchased and installed for purposes of a quick nap now and again, he said, "You don't know what you've done, do you?"

I said that I had done a high-school football game at Evans-Collins Field in Knoxville, Tennessee.

And Charlie said, "No, no, you have just done the best football broadcast ever heard in this town. The very best!"

I went home and patted my spotter's boards gently. They had been to the Rose Bowl. Maybe I could someday work in the Rose Bowl. Wouldn't that be something? Like the lyrics say, "If you don't have a dream, how're you gonna have a dream come true?"

I was discovering, though, that no matter what thrills I found at the stadium or the ball park, they never managed to wash away my continuing awareness of the experiences I had had in the war. It was a continual reaffirmation of James Jones's dictum in *World War II* that "none of them would ever really get over it."

I knew that I never really got over it. And one day, years later, I picked up a volume authored by my good friend W. C. (Bill) Heinz. It was titled *Once They Heard the Cheers.*

In one early chapter, Bill described a particularly difficult time he had had at one period in coping with the war and he was recalling some of his thoughts:

> It was late September, and we were inside Germany now. That day several of us had gone up to the Ninth Infantry Division, and a captain named Lindsey Nelson had taken us up to a battalion command post in the Huertgen Forest. Nineteen years later I was

> driving north out of Manhattan one night, and when I got on the Major Deegan Expressway in the Bronx, I could see, across the Harlem River, the lights of the Polo Grounds. That was after the Giants had gone to San Francisco and the Mets had moved in, and I turned on the car radio and I heard Lindsey doing the game.
>
> There were two hundred square miles of it in the Huertgen, the fir trees sixty feet tall and planted ten square feet apart in absolutely straight rows. It was a picture forest, and there in the cool, soft, and shaded dampness, in a place that had once known the cathedral quiet that is the forest's own, they were dying between the trees and among the ferns.

It was not just me, then, who was left with an overriding memory of all that had happened there. Bill Heinz had since written of athletes and surgeons and had experienced the pain of creation in toiling long hours over novels. But his feeling for that scene in the Huertgen Forest was just beneath the skin and would come bleeding through at the slightest prick of memory.

A soldier's feeling for any such experience is one that cannot be shared with anyone who was not present. It cannot be conveyed. It is possible for an individual to tell a friend, male or female, how it was at a football game years ago, what the feeling was. It is possible to transfer that emotion. But a soldier cannot do that. And it may become a feeling of resentment between him and the woman with whom he chooses to spend his life. She may reasonably expect that the deepest feelings of his lifetime will be some that he has shared with her. And it is not likely that this will be true. And it is less likely that he will ever be able to explain that to her.

I was still struggling at readjustment, and by the summer of 1948 I had made the move from the *News-Sentinel* to the radio station full-time. And I was now into football, baseball, and basketball. And I was also broadcasting boxing and automobile racing.

I was doing the midget auto races at the Knoxville Raceway, and one Sunday we barely averted tragedy when a budding senatorial candidate attempted to cross the track from the infield to our position on the far side, not knowing that the race had begun. He was caught in a cluster of on-rushing Offenhauser racers and barely escaped as he scrambled through the dirt, gravel, and dust. His name was Estes Kefauver.

This seemed now to be building toward a busy summer. The Tennessee football games were sponsored by the Aluminum Company of America (ALCOA) and had been carried on WNOX. Now the new station, WKGN, made a pitch. Actually, it was a case of ALCOA owning the rights and, through an advertising agency, placing the broadcasts wherever they wished. If ALCOA chose WKGN, I would presumably be the play-by-play announcer. That was the basis on which the pitch was made. But one day Charlie DeVois called me in to say that he was terribly disappointed and he knew I would be, but ALCOA had chosen WNOX. It really was not that big a surprise. We were a new 250-watt station, and WNOX was a 5,000-watt CBS affiliate. So we set about the business of making our plans for a lot of high-school football coverage for another season.

Meanwhile, the date was approaching for the expected birth of our first child. And we were excited about that. The big event came in the early-morning hours of July 17, 1948. We named her Sharon. And now we were a family.

Mickie was still recovering in the hospital, and I was making daily trips to see her and Sharon in between broadcasting assignments. Then one morning I got a call from the pediatrician who was attending Sharon. He asked if I could come to his office. He gave no indication of what he wanted. I should have known that this was a little unusual, but I didn't.

I should have known that a doctor doesn't call the father of a newborn child to his office midway through a working day unless it is something important. But I had been right on top of a cloud ever since I had become a father. I had gone to Walter Blaufeld's shop on Gay Street and bought a box of cigars, on which was imprinted, IT'S A GIRL! I had my chest out a foot.

The pediatrician sent me away in a shambles. First he reached up into a bookcase against the wall and pulled out a book. He turned to a section that said "Mongoloids." The term did not mean a thing to me. I had never heard of a medical application of the term. He didn't mention Down's syndrome. The doctor slowly began to explain the nature of retardation, the fact that the position of the dainty little finger, which we had thought so cute, was one of the clues. So was the spacing of the eyes, he said. And gradually it began to sink in, slowly at first, then deeper. He was telling me that our daughter was irrevocably retarded. Her learning capabilities were severely damaged, he said. And then he said something that puzzled me: "Fortunately, these children do not live very long."

I didn't know what he meant by "fortunately." He was telling me that my daughter would soon die and that I should consider it fortunate. And he thought that he would leave it to me to tell Mickie when she came home from the hospital.

I was still dazed when I got into my car and started to drive back to work at the radio station. As I drove down Broadway toward the center of the city, there were tears streaming down my face. I couldn't define the cause of my tears. I didn't know whether I was crying for Sharon, or for Mickie, or for me. I suppose it was for all of us. And I knew that in the war I had seen men killed in all kinds of terrible ways and I had never been moved to cry. Now I couldn't stop.

The next few days were sheer torture. I would go by the hospital to visit Mickie and Sharon. Mickie was so happy with our daughter. And it tore me up to watch, knowing that I would have to tell her the tragic news when she came home.

Tom Anderson of the *Journal* sent a photographer, Tommy Greene, to the hospital to take a picture of mother and daughter for our baby's book. George Cafego, a schoolmate who had been a famous football player, came by the house and spent the night.

When Mickie came home and I finally told her that our daughter was retarded, her reaction was predictable. At first, she was disbelieving. There had been a mistake. This just wasn't true. If it was true, why had it happened? The doctors didn't know the causes of retardation, they said.

Mickie and I both agreed that the first thing we would do would be to get another doctor. We would never stop trying for some other verdict. We would have Sharon examined again, and again, and again. This couldn't be true.

But in quieter moments, alone, we admitted to ourselves that it was true, and we acknowledged the despair that we faced.

It was harder on Mickie than on me. She was there with our daughter every moment of every day and night, knowing that there was really nothing she could do about it.

But Mickie did do something about it. She was determined that her daughter was going to be "something" and she wasn't going to die right away, either.

I plunged into the work at the station. Charlie DeVois suggested that maybe I would want to take some time off. I declined, and instead I worked all the time. And I have been overscheduled ever since.

Sharon might be retarded, but she was ours. And she was little, and fragile, and very dear. Deep inside we acknowledged to ourselves that severe signs of her retardation might show up later, but for now she was a little baby girl and we loved her. We would always love her, and a doctor years later would say, "Mickie reached down, pulled her up by the bootstraps, and made a person out of Sharon."

She has always been severely retarded, she has never weighed more than seventy-three pounds, she has physical disabilities, she has trouble with speech. But she is now 37 years old, and has been a central figure in our family since the day of her birth that July day of 1948. She has taught her parents more about tolerance and compassion than they had ever known or ever would have known. Sharon has been and is a joy.

I particularly remember occasions like the night she sat in Danny Kaye's dressing room at the Imperial Theatre in Manhattan after Danny's evening performance in Richard Rodgers's *Two By Two.* Sharon and Danny entertained each other there with their pantomimes and funny faces and laughter. And I remember riding home after a day at Shea Stadium when Danny, in the broadcast booth with me, and Sharon, in a box behind the dugout, had waved to each other during the game. And now Sharon said softly to me, "Danny Kaye loves me." And the night on the liner *Maasdam* in the Atlantic, when she sat at dinner with her sister and her parents and would tentatively put her small hand on each successive piece of silver until her father nodded, and then she would select that fork and eat.

One would not have chosen retardation for Sharon, but how much we all would have missed, how much poorer we would have been, if she had lived only the short life predicted for her.

In later years, Sharon went with the family to almost every baseball game of the New York Mets at Shea Stadium. Many of the players knew her and spoke to her when they came on the field. She was always in the box just behind the dugout. And there was the night she had been with me at a game in Atlanta. A heavy and steady rain had finally forced postponement of the game, and now the players were ready to get on the team bus. Lou Niss, the traveling secretary, said it would be okay for Sharon and me to ride back to the hotel, although there was a club rule against females riding on the team bus. Sharon and I sat up front, and as the players loaded, many of them patted her gently on the head and said, "Hi, Sharon." After that road trip, which had lasted several days, I said, "Sharon, what did you enjoy most of all?" And like any sensitive female, she said, "I liked the team bus."

Some years ago, Sharon was enrolled in a special school, where she has undergone continuing and competent instruction, worked in a sheltered workshop, and lived a generally satisfactory life.

Often, when I have visited her, she has gotten so excited that she has run in my direction. And from several feet away, she has flung her little body into the air and clasped her hands around my neck while she squealed with delight. It is an exhibition of pure love. Perhaps a completely normal child is incapable of such unqualified, unreserved love and affection. I don't know. But I do know that from Sharon I get the purest form of love that exists on the face of the earth. And I thank God for her. From me, she gets that affection returned, admittedly to a lesser degree. Perhaps I am incapable of the purity of her emotion, but it is the act of loving that is the great blessing, and Sharon has been the object of my pure love. One of my greatest blessings is that of having had Sharon for a daughter.

CHAPTER 12

My Break into Broadcasting

In that summer of 1948, Charlie DeVois called me one morning to ask if I could hurry down to the radio station. When I got there, he was all aglow. "ALCOA has changed its mind," he said. "The Tennessee football games will be carried on WKGN and you will be the play-by-play announcer."

I was pleased. It was a surprise. A few months earlier I might have been ecstatic. But after Sharon's birth, I would never again get that excited over good fortune or feel the terrible despair of what I presumed to be bad fortune. In the trade, I got the reputation of being imperturbable. I earned it.

After that first season, Coach Neyland, who was now a retired general, put me in charge of marketing the Vol football rights. So I went on a sweeping automobile safari from one end of the state of Tennessee to the other, setting up the football network. Tom Anderson went along for the ride.

I thought we should call it the "Volunteer Network." I sat in the living room of my home out on Valley View Road and practiced. "We pause for station identification, this is the Volunteer Network!" I thought it sounded beautiful.

I went to Neyland and said, "General, I have a great name for our network. Let's call it the Volunteer Network."

He said, "Let's call it the Vol Network."

I said, "Yes, sir, let's call it the Vol Network. We pause for station identification, this is the Vol Network!"

It is still the Vol Network and it is always going to be the Vol Network. General Neyland said so.

I would also select the play-by-play announcer, and I already had somebody in mind for that. I had done the games for WKGN, of course, but twenty-five dollars per game somehow seemed a little light to me.

"I think the announcer should get a least a hundred dollars," I said.

General Neyland looked pensively out the window, then said, "Well, let's see. The referee gets a hundred dollars a game. Do you work as hard as the referee?"

"Harder," I said.

"Okay, you'll get a hundred dollars a game."

Independent of my football operation, at about this time I also got offers from two other radio stations for staff jobs. And I moved from WKGN to WROL, which was an NBC affiliate. With a little urging from me, WROL now submitted the high bid for Vol Network coverage of Tennessee football and basketball, so that now all my games were heard on the NBC station. I was also doing some baseball games of the Knoxville Smokies of the Tri-State League, and I was doing some major league re-creations. I was right up to my neck in sports broadcasting.

In 1950, the Tennessee football team opened with a 56–0 victory over Mississippi Southern. The next week, the Vols surprisingly lost to Mississippi State in Starkville, Mississippi, by a score of 7–0.

The Vols recovered, however, and moved toward the big game against Alabama in Knoxville. It was a game with national implications and the networks made plans. By now CBS was into the "roundup" format. Crews of announcers would be stationed at several games around the country, and Red Barber would anchor in New York, switching from one game to another. The young announcer whom they sent to Knoxville was a bright redhead named Vin Scully. He had been a junior member of the Brooklyn Dodgers' baseball broadcasting crew in the season just completed. As we watched practice on Friday, we talked of baseball and the Dodgers and many things.

And then we walked from the stadium to Scully's hotel. He was staying at the midtown Hotel Farragut. WROL was situated just across the street. Scully and I went into details of the buck-lateral series that Neyland had added to his single-wing offense to give it a multiple-option capability.

Following a victory over Alabama 14–9, Tennessee, with only that one loss, was building toward what would be the biggest game of the season, that against Kentucky. The Wildcats were coached by Paul (Bear) Bryant. They were undefeated, untied, and already had clinched the Southeastern Conference championship. But Bear Bryant had never beaten Bob Neyland—and he never did.

Let me observe here that when you are waiting, and working, and hoping that maybe someday a chance will come along to advance in your profession, your greatest enemy is discouragement. Neyland and I had frequent talks about broadcasting. He told me that a fellow should always work at his trade so that he is a little more skilled today than he was yesterday and a little less than he will be tomorrow. Neyland told me that an announcer should be able to broadcast Class B baseball with the same skill that he would the World Series. The trick, he said, was never to give in to the temptations of despair, never to stop trying, always to be ready for the time when that break would come. One of his famous game maxims was "Play for the breaks, and when one comes, SCORE!" Well, that was the philosophy he was teaching me. And I was playing for the break, I was waiting for the break, and when it came, I hoped to score big.

It came there in 1950. A fellow named Gordon McLendon, who billed himself as "The Old Scotchman," had built the Liberty Broadcasting System in Dallas, Texas. His principal product was re-created major league baseball. A strange gadget called television had come along in the world of communications, and Madison Avenue advertising agencies had generally declared network radio dead.

There was no longer any need for network radio, they said. And so Gordon McLendon had stepped into that void and built LBS to a strength of 431 radio stations.

Liberty did baseball and an awful lot of football as well. I knew that he carried the Army games, broadcast by the great Ted Husing. And I also knew that neither Army nor Navy had a game scheduled the Saturday before the annual Army-Navy game. That was the Saturday that Tennessee was scheduled to play the Kentucky Wildcats in

Knoxville. It was a big game. Both teams were strong. Kentucky actually was on the way to the Sugar Bowl, where the Wildcats would upset one of Bud Wilkinson's strongest Oklahoma teams, and Tennessee was on the way to the Cotton Bowl, where the Vols would upset Texas.

I offered to sell the outside-the-state rights to my broadcast of that game to LBS for five hundred dollars. I closed the deal with the network's director of sports, a fellow named Jerry Doggett, who would later team up with Vin Scully on the broadcasts of the Dodger baseball games, first in Brooklyn and then in Los Angeles. At that point, I knew Doggett and I knew Scully, but they didn't know each other.

That 1950 Tennessee-Kentucky game was played on the Saturday after Thanksgiving. And I had that old feeling that this was going to be somehow a big day for me and my career. My broadcast would be carried coast to coast.

Previously, I had not been carried very far. I had once received a fan letter after one of my earlier football broadcasts had been picked up by the Armed Forces Radio Service and carried overseas. The letter was from a woman in London. The employees at the station were thrilled, and wanted to know why I wasn't more excited about getting a fan letter from London. I tried to explain that, as I recalled it, my social conduct in London during the war years had been predicated on the basic premise that I would never, ever be heard from or of again.

By the time that Saturday rolled around, there were problems. The weather had taken a plunge and we had endured a snowstorm. It was bitter cold and a blanket of snow covered everything. A train bearing Kentucky fans did not arrive in Knoxville until well after the game was under way. Among those who did not arrive was my Kentucky spotter. I had my big chance and I didn't have a visiting spotter. Announcer Jack Britton volunteered. His handicap was that he had never seen this team play before. But when the big break comes, Neyland hadn't said anything about grumbling over details. When the big break comes, you SCORE!

If you are a singer, you select a suitable song, and you sing it to the biggest audience you can find. That's the way you get attention. If you are a football announcer, you hope for a thrilling game, and I had one. Tennessee won by a score of 7–0 on a touchdown pass from Hank Lauricella to Bert Rechichar. It was an exciting day under trying conditions.

After the game, I hitched a ride back to town with country comedian Archie Campbell and met Mickie at the radio station. Then we had dinner and went to a movie at the Tennessee theater. When I came back to the station after the movie, there was a stack of telegrams. Gordon McLendon called my broadcasting of the game "sensational." There was a message from the Natalie Kalmus Company, which had sponsored the broadcast on 50,000-watt KMPC in Los Angeles. They said they were "proud to be the first to present Lindsey Nelson on the West Coast."

I was rather proud to be presented almost anywhere, and I was very pleased to be sensational. And I was also pleased to be Tennessee's radio broadcaster. I did not know, of course, that I had just done the last radio football broadcast I would ever do from that stadium.

But it was plain to see that the Tennessee-Kentucky game of 1950 had been my big break. Now I would have to wait awhile to see how big I had SCORED!

From Knoxville I kept in touch by mail with General Matt Eddy, who was now commanding the U.S. Army in Europe. One day, he wrote, "I took a tour of inspection last week with Correspondents Drew Middleton of the *New York Times* and Bill Stoneman of the *Chicago Daily News.* I took the liberty of showing them your last letter and they both send best regards."

Okay, Eddy was in Europe, so were Middleton and Stoneman. Don Whitehead was still in Honolulu and I was in Knoxville. Oh, I missed association with some of those wartime people. I could not deny that. For instance, there was the night when the long-distance operator said I had a call from New York. There was a little wartime reunion party in progress at Mamma Leone's restaurant on Forty-eighth Street in Manhattan. And they had decided to ring me up. I talked with Hal Boyle of AP, George Hicks of NBC, and Roy Wilder of the *Herald Tribune.* They were having a great time, and they wanted to know when I would be coming to New York. Coming to New York, I thought. I saw no indications that I would ever be coming to New York. I had thought enough about it, but I didn't see how I was ever going to make it there. No one in New York was offering me any jobs, and it took money to live in New York. The song after World War I said, "How're you gonna keep 'em down on the farm after they've seen Paree?" Well, I had seen Paree, and more than that I had worked with some of the world's great names in journalism—Hal Boyle, H. R. Knickerbocker, Harold Denny, A. J. Liebling, Ernest Hemingway. That stimulation is habit forming, and I had formed the habit. But they seemed to have kept me "down on the farm" all right. I was working for a 250-watt radio station in Knoxville and was making seventy-five dollars per week plus football fees.

I was thirty-one years old, married, the father of a handicapped daughter. I thought that I should be moving a little better in the trade, but I didn't know how to engineer it. It was plain that if you were to seek success in the top echelons of the broadcasting business you had better seek it in New York. Los Angeles, maybe? Not yet. That would come later, but in 1950 there was no doubt about the location of the seat of power in the broadcasting business. It was New York City.

In the meantime, Gordon McLendon at the Liberty Broadcasting System in Dallas was a positive factor. He wanted his network, coast to coast, to take a feed of some of my Tennessee basketball broadcasts. And the Vols football team was on its way to Dallas to play Texas in the Cotton Bowl on New Year's Day. Bill Stern was doing the broadcast and wanted to know if I could be his spotter. NBC would pay all my expenses. That was something new.

First I went to Philadelphia to broadcast the Tennessee vs. Villanova basketball game from the Palestra on the campus of the University of Pennsylvania, and then I took an overnight flight from Philadelphia to Dallas.

The day before the game I went on a network radio show in Dallas originating at WFAA, the NBC affiliate. The show included a tape recording of my call of the big touchdown play in the Tennessee-Kentucky game. Then on the Cotton Bowl game next day, Bill Stern called me in for a few words at halftime. It wasn't much, but I was on there from one side of this great big land to the other. I got letters from old army friends who didn't know I had survived.

When I returned to my daily staff duties at WROL in Knoxville, I was in for another surprise. I got fired.

Oh, they tried to make it painless and to disguise it, but any way you looked at it, I got fired. The general manager, the boss, was Henry Linebaugh, and Henry called me into the front office and carefully closed the door. He said, "You know, I've been giving your situation a lot of thought. You are an outstanding sports broadcaster and you ought to be making a lot more money. But we can't pay you any more money. You could stay here for years and not make much more money. We have people who have been here forever and they're not making much more than you are. And I think you ought to be working somewhere else and making more money."

I was perceptive. I realized that the key phrase there was "working somewhere else."

"You can take as long as you like," he said. "And I will give you the strongest possible recommendation when you find something you want to go after, but there really is no reason for you to stay here any longer."

I said, truthfully, "I appreciate your attitude, Henry. I have never been fired more gently in my life." And I had been fired some.

Meanwhile, I had struck up a pretty steady arrangement with the Liberty Broadcasting System. I was doing basketball games, and I was re-creating various sports events. I would do the voice track, and their people would add the crowd to the re-creations.

Of course, I was running the Vol Network, doing the Tennessee basketball games, and I still had the continuing arrangement for the football games. And Tennessee was looking for a sports-publicity director. Tucker Musser had been doing the job, but he had resigned to go into business.

One day, General Neyland called me in to ask if I would be interested in combining my Vol Network duties with those of the sports-publicity director, and I supposed that I would. Neither one of those assignments paid very much money, but in combination the position would be respectable, so respectable that the general asked me not to divulge what the total arrangement would be. "There might be a lot of unhappy assistant football coaches," he said, "if they discovered that you would be the second-highest-paid man on this athletic staff."

We did not strike an immediate deal. We both wanted to think about it a little more. I didn't want to think about it for long, because my income was terribly small and rapidly disappearing. Next day, I was there in the office of the business manager for athletics, Mrs. Edna Callaway. And I was ready to sign on.

I remember the scene in detail. Mrs. Callaway's office was on the first floor near the entrance. Coming down the steps from the general's office, one had to come right by her open door. And here he came.

The general was on his way out to lunch. It was January and he was wearing a tan topcoat with a wraparound belt and gray felt hat.

"Have you thought about what we discussed?" he asked.

I said I had.

"And do you want the job?" he asked.

I said I did.

And then he walked all the way across the room to the windows on the far side. For a long time he looked out into the parking lot and didn't say anything.

I didn't say anything, either. I wouldn't have interrupted the general's solitude for a cash endowment.

Then he turned slowly and looked straight at me. I felt like I wanted to look behind me to see if anyone might be standing there, because when the general looked at you, he gave the impression that he was looking through you.

"The only problem is—" he said. "The only problem is that if you keep broadcasting football games the way you've been broadcasting football games, one of these big networks is going to snap you up, and I'm gonna be right where I am now—looking for a publicity director."

That was to me the most preposterous thing I had ever heard. One of those big networks was going to snap me up! They hadn't been exactly standing in line. I knew that there must be little clues that an announcer would pick up, things that would happen to indicate that he was being sought after.

As for myself, I was still doing the show once weekly from the Berry funeral home out on the Chapman Highway. Once a week, we'd crank up the old portable tape recorder and go out to the funeral home. The organist in the chapel would play some mournful music, and in my most ecclesiastical tones I would read the commercial, ". . . and for the seventy-five-dollar funeral . . ."

Somehow I didn't think that was the kind of work that an exciting play-by-play man did just before he was snapped up by one of those big networks.

Still, the general had said it, and the general was never wrong, as far as I knew. And if I ever knew, you could bet that I wouldn't tell him. I came out of my reverie to hear him saying, "But we'll worry about that when we come to it. You've got the job."

And that is how I became the director of sports publicity for the Volunteers of the University of Tennessee and on the staff of General Bob Neyland.

Everything was surely optimistic because we would now be building for the college football season of 1951, when the Vols would win the national championship.

I wouldn't be there to share in the joy. I would be gone to a network.

For the moment, though, still in Knoxville I was doing some baseball re-creations for Gordon McLendon, famous games from years past, for which one dug up the details from old books and records. Regular-season games were done on the basis of information received by Western Union. Re-creating baseball games was an honorable practice of the time. A fellow doing it in Des Moines was named Ronald Reagan, and he has frequently regaled guests at the White House with stories of his troubles in doing "make-believe baseball."

I kept in close touch with the Liberty Broadcasting System, and one day somebody mentioned that Gordon was considering me for another assignment. Liberty also handled the broadcasting arrangements for the St. Louis Browns and would presumably have a lot to say about announcers. The program director at Liberty was Glenn Douglas, and he said Gordon was considering me for a spot on the Browns' announcing crew. I was excited at the prospect of graduating to the major leagues, but I wasn't excited for long. One day, I said to Glenn Douglas, "What does a job with the St. Louis Browns pay?"

He said, "Oh, I'm not sure, but I'd say somewhere between five thousand and seventy-five hundred."

I needed further clarification. I knew that these big networks paid big money, but I just wasn't sure how big. "Five thousand a week," I asked, "or five thousand a month?"

There was a slight pause and he said, "Five thousand a season."

My excitement subsided somewhat.

Just the same, I stayed in touch.

CHAPTER 13

Now the Networks

I attended all of the college baseball games with regularity. And one afternoon in the spring of 1951 I was standing on the gravel road that led to Hudson Field where the games were played. I was talking to a fellow who said that he was a scout for the Brooklyn Dodgers.

Nearby, on a corner of the football practice field, there was an equipment shack, and inside there was a telephone. A fellow yelled to say there was a call for me. I jogged across the gravel and stood there outside the shack in the hot afternoon sun talking to a fellow who said that he was "Jim Foster, vice-president and general manager of the Liberty Broadcasting System." I think he had been practicing in his room at home at night. His manner of speaking was too pat to have been altogether ad lib.

But I got the message. LBS was offering me a job. They wanted me to come to Dallas, Texas, just about as quickly as I could get there. They wanted me to re-create major league baseball games right away and to do football games in the fall. They were doing a baseball game every afternoon and night. And in football season they would do six games per weekend, college and pro. That sounded like work enough for everybody. And he said that they would pay me $125 per week. Since I had been making $75 per week a short time ago at WROL, I was ready.

General Neyland was out of town, but we talked by phone. I told him about my offer and my inclination to take it. He was supportive. This wasn't the biggest of those networks, but it had snapped me up at a bargain rate, and I was off to Dallas, Texas.

Mickie and I decided that I would hasten on to Dallas alone, and that in a short time I would find an apartment. Then Mickie and Sharon would drive to Dallas, leaving our house in Knoxville to a rental agent. We were wrapping up a period of almost five years of our married life in Knoxville. They had been essentially very happy years. We had survived the trauma of Sharon's birth, and were adjusted as a family. We had struggled financially, but we had managed well enough to enjoy life. We had lots of friends whose love we treasured.

On a Sunday afternoon, Mickie walked me to the gate in the wire fence at the Knoxville airport. I was ready to board my plane. And as I bent down to kiss Mickie good-bye, there were tears on her cheeks. I understood. They were not tears of parting. We'd be together again very soon. These were tears for the end of a portion of our lives that we loved. We didn't know what was out there waiting for us.

In Dallas, I lived for a few days at the Baker Hotel, and then in the interest of economy I moved to the Southland Hotel. In further interest of saving money, I prepared to move into the YMCA on Ervay Street, where the rates were more akin to my resources.

But I soon discovered that you don't just show up and move into the YMCA. You must present references, or at least one acceptable reference, and I was not overly acquainted in Dallas.

Already I had begun my broadcasting chores, and at nights I had gone out to Burnett Field to watch the Dallas Eagles baseball team, a Texas League entry. The broadcaster was Jerry Doggett, who also worked at Liberty. He had been doing the Dallas games for years. We got along fine. Everybody got along with Jerry.

Now I was standing there at the desk of the Y, and this fellow was asking for references. I mentioned Gordon McLendon, who was president of LBS. This fellow had never heard of Gordon McLendon. He also had never heard of LBS. You see, the flagship station of the network here in Dallas was KLIF. This fellow knew KLIF, but he didn't know LBS. And he wanted another reference. I mentioned Bob Bumpus, who was now vice-president in charge of programs for LBS. My man had never heard of Bob Bumpus. I didn't press my case. I hadn't heard of him, either, until the day before. And then, sort of in desperation, I casually mentioned Jerry Doggett. "Wait a minute," the fellow said, "you know Jerry Doggett?"

"Yeah," I said, "I know Jerry Doggett. In fact I did a couple of innings of the Eagles game with him last night. I know Jerry Doggett."

It was magic. I was in at the Y. I didn't get any reduction in rates, a room with a private bath, or anything like that. But I had a reference, and I was in off the street.

Life at the Y was a little depressing. That room was so small! And there wasn't much furniture—just a table and a chair and a small bed. During all waking periods I had a great urge to be out of that room, and I began to invent reasons not to go to it in the evening.

When the first Saturday night rolled round, I had that old lonely feeling. I didn't know enough people to get invited anywhere. I ate all my meals in the greasy spoons, and if there is any one thing that Dallas had then and has now it is greasy spoons.

At six o'clock, I went to a movie, partially because it was "fifteen degrees cooler inside." When the movie was over, I took a walk around downtown Dallas and stopped for a bite of junk food here and there. And it seemed to me that the best thing to do here at nine o'clock was, perhaps, to go to a movie. So, I chose another theater and settled in for another few hours. After I had sat through my second picture, I again hit the streets. Downtown Dallas on Saturday night was all abuzz in those days. There was jukebox music blaring from the open doors of the beer joints and hustlers on the sidewalks. In fear of the many obvious threats to health and safety, I decided to hit a midnight show, my third consecutive movie. But at least I had delayed my return to that cell at the YMCA.

As soon as I could, I rented an apartment in the Wynnewood section of Oak Cliff and sent for Mickie and Sharon.

And so we settled into life in Dallas, Texas, for that summer of 1951. It was hot. Our place had no air conditioning. And every payday we bought another fan.

And now the football season was coming. In the game sponsored annually by the Salesmanship Club, the New York Giants were matched with the Detroit Lions in a night game at the Cotton Bowl. There was method in the arrangement. The star running back of the Lions was Doak Walker, who was a folk hero in Dallas following his career at Highland Park High School and then at SMU. And the first draft choice of the Giants and a red-hot rookie was Kyle Rote of San Antonio, who similarly had starred at Southern Methodist right there in "Big D."

Jerry Doggett and I shared the broadcast, and it went well. I knew it had gone well the next day. That was when Bill Weaver, the general manager of KLIF, came in and took me by the hand. As he shook it, he said, "I owe you an apology."

"For what?" I asked.

"For not knowing," he said with a smile. "For not knowing that we had a man on the staff of your talent and capabilities. I never heard a better football broadcaster. And I want to apologize for not knowing about you."

I knew that Bill was exaggerating. I knew that no Texan could really mean what he had said. But I had appreciated it nonetheless. Everybody in Texas knew who the greatest football broadcaster in the whole world was. And I was not about to presume greatness beyond that conferred daily by the constituency on Kern Tips. Kern Tips had been the "voice" of southwest football for a lot of years, and to presume an encroachment would be self-destructive heresy. Kern and I would become close friends.

And LBS was preparing to broadcast a lot of football games. While they did most of the baseball by re-creation, most of the football was done live. I liked that. I wanted to get out there where the troops were. And my first stop was LSU vs. Rice, in Baton Rouge, Louisiana.

What I liked most about this assignment was that there was nothing provincial about it. It wasn't a Tennessee game. I had no allegiance of any kind. My job was to broadcast the football game, and my efforts would be heard, and judged, from coast to coast. That was the challenge.

On Saturday afternoons, LBS carried Ted Husing's play-by-play broadcasts of the Army games. The originating station was WMGM in New York, which had a loose arrangement with Liberty. Bert Lebahr was handling details for WMGM, and it seemed that he and Gordon were having some difficulty with the arrangements. Late on Thursday afternoon, word came down that I was to head to New York and broadcast Saturday's game between Dartmouth and Army at West Point. Husing would still do the WMGM origination, but I would do the network feed. The idea of working beside Ted Husing on a football game was overwhelming to me.

I had been to New York City that time in the army just before

I went to North Africa in 1942. I had been there in 1946. And I had been there on vacation in 1949. That was it. I wouldn't say that I was frightened of New York City, but I was not overconfident either. Harold Vertel was one of our vice-presidents, and he volunteered to help me with arrangements. He asked what hotel I preferred. And I chose the New Yorker at Eighth Avenue and Thirty-fourth Street, a better neighborhood then than now.

Early Friday morning I went about the business of preparing for my broadcast, and that meant that I somehow had to get to West Point and find out some things about that football team, not to mention the Dartmouth team. LBS pretty much left its announcers on their own, in more ways than one. First of all, they didn't have a lot of money for expenses. They had carefully explained the advantages, all financial, of the subway over the taxicab. So, now I went up Eighth Avenue in search of a bus station. Imagine my feeling of good fortune when I came upon the Port Authority Terminal. Shortly I was aboard a rattling and experienced bus, headed up the Hudson for Highland Falls. Alighting there, I inquired about the schedule of buses leaving for the return to Manhattan in the late afternoon, and I was off and hoofing my way across the post of the United States Military Academy.

I was thrilled to my toes. I had grown up on all those marvelous movies made about West Point. I had sat bug-eyed and watched Dick Powell in *Flirtation Walk,* and I knew all about those great Army teams of the war years, Red Blaik's "Black Knights of the Hudson." I walked up past the Lusk Reservoir and there was Michie Stadium.

At this early moment there was not a soul stirring in Michie Stadium, so I climbed up to a seat alone and soaked up the feeling of being right there at West Point.

Having made inquiry about the location of the publicity director's office, I walked down to the gymnasium and then into his office. For a rookie announcer trembling on the brink of breaking into the really big time, to be placed into the kind and capable hands of this Joe Cahill was good fortune indeed.

Cahill answered questions before I asked them and made me feel that I had directed him. He always smiled. He took me to see Coach Blaik. He showed me motion pictures of Army games and Dartmouth games. He gave me something the likes of which I had never seen before. They did not yet call it a "flip card" or a "speed card." As I recall, they didn't name it anything. But it was a printed card with the starting lineups indicated by name and number at proper position, and there were numerical squad lists. And that card had just about all the information on it that anyone, writer or broadcaster, would need to cover the game. I had not seen anything like this at the Rose Bowl or the Sugar Bowl. But I've seen a lot of them since.

Joe Cahill steered me to the officers' club, and he took me to practice, and he sought out track coach Carlton Crowell, formerly of Tennessee, and Carlton said that he would be my Dartmouth spotter next day. Joe had a Cadet to serve as my Army spotter. By the time I started walking again to the Highland Falls bus station, the late-afternoon fall shadows were lengthening on that lovely scene at West Point. I am still thrilled every time I see it.

I am sure that Joe Cahill would have had me driven back to the bus station, perhaps all the way to Manhattan, had I mentioned that I was headed to that destination. But I had made no big point, no point at all, of my mode of travel. I was tasting the heady wine of the big time and I did not want to sour it. Not many people expected to find us big-time announcers traveling by bus.

But the bus delivered me triumphantly back to Manhattan, where I went confidently into the big dining room, watched the ice show, and ordered a dinner that later sent the LBS auditors scurrying. I actually didn't think the dinner charge was excessive. After all, it was the only meal I had eaten all day and I had had considerable exercise.

The offices of the Liberty Broadcasting System in New York were located at 509 Madison Avenue. There were essentially two rooms. One could be used as a reception room, a sales room, a copywriters' room, or an announcers' lounge, depending upon your particular needs at the moment. The other room was a studio, or, if not in use, any one of the above. I had checked in for the first time and discovered that our engineer, whom I would accompany to West Point on Saturday morning, was authorized to rent an automobile. I was particularly pleased at the news because, although I had been served well on the previous day by the bus line, I suspected that continued use might deplete continuing admiration. And besides, it would look better arriving by automobile to Michie Stadium.

We got there so early that we were in position to watch everyone else arrive. And I was so pleased that we would be permitted to watch the entrance of Ted Husing.

One of Ted's most obvious qualities was his absolute arrogance. He did nothing to conceal it. And I was never offended by it. In fact, I came to consider Husing attractively arrogant. There was, in those days, a little concrete ramp that ran from the back of the press box, where the radio booths were located, out to the gravel road behind. And the ramp was bordered with black pipe railings. Early arrivals would perch on the pipe railings to watch for Husing. When he arrived, I was among the railbirds. He was in a Carey Cadillac, and he had the chauffeur drive it practically onto the ramp before he prepared to alight. As his alligator-loafer-clad feet touched the ground, his eyes were straight ahead, and he wore a black French beret at a jaunty angle. He had a cigarette in a long holder, and as he strode unhesitatingly toward the booth, dismissing all cries for autographs, every fiber of his being seemed to shout, "Get the damned peasants out of the way and make way for the king!" I loved it.

Once we were into working position, my booth next to Husing's, he seemed puzzled. I noticed that there was some hurried whispering. And Husing was pointing toward me. Then he came in and was cordial enough as he said, "Lindsey, I'm Ted Husing." I refrained from saying that I knew who he was, that I had known who he was since I'd listened to the radio during the years of my extreme youth. He then said, "I thought I was doing the network broadcast." I said, "No, I think I'm doing the network broadcast and you are doing WMGM local."

He said, "Oh." And that was all. We went to work.

Joe Cahill, competent as ever, came by to ask if I would require a halftime guest. When just about the only man in the whole stadium whom you know by name is your engineer, and you aren't too sure about that, you need a halftime guest. And Joe delivered one, a sportswriter. I had met him briefly the day of the Tennessee-Kentucky football game of 1950. Now he was saying that this was his first football game this season because he had been busy covering the World Series, and we talked about baseball and football. He was super gracious and courteous to a neophyte broadcaster. His contribution was considerable that day, and his continuing contribution to the quality of my life through his writing and friendship for years to come was even more considerable. He wrote for the *New York Herald Tribune.* And his name was Red Smith.

Back in Dallas, I was advised that my next assignment would be an NFL game, the New York Yanks and the Detroit Lions at Briggs Stadium in Detroit. The Yanks were coached by Jimmy Phelan, a delightful man, and the Lions by Buddy Parker, a similarly talented coach and character.

I had never worked in a major league ball park. I had listened to the World Series in 1934 when Joe Medwick and Marvin Owen had their ruckus in the final game, and Commissioner Kenesaw Mountain Landis, sitting right there in a box, ordered Medwick removed from the game to prevent a riot.

And more than that, this was the ball park that my wife, Mickie, and I had talked about so many times. As a kid growing up in Detroit, she had idolized the Tigers. She had scoured the neighborhood for empty soft-drink bottles that she could turn in at the grocery store for two cents each, and thus get twenty-five cents for a seat in the left-field stands. This was her shrine. Not a lot of our close friends knew that her square name was Mildred. Everybody called her Mickie. She had arranged the last two letters, the *ie,* as her version of the feminine of "Mickey." This was for Mickey Cochrane, who had been the catcher, manager, and heart and soul of the Tigers in her time there.

Well, I was sailing now—on stilts, as they say. I was flying to New York and Detroit and doing football, college and pro, from coast to coast. I was getting the usual cautionary memos from the front office of the network, "Don't call 'em New York Yankees—there's a legal point involved, the football team is the New York *Yanks.*" And, "Be careful about the music—you can pick up the background music and take it to an interlude, but don't make a big deal about announcing it; then it becomes a part of the show and we are liable for a music fee." There was a lot to be learned, and I was learning.

I was also learning about doubling up. Before the airplane became so available, announcers took a leisurely train to the city of assignment, did the ball game, and took a leisurely ride back the next day. Then came the airplane, and instead of taking advantage of the new fast means of transport, announcers simply started doubling up. So, LBS said, "Go to West Point and do the Army vs. Columbia game, and then take the plane Saturday night to Chicago and do the Chicago Bears and the New York Yanks at Wrigley Field on Sunday."

Yes, sir, yes, sir! This was the start of a pattern that began then and continues now. Tote that barge, catch that cue, ride that plane, who's playing, where are we, what's the name of this stadium, what's the name of this hotel, what's the name of this city?

Everybody seemed to be going somewhere. The midnight flight to Chicago was a DC-3. There was one fellow aboard who was going home after having been in New York to work on arrangements for a television show that would be called *Make Room for Daddy.* His name was Danny Thomas.

There was another passenger, a larger fellow, who was returning home to Chicago after having been in New York to work on arrangements for a television show that would be called *The Today Show.* His name was Dave Garroway.

I was going to Chicago to do a broadcast of a Chicago Bears game and to do some work toward building a career as a sports broadcaster.

That Sunday afternoon out there at Wrigley Field was another thrill. Television was in its infancy, but the Bear games were being televised in Chicago. There were not a lot of TV sets in use, but there was a telecast. And the announcer was the immortal Red Grange, the "Galloping Ghost of the Illini." Red Grange, whose name had intrigued me when I was a kid. And there he stood! It was the first time that I ever actually saw him.

And there was yet another thrill. One of our top producers at LBS in Dallas was John Kieran, Jr. He had been a classmate of Gordon McLendon when both had been first at Yale and then at Harvard Law. Johnny and I were neighbors in Dallas. We had become close friends, and our families were close. John's father, of course, was world famous as a former sports columnist for the *New York Times,* a member of the *Information, Please* panel on network radio, and a man of many sterling talents. John had given me his father's phone number in Riverdale and told me to call him when I was in New York. I did and during our cordial conversation he asked where I was going next. I was already at LaGuardia, and I told him I was on the way to Chicago to do a Bear game the next day. "Okay," he said, "you find George Halas and you tell him that I defy him—tell him that John Kieran says—I defy you!"

When I had finished the broadcast the next day, I discovered that there was a sort of press lounge, The Pink Poodle, on the mezzanine, where Halas met the press after the game. I delivered Kieran's message and Halas roared. I don't know what it meant. It was an inside joke, alluding to something in their past relationship. I don't know what. But it was the start of a long, fruitful relationship for me with George Halas.

The Liberty Broadcasting System did not dispense a great deal of money among its employees, but it was extremely liberal with titles. And somewhere in that cyclone fall of 1951, I became director of football. It meant that I would call a college director of athletics or a pro general manager, offer the least possible amount of money, procure the broadcast rights, then get on an airplane, and proceed to broadcast the game myself. For a fellow who liked to broadcast football games, it was a pretty nearly perfect arrangement.

Gordon wanted me to try to get the rights for the game on Thanksgiving Day between the Green Bay Packers and the Detroit Lions in Detroit. I got General Manager Nick Kerbawy on the phone and explained that we were loaded with exposure from coast to coast, which would be of great benefit to his Lions, but that we were a little short on cash. Nick assumed I knew that the game was being televised by the Dumont Television Network, a pioneer network in the field of TV. I actually didn't know, and I didn't care. I could offer all the way up to five hundred dollars for the radio rights, and I did. Kerbawy accepted, with a provision not altogether uncommon in pro football operations of that day. He asked that I bring the check with me, indicating that the booth would be more accessible to me after the Lions had received the money in hand. It wasn't that they were distrustful. They were just careful. The Lions weren't in a lot better financial shape than we were.

Of course, there on that very afternoon they were into something that would change the fortunes of pro football, financially speaking. It was television.

Things in Dallas seemed to be going well until, after about a year, the financial status of our network began to get a shade shaky.

It soon became apparent that old LBS was not long for this world. Chuck Comiskey of the Chicago White Sox had been in a squabble with his mother over the stock in the club, and he had defected to Dallas to hook up with us as vice-president in charge of sports. But he was now on the phone daily working on a reconciliation and his imminent return to the White Sox. Jerry Doggett had bailed out full-time to the Dallas Eagles baseball team, where he would be broadcaster and publicist. Don Wells was on his way to a broadcasting job in Houston, then to the White Sox, and later to the California Angels. And I prepared to go temporarily to Memphis to do some broadcasting for WHHM, owned by a friend named Cecil Beaver.

So all my big network plans had suddenly come crashing down. I had been involved in just enough of big-time broadcasting to make it attractive to me, and now it was all gone.

On my last day at LBS, I went by the office at 2100 Jackson Street, hoping to pick up a check. I had a ticket for a roomette on the five P.M. train to Memphis. And now Mickie and Sharon and I were driving through downtown Dallas toward the railway station. We went down Elm and turned left on South Houston at a building that would become infamous a decade later as the Texas Schoolbook Depository, where President Kennedy's assassin had lurked.

This was one of the darkest moments of my life. I had liked Dallas, but that was all over. I was back into the business of scratching out a living at a small radio station. I was leaving my wife and daughter temporarily at the apartment in Dallas. I would live in a hotel in Memphis. I did not look forward to the lonely life. I had endured that when I had come ahead of my family to Dallas.

I did not think I would ever be in Dallas again. But there were many things I did not then know; there were forces at work. Matty Brescia was our public-relations director at LBS and a good friend. Matty had volunteered to get me employed. He had a lot of contacts in the broadcasting business and he had called first Tommy Velotta at ABC, and then NBC. At NBC he was acquainted with the new director of sports, Tom Gallery, who had just taken over the department from Bill Stern, who was now strictly an announcer.

If you are going to make it in a big business, there will come a time when somebody, somebody of reputation and position, will have to step forward in a meeting somewhere and say to all the rest, "I think this man can do the job. I will stake my reputation on it." If you progress, you must have the help of that man. And my man was Tom S. Gallery, the director of sports for the NBC radio and television networks.

To paint a word portrait of Tom Gallery is a challenging task. But let me start by acknowledging that he was easily the most influential figure in the early days of sports television. Dumont and NBC were the early sports network leaders and each time Gallery was the man in charge. And the industry has followed the trails that he originally blazed ever since. He had the rights to the headline events—the World Series, the Rose Bowl, the National Open golf tournament, the top boxing matches—and he was creating a pattern of coverage for sports on television in days when there were no precedents. But before television he had already led an intriguing life.

A native of Chicago, he served in the Tank Corps in World War I. Then he went to Hollywood and became a silent motion-picture star, playing the male lead in a string of pictures starring the dog Rin Tin Tin. He was married to and divorced from comedienne ZaSu

Pitts. They made and distributed two independent pictures of their own. And Tom was an outstanding squash and tennis player.

Boxing was the big sport of those times, and a weekly card was presented at the newly constructed Hollywood Legion Stadium. Gallery was invited to manage that operation, and for three or four years he continued to work in the movies and promote the fights at the same time. "I really wasn't all that interested in acting," says Tom, "and I'm still not."

But before long, Gallery had built the Friday night fights at Hollywood Legion Stadium into the "in" thing to do. If you wanted to see or be seen, you went to the stadium and got yourself into one of the four thousand seats available, if you could. The place was almost permanently sold out. And it was exciting.

For example, there was the Friday night when Al Jolson punched Walter Winchell in public. There was no bigger film star than Al Jolson, and there was no bigger journalist than Walter Winchell. But Winchell had written something in his column about Ruby Keeler, who happened to be Mrs. Jolson. And when Jolson encountered Winchell at the Hollywood Legion Stadium, he slugged him. It got more publicity than all the fighters on the card. The demand for tickets was even greater. If you had a chance to see an attractive bill of fighters, plus sidelights like Al Jolson punching Walter Winchell, it was irresistible.

Tom's younger brother, Dan, had come out from Chicago to go to law school at Southern Cal, and had fallen into some lifelong friendships, as people frequently do in college. And if you couldn't get along with Dan Gallery, you couldn't get along. He was the original happy Irishman. And he fell into a triumvirate. The three went everywhere together and did everything that college boys did—Dan Gallery, Ward Bond, and Marion Morrison. In pictures, Morrison's name got changed to John Wayne and everybody called him the Duke.

In 1932 the Olympic Games came to Los Angeles, and you could bet that Tom Gallery would be there every day.

In pictures he had known a charming actress named Corinne Griffith. They had been very good friends. And Corinne had married a fellow named George Preston Marshall, who would become best known as the owner of the Washington Redskins and a pioneer of pro football.

But back there at the Olympic games, George Marshall had the contacts and the tickets. And Gallery knew Corinne, who arranged for Gallery to get four tickets for the whole program of events.

While Corinne and George Marshall used two of the tickets, the other two were used by a handsome, wealthy young sports impresario named Dan Topping. As they sat there day after day, he decided that he liked Tom Gallery.

Meanwhile, George Marshall liked Gallery, too. The fact is that Gallery and Marshall had a lot in common. They were both promoters at heart.

Gallery convinced Marshall that it was fairly stupid for professional football to overlook such gold mines as Los Angeles and San Francisco. And Gallery promoted exhibition appearances. He also convinced Marshall that his Redskins should be training at Occidental College. Although colleges in those days took a stance of having nothing to do with professional football, Bill Henry was prevailed on to influence his alma mater. Bill Henry was sports editor of the *Los Angeles Times,* and he was an alumnus and former quarterback who was able to persuade the college that nothing very bad would come from having the Redskins train on campus and use their facilities at a time when they would otherwise be unused.

Gallery also had an idea for an all-star football game that would involve two squads of outstanding NFL players. And one day Gallery, Henry, and Marshall sat at the Brown Derby and worked out the details. Henry would sell the *Los Angeles Times* on the idea of backing the event as one of the *Times* charities. And so the Pro Bowl was born.

The first year it was held at the Los Angeles baseball park. The second year it was held at Gilmore Stadium in Hollywood. And then it was scheduled for the Los Angeles Memorial Coliseum.

But then the Japanese bombed Pearl Harbor. Public gatherings on the West Coast were banned by the military. And if you can't have public gatherings, that is no place for a promoter.

Tom, who had been a constant column item with film star Madge Evans, was now married to Lillian Fette, an airline stewardess who was a Texan, and she and Tom moved to Miami and went into the wartime boat business.

Soon, though, Tom got word from Dan Topping that he was in the Marine Corps headed overseas and he wanted Tom to go to New York and take over his sports enterprises, including his football team, the Brooklyn Dodgers. Then, in association with Del Webb and Larry MacPhail, Topping became an owner of the New York Yankees baseball team.

Gallery was now into the New York phase of his life. He had

given Hollywood and motion pictures the full treatment and he had been a boxing promoter. It had been interesting, but now that was all over.

There was another incident that impressed Gallery. During a trip to Los Angeles once, he had been invited by Don Lee, who owned radio station KHJ and the Don Lee Network, to witness a demonstration of something new called "television," which was barely on the horizon. And so Gallery joined him as they watched a demonstration of a little box with a one-inch screen that showed pictures. Gallery thought that this was going to mean a whole new world of communications and entertainment. (Looking back at his career in sports promotion and in communications, Gallery says now, "I didn't have the background for those things, but I had vision.")

But now Gallery was in New York, representing Dan Topping who, with his associates, had gained control of the New York Yankees. One day, he went to the stadium. The first thing he noticed was that the public-address system was easily the most ineffective he had ever heard. "It crackled and it popped and it was inaudible," he said. "Even Joe DiMaggio's name came out garbled.

"I knew that something had to be done, and all I knew was that RCA made sound equipment, so I phoned and asked to speak to the president of the company and I got him—David Sarnoff. I explained that he didn't know me but that I represented Dan Topping, who had gained control of the Yankees, and I explained my problem. General Sarnoff said for me not to worry, that RCA would install the very best sound system, and they did. Of course, RCA owned NBC. Television was in its infancy, and Sarnoff at one point asked if I would be interested in working at NBC. I told him I was then more interested in staying on the promotion side of sports."

But Gallery had been bitten by the television bug and soon began to work with Dr. Allen B. Dumont in setting up television coverage of sports events, like Yankee baseball.

Soon after Gallery joined the Dumont Network, he signed two heavyweight championship fights for showing. But it occurred to him that the industry, the other television-set manufacturers in addition to Dumont, like RCA, were doing nothing to promote the sale of television sets. So Gallery called General Sarnoff. And he persuaded the general to join other set manufacturers in buying commercial time on Dumont to promote the sale of television sets, despite the fact that RCA owned NBC.

The rights to the World Series were held directly by Gillette. So one day Gallery got on a plane and flew to Cincinnati, Ohio, where Happy Chandler reigned as commissioner of baseball. Before that conference ended, a change had been made in the manner in which the rights were bid upon and awarded.

And Gallery also worked out with Commissioner Bert Bell of the National Football League an arrangement whereby Dumont televised the games of the NFL.

And it was along in there somewhere that General Sarnoff said to Gallery, "You're not at the Yankees anymore, you're in television. How about coming over to NBC?"

At the beginning, the radio networks just made television an addition to the existing structure. Generally speaking, the top sports announcers were also the heads of the sports departments of the networks. Accordingly, Bill Stern was director of sports at NBC. Bill personally was not yet much interested in television. He was still the nation's number-one radio sports announcer, so he was content to let television struggle along under the eyes of such as Jimmy Dolan, Bill Garden, Lew Brown, Ad Schneider, Jack Mills, and Jack Dillon.

But now NBC was taking a lively interest in the new medium, and General Sarnoff had the man he wanted in charge—Tom Gallery.

It was January 1952 when Gallery officially became the director of sports for the NBC radio and television networks. Bill Stern was signed to a performer's talent contract. He was not very happy at the turn of events, and as it developed, he had problems larger than his mere professional frustration.

I next heard from Gallery when he called and asked if I would represent him in taking over the NBC radio coverage of the National Open golf tournament in Dallas. The principal sponsor would be General tires, handled by the D'Arcy Agency, which also handled Coca-Cola. The agency rep in Dallas would be Newt Stammer, out of the New York office.

The announcers assigned to coverage of the National Open were Bill Stern and Dizzy Dean. Gallery instructed me to produce the broadcast and to use myself as an announcer however I chose.

Dizzy Dean was delightful, but not terribly well disciplined. Getting ready for the broadcast of any segment of the coverage that weekend, I never knew how many announcers I had or where they were.

A corps of Pinkerton's detective agency men had been retained to handle the crowd control. Diz was constantly losing his credentials and identification and then complaining to me that those damned "Pinkston men" wouldn't admit him.

Bill Stern's coverage was interesting. One day, he got me on our intercom (I was stationed as the anchor in the press tent) to explain that he had veteran golfer Dutch Harrison out at the eighteenth green. "Dutch just finished," said Bill, "and I want to interview him and see how the course is playing."

It sounded like a good idea to me, so I said, "Now, let's switch out to the eighteenth green and Bill Stern."

Bill said, "Well, we have Dutch Harrison here. He is a veteran golfer who has just finished his round for today. Dutch, how is the course playing?"

There was a lull, a silence, and then a voice said, "I'm not Dutch Harrison."

I quickly resumed from the press tent. I never knew whom Bill Stern almost interviewed.

I do know that our credibility never got much better. Bill identified George Fazio as a golfer who came into the eighteenth with successive threesomes. On the intercom, a frustrated Newt Stammer said to me, "What the hell is Fazio doing—hiding in the creek and coming in with every threesome?"

After every broadcast, we would call Gallery on the phone at his home in Scarsdale. Now he was depressed. "We really fell apart," he said.

We did manage to get the right winner. It was Julius Boros.

Back in Memphis, we decided that, in the interest of economy, Mickie and Sharon would go to the home of our parents in Columbia, Tennessee, and I would move into the Peabody hotel. The monthly rate for a single at the fashionable hotel was $160.

One day, two fellows came knocking at my door. They said they were representatives of Lang, Fisher, and Stashower Advertising in Cleveland. They represented Carling's Black Label beer and ale. It so happened that Carling's sponsored our baseball re-creations there in Memphis, and these fellows wanted to know if I could broadcast football as well as baseball.

Carling's sponsored the broadcasts of the Cleveland Brown games on WTAM, which was an NBC-owned-and-operated station in Cleveland. Bob Neal had been their broadcaster, but some sort of rift had developed and the job was open. They wanted to know if I would be willing to come there for a personal interview with Paul Brown, who was head coach and general manager of the Browns. He was, in fact, even more than that. The team had been named for him.

While I waited for pending events to untangle themselves, I made my move into the Peabody, gently recalling all the nights of my college years, when I had sat in front of the radio and listened to the big-band music of Clyde McCoy and his trumpet broadcast from the roof of the Peabody.

During those years when we would come to Memphis for a sports event, the Peabody was simply an edifice on which we gazed in awe, somewhat after the manner we presumed we would approach the Taj Mahal in Agra, India. When night fell and the necessity arose for us to seek shelter, we settled into the Gayoso, the Chisca, or, stretching our budget, the Claridge. But the Peabody was simply a subject for conversation. Now, I was residing there.

Each morning I would arise and go up the hill to the Sterick building, where I would put in my day's work at that stalwart radio station operating on 250 watts, WHHM. When day's work was done, I would retire to the confines of the Peabody, perhaps arriving in time to witness the retreat formation of the ducks who had spent their day on display in the lobby pool. A late-afternoon imbiber making his necessary way from the cocktail lounge to the men's room might come upon this unlikely afternoon ceremony and pause to watch this single file of ducks making its way to the elevator much in the rigid manner of the Coldstream Guards on parade at Sandhurst. It was said with some truth that the unlikely sight of the marching ducks at the Peabody in Memphis probably did as much to promote future sobriety as the Volstead Act or Alcoholics Anonymous.

One morning I read a small box on the sports page of the *Commercial Appeal* that said simply that the television rights to the NCAA college football games for the coming season had been awarded to NBC. I was sure that I would be getting a call from Tom Gallery at any minute inviting me to New York.

I did not know then what I know now about networks and the way they work. They are not likely to do anything quickly, easily, or logically. Tom Gallery would likely have called me, as he had promised, but he didn't have anything to tell me. For him to be able to hire me would require the approval of a lot of other people. Just getting them to agree to any one thing, much less me, would be a tedious accomplishment.

So, in the hot and humid good old summertime, I just waited down there on the banks of Ole Man River.

CHAPTER 14

Me to NBC

I waited and I waited until the day before the 1952 major league All-Star baseball game, which would be played at Shibe Park in Philadelphia. It would be televised by NBC, and I knew that Tom Gallery would be there. I decided that I would be there, too. For my far-flung operations I was capitalized at four hundred dollars, the amount of my fee for having worked the National Open on NBC Radio.

In Philadelphia Gallery and Bert Bell, the commissioner of the NFL, were staying at the Racquet Club. I phoned and aroused Gallery from a sound sleep. He said that there would be a baseball luncheon at the Warwick Hotel at noon, and he would be glad to meet me there if I would just hang up the damned phone and let him get back to sleep.

Once outside on the street, I noticed that it had begun to rain, and it just kept right on raining. But I made it to the Warwick and I met Gallery on the crowded mezzanine. He was cordial, and commented that this was hardly the place to have a serious conversation. He suggested that I come on to New York and meet him at his NBC office the following day.

But there was a conflict developing. The football people in Cleveland had called again to urge me toward that visit and interview with Paul Brown.

I went to the All-Star game with Chuck Comiskey, who had rejoined the White Sox when Liberty folded. He rented a chauffeur-driven Cadillac to get us to and from Shibe Park. It had rained all day, and the game was called at the end of five innings. Ballplayers scattered in the rain. We picked up Eddie Robinson and Minnie Minoso, who played for the White Sox.

Later I headed for the North Philadelphia railway station to board the train for New York, as did a number of ballplayers and American League manager Casey Stengel. Casey had made the dash through the rain to get to the railway platform, and like the rest of us, he was drenched. His face had also taken on a bright orange hue. He had just begun to color his hair, and the rain caused the dye to run onto his face. I was to learn that coloring the hair was not all that unusual among athletes and performers, like Leo Durocher and Bob Hope and Pete Rose and, eventually, me. Gray hair may attract women who think it is a mark of distinction. I wouldn't know about that. But it does not attract employers in the sports and broadcasting trades.

In New York I checked into the New Yorker Hotel, and next day I made my way to the RCA building where the offices of NBC were located. There were a good many people lined up to see Tom Gallery. And he was seeing them one by one. When I finally got the word to go in, it was past noon. And the first thing that Gallery did was apologize for keeping me waiting so long, and explain that he had done that so we could go to lunch together. It was still raining. We would go to the French Grill of the Promenade Café, fronting on the plaza, which in the wintertime doubled as a skating rink. We were joined by Mike Dann, a junior executive who would later become a giant figure in the business as programming boss at CBS-TV.

During our conversation, Tom suggested that I go on to Cleveland for the weekend. I was surprised that he knew about Cleveland. I hadn't mentioned it. But the Cleveland Browns games would be carried on WTAM, the NBC station in Cleveland, managed by Hamilton Shea, who had called Gallery to inquire about me. I was beginning to suspect that there were not many secrets in the broadcasting business.

So I flew out to Cleveland. Ham Shea met me at the airport. We went to Paul Brown's home on Saturday morning for what turned out to be the most thorough examination on the subject of football that I have ever undergone. I had done a game between the Cleveland

Browns and the New York Giants at the Polo Grounds, and Coach Brown wanted to know what I remembered about it. Among other things, I remembered that the Browns had stopped Giant fullback Eddie Price on the one-yard line. Brown smiled, still proud of that goal-line stand. Great coaches will always tell you about their defense.

And then we drove out to Al Fisher's farm for an outdoor lunch and more conversation. He was the middle member of the advertising firm of Lang, Fisher, and Stashower. At the end of the day, I was offered the job. I would get $350 per game and Ham Shea would put me on the payroll at WTAM for $100 per week just to pad things out. I would fly back to New York on Sunday and let them know on Monday. WTAM would pay my expenses for the Cleveland trip, but they saw no urgency about the reimbursement. I did. The National Open's four hundred bucks was running very low indeed.

Very early on Monday morning, I was back in Gallery's office to report on my trip to Cleveland. And he had set up some more interviews for me at NBC. Up to now I had been interviewed by everybody but General Sarnoff.

I explained to Tom that I had promised to let Cleveland know my decision by sometime Monday. So Gallery phoned Ham Shea to say we would be a day later with the word, promising to call on Tuesday.

On Tuesday Gallery left me in his office while he went upstairs for more meetings. When he came back, he said nothing directly to me. He picked up the phone and called Ham Shea in Cleveland. And all he said was, "We've decided that Lindsey will stay here." Then Tom turned and stuck out his hand. "Welcome aboard," he said.

Years later, when Gallery was asked why he had hired me, he said, "Well, among other things, Paul Brown in Cleveland was about to hire him, and Brown is no dummy." But I was now set to move to New York, and Ken Coleman was soon on his way to Cleveland from Boston and would have a long and distinguished career as the voice of the Browns.

I had had quite enough of the loneliness of those break-in days in Dallas, and I had decided never to do that again. We would leave Sharon temporarily in Columbia, and Mickie and I would drive to New York together.

I had made a major move and purchased a dark blue, summer-weight Palm Beach suit to wear to my new post with the big network folks in New York. During my years in Tennessee and Texas we had run heavily to seersucker or maybe light slacks and a sport shirt. But this was different, and I felt suitably attired as I walked down Fifty-fifth Street to Sixth Avenue (why did the sign say AVENUE OF THE AMERICAS?). A right turn then took me along to the RCA building. In the center section of the building, I took an NBC elevator to the second floor, and thence down the long dark corridor to the door that led into the sports department. In fact, in gold leaf on the door it said SPORTS DEPARTMENT. And underneath that, it said TOM S. GALLERY, DIRECTOR. And underneath that, it said BILL STERN. That's all it said. Very impressive in its stark simplicity, I think. I also thought that if I were the Radio Corporation of America, with all those electronic geniuses on the payroll, I would work out some way to light that dark corridor, like maybe putting in a few larger bulbs.

The next thing I observed was that there seemed to be no office or desk for me, not even a cubicle. Networks deal heavily in cubicles. Bill Stern had the office on the left, the one that was paneled. Dave Cammerer had the office in the middle. He had just been hired to publicize the NCAA football series. Tom Gallery had the office on the right. There were desks for writers and secretaries and room for file cabinets. And no room for me.

Mickie had asked me a couple of pertinent questions about my employment at NBC that I was unable to answer. First, in the interest of planning a proper family budget, she wanted to know what my salary would be, and I didn't know. It had never really come up in our discussions. I wasn't anxious about it because I had decided that I was in the broadcasting business for good. And if the National Broadcasting Company offered me a job sweeping out the office at ten bucks a week, I wasn't going to turn it down. I thought the amount of starting pay was unimportant.

Mickie also wanted to know what kind of duties I had, whether I had any sort of job description or title. I told her that that had never come up, either. My arrangement with NBC up to now was obviously very loose.

Now I sat there in the chair where I had waited that first day for my interview with Gallery. And I was ready to begin my network career. It was July 21, 1952. And I seemed to be a lot more impressed with this development than NBC was.

My life at NBC was off to a slow start, but I soon discovered that I was involved in a sudden and continuous learning process.

About every twenty seconds I was being confronted by something that I didn't know.

Something I did know was that I could not long afford to live at the Park Sheraton Hotel. Since it was a matter of some concern to me, I inquired around NBC about the exact date of the next payday. I was told that a new employee did not get paid right away. It took several weeks, they said, for all the papers to clear. And it occurred to me that they had at least one new employee who might face starvation before that first check arrived.

Of course, as a prospective homemaker in expensive New York, Mickie was horrified to learn she was married to a man who didn't know how much he was to be paid or when. When I had told her that it wasn't important, she pointed out that it might not be important to me but she suspected that any day now it was going to become important to the Park Sheraton.

We didn't know anything about the geography of New York, except that there seemed to be a lot of it. We surely didn't know what the most desirable suburban residential areas were. But John Kieran had confidently touted us on the Scarsdale-Hartsdale area. So when I went to NBC each morning, Mickie was driving off to Westchester in search of quarters. For openers, she found us a room in White Plains in what was essentially a rooming house. The bed was soft and the rates were cheap. Now I was into the fascinating life of a commuter on the New York Central run, Harlem division. Like hundreds and thousands of others, I got on the train each day with my morning newspaper. I promptly put my head into the paper in the approved manner and looked neither to the right nor to the left until we had arrived safely at Grand Central.

Speaking to a fellow traveler, I discovered, was forbidden. If you chanced to say something to the fellow sharing the seat with you, he might look at you blankly, but he would not see you. You could wave your hand in front of his staring eyes, but there would be no recognition of your being there.

I was sort of juggling things, too, waiting for some development. The possible developments included arrival of a check from WTAM in Cleveland, reimbursing me for my expenses out there, or a payroll check from NBC.

I did make one interesting discovery. One day Gallery asked me to come with him and we went up to the office of Sid Eiges, who was vice-president in charge of the press department. He was the man who handled the dissemination of information about the network to the press. And we were going up to tell Mr. Eiges that we now had a new man in the sports department named Lindsey Nelson. Eiges was not as thrilled by that news as I was. He said, "What title?"

Gallery said, "Assistant director of sports, radio and television networks."

I don't know if any of the people who read the press release were impressed, but I surely was. I wasn't rich, but I was titled.

One morning a few days later, I came in to a shocking surprise. When I got to the door of the sports department, it was apparent that the sign painter had been at work. I guessed that the busiest man at the network was the sign painter. NBC believed in putting those names on the doors, and there were changes every day. You couldn't get paid but you could get advertised. Right there on our door it said, SPORTS DEPARTMENT, TOM S. GALLERY, DIRECTOR. And just beneath that, in impressive gold leaf, it said, LINDSEY NELSON, ASSISTANT DIRECTOR.

Beneath that, it said, BILL STERN.

Well, it looked good to me, although I wondered how it was going to look to Bill Stern.

Tom must have wondered, too, because he ordered all names removed from the door and just the words *Sports Department* to remain. It seemed like a judicious move. I was surely glad, though, that Mickie hurried in and got a picture of my name on that door before they took it off.

One of the first people I met around NBC was a good-looking young fellow who seemed to be into all sorts of projects. He was in the business of handling talent, and he did some things for NBC Radio, at one time handling a nationwide search for new talent.

The young man moved on into the agency business. I remember one phone conversation we had about talent. He was looking for a male type to represent a certain shaving product, and we discussed Jack Gregson.

In 1962 this friend would come back to NBC as a vice-president. I got a call from him one day. "Since I came back," he said, "I've received calls from most of my friends welcoming me back. I haven't heard from you. What's the matter?"

I laughed and explained that it just so happened that I was about to leave to become a baseball announcer.

We chatted for a while and I subsequently went away to the world of baseball. This friend was named Grant Tinker, the man who married Mary Tyler Moore, built MTM Enterprises production company into one of the most influential in the business, and became chairman of the National Broadcasting Company. He has certainly been busy while I've continued to be a sports announcer.

Back there in the fifties, though, I was doing whatever one could do in those early days of television. During one period, I teamed up with a newsman and a weatherman to present a daily fifteen-minute show on Channel 4 in New York. This was what you would call your basic low-budget show. We worked in a studio on Sixty-seventh Street, and we knew it was low budget when the comptroller insisted that we take the subway instead of a taxi from the RCA building. Have you ever tried to take big cardboard cue cards onto a Manhattan subway car in midtown at five P.M.?

The news segment was done by Kenneth Banghart, and the weather by Tex Antoine. We had one small desk, one chair, and one camera. When Banghart finished five minutes of news, he would say, "Now stay tuned for Lindsey Nelson and the sports." They would throw up a slide, and while they were on that, Banghart would slip out of the chair and I would replace him. And we'd do the same thing with me and Tex Antoine.

There were frequent changes in the crew, and one day the floor manager was a young, pleasant fellow who wanted to talk sports. On the show, he handled the duties of relaying information from the director. This was before the days of the Telex in your ear and direct communication. So this fellow would count down the time remaining, doing it on his fingers in the approved manner.

He later advanced to the position of producer there at Channel 4, doing a show called *Hi Mom.*

I would see him again and again, and he would have a profound effect on sports on television and news, too, for that matter. That was Roone Arledge, longtime president of news and sports at ABC.

The sports department of the NBC Television Network had been loosely run up until now. Bill Stern had been the nominal department head, but he had been spending his time as an announcer on both television and radio, mostly radio. Jimmy Dolan, who had once been an assistant and spotter for Ted Husing at CBS, had come over as the assistant director. Gallery had been running sports at the Dumont Network, and when he came to NBC, Stern reverted to a talent contract and Dolan was out. That is where I came in.

If I had been working for a station in or near New York, I don't think I would have come to Gallery's attention. But he knew that if he hired me, I wouldn't have any bad big-city habits to break. That RCA building was full of cliques and politics. I'll bet it still is. But I didn't belong to any of them. I was there to do what Gallery told me to do. That's why he hired me. And he didn't hire me to be an announcer. The fact was that Gallery couldn't stand announcers.

Ad Schneider was producing a good many of the sports events. And the directors were Jack Mills, Lew Brown, and Jack Dillon. They had become accustomed to running things under the Stern banner without interference. Stern didn't care what they did. Gallery intended to change all that.

Before long, it was obvious that Gallery's operation had become the leader in the sports field. NBC had most of the top events—the World Series, the Rose Bowl, NCAA football, the National Open, the NFL championship.

One day I was invited to lunch at Toots Shor's restaurant on Fifty-first Street. Everybody knew about Toots Shor's popular restaurant.

When I walked in, there was Hal Boyle of the AP, Neil Sullivan of *Pathé News,* and Bill Heinz of the New York *Sun.* They were all friends from the war years. "Where have you been?" they said. "When the war ended, we thought we'd all be back in New York together, but you never showed up. Where have you been?"

"I was away," I said.

And years later when I heard from Willie Morris an autobiographical remark attributed to writer James Jones when he was in similar circumstances, I understood what he meant. Jones had said, "I was getting over the war."

To get over a war, some take a long time. And some take forever.

Mickie and I had moved into an apartment in the Kenilworth on Garth Road in Scarsdale. It had two bedrooms and cost $140 per month. And now we sent for Sharon. My sister would bring her up on the plane from Tennessee, so once again we could have our little family together.

There was another purpose in that, too. Mickie and I had never really given up hope that somewhere, some way there would be a possibility of getting further medical aid for Sharon. We had systematically exhausted every possible facility in Knoxville and then in Dallas.

There was just not a great deal of assistance available for the retarded.

But we were sure that in New York, in that big sprawling city full of talented people, there would be some help. We had searched for information and had discovered that there was a doctor on Central Park South who was said to be world famous. She specialized in retardation. We would have to wait a month for an appointment, but we anxiously, and dutifully, and hopefully, got in line.

Our appointed day came early in the fall. There was just that first little hint of autumn in the eastern air. It was still bright and sunny. But there was notice that cooler days were ahead.

It was midmorning when Mickie, little Sharon, and I marched into the office of this celebrated doctor on Central Park South. The reception was cordial, and the first pronouncement was that they didn't really have any further need for father.

The doctor would conduct a detailed examination, and Mickie would be there to encourage Sharon in the things she would be asked to do with blocks and cards.

The doctor suggested that I take a walk. It would have been more to the point, I think, if she had suggested that I take a hike. Maybe she did.

Anyway, I did as ordered. Soon I was strolling down Central Park South to Sixth Avenue and around the block and back and forth. I was lost in thought. What would the doctor tell us? Would she be able to prescribe some miracle medicine that would help our tiny, fragile daughter? Would there be some special exercises? Could we work with her at home on the basics of reading and spelling? And could she go to a speech therapist to relieve the frustration of her inability to communicate?

At one point, I went into a bar and ordered a Coke. I sat there and watched the television set behind the bar. Although we had had our first television set in Dallas, that glowing screen was still a novelty to me.

Presently, it was time for me to go back to the doctor's office to hear the wonderful news and instruction about how we would help Sharon.

When I went through the door and saw Mickie and Sharon, one glance told me that the news was not going to be all that wonderful. Mickie was solemn, and a little determined. Sharon was smiling and happy. The doctor was all business. She either invited or ordered me to sit.

She hastily explained that she had done a thorough examination, and that she really didn't have anything specific she could suggest. She knew of nothing in particular that would improve Sharon's situation. She thought it best that we place her immediately in an institution. There were several in the area, she said, including one in Vineland, New Jersey. She said that Sharon would be better off there, and that it was not terribly expensive. There were places that charged as little as three thousand dollars per year, she said.

I had learned from NBC that my annual salary was $7,500.

Mickie and I were stunned as we walked toward the garage where we had left our car. We had not been prepared for an absolute capitulation, a declaration of defeat. Of course, we had raised our hopes too high. But the more we talked of it as we walked, the more we were resolute in the decision we were about to make. By the time we got to the car, we knew exactly what we were going to do. We were not going to place Sharon in any institution in any Vineland, New Jersey, or anywhere else. We would just take her on back home and love her.

We did not then perceive that the love we would get in return would far exceed anything that we were going to get from television, or NBC, or New York, or anything else. And a little later on, the God who had created Sharon had something else in mind for us: another daughter.

I got rather quickly into the daily work of the sports department at NBC. In my role as assistant department head, I got a liberal education from my attendance at the administrative meetings.

One day it was announced that it had been decided to bring a young fellow from California and install him as the anchor in New York for the nightly news. He would be teamed up with David Brinkley, who was already anchoring the news from Washington. The new man's name was Chet Huntley. And that became *The Huntley-Brinkley Report,* which soon went to the head of the class in the network-news field.

We discovered that the most reasonable of people would sometimes become ardently unreasonable in competing for a favored position on the network-television schedule. The man in charge of religious programs was a mild-mannered fellow named Ed Stanley. One day, he arrived at one of the program meetings a little late and a little harassed. When he was asked what the matter might be, Ed Stanley said quietly, "I have had just about all the Norman Vincent Peale I can take in one morning."

In many areas my tutor was Gallery's secretary, a talented lady named Zena Bier. She had worked for NBC for quite a while, and she knew the inner workings of this complex company. Every department, of course, requires the services of such a person if it plans to survive and prosper. Zena had served in the WAVES, I believe, during the war years, and she had retained some of the mannerisms of a drill sergeant.

I do not mean that to be harsh. Zena was a good-looking, extremely intelligent lady, and I am indebted to her for assisting a green rookie. She saved my administrative neck more than once. I am just trying to convey that your chances of getting past Zena and in to see Gallery without an appointment were roughly the equivalent of getting safely past the guns of Navarone.

My biggest project, of course, was involvement in the NCAA football package. From the time that television had raised its black-and-white head, there had been fears among the college football folk of just what effect it might have on the college game. It was thought, not unreasonably, that if a fan could claim the option of sitting at home and tuning in one of a variety of games on the television, that he might decline to attend in person. Worse still, he might lose the habit. Some far-seeing folk thought they saw the distinct possibility of "studio football"—games played before a few fans in the stadium and carried to a lot more on the tube. They thought it indicative that when more movies showed up on television at home, more movie theaters downtown closed their doors.

And back there in 1950, Tom Gallery, on behalf of Dr. Dumont's network, made a monumental move.

He signed the entire home football schedule of the Fighting Irish of Notre Dame, sold the entire package to Chevrolet, hired announcers Mel Allen and Jim Britt, and put the whole thing, live, on Dumont television.

The fathers of college athletics across the length and breadth of this land were struck with fear. You see, during the war years, not long past, the service academies had fielded football teams that drew large national followings. They featured such stars as Felix (Doc) Blanchard, Glenn Davis, Clyde Scott, Barney Poole, Don Whitmire, and more. Some directors of athletics awakened from nightmares in which they saw, each Saturday afternoon, Notre Dame on Dumont,

Army on NBC, Navy on CBS, the infant Air Force Academy on ABC, and large patches of green grass, maybe even beans and potatoes, growing in the unoccupied stadiums of the land.

This called for urgent action. This called for organization. This called for the NCAA, the governing body of college athletics and protector of the welfare of the individual institutions. There would have to be some restrictions right away. Not soon, but right now, for the 1951 season. It was the colleges who were clamoring for restrictions and protection. It was a hastily arranged and ill-conceived plan, and like most hastily arranged plans, it had major faults.

In general, the plan said that games would be picked up in the eastern half of the nation and televised to the West. And games would be picked up in the West and televised to the East. In that way, attendance at the stadium would not be damaged, since the games would be seen on television in remote locales. That was also the fatal weakness of the plan. Games were televised only to areas where nobody cared. That cut down on the interest of television sponsors, too. And this was to be one of the difficulties with which the colleges wrestled through the succeeding years. They found it difficult to have their cake and eat it, too. But it did not stop them from trying. In an effort to protect the home gate by limiting the number of appearances of popular teams, they sent games to audiences that did not want to see them.

The colleges then were faced with a many-faceted problem. They wanted to get their best games on television, to present the product in its best light, such as Notre Dame against Southern California and Oklahoma against Texas. They wanted to attract the revenue that such telecasts would surely bring. But at the same time, they wanted to protect the in-stadium attendance of smaller schools whose attractiveness was limited, and they wanted to protect in-stadium attendance in general. They did not always seem to realize that the large amounts of money available from the television networks were based largely on exclusivity. If the number of televised games went up, the resulting price was likely to go down.

In time, greed seemed to intercede. There was less interest in protecting the smaller schools and more interest on the part of some of the more attractive schools in getting as much exposure and as much money as possible. Finally, in 1984 the United States Supreme Court held the NCAA plan to be in violation of the antitrust statutes (it had been for thirty-two years), thus allowing colleges to control their own television rights. It may be several years before we know whether this has been good or bad for the colleges. We do know that we have more football on television, and anxious administrators are checking between the stadium seats for the first signs of sprouting grass.

But back there in July of 1952, before I had made my quiet arrival at NBC, the entire NCAA football package was sold. One cloudy morning, NBC president Joe McConnell, with Tom Gallery and a bevy of sales minions, flew off to Detroit, Michigan, and peddled the whole package, a nine-game schedule, to General Motors for a grand price of four million dollars. It was reckoned at that time to be a milestone event in the business. It would be reckoned now to cover not quite the first quarter of the Rose Bowl.

Everybody then got busy making schedules. It was a lot like a jigsaw puzzle. You could get an attractive schedule laid out and then discover at the last moment that you had committed a disqualifying omission of one of the basic requirements of the complicated plan. Many long hours, day and night, were spent by all members of the NBC Sports staff and by the NCAA committee members, who were supposedly standing by in a role which would confer approval upon whatever was submitted by NBC. The role of the NCAA committee is not to be underestimated. While the schedule did have to be devised and submitted by NBC, the NCAA did retain the right of approval. That is a powerful right.

For that first season under the new NCAA television plan, our talent lineup had Dick Kazmaier in the leadoff spot doing the pregame show. We had Mel Allen and Bill Henry doing the game, Russ Hodges doing the commercials, Herman Hickman and Andre Baruch doing the postgame show, Ad Schneider producing, Jack Mills and Jack Dillon directing, and me supervising.

We had held a business meeting in the department before the start of the season to set the fees that would be payable on this series. Les Vaughan was our man from business affairs, who recorded the amounts as Gallery intoned them. It was decided that Bill Henry would get one thousand dollars per game. There was a reason for that. Bill was being paid for prestige. His sports background was impeccable. He had been sports editor of the *Los Angeles Times* and had done color on the West Coast broadcasts of the Rose Bowl for years. But more than that, he was a television pioneer and he was NBC's anchorman at such things as political conventions and the elections.

He was our "host." I remember that at one of our meetings with General Motors in Detroit it was explained that "Bill Henry will be our frame around the entire picture." I thought I was getting into agency and network jargon. In Texas we would not have felt required to explain Bill's position. When we saw that he was getting a thousand bucks, we would have known that he was the frame and the host and anything else we wanted to call him. In Texas, the top hand gets the top buck, and you can bet on it.

Mel Allen was our play-by-play man. He was the voice of the Yankees and was frequently on the World Series. Many thought he was chosen to do the World Series each year by some kind of competition. The fact is that the announcers representing the two competing teams did the World Series, and Mel's team, the New York Yankees, seemed to be there almost every fall.

That had added to Mel's national fame and prestige. He was down for $750 per game. Next year, when Bill Henry would be doing something else, Mel would move up to the thousand-buck class.

Russ Hodges, doing the commercials for General Motors, would draw $400 per game. Ad Schneider, the producer, would get $200. Mills and Dillon would get $100 each. And I, the supervisor, was a staff member of management who was already drawing a regular salary from the company. The fact that my regular salary from the company was $150 per week was ruled irrelevant. I got no football fee.

Suppose we look back at it now. You have this new medium called television, which has the power to show off the game of college football to the millions of fans across the nation. By showing outstanding teams with exciting traditions to areas of the country where they have been unknown, you can build a new and receptive audience for the game. You have the power with this magic carpet to take the game live from some stadium in this country, some football shrine like the Yale Bowl or Notre Dame Stadium, to everybody else. So, where and between what teams is your very first game?

Well, you have studied night and day with the best football advice you can get, and you announce that your opener will be—are you ready? Roll the drums and sound the trumpets! It is: TCU versus Kansas from Lawrence, Kansas. Yeah, well.

Looking for things to promote, there was the fact that TCU was coached by an exciting and delightful fellow named Dutch Meyer. He was a legend who had gone 6–4 the previous season, and then in the Cotton Bowl lost to a Kentucky team quarterbacked by Babe

Parilli and coached by Bear Bryant. But now, we didn't have Parilli and Bryant in our game. We had the Dutchman, and we were glad to have him. Because Kansas was coached by J. V. Sikes. He was competent, but his fame was local, very local.

Kansas won by a score of 13–0. And there were some sections of the nation that exhibited something less than fervent interest in those proceedings.

When reactions to that first telecast were in, there were some changes made. Gallery's immediate superior in the hierarchy at NBC was Davidson Taylor, director of public affairs, a tall, thin, soft-spoken gentleman who had once studied at the seminary in Louisville, and who had been a top executive in his radio days at CBS when he had worked with the likes of Edward R. Murrow and Ted Husing. Gallery and Taylor were spending a lot of time together, but communication between them was not easy. Personally, they were absolute opposites.

Gallery had not been altogether pleased with the production work on the first game. It appeared to him that there were still lingerings of the old regime in the sometimes seemingly surly attitude of some connected with the presentation. Gallery was a strong man, and if there was one thing that he intended to have completely, it was the assurance that things were going to be done his way. He would take all the responsibility and if need be the blame, but in the bargain he would require all the authority. He and Mr. Taylor informed me that henceforth I would retain my title as supervisor but that I would in fact produce the games. And then they spoke the sweetest words that I had heard in my network career up to then. They said, "And you get the two hundred dollars per game budgeted for the producer."

To a man who is making a hundred and a half per week, that is a marvelous announcement.

CHAPTER 15

College Football

Networks did not have a lot of sports announcers on staff or under contract in the 1950s. The days of the radio networks, when each had a sports announcer who doubled as director of sports, were gone. Most of those sports events on radio had been carried "sustaining." That means "without sponsors," and that means "without income," and to the network brass that meant "unimportant."

Sports had constituted the "toy department" of the network. It was fun and games. Now television came along to lend another tone to the proceedings. When the football package was peddled for four million dollars, the network brass showed immediate and continuing interest. The bastard child had just found a birth certificate. And respectability was on the way.

When a big sports event was scheduled, the final decision on the announcers would likely be made by the advertising agency handling the sponsor. The network retained a sort of right of approval, but they did not intend to disapprove anybody unless he committed incest in Macy's window, or maybe was just physically unfortunate, like Russ Hodges.

The Kudner Agency had the General Motors corporate account,

plus that of the Buick division and GMC. It was an affluent member of Madison Avenue society. And when it was casting the crew for the NCAA football games, Russ Hodges had been chosen to do the commercials. Russ, of course, was doing the New York Giant baseball games, and did not personally have time to get to many of the agency meetings. I came to believe that the people at Kudner had never actually *seen* Russ Hodges.

But I remember the commercial opening of that first game so well. Kudner had spent a lot of money on it. And it was impressive. It impressed me. And it impressed General Motors, too, although in a different way. First there was this big distinctive General Motors key. It's the kind you got when you bought any General Motors car. And up at the top there was a little hole for your keychain. The camera moved tantalizingly toward that aperture. And as the scene behind the hole became apparent, there sat Russ Hodges, smiling. And as the camera moved to show him full-face, Russ said, "Hi and welcome from General Motors."

Shocked executives from Flint to Pontiac to Detroit to New York scrambled for telephones. How could this have happened? Who was responsible? Could they possibly get that man off there before he came on again? He would surely have to be gone before next week. And he was.

You see, Russ Hodges looked exactly like Walter Reuther. They could have passed for brothers. And Walter Reuther was the president of the United Automobile Workers, the union that seemed to be in constant conflict with corporate General Motors. When the GM folks had seen their opening commercial seemingly done by Walter Reuther, they had fainted.

On Monday there was an anxious meeting to cast Nelson Case as the commercial announcer and to put Russ Hodges in the booth with Mel Allen for commentary. After all, he didn't *sound* like Walter Reuther.

But that incident is illustrative of the things that can happen to an announcer over which he has no control.

Viewers do form definite opinions about announcers. When my mother and father came to New York for a visit, it was their first trip to the Big Apple, and we made most of the tourist stops. And on Sunday, we went to Yankee Stadium for a baseball doubleheader. First we had lunch in the Stadium Club, and then we went up to the NBC box on the mezzanine just behind the working press. Between games, I asked my mother if there was anything in particular that she would like to do or see. "Yes," she said, "I certainly would like to meet Mel Allen. I listen to him on television and I think he is just marvelous. Could I meet him?"

I assured her that she could, without assuring her that Mel Allen just happened to be my biggest competitor in the sportscasting trade. When I got the word to Mel, he was as gracious as ever, and came up to the box to meet my mother. She was delighted.

In many ways we proceeded through that initial NCAA football season of 1952 on television in a sort of catch-as-catch-can manner. Often Jack Dillon and I would sit on the running board of the control truck about an hour before kickoff and work out commercial placement and roll cues. We handled a succession of small emergencies. There was that day at Notre Dame, for instance, when the Irish band was marching up the field, into the verse of a very familiar fight song, and I heard director Jack Mills say, "Okay, cue the commercial." I declined to cue the commercial because I knew what was about to happen.

But Mills was getting a little heated. "All right, dammit," he said, "cue the commercial!" At that moment the Notre Dame band broke into its traditional pregame rendition of the "Notre Dame Victory March." Mills then said to me on the headset, "And I thank you very much." One does not cut to a commercial in the middle of the "Notre Dame Victory March." If one does, there will be a lot of mail from Notre Dame fans, and they abound by the millions. And then there will be another meeting with the agency and the sponsor.

But we were learning. And there came the day we were doing the University of California at Berkeley versus Ohio State in the California confines of strawberry canyon and "tightwad hill" (an area from which spectators can watch without paying admission).

The way the game was played in those days, if a team called time it was not necessary for them to utilize the full period of the time-out. After any length of time, say twenty seconds, if the team that called the time-out was ready to play, then they played.

General Motors had spent some forty thousand dollars on a special animated commercial for this game. And during a time-out we rolled it. The problem came when the teams began playing again after only twenty seconds. We had to cut out of the commercial and get back to the game. This upset General Motors, and they applied for a sizable rebate.

It was the NCAA television committee that then recognized the necessity for instituting some kind of on-field controls. I remember one member at a meeting remarking that time-outs involving sums like forty thousand dollars were far too important to be left to the discretion of a college boy.

So, it was the NCAA television committee that devised the system of placing a man on the sidelines. He has come to be known as the "red hat." Through the years he has worn white gloves, a red hat, or some other distinguishing color of clothing so that he can be easily seen. And he has been in touch with the officials and the control truck to be sure that play is not resumed until the commercial is through. The duties of the red hat have been expanded to include getting word to the referee that a television time-out is needed.

It was the NCAA television committee that realized in that regard, too, that if the package were to remain marketable, it would have to include places for commercials to be inserted. Otherwise no network would be interested in bidding all that money.

Our directors in the control truck were discovering also that they had trouble picking the referee out of the staff of officials milling around out there on the field when a confusing penalty had been called. The referee, admittedly, was the boss, and he was the official who would finally signal and enforce the penalty. But which one was the referee? They were all dressed alike, and the director out there in the truck scanning his monitors was having a problem. Since all the college officials wore black caps, we suggested that the referee wear a white cap to make him more readily visible. In college games, the referee still wears a white cap.

As we all know, it is difficult to get people to agree on anything. In baseball, the National and American Leagues have been unable to agree on proper dress for the umpires and even on how many players there are on a team, with the American League presence of the designated hitter. So the NFL decided that the distinguishing cap for the referee was a good idea, except the NFL put their man in a black cap. He still wears a black cap.

We did a marvelous game at Notre Dame in which Frank Leahy's Notre Dame team defeated Bud Wilkinson's Oklahoma Sooners 27–21, a matchup of Johnny Lattner vs. Billy Vessels. I have never seen a better football game.

And we had a memorable game at Illinois involving Illinois and Purdue. Since we were in the Midwest, General Motors had a goodly number of representatives on hand, and they had gathered outside

Memorial Stadium in Champaign-Urbana the morning of the game. It was bright and sunny as the early arrivals pulled up in quest of the parking lot. Russ Hodges had been in town for a couple of days and had rented a car. But he had no previous reservation and the garage was just about out of cars. In fact, they had only one rental left—a Hudson. Russ took it. And when he drove up there the morning of that game and was seen by this gathering of General Motors officials, it was more than they could reasonably bear—Walter Reuther in a Hudson for General Motors.

As we approached the Army-Navy game, we were also approaching the end of the season. In those days, the Army-Navy game was an enormous attraction. It was played to 102,000 fans out there on the windswept field of Municipal Stadium in Philadelphia. Along with Soldier Field in Chicago and the Memorial Coliseum in Los Angeles, I considered this the most difficult place from which to announce a football game. Unbelievably, the photo deck, full of large people with even larger cameras, was in front of the booth, between the announcer and the nearly invisible field.

And it was along about here that I got into the network-announcing act—radio announcing. All through that season of 1952, Bill Stern had been doing a series of games on radio, assisted by Joe Hasel, and it was *co-op'd.* To *co-op* means to sell the game commercially to local sponsors in the markets where the game is broadcast. Now, General Motors had decided that it wanted to sponsor the radio broadcast of the Army-Navy game as well as the telecast. NBC Radio, then, would carry two games—the Army-Navy game for General Motors and the Tennessee vs. Vanderbilt game in Nashville done by Bill Stern.

After I had dropped numerous hints, Gallery asked if I wanted to do the play-by-play of the Army-Navy game. He wanted to know if I needed Jim Gibbons from Washington to do color. I said I did.

I also imported old friend John Kieran, Jr., as radio producer, because it was apparent that I was about to get spread a little thin. I thought maybe I was about to get spread even thinner when word came from New York that Kieran and I should get out to the railway siding behind the stadium the next morning and personally deliver an armload of programs, compliments of NBC, to President Harry S. Truman and his entourage. We had all this and a president, too.

On Friday afternoon, I went to the stadium and attended the workouts of Army, coached by Red Blaik, and Navy, coached by

Eddie Erdelatz. Then I checked the TV booth to see that the monitors were properly placed, and checked with Jack Dillon about the placement of commercials. I wouldn't have time the next morning. I would be out there in the South Philly brush looking for a railway siding and Harry Truman.

Navy won the game by a score of 7–0. I had made my debut as a play-by-play football announcer, coast to coast for NBC, on the Army-Navy game. It was a prestigious way to break in. And I had felt strangest when I read a fourth-quarter promotional announcement, "Stay tuned to this NBC station immediately following this broadcast of the Army-Navy game for Tennessee vs. Vanderbilt in Nashville with Bill Stern."

Bill Stern and I had switched roles.

Soon afterward, I was sent to Los Angeles to produce the telecast of the NFL Pro Bowl game. Professional football was not then the big deal that it eventually became. The game was to be played at the Los Angeles Memorial Coliseum, and I was sitting there at the Sheraton-Town House on Wilshire Boulevard in social conversation with Manager Ed Crowley. It was Friday morning, and I was awaiting word from NBC's West Coast sales department. They had advised that they still had one hot prospect for a partial sale and that I should delay making up my sustaining format. They said that they were still talking to Beacon Wax. They may still be talking to Beacon Wax, because we never sold a dime's worth of the Pro Bowl to anybody. We could not sell one spot announcement. Sponsors were not interested in an NFL professional all-star football game.

My announcers were Bud Foster of Berkeley and Mark Scott of Hollywood. Our director was Bill Bennington of NBC's West Coast division. As we were getting set in the booth and mostly just standing by, Foster and Scott came to me, giggling almost, and said, "Can we ask you a question?"

I said, "Of course."

Bud said, "Well, Mark and I are glad to be working, but why aren't you announcing this game?"

I explained that they were apparently unaware that I was a big front-office network executive, and that we generally didn't associate too much with working-class announcers.

But at dinner I confided to director Bill Bennington that I certainly would admire to announce some football games. I would particularly admire to announce a game on television, a medium on which I had never announced a football game.

Later in December, we would be doing something called the Poinsettia Bowl. You may not have heard of that one. It was a game for the service championship between San Diego Naval Training Center and Bolling Field, an air force installation. It was to be played at Balboa Stadium in San Diego. And NBC would carry it from coast to coast on both radio and television.

The radio had been cast first. Tom Harmon would do the play-by-play and a staffer named John Storm would do the color. We were in Gallery's suite at the Town House when we discussed the television announcers. Gallery said that he had already talked to Roy Neal and would use him on color. Neal was a newsman on the West Coast who has since become a top authority on space and rocket events. Now we only needed to come up with a play-by-play man for television.

I do not know what prompted Bill Bennington, but I have blessed the memory of the moment when Bill Bennington said to Gallery, "Why don't you let Lindsey do it?"

Gallery looked surprised. He turned and said to me, "You want to do it?"

I said, "Sure."

He said, "Okay, you do the play-by-play, and we'll have Bill Kayden produce and Bennington direct." I was on my way to football announcing on television.

I might as well go ahead and tell you here that the event was not exactly a howling success, and the Poinsettia Bowl was right then in the act of dying as it began. It struggled for future renewals, but in relative obscurity and never again on national television.

First of all it rained. I do not mean that there was a shower or what we in the South call a sprinkle. It rained like a continuing and ever-strengthening tropical storm. It was the most consistent rain I ever saw. It started about daybreak on the day of the game and it just rained and rained.

We were staying at a big white hotel on a hilltop in the center of town, the El Cortez, and I went down to the breakfast room. There was a big skylight there, and when those big raindrops in great quantity hit that glass you couldn't hear what the waitress was saying. Gallery was having breakfast in his room upstairs. He could tell that this was getting pretty serious, but he decided to ask for a second opinion. He had me called to the phone in the dining room. I could hardly hear what he was saying for that rain hitting the skylight. He said, "How does the rain look?" And I said, gritting my teeth, "Oh, it seems to be letting up." He said he'd see me at the stadium.

He could have seen me easier at the stadium if he had come by boat. They had taped great stalks of poinsettias to the concrete of the stadium. They had all just dropped off into the running water.

Bill Bennington had devised a camera situated on a rubber-tired mobile stand. It would be something new and revolutionary in this new medium, a moving camera. It was now a sunken camera, right up to the hubs of the rubber tires.

My spotter for the Bolling Field team was Mike Walden, who did not learn anything that day to assist him in his later duties as a topflight sportscaster with the Milwaukee Braves, the Los Angeles Dodgers, USC, UCLA, and points west. That day, he just got wet.

As kickoff time approached, we became aware of another interesting development. There were no spectators.

I do not mean that there were only a few spectators. I do not mean that it was a small crowd. I mean that there did not appear to be one single paid admission. We were about to televise from coast to coast on NBC a football game to which nobody had come. Admittedly, they would have drowned, but you would have thought that some soul with a spirit of adventure would have shown up. But they hadn't. On a day like this, they were all in the movies and the bars.

There was an idea. Gallery gathered the military for a quick strategy conference. He explained rather patiently, I thought, especially for a wet Irishman who appeared likely to drift downstream at any moment, that we simply could not televise a game without any spectators at all. We had to have a crowd shot of some sort. He proposed that the military devise some way to get some people into that Balboa Stadium. I personally did not deem this possible unless we sought the services of General Lewis Hershey and the citizens' military draft, which was no longer in force.

But the military knew things that we did not know. The military knew that there are always means with which the military can deal with the military. It is when they deal out of the military that the difficulty comes. And here was an officer stating a perfectly logical solution.

We would send the Shore Patrol, billy clubs at the ready, out into this great city of San Diego. They would have been empowered to cancel on the spot the weekend pass of any soldier, sailor, or marine that they encountered. They would concentrate particularly on the movie theaters, boot camp, and the bars. And they would report back with the fruits of their mission.

To:- Lindsey Nelson-
my idea of the
best "spotter" in
the U.S. and a
grand guy
Bill Stern
KNOXVILLE
1940

In Knoxville the day before the 1940 Tennessee vs. Duke game. I am seated on tarp with Bill Stern, center, who would announce the game for NBC Radio. I was a college senior and his spotter. After World War II, I would succeed him as NBC's top sports announcer.

Shortly before D-Day, troops of the 9th Infantry Division are reviewed by, left to right, Major General M. S. Eddy, commanding the division, General Dwight Eisenhower, and Prime Minister Winston Churchill. Eddy and Eisenhower signed the photo for me. It says, "To Lindsey Nelson—A very busy man the day this picture was taken." I was in charge of the war correspondents there. There were lots of them. U.S. ARMY PHOTO

With Russian officers, 1945. This was an "official" linkup of the Russian and American armies on the Elbe River at Pratau. I had already been with the Red Army for several days. U.S. ARMY PHOTO

Euskirchen, Germany, soon after crossing the Rhine at Remagen, 1945. Left to right: Roy Wilder, Jr. (former *New York Herald Tribune* staff writer), me, and war correspondent Don Whitehead of the Associated Press.

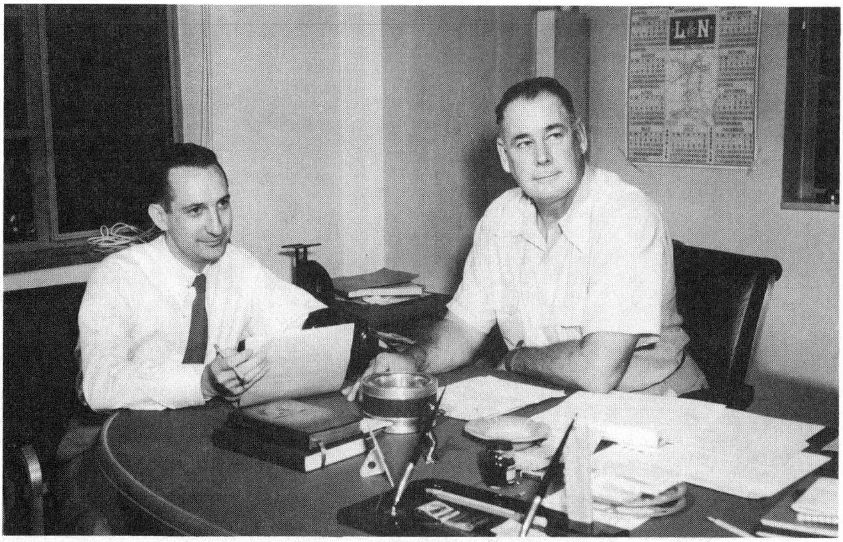

With General Bob Neyland, 1949. He was one of the great college-football coaches of all time. At the University of Tennessee, I had the good fortune to serve on his staff as sports information director and director of radio broadcasts. THOMPSONS PHOTO

With Mel Allen, 1953. We were the announcers on the NCAA college-football series on NBC-TV. There was no doubt that at that time Mel Allen was the top-rated sports announcer in the country. He was best known then for doing the New York Yankees baseball games and, usually, the World Series. NBC PHOTO

Leo Durocher and I teamed up to announce the NBC-TV major league baseball games in 1957 and spent three seasons together. Whatever else he was, and he was lots of things, Leo was never dull. If I wanted to pick the winner of one single baseball game, I'd go with the team managed by Leo Durocher. He might bluff it, or finesse it, or even steal it—but I think he'd win it. NBC PHOTO

Curt Gowdy and me attending a practice of the basketball New York Knicks. We teamed up to announce the NBA game of the week for several years in the 1950s. Curt came to NBC, and great fame, from baseball (the Boston Red Sox). I went to baseball (the New York Mets) from NBC. NBC PHOTO

Red Grange and me at old Archbold Stadium, Syracuse University, 1956. We teamed up to announce the NCAA games on NBC for five straight years. Grange was the most modest hero I ever knew and one of the really great figures in the history of American sports. NBC PHOTO

In 1959 I was named the top radio sportscaster and top television sportscaster in America in the *Radio-Television Daily* poll of 487 critics from coast to coast. It was the greatest recognition I could get.

The very happiest times were the years when there were gentle little folks around the house, Sharon, left, and Nancy.

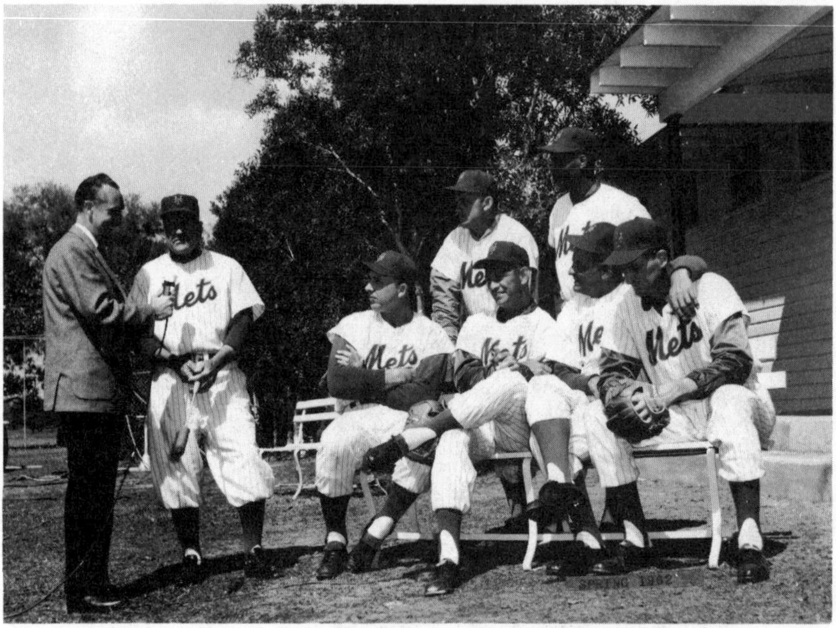

St. Petersburg, Florida, 1962. I interviewed all the former Brooklyn Dodgers at the first Mets' spring training camp. I am talking to Casey Stengel. On the bench, left to right: Gil Hodges, Clem Labine, Cookie Lavagetto, and Roger Craig. Standing: Don Zimmer and Charlie Neal. In this picture are five men who managed major league teams: Stengel, Hodges, Lavagetto, Craig, and Zimmer. With all that brain power, the Mets that first season won 40 and lost 120.

At the National Sportscasters and Sportswriters annual awards dinner, Salisbury, North Carolina, 1962. The Lindsey Nelsons and the Red Smiths dance the "winners' waltz." For the third consecutive year, Red and I had been named the top sportswriter and sportscaster in the country by a vote of our contemporaries. When we started onto the floor, Red said, "You go first this year, and I'll go first next year."

Al Lang Field, St. Petersburg, Florida, the spring of 1962. Manager Casey Stengel, left, of the Mets goes over his starting lineup card with me and broadcaster Ralph Kiner, right. The 1962 Mets were pretty funny. Some said they were a joke. The season hasn't begun and we're laughing already.

In 1962, I visited with Willie Mays at the batting cage. When young Met outfielders would misplay fly balls and blame it on the errant winds, Manager Stengel would say: "It don't bother Mays none." Nothing bothered Mays. He was the best baseball player I ever saw. BILL MARK

The banquet circuit can put one in some legendary company. Here in 1964, for instance, I am sharing a dais with, left to right, the Finnish runner Paavo Nurmi; the hero of the 1936 Olympic games in Berlin, Jesse Owens; the Olympic swimming star who became Tarzan in the movies, Johnny Weissmuller; and U.S. runner Horace Ashenfelter. Some of my most treasured friendships were formed on occasions like this. BILL MARK

With, left to right, Mickie, Sharon, and Nancy at the Polo Grounds, 1963. For us, the Mets were a "family affair." We bought a season's box of four seats, and we were all there most days. LOUIS REQUENA

With Arnold Palmer and Bob Hope, 1965. I covered a lot of golf for NBC-TV, such as the Bob Hope Desert Classic at Palm Springs, California, where a fellow might meet golfer Arnold Palmer. Usually I worked with Hope, and the opportunity to hear his steady stream of ad libs for several days was worth the price of admission. NBC PHOTO

On a day in April of 1964, Bob Murphy and I went out to look over Shea Stadium. Construction workers were still putting on the finishing touches. The stadium opened the next day. It was my "home" for fifteen years.

Shea Stadium, 1965. I spent a lot of time with Bob Murphy, center, and Ralph Kiner, right. Here we are wearing our "Rheingold jackets" on the steps of the Mets' dugout at Shea. By contract, I was designated "Chief Announcer." We worked together for seventeen seasons and remained close friends. We never had a serious disagreement. LOUIS REQUENA

A Christmas party at the Diamond Club, Shea Stadium, 1967. I am talking to Met coaches Joe Pignatano, center, and Yogi Berra, right. Yogi had already been the manager of the Yankees. He would become manager of the Mets, and subsequently manager of the Yankees again. In case of danger, I want to be near Yogi. He is the luckiest man alive.

Candlestick Park, San Francisco, 1968. Russ Hodges and I were friends and neighbors in Westchester County during his time as the voice of the baseball Giants in New York. Here we are in the Giants' dugout at Candlestick Park on opening day of the 1968 season, the Giants vs. the Mets. Eleven years later, I would become the voice of the San Francisco Giants. RUSS REED, *OAKLAND TRIBUNE*

Shea Stadium, 1970. Here Casey Stengel is acknowledging the crowd that has packed the park to celebrate his eightieth birthday. And he is putting them on, as he strikes a dramatic pose. Commissioner Bowie Kuhn and Mets General Manager Bob Scheffing (behind Stengel) are obviously amused, and I am broken up. My greatest reward in making the switch from network announcing to baseball-club announcing was the time I spent in the incomparable company of Casey Stengel. There was never another like him. LOUIS REQUENA

Shea Stadium, 1970. The broadcast booth at Shea was my home away from home. I found that watching baseball games from there day after day was a mighty pleasant way to spend the summer.

On the set at WOR-TV in New York in 1972, doing a memorial program for Gil Hodges, the Met manager, who had died of a heart attack. There were few New York baseball figures ever as popular as Hodges. He played for the Dodgers, played for the Mets, then managed the Mets to the world's championship. DOMINIQUE

Shea Stadium, 1971. Mel Allen and I share a microphone on the field at Shea during an Old Timers Game. For many of us, the circumstances and reasons for the Yankees' firing of Mel remain a mystery. But for a generation, that rich, mellow voice was the voice of Yankee baseball. DENNIS BURKE

St. Petersburg, Florida, 1973. Give me spring training in the sunshine at Huggins-Stengel Field, and baseball conversation with Joe Garagiola, left, and Casey Stengel, center, and there will be happy times. I guarantee it, if I can stop laughing long enough.

Shea Stadium, 1973. With some teams, the newspapermen and the announcers don't get along very well. We, fortunately, never had that problem. Left to right: announcer Ralph Kiner; writer Jack Lang of the New York *Daily News,* writer Joe Durso of *The New York Times;* me, I'm an announcer; announcer Bob Murphy; and writer Dick Young, then of the *Daily News,* now of the *Post.*

Shea Stadium, 1973. My guest on the pregame show this day was Henry Aaron of the Atlanta Braves. He hit more home runs than anybody, of course. I had become an Aaron fan when he was first riding high with those great teams in Milwaukee. On this show, he explained that when he first started playing he batted "cross-handed."

At a birthday party for legendary Manhattan restaurateur Toots Shor, I had a chance to visit with one of my all-time heroes, boxer Jack Dempsey. The first sports broadcast I remember hearing on radio was announcer Graham McNamee doing the Dempsey vs. Gene Tunney heavyweight championship from Chicago in 1927. BILL MARK

In the booth at Candlestick Park, San Francisco, 1979. Disc jockey Carter B. Smith at KNBR invited fans to send in scraps of material that might be assembled into a jacket for me. This was the result. It was what Andy Rooney had in mind when he said that of all his old army friends, I was the only one better dressed then than now.

At Atlanta-Fulton County Stadium for Los Angeles Rams vs. Atlanta Falcons, November 1973. Left to right: Spotter Bill Friel, me as play-by-play announcer, and analyst Pat Summerall. Summerall has since switched to play-by-play and is CBS's top man in that field on NFL games, including the Super Bowl. BILL FRIEL

Paul (Bear) Bryant was one of the truly distinguished men in sports. It was my pleasure to know him for forty years. Here I am introducing him at a luncheon before the Cotton Bowl game in Dallas in 1980, where his Alabama team defeated Baylor. Slightly more than two years later, he was dead of a heart attack.

In the booth with Pat Haden, 1982. In recent years, my analyst was frequently Pat Haden, who played for Southern Cal and the Rams. He has a bachelor's degree from USC, a degree from Oxford University in England as a Rhodes scholar, and a law degree. I figure that's about even up with my BA from Tennessee plus my time in the army and on the road.

Red Grange was eighty-one years of age when I stopped for a visit at his home in Florida in the summer of 1984. I spent five seasons in the booth with Grange. He was the most modest hero I ever knew. I tried to learn all I could from him about how one charts a steady course, without controversy and furor, when cast into the glare of the public spotlight. No one ever did it more becomingly.

This was in the booth and on the air for the opening of the 1984 Cotton Bowl game between Pittsburgh and SMU. On radio or television, I have done the Cotton Bowl game twenty-five times. It is the longest association of any announcer with any bowl game. Before the 1985 game, the Cotton Bowl presented me with a marvelous jacket and the CBS crew gave me a watch and a cake. Longevity does have its rewards, but the most treasured ones are the valued friendships formed over the years. CBS SPORTS

Shea Stadium, 1984. A marvelous day for me came in September 1984 at Shea when I was inducted into the New York Mets Hall of Fame along with Bob Murphy and Ralph Kiner. And it was great that my family could be with me—left to right, Nancy, me, Sharon, and my son-in-law, Andy Wyszynski.

The rain had let up not one bit when the Shore Patrol reappeared with about two hundred bedraggled, wet, and protesting members of the military. Bennington directed that they be placed in a tight little square of seats in the stands across the field. A member of the Shore Patrol stood at each corner of this unhappy little group to discourage any thought of departure. And thus the game began.

Whenever there was a big play, which wasn't very often, Bennington would cut to his crowd shot, which showed two hundred mad members of the military with their faces frozen in a permanent frown and water running into and out of the crevices in their clinched visages.

Years later I told that story at a gathering of college football people at Caesar's Palace in Las Vegas, and when I had finished, Hayden Fry came up and introduced himself. I knew who he was. He had played at Baylor, and coached Southern Methodist, North Texas, and later, Iowa. Hayden said, "I am so glad to hear that story. Because I was one of those from boot camp that they marched in there that afternoon, and I never knew why they made us watch that football game."

That was my television debut as a play-by-play football announcer—in a pouring rain between two service teams in San Diego. And I have never talked to anybody who claims to have seen that telecast.

In those early years, I discovered that traveling around the country as a representative of a television network opened up all sorts of doors. And it enabled me to make acquaintances that were to me unbelievably thrilling. I watched Minnesota football practice with their former coach Bernie Bierman. I watched Yale practice with a bright businessman from Chicago named Clint Frank. I was at Texas A&M with John Kimbrough, at SMU with Doak Walker, at TCU with Davey O'Brien, and at Notre Dame with Johnny Lujack.

Of course, I didn't travel all the time. Sometimes I took my sports on television from the easy chair. One night at the RCA building I watched a pretty good boxing match on television, watched it with two fighters while we were waiting to do a live show. I watched it with Joe Louis and Jimmy Braddock, twenty years after their memorable fight for the heavyweight championship of the world.

In New York, I was working the regular nine-to-five shift in the office. And I was doing broadcasting when called upon. I was more than available; I was eager. But I still was not finding the trade very remunerative. The radio network had decided it wanted to program a Saturday night sports show of fifteen minutes' duration entitled *This Week in Sports.* It would actually consist of feature presentations of the big developments of the week in sports. I would be in charge of producing, directing, and narrating. My total fee would consist of nothing.

I mentioned that a lot of people got paid for work like that, but they said that I was already an employee of NBC, that I was the assistant director of sports, and that since this was a sustaining show (no commercials, no income) I would be expected to work for nothing.

They did such a good job of selling me on this very illogical idea that I went out and sold it to a good friend named Barney Nagler. Barney was a first-rate newspaperman and author. He did a daily column in the New York *Morning Telegraph* and he did some writing for NBC. He was frequently in the sports department just as a means of keeping his contacts going, and I prevailed upon him to drop by on Saturday evenings to write *This Week in Sports.* I explained to him that since he was already there a lot of the time and since it was sustaining, that he would be expected to work for nothing. Barney said okay.

They assigned us a staff announcer named Howard Rieg. He was on a staff salary and did not expect to be paid extra for sustaining performances.

Our show, *This Week in Sports,* appeared to be a shoo-in for the award for "this week's cheapest show." It wasn't even close.

Howard usually didn't come in until after the dinner hour, so sustenance was no problem for him. But it was a problem for Barney and me. We had figured out how to run a network radio show from coast to coast without spending or earning a penny. But we had not learned how to survive without eating. That brought us to the English Grill of the Promenade Café on the ice-rink level of the RCA building. Two suitable dinners came to the grand expenditure of eleven dollars per Saturday night, an expense that I felt called on to bear as the producer, director, and narrator of *This Week in Sports.*

Our show did not run many weeks. I protested that I really couldn't afford to do this show with this sort of arrangement much longer. I was a "star," but this kind of stardom would have me back in Knoxville before spring. One week *This Week* died. There were no ceremonies and no mourners. Only the memories and the scars survive.

Our family life was delightful. We had Sharon enrolled in a private day school on Split Rock Road in Pelham. She was picked up each morning and delivered back to us in the afternoon. I soon became a director of the school.

Mickie and I were having a marvelous time exploring Manhattan. On weekends we went to the theater or we went to the Roosevelt Grill for dinner and danced to the lovely music of Guy Lombardo and His Royal Canadians. That was not only "the sweetest music this side of heaven," as advertised, but maybe just about as close to heaven as a fellow ought to get.

One night I was sitting with a few friends at Bleeck's, the famous journalists' bar on Fortieth Street. The door swung open, and in out of the night strode a rotund fellow with thick glasses and a wide grin. I had not seen him in years, since the war in Europe. I somehow remembered the day he had looked at a lone brothel standing unscarred in the midst of complete destruction in Nancy, France. And he had said to his companion, Roy Wilder, "The Lord protects the pure in heart." Now he was walking straight toward me in Bleeck's bar, pointed a finger, and said, "Captain Lindsey Nelson of the Ninth Infantry Division." That was my greeting from author Joe Liebling.

Mickie and I went to baseball games and to basketball games. And we tried to learn hockey. But we didn't make it.

John Kieran, Jr., had moved back to New York at our insistence and blessing, and Johnny had been hired by NBC Sports as a writer and producer. He, of course, had grown up in New York. He knew everything about the city, and I suggested to him that he teach me all about hockey. I explained that when I was growing up in Tennessee, people just hadn't been inclined to play a hell of a lot of ice hockey. I had watched on television, but I couldn't understand the terminology.

The agreement was that John would get the tickets for his father's box at Madison Square Garden at stated intervals when the Rangers were playing home games. John and his wife, Lee, would go with Mickie and me to dinner. I would pay the check, and then Johnny would furnish the tickets plus the education at hockey.

My money ran out before John's instruction penetrated, and I have been left forever since, and presumably for all time to come, in a state of hockey ignorance. I know some terms. There is something,

I think, about "high-sticking," somewhere there is a "blue line," and maybe a "face-off" is something.

Our apartment building on Garth Road in Scarsdale did not have very much of a playground for children. There just wasn't much room in the area for the kids to cavort.

But Mickie and I had friends at West Point whom we visited often, and very soon we were visiting them more often. We had discovered that spacious parade ground at the Academy, and little Sharon just loved to be turned loose where her short legs could carry her hither and yon on the grassy surface, running and laughing and having a marvelous time.

It got so that we drove up every weekend, up the Taconic Parkway and across the Bear Mountain Bridge. Although in no sense an army brat, Sharon was literally brought up on the parade ground at West Point.

Soon we were into the discussion of possible announcers for the NCAA football games of 1953. Usually, such a discussion starts with an executive saying, "My wife doesn't know anything about sports, doesn't care anything about sports, but she says that Joe Doakes is a terrible announcer."

I can tell you from painful experience that at this specific moment and on this flimsy evidence alone, Mr. Doakes was about to be forced into some other line of work.

In this instance, I recall that we were there in the boardroom of General Motors in Detroit discussing the possible color announcer.

At a propitious moment, Bernie London, an agency man, had risen and said sarcastically, "Why don't you mention Lindsey? You don't have to be ashamed of him. We think he's a good announcer. Why don't you let Lindsey do the color with Mel Allen?"

Well, there was a slight ripple of affirmative conversation in the room. Nothing like an ovation, mind you. Just a murmur here and there from people who apparently knew that there had been a time when I announced football games.

Gallery did nothing to encourage further conversation in that direction when he said, "Oh, I don't know if we could spare Lindsey."

Under my breath, I was saying, "Please spare Lindsey," but I said nothing aloud, and the subject died without our having arrived at any definite color announcer.

We went straightaway to the railway station and boarded the *Detroiter* for our return trip. We had our dinner in the diner, and then some went to the club car. I knew that Gallery would be in his compartment, and I waited until he had had time to settle down.

When I knocked on his door, his quiet voice said, "Come." When I entered, he didn't seem surprised.

"Can I talk to you?" I said.

"Sure," he said, "what is it?"

I had given my speech a lot of thought. I knew exactly what I wanted to say and how I wanted to say it. So I began.

"On the NCAA series," I said, "if you really think that I am of most value as a producer and if this is where you definitely want to keep me, then disregard the rest of what I have to say."

I paused, and he said nothing.

So I continued, "I just think you should know that I really do enjoy announcing football games. I like to go out to the stadium and to mix with the crowd and to watch the players and to announce the game and its strategies as it unfolds. To some this might be work. It is not work for me. I love it. I have been into football for a long time, and unless you have other unchangeable plans I would like to announce the games with Mel."

That was the end of my speech.

For a moment, Gallery still said nothing. He had been reading the newspaper when I came in. Now he slowly took off his glasses, turned more directly toward me, and said, "Is that possible?"

The truth is that Tom never did have that high a regard for announcers. He had been in movies where directors hated actors. He didn't understand how anybody could actually want to be announcer. He said, "We had hoped to fix it so you'd never have to do that."

"I know," I said. I knew that he was moving me into a young executive's slot at the network and he expected that I would advance in that direction. I suppose his disappointment must be like that of the father whose son tells him he has decided to go into the business world by opening a bawdy house.

But, slightly shaking his head and still obviously puzzled, Tom said, "Well, we'll see if we can't work that out for you."

By late summer I suspected that he had worked it out, but he never said anything. What he did do was announce that he was going to Detroit with Bernie London and the Kudner people on the RCA plane, and I was pointedly not invited. When the supervising producer does not make the trip, he had better count the savings bonds and see if he is financially backed up, because he may be about to be in some other business.

The next afternoon late, I was with Sharon in the playground when Mickie came out looking like the cat that had eaten the canary. "Tom Gallery called," she said, "and he wants you to meet him at Teterboro airport in New Jersey after nine. He is coming from Detroit on the RCA plane."

Well, this was unusual. Tom never asked to be picked up. Either Fette picked him up or he arranged for a limo. Now he wanted me at the plane.

Mickie was plainly about to burst, and it wasn't those early stages of pregnancy. "I've got to tell you," she said. "Tom said that I was not to tell you so that he could surprise you at the plane, but I can't keep a secret like this away from you. I know how much you want to do the football games, and you are going to do them."

I wanted to leap to the rooftop. Mickie was as excited as I.

"They set it at General Motors this afternoon. You and Mel Allen will be the announcers. And when he tells you at Teterboro tonight, please be surprised." At Teterboro, I waited in a hangar and watched Mary Martin and Ethel Merman on television.

When Tom came off the plane that night, he said, "Well, it's nice to be met by a member of NBC's top football announcing team."

I did my very best. But I am not a very good actor. I think he knew that I knew. Besides, Tom Gallery hates actors. And announcers.

During that season, there came a date when we scheduled regional games, and Gallery decided I would do play-by-play of the Georgia vs. Florida game, and my color man would be Bill Munday.

Bill Munday was a part of the history of sports broadcasting. He had been working with Graham McNamee and Carl Haverlin on the NBC broadcast of the Rose Bowl game New Year's Day 1929 when California center Roy Riegels recovered a Georgia Tech fumble and ran the wrong way. Munday soon became a national star. The three top football announcers in the country were Graham McNamee and Bill Munday for the NBC Red and Blue networks, and Ted Husing for CBS. (NBC had two networks, said to have been named for the colors of the pencils used in plotting them. The Blue Network became ABC.)

But somewhere in all the glamour and excitement of that life, the booze had gotten Munday by the throat, and after five years on the network he was gone.

After some years, he made a recovery through the help of Alcoholics Anonymous, and Red Barber put him back on the football radio roundup on CBS.

And now Gallery had decided it was time to cast him on television with me. Gallery said, "If you want to give him a shot at a little play-by-play, it's up to you. I certainly want you to open and do the first part of the game, but if you get the feeling that he can handle it, bring him in for a few plays."

Early in the second quarter, I brought Bill Munday in on play-by-play, and he was ready. He was back on NBC, this time on NBC Television. Television had been invented while he was drunk. Now he loved it. Those eyes sparkled and those creased old cheeks broke into a smile. Telegrams began to pour in, many from people who had thought he was dead. For me, it was only my second game as a play-by-play man on television. But this was not my day. This was a day for Bill Munday who had been to hell—and back.

As a part of the NBC competitive bid for the NCAA package, it was customary for the networks to include a number of supporting activities and programs designed to promote college football. In the bid, the approximate dollar worth of these programs would be interpreted in order to put the actual money bid in perspective. Over the years, it occurred to me that some committee members managed to get rather quickly through the prelude and right to the bottom line—how much cash? But in the early days we were still naïve. We had devised a Friday night interview show on the NBC Radio Network that I would do from the site of the television game. And this was a part of our pitch on behalf of college football.

It was an enjoyable task for me. That was good, because it was unsponsored and I didn't get a dime for doing it. But I had great guests. I had sportswriter and former football official Austen Lake of the Boston *American.* I had known him in Europe, where he had been a war correspondent. I interviewed Admiral Tom Hamilton in Chicago, the man who had run the navy's training program in World War II. I interviewed a rookie coach named Woody Hayes of Ohio State, and a running back named Howard Hop-a-long Cassady, who won the Heisman Trophy. And, most memorable for me, I interviewed Bill Nicholas, who was general manager of the Los Angeles Memorial Coliseum and a member of the Rose Bowl football committee.

NBC Radio was still operating in those studios at Sunset and Vine in Hollywood, where I had gone with Bill Stern in 1939 for his Friday night show. Now all arrangements had been made for me by New York, and I was a little excited as I prepared to make my journey to that same building to do my NBC Friday night show with Bill Nicholas. I was in a Cadillac limousine with a chauffeur as we pulled up to the curb in front of the entrance on Sunset Boulevard. I was met by a doorman. Inside, I was met by a female uniformed page, who said, "Right this way—your studio is ready, Mr. Nelson." And she led the way down the hall to the studio where Bill Nicholas was waiting. I looked around and smiled. It was the very same studio where I had gone with Bill Stern. And now I had returned, this time to do *my* Friday night show.

Of course, as we neared season's end, I was aware that we had the old Cotton Bowl waiting out there. Bill Stern was no longer at NBC. He had departed for ABC in a rather bizarre series of events.

Although still under contract to NBC, Bill had been working on the possibility of doing a sports show for ABC. In fact, he had personally talked to Gussie Busch at Anheuser Busch about doing the show for Budweiser, and he had talked to ABC about placing the show there as part of a lucrative overall contract for Bill. NBC was not aware that these arrangements were in progress.

Gallery was out of town and I was running the office, when I got a frantic call one afternoon from NBC Chicago. It was the sales manager. He had heard a rumor that Bill Stern was trying to arrange to do a show for ABC. Didn't we have Bill Stern signed to an exclusive contract? I told him we did. Well, he wanted to make a quick and desperate pitch to Budweiser for a show starring Bill Stern to run on NBC Radio. Could I give him a quick talent fee for Stern that he could use in pricing his package? When I delayed my answer slightly in an effort to get a figure that would be close, he named his own figure ($1,500 per week), thanked me, and hung up. But it was all too late for NBC.

Bill Stern came in a few days later to announce that he was resigning. By this time NBC was not all that surprised, and the boys upstairs knew exactly why he was resigning and they were not happy. They decided that Bill Stern was under an exclusive, binding contract, from which he would not be released until the end of the term, a year hence.

Bill was at first surprised, then he was furious, and then he was desperate. Everything had been set up at ABC. He had signed a contract. They were ready to go. But Bill wasn't.

Finally, Bill decided that he would play his trump card. He made an appointment and went up to see General Sarnoff. By this time the general was not dabbling too much in the daily doings of the network, particularly the radio network. But he received Bill and listened to his plea. And the general told Bill that he would be released from his contract and that he would be expected to vacate his office by that evening. The general was not too cordial. He had been briefed. He knew where Bill was going.

Bill came down to his office and immediately began to pack up his things. He called a moving company and they sent a truck, which was parked at the subterranean level of the RCA building, and they sent up a couple of packers.

By now everyone in the department was gone for the day except me. The writers were gone, the secretaries were gone. I was still there because I had received a call, just after Bill had left the general's office, from Manny Sachs, the general's staff assistant. He had various titles, but mostly he worked for General Sarnoff. When you heard from Manny you were hearing from the general.

Bill was now doing a nightly radio show and two nightly television shows. The word from Manny—from the general—was that Bill Stern was not to be allowed to go on any of them. He was not to appear behind an NBC microphone for any purpose. I was instructed to do all of his shows until further notice.

I called Mickie at home to say that I would be a little late.

When I looked up, Bill was standing in front of my desk leaning heavily on his cane. "Come here a moment," he said softly. And he walked in the direction of his office. The movers were gone and so was all the furniture. Only the telephone sat on the bare carpet. The walls were paneled. That had been a stipulation in Bill's talent contract, an office with paneled walls. Now, as I stood in the doorway, somewhat bewildered, Bill walked dramatically around the room, tapping the walls with his cane and saying to no one particular, "These are the things that make the difference." Then he sat heavily on the carpet, picked up the phone, and made a long-distance call to St. Louis. It was, I thought, one final act of defiance or of frustration. Then Bill Stern got up slowly, still leaning on the cane, and walked quietly down the shadowy corridor toward the elevator that would take him to the exit. As far as I know, Bill Stern never came back to NBC.

This was all an emotional scene for me. In college, I had been a student spotter for Bill Stern. I had worked with him at the Rose Bowl. During the war years when I was in Europe, we had corresponded. When I felt the strong urge to reach out and see if the real world was still there, I would write to Bill Stern, and he would invariably respond. As a sports announcer, Bill Stern had been my role model. I copied his delivery, his dramatic inflections, and his pace.

When I got to New York I had been surprised and disappointed to find that he wasn't very popular, either around NBC or among the sports people of the town.

I did not then know what Bill later wrote, that he was battling an addiction to morphine that at times absolutely incapacitated him. A few years later, at the Sugar Bowl, he would have to be taken off the telecast and replaced by Ray Scott. I didn't know much about all that. I only knew that there were times there in the office when I thought he had gone nuts.

Tom Gallery recently provided an amplification of the Stern story of which I was not previously aware.

Tom lived in Scarsdale, New York, and one night his youngest daughter, Michele, was suddenly very ill. Her parents thought that she needed medical assistance immediately, and they set about calling doctors. Finally they found one who said that he would be willing to make a house call.

The doctor administered medication and treatment that soon had Michele at ease and on the way back to comfort and good health. Gallery was expressing his gratitude as they stood at the door and talked. The doctor, a little hesitantly, said, "Mr. Gallery, could I talk to you at lunch tomorrow about one of your employees?"

Gallery would have done anything for a doctor who had made a house call, and they quickly set the date for the next day in New York. They met in Gallery's office at NBC, where the doctor got right to the point. He said, "Mr. Gallery, you've got an addict on your hands. It's Bill Stern."

He then explained that he had been treating Stern, who had become more and more addicted to drugs, and explained further that he thought he had convinced Stern to place himself in a Connecticut sanitarium. Bill, however, had apparently balked when he feared that he would be without income for the period of his hospitalization. Gallery assured the doctor, and later, Bill, that his salary would continue, and Bill was subsequently admitted.

Gallery said that he was always grateful to the Scarsdale doctor. He was Dr. Herman Tarnower, who was to devise the famous Scarsdale Diet. And he would still later be shot and killed by Jean Harris in a bizarre episode.

Those were all bizarre days for a very famous Bill Stern.

* * *

I was learning as I went along that things do not always go as they are planned in the world of television. For instance, there was the night that I was set up to interview former major league baseball pitching star Schoolboy Rowe. It was a show that followed the fights on Friday nights, and Schoolboy was to be my guest.

We had gone to lunch and discussed what we might talk about. Rowe had had a teammate on the Detroit Tigers staff named Tommy Bridges, and Tommy had obtained quite a bit of attention with a magazine article he had just done, saying that he had thrown an illegal pitch, a spitball, during his later years. So I said to Schoolboy, "Did you ever throw a spitball?"

He smiled and said, "Oh, sure."

That interested me. I said, "Where, when?"

"Oh, when I won the sixteen straight in Detroit I was using a spitball," he said. "And that last year with the Phillies when I won seven, the spitball was just about all I threw."

"Do you mind talking about it on the air?" I asked.

"No," he said, "I'm out of baseball now. I don't mind."

All right, I thought, I've got the kicker for my interview tonight. And as we went through the routine questions on the show, I was keeping in the back of my mind that I would finish with what amounted to a confession.

The floor manager showed me four fingers, meaning four minutes to go. I lowered my voice, leaned forward and said, "Well, Schoolboy, your famous teammate, Tommy Bridges, has admitted that he threw a spitball. Did you ever throw a spitball?"

The director, Craig Allen, had been alerted. He moved in to a full-face shot to get all the emotion of this revealing answer. But the expression on that face was strangely calm. And I heard him saying, "No, I never threw a spitball in my life."

I was urgent. "What about when you won the sixteen straight at Detroit, what about when you won the seven at Philadelphia?"

"No," he said, "I never threw a spitball in my life."

Obviously, sometime during the afternoon or early evening, Schoolboy Rowe had changed his mind. That was all right. I just wish that he had told me that before he allowed me to hang myself out to dry.

We stammered around for three more minutes, wrapped up the show, and I went straight to the elevator on the eighth floor of the RCA building. I never saw Schoolboy Rowe again.

* * *

Nonetheless, these were busy times. I did the National Open golf tournament at the Oakmont Club near Pittsburgh with Ray Scott and Joe Hasel for NBC Radio. And I had a visit there on the course with an announcer named Herb Morrison. He had done one of the milestone broadcasts in the history of radio and, in fact, in the history of news. In 1937, he was at Lakehurst, New Jersey, on assignment from WLS in Chicago to describe the arrival of the German airship *Hindenburg.* As the big dirigible tied up to the mooring mast, it burst into flame and was destroyed, killing a number of passengers and crew. Herb Morrison described this scene before his eyes in all the emotion of that tragic moment, finally breaking down and saying, "I can't talk . . . it's the worst thing I've ever witnessed." He was far more composed on the golf course, and I was particularly pleased to meet Herb Morrison as a part of my continuing education in the history of electronic communication.

Then I got an assignment to do a Monday night show on Channel 4 called *Monday Quarterback,* starring Jackie Robinson and Lindsey Nelson.

Jackie was knowledgeable in all sports. At UCLA he had played football, baseball, basketball, and was a track man.

We would usually meet at the studio on Sixty-seventh Street around 5:30 in the afternoon and do a sort of walk-through of the show. It was ad lib, but we didn't want it to be too ad lib.

Then we would go to a little restaurant across the street, usually Jackie and his wife, Rachel, and me. We'd have a bite to eat if Jackie could get a moment off from signing autographs.

Several years later when he had retired from baseball, I was aware that Jackie's health was not the best. I would see him around town in the company of some of the city's political figures. Then there was word that his eyesight was failing and that he was not well. His son had died a tragic death, and friends said that he never fully recovered from that.

I was doing the Sunday afternoon segment of *Monitor* some years later on the NBC Radio Network, and I came in one day to be told by the producer that there was a project afoot to induct certain veteran black baseball players into the Hall of Fame. Jackie, of course, was already a Hall of Famer, but the producer wanted me to call him and get his reaction on tape.

I got Jackie on the phone at his home in Connecticut, and I

opened up by saying, "Let's bring back the *Monday Quarterback* show." Jackie had sounded tired when he came to the phone but apparently this memory was a good one. He laughed and said, with some enthusiasm, "Yeah, let's bring it back!"

Then I told him about the project to induct the veteran blacks into the Hall of Fame, and for one brief moment, he was the old Jackie Robinson. He was on fire. "It's about time," he roared. "They should have been inducted years ago."

The later years were not kind to Jackie. He had diabetes, high blood pressure, and he suffered a heart attack. In a characteristic manner, he told writer Roger Kahn, "That's because I never drink and I don't smoke."

I did not see much of Jackie in his last years, but I never forgot the exciting experience of *Monday Quarterback.*

CHAPTER 16

Galloping Ghost of the Illini

I got a great many of my announcing assignments from Tom Gallery during our travels to and from our homes in Westchester County and the office.

And I remember so well the time when we were driving through the thick late-afternoon traffic of Manhattan and Gallery said pensively, "I think that on the Cotton Bowl game we'll have you do the play-by-play and Red Grange do the color."

Me and Red Grange! I was afraid to say a single word. Any spoken opinion of mine, I thought, might jinx the arrangement. But that's the way it worked. And Red Grange and I teamed up for the first time on the game in January of 1954. It was Alabama vs. Rice.

This was still in the era of black-and-white television, and both teams had gone out and bought brand-new jerseys to make a good impression on the football fans of the nation. Early in the week, though, we realized we had a problem. Alabama had beautiful new crimson jerseys and Rice had beautiful new blue jerseys. And on black-and-white television, they looked exactly alike. You couldn't tell one team, or one player, from another.

We requested that somebody switch to white, but nobody wanted to change. So Commissioner Howard Grubbs of the Southwest Conference stepped in.

He invited Red Drew, the Alabama coach, and me to come to his room at the Baker Hotel. He got Jess Neely, the Rice coach, on the phone. Because of heavy rains in Houston, Neely had taken his team to Abilene for workouts.

Commissioner Grubbs explained that we were going to flip a coin to determine who switched to white jerseys. Then he handed me the phone so that I could keep Coach Neely informed while the Commissioner flipped the coin and Coach Drew called it. Coach Drew won.

On the phone, I said, "Coach Neely, you lost."

He didn't hear me clearly. "What?" he said.

"You lost," I said. "You lost the flip of the coin."

There was silence for a moment, and then rather crustily Jess Neely said, "Well, I didn't think I was going to win out here in Abilene, on the phone."

He lost the flip and Rice wore the white jerseys but won the game.

In the second quarter, a very strange thing happened. Alabama had driven down deeply into Rice territory, where their quarterback had fumbled away the ball on the five-yard line. He was a relatively unknown junior from Montgomery named Bart Starr. From the five, Rice ran a hand-off to halfback Dickie Moegle (he later legally changed the name to "Maegle"), who got to the outside and raced up the sideline. It looked as though he might be able to break it into the clear. There were Alabama players angling on him but they were not the speediest men in the world. And then just as Moegle got in front of the Alabama bench, he inexplicably went down in a heap. I wondered if somebody had shot him, until I saw a helmetless figure named Tommy Lewis scampering back to the bench.

Moegle had been tackled by a player who had come off the bench. Coach Neely was in the middle of the field, and Coach Drew was on the field. Referee Cliff Shaw was in the middle of the field. Shaw shot his hands skyward, awarding a touchdown to Moegle.

There had been a strange and eerie prelude. The night before the game, Grange and I sat in the Adolphus Hotel discussing football and the new medium, television. We remarked that radio coverage of football had certain safeguards, the most valuable of which was the fact that the listener could not see the game being described. Now television had taken away that protection. If something unusual happened on the field, it had to be explained immediately. The guy at home could probably see it better than the announcer. We talked about unusual things that could happen.

For no reason, Red absently said to me, "Have you ever seen anybody come off the bench to make a tackle?"

I said I hadn't.

"I did, one time in Canada," said Red. "Do you know what the ruling is?" I said I didn't.

Red explained that most football penalties are designed never to award points. Severest penalties are half the distance to the goal line but not across the goal line. "In this case," said Red, "if in the opinion of the referee the runner would have gone all the way, he is empowered to award a touchdown."

In our booth that afternoon in Dallas, as the play happened, Red turned to me with a smile on his face and his palms turned upward, as though to say, "It's all yours, take it and run." And I did.

I said, "The rules of college football provide that the referee is empowered to award a touchdown if in his opinion Moegle would have gone all the way." As I said that, we had a picture of Referee Shaw lifting his arms skyward in the signal for a touchdown.

The chairman of the NCAA rules committee was Matty Bell of SMU there in Dallas. Next morning, there was a knock on my door and there stood Matty Bell. "I just want you to know that we heard about your handling of the play off the bench yesterday, and on behalf of the rules committee I want to congratulate and commend you." I thanked him and smiled and did not then give Red Grange the credit he deserved.

Red never asked for credit. He did write a book, an autobiography that came out a month or so later, and he sent me a copy inscribed, "To my good friend, Lindsey. It was a great pleasure to work with you—hope we can do it again. You are the first guy who knows the rules."

That day was the start of a long association between Red Grange and me. We did it again, over and over again, as NBC's football commentators on television for the next five years—"Lindsey Nelson and Red Grange." We traveled the length and breadth of this land by train and plane and bus, and we never had a cross word. Through the 1959 season, we roamed the stadiums of this land, doing bowl games and all-star games, and the NCAA regular-season games. We were the voices of college football. Everywhere we went, fans formed long lines to meet or just to see Red Grange, perhaps the greatest star the game of football has ever known. His magnitude was immense.

For his generation, Red Grange was a lot like Pearl Harbor day was for a later one. Everyone could remember exactly where he was and what his detailed circumstances were when he heard or read about the exploits of Red Grange.

Maybe there have been others who played the game better. I wouldn't know. I do know that we have had no performers in the gridiron sport whose flame of fame burned more brightly or longer than that of "the Galloping Ghost of the Illini."

Even today, more than half a century after Grange played his last game at Illinois, a golfer coming off the course at some obscure location will say to his partner, "What did you shoot?" And the partner will reply, "Red Grange."

And it is understood that he shot a seventy-seven, because that was the number that the "Wheaton Iceman" (he worked on the ice wagon in Wheaton, Illinois) made so famous and with which he has been associated ever since.

My accolade is not of deeds done on the gridiron. The simple fact is that I never saw Red Grange play football. He was a tad before my time, or I was slightly after his. But I spent five years as his broadcasting partner. We spoke at dinners and luncheons and breakfasts. We spent long hours spinning stories and entertaining each other. We had at least one deep-sea-fishing trip during which we both became deathly seasick. And on the evidence of this association, I am positive that no more modest hero than Red Grange ever lived.

But for some who may have forgotten, or perhaps never knew, let me digress to recount some of the achievements of Red Grange.

In October of 1924, against a heavily favored Michigan team and before a crowd of sixty-seven thousand fans, at that time the largest crowd ever to see a football game in the Midwest, Red Grange took the opening kickoff 95 yards for a touchdown. In less than twelve minutes, he scored three more touchdowns, from 67, 56, and 44 yards out. Coach Bob Zuppke took him out of the game to rest him. But he came back in the third quarter to score from 15 yards out. In the final quarter, he passed for still another touchdown. Illinois won 39–14. He had handled the ball twenty-one times, gained 402 yards, scored five touchdowns, and collaborated on a sixth.

Coach Amos Alonzo Stagg of the University of Chicago later wrote, "This was the most spectacular single-handed performance ever made in a major game."

W. C. Heinz wrote, "Red Grange was the most sensational, the most publicized, and possibly the most gifted football player and greatest broken-field runner of all time." He was three times an all-American. He grossed a million dollars in his first three years out of school from football, motion pictures, vaudeville appearances, and endorsements, in an age when this was reckoned to be an astronomical amount of money.

It was written by Paul Sann in his book *The Lawless Decade* that "Red Grange, No. 77, made Jack Dempsey move over. He put college football ahead of boxing as the Golden Age picked up momentum."

The following season, Illinois came east to play Pennsylvania at Franklin Field in Philadelphia, and the eastern press had its first opportunity to see Grange up close. The effect was monumental. The first time Grange carried the ball, he went fifty-five yards for a touchdown. He returned the next kickoff another fifty-five yards to the twelve, from where Illinois scored again. In the third quarter, he ran twenty yards for a score. Illinois won 24–2. That red-haired comet had continued a streak across the football sky that would make his impression indelible forever. When the return train arrived at Champaign two days later, it was met by a crowd of twenty thousand fans, and they carried their hero two miles on their shoulders to his fraternity house.

Professional football had been an unnoticed minor sport. But in a span of ten days, during which Grange played five pro games, all of that changed forever.

Following his last Illinois game, he signed a professional contract with the Chicago Bears, and agreed to go on an immediate barnstorming tour. The deal would be 50 percent of the gross for the Bears, who would pay the expenses, and 50 percent for Grange.

In the first game, played in a snowstorm at Wrigley Field in Chicago, they drew twenty-eight thousand. And at the Polo Grounds in New York they drew seventy-three thousand.

The world of sports had never seen anything like Red Grange. Fans poured out to see him, and professional football prospered as they stayed in later years to see Nevers, Baugh, Conerly, Walker, Rote, Huff, Starr, Hornung, Butkus, Sayers, Brown, Simpson, Harris,

Sims, Montana, Walker, Flutie, and all the rest. When they see a picture of Grange, they should salute.

He went to Hollywood and starred in a full-length motion picture, *One Minute to Play.* The studio was owned by Joseph P. Kennedy. Kennedy tried to talk Grange into giving up football in favor of a movie career (something the great Jim Brown would do years later). Red declined, although he did later do a serial called *The Galloping Ghost,* and another full-length picture named *Racing Romeo.*

His manager was C. C. Pyle of Champaign-Urbana, Illinois. The press called him "Cash and Carry," and he was a promotional whiz. He formed his own pro football league in opposition to the National Football League, and he and Red co-owned the franchise in New York, called the New York Yankees (not to be confused with football's later New York *Yanks*). They played home games at Yankee Stadium.

It was on October 16, 1927, that the Yankees played the Bears in Chicago. As a pass receiver, Grange reached high for the ball and collided with Bear center George Trafton. Grange's cleats caught in the sod, and Trafton fell and twisted Red's right knee. Although he played for eight more seasons, the Galloping Ghost was through galloping. He could play, and actually became an outstanding defensive player, but he could no longer make the disappearing cuts that had made him the ghost of the gridiron. But fans still filled the stadiums just for a glimpse of Grange.

He played his last game in January 1935 in Gilmore Stadium, Hollywood, California. It is an area that now houses CBS's Television City.

Grange then built up a lucrative insurance agency in Chicago, and became a headline football commentator, first on radio and then on television.

It was the age of the Roaring Twenties. They called it the "golden age of sports," and the stars were Babe Ruth, Bobby Jones, Jack Dempsey, and Red Grange.

What did others have to say of Grange the player? His coach, the famed innovator Bob Zuppke, said, "On the gridiron, Red Grange was a football stylist, a symphony of motion. Grange's modesty was the lifesaver of his team's morale. Jealousy on the part of his teammates could have developed. It was Grange's tact, bred by his modesty, which caused his teammates to remain consistently strong and loyal."

Zuppke went on, "The qualities of character which contributed toward making Red Grange the greatest name in football are those same qualities which have made him the outstanding citizen that he is, long after his playing days are over. He continues to be a credit to football, his university, and his former associates. He has proven himself to be a durable character on and off the field. I know of no finer example of true American sportsmanship than 'the Galloping Ghost' of Illinois."

One sportswriter wrote, "Grange was Jack Dempsey, Babe Ruth, Al Jolson, Paavo Nurmi, and Man o' War rolled into one."

This, then, was the man with whom I had formed a partnership.

One weekend we were assigned to do a game at the University of Illinois, and I could hardly wait to get into the experience of going back to Illinois with Red Grange.

First we got a taxi and Red took me on a tour of the campus and of the whole Champaign-Urbana area. We came to one large open area on campus and Red said, "That's where I took ROTC. I was in the cavalry, and I made great grades. I didn't know anything about the army, but I had an old horse that knew more military than MacArthur. I just went along for the ride and this old horse went through the maneuvers perfectly."

I was in my room at the Urbana Lincoln that afternoon, when Red came in and said, "Get your coat—we're going to see Zuppke."

I knew the story of the relationship of Red and his coach. When Zup had heard that Red was going to join the professionals and play for money, he had been furious. He had earnestly tried to talk Red out of the idea. "Football is not a game you play for money," he had said. Red had trouble following that logic. He had said, "Why is it okay to coach for money but not to play for money?"

For a while there had been a serious breach in their relationship, but it had healed over the years.

I knew that Zuppke was not well and that he had been confined to his home for some time. Still, I was thrilled at the idea of a visit with Coach Zuppke, the man who had advised his young college players, "Aim for the stars. If you don't make it, you'll still land pretty high." His best example was Red Grange, who had aimed for the stars and made it.

When we got there, Zup was seated in a big chair and had a lap rug over his knees. The doctor said we should stay for only a few minutes because he didn't want the coach to get excited.

Red and Zup talked about a variety of things, and then Zup said, "Red, do you realize that on the television you are seen every weekend by more people than ever saw you play? Do you realize that?"

I had been content to listen, but now I said, "Coach, do you watch football games on television?"

"Sure," he said, "I watch every weekend."

And I said, "Do you like what you see?"

"No, I don't like it," he said. "Nobody invents anymore, nobody improvises. Somebody comes up with a formation and they go to the coaches' convention and diagram it, and next season everybody uses it. Nobody invents, everybody borrows."

That was an interesting comment from one of the great inventors of all time. He had been variously credited with inventing the spiral pass from center, the huddle, the practice of pulling both guards to protect the passer, and the screen pass.

Now he was in his late seventies and ill. I said to him, "Is there anything you can think of now that you'd like to try, as a coach?"

His eyes sparkled and he could hardly wait to reply. "Sure, sure," he said, "I'd like to put the quarterback about a yard or a yard and a half back of the center, and give him a short, direct snap. Now, he doesn't have to pivot out, or slide down the line. He's already out and ready to execute a variety of options from there."

Zup never got to try his formation, but it wasn't so different from the principles of some of the triple-option offenses that came later.

Red and I looked at the doctor. He smiled and said that the coach was having such a good time, he thought we could stay awhile longer.

I looked around the house at some of the trophies and awards. In a prominent place was a framed copy of Kipling's "If—":"If you can keep your head when all about you/Are losing theirs and blaming it on you . . ."

It occurred to me that Kipling probably never saw a football game or knew a coach, but he had devised a pretty good philosophy for a coach. Bob Neyland loved to quote from that same poem, "If you can meet with Triumph and Disaster/And treat those two imposters just the same."

We said our good-byes. There was a feeling of love and sincerity as Red Grange said good-bye to Coach Zuppke, and now we went back to the hotel.

Purely by chance, Red's class was having a reunion and he invited me to go with him to the dinner, which was being held at the cafeteria.

The second most famous player on those great Illinois teams

was Earl Britton, who had been known as Grange's blocking back and was the placement kicker.

Most of the class had gone in and started dinner by the time that Red and I arrived. When we got to the door, the ticket taker explained that we would have to go back to the booth at the outer entrance and purchase tickets. Grange nodded and we started out. About this time, the extroverted Mr. Britton was coming in. "Hold it, hold it, you're going the wrong way," he said. "The dinner is that way."

"We know," said Red, "but we've got to go back and buy tickets."

Britton started to laugh. "Here, take mine," he said, producing a pair of tickets. "I'll go out and get some more. That's a great bunch we've got. The famous Red Grange comes to our reunion and we ain't gonna let him eat."

We ate.

And we once went to Champaign for another game between Illinois and Minnesota. On Friday afternoon, Ray Eliot, the Illinois coach, came over and asked if Red Grange would say a few words to the squad. Red said that he would. While we waited for the boys to dress, Ray wondered out loud how he should introduce the Galloping Ghost to his players.

"Just say," I suggested, "that thirty-three years ago today, on the afternoon that this stadium was dedicated, Red Grange gave the greatest individual performance in the history of collegiate football until that time, against a Michigan team favored over Illinois just about as much as Minnesota is favored tomorrow."

"Holy smoke," shouted Ray, "was that the day this stadium was dedicated?"

I assured him that it was.

As Grange and Eliot disappeared into the Illinois dressing room, I slipped out to watch Minnesota practicing. They were coached by Murray Warmath, an old friend from Tennessee days.

I said, "I thought you'd like to know that Red Grange is inside giving the Illini a pep talk."

"I don't care how many pep talks he gives 'em," said Warmath, "just as long as he's not in there at halfback for them tomorrow."

Grange didn't play, but they didn't really need him. Illinois scored an upset victory, 34–14.

* * *

There was no doubt that we were now moving in the higher circles of big-time television. Ed Sullivan's *Toast of the Town* was the big show on Sunday night. He effectively used the threat of his newspaper column to line up performers who might otherwise have been a little reluctant. And *Look* magazine developed awards in various fields for deserving performers, and the awards were presented on Ed Sullivan's show. After the 1956 season *NCAA Football* received the sports award, and Red Grange and I were instructed to appear for the show. It was a heady experience. The show was held in the Ed Sullivan Theater on Broadway, and Red and I had to appear early for a brief rehearsal of procedure. Backstage we were wandering around amidst a "Who's Who" of television. Actor Cyril Ritchard was there for his role as Captain Hook in Peter Pan, Bishop Fulton Sheen was there to pick up an award for his Tuesday night show, Ed Murrow got the news award.

Red and I got through our brief appearance on the show without a bobble, and when the formalities were over we retired to the Palm Court of the Plaza Hotel with Tom and Fette Gallery, Davidson Taylor, and Mickie. Red and I presented the plaque to Gallery. We figured it belonged to him a lot more than it belonged to us.

I had the good fortune now to develop a close association with the famous "Four Horsemen of Notre Dame." When Grantland Rice had penned that famous lead after the Army–Notre Dame game at the Polo Grounds in 1924, he immortalized that quartet: "Outlined against a blue-gray October sky, the Four Horsemen rode again. In dramatic lore they are known as Famine, Pestilence, Destruction, and Death. These are only aliases. Their real names are Stuhldreher, Miller, Crowley, and Layden."

The student publicity director of Notre Dame phoned back to South Bend and arranged to get the four players pictured riding four horses. The picture ran in newspapers from coast to coast, and their fame ran forever. The publicity man was George Strickler, who later was the sports editor of the *Chicago Tribune,* and we became close friends. Strickler had told me the story behind the Four Horsemen nickname. It seems that Strickler had recently seen the movie *The Four Horsemen of the Apocalypse,* starring Rudolph Valentino.

At halftime of that game at the Polo Grounds, Grantland Rice and some of his colleagues of the press were stretching their legs and talking about the sparkling play of the Notre Dame backfield. It was Strickler who contributed to the conversation by saying, "They look like the Four Horsemen." Grantland Rice obviously heard, but he said nothing. When the game had ended and Notre Dame had won and Rice sat down to write, however, what he pecked out on his portable typewriter was a reference to the Four Horsemen. It was the most famous football lead ever written.

Crowley told me that the most dangerous part of the weekend for him was mounting the horse at the livery stable in South Bend for the famous picture. "I had never been on a horse before," he said, "and I thought that any moment I'd come tumbling off."

The legend prospered, as did the quartet. Stuhldreher became head coach at the University of Wisconsin and a vice-president of United States Steel. Crowley became head coach at Michigan State, at Fordham in New York City, and commissioner of the All-America Conference. Don Miller became a distinguished federal judge in Cleveland. And Layden became head coach at the University of Notre Dame and commissioner of the National Football League.

One weekend, Red and I went out to Michigan State to do a telecast, and a professor asked if we would mind doing an informal seminar for his class. One of the students in that group was Gene Jankowski, who is now the president of the CBS Broadcast Group.

Another weekend, we went out to Penn State to do a game between Holy Cross and Penn State. Dr. Eddie Anderson, an old Notre Damer, was head coach at Holy Cross. In fact, it was his second time around. He had been the coach at Holy Cross before he had gone out to coach an Iowa team that starred Heisman winner Nile Kinnick, who was killed in World War II. And then Dr. Anderson had come back to Holy Cross.

The head coach at Penn State was Rip Engle, who had come from Brown, bringing with him as an assistant the little fellow from Brooklyn who had played quarterback at Brown, Joe Paterno.

The referee for the game was one of the top officials in the east, Albie Booth, who had earned immortal fame at Yale. He was "Little Boy Blue," the personification of Frank Merriwell, one of the greatest of all the Yalies.

When the game was over, Red and I went back to our rooms at the Nittany Lion Inn to pack. And I called a taxi to take us to the Philipsburg airport. It was a typical postgame scene. It was a fall day, brisk, with leaves blowing about. And people were gathered in front of the inn, talking in little clusters.

As our taxi pulled up, Red Grange and I walked out carrying our bags. And a fellow yelled from one of the groups, "Are you going to the airport?"

It was Albie Booth, and I invited him to join us. Red had already taken his seat in the cab as Albie shoved in beside him. I always assumed that everybody in football knew everybody else, especially the immortals. So I said, automatically, "You two know each other, of course." They looked at each other, shook their heads, grinned, and said, "No, we've never met."

Grasping the drama of this little scene, I said, "Then let me have the honor." And out there in the shadow of Mt. Nittany, I said, "Mr. Grange, meet Mr. Booth."

As I have continued to work football games through the years, the colleges and the pros, the players have come on in a steady stream, always bigger, stronger, and faster. And that has given us a better game than ever. Greatness must always be measured against the standards of one's own time. Their greatness was established against the obstacles and defenses of their time, and it is foolish to try to compare performers of one era against performers of another. You can only guess and dream. If you ask any man to pick the greatest players he has ever seen, they will likely be chosen from among his contemporaries—something about reflected glory and all that. For instance, if you ask me who is the greatest lineman I ever saw, I will tell you Bob Suffridge, a guard at Tennessee. We were classmates, and I was an usher in his wedding.

The heaviest of the Four Horsemen weighed about 170 pounds, sometimes said to be nearer 165. I know they were great, they contributed so much to the game of football, and no one admires the memory of that quartet more than I. As this is written, only Crowley survives. But I would have to tell you that I doubt that any of the four could get a scholarship at any major school today. And what does that mean? It means nothing except that those muskets they used at Gettysburg wouldn't help a lot in a battle involving atomic weapons. The march of time really is relentless.

CHAPTER 17

Baseball in the Big Apple

In the spring of 1954, by far the most important thing in our lives was the impending addition to the family. We realized that we had been extremely fortunate for Mickie to have achieved pregnancy after a previous ectopic pregnancy.

One Saturday morning, Mickie announced that she was having labor pains. We called the doctor, who told us to meet him at Lawrence Hospital in Bronxville. We gathered up the necessary clothing and toilet articles, and hastened away down the Bronx River Parkway. Mickie was duly installed, and we waited. And we waited, and we waited. And then the doctor announced that it was a false alarm. There were no additional signs of impending birth, and he suggested that we return to our apartment in Scarsdale and await further developments.

More than anything, Mickie was embarrassed. Everybody in the building had been following the progress of the "little mother," and they all knew that she had gone away to the hospital. Mickie would just as soon they didn't know that she had returned from the hospital on the basis of premature arrival—not of the baby, but of the mother. Mickie asked if she could wait in the car in the garage until I checked to see if the coast was clear. And then she slipped surreptitiously back into our place. We waited until after dark, when we could make our move undetected, before we slipped out to a movie theater in White Plains to see Marilyn Monroe, Betty Grable, and Lauren Bacall in *How to Marry a Millionaire.* It was a little late for Mickie to entertain any ideas about marrying a millionaire. I suppose that in her state she felt fortunate just to be married. We were products, you see, of middle-class morality.

Several days later, Mickie somewhat quietly announced to me that she thought her time had come again. This time we made a quieter departure for the hospital. It appeared that we had made a proper move. The doctor said that birth was imminent. I stayed at the hospital until around midnight, when the doctor suggested, rather strongly I thought, that I get the hell out of their way and go back to the apartment. They would call me if and when I was needed.

In the gray hours, they called to say that Mickie had safely delivered and I was quickly on my way. When I got to Lawrence Hospital, the doctor met me in the corridor and we walked together back toward Mickie's room. Nobody had yet told me boy or girl. As we walked, the doctor said, "This is your second child?" I assured him that it was. He said, "What do you have at home?" I told him we had a girl. And he said, "Well, you've got another one."

I was delighted. That was fine. "Your wife is still asleep," he said, "and your brand-new daughter is normal in every way."

Hallelujah! It was easily the greatest moment of my life.

Like all parents, we had discussed names, and we thought that "Nancy Nelson" would be a nice alliterative name. Mickie thought we should add something of my name. This was before the custom of using "Lindsey" for a girl's name had become popular. Mickie thought we should just choose something close, like "Lynn." And she said, "Let's put an *e* on it to emphasize that she is feminine. Make it 'Nancy Lynne Nelson.' " And so that was her name.

As I rode the New York Central in to work, I felt that there was no father prouder than I. I was bursting. As I walked up Fifth Avenue, coming from Grand Central toward my office in Rockefeller Plaza, I decided that I must get some cigars right away. Where did one buy cigars? I didn't know. I had not bought any cigars since Sharon's birth. I didn't smoke. Then I remembered Dunhill's on Fifth Avenue at Fiftieth Street. I strode proudly in to announce to the world at large, and the gentleman behind the counter in particular, that I wanted to buy a box of cigars. He asked what kind of cigars, and he had me there. I didn't know what kinds they came in. I told him that I wanted one about this long that you lighted at the end.

The clerk did not appear impressed with my description. He suggested that we repair to a room in the back, a sort of humidor compartment, where they kept the good stuff. I knew we were in the good-stuff department, and out of my neighborhood, when he mentioned that these were seventy bucks a box. Seventy bucks! That was almost a half-week's pay. How about a good old half-box? That, he said with logic, would be thirty-five dollars. I had the feeling that I'd prefer to be out of that humidor room and into a cheap drugstore, but I had gone too far to turn back. So I made the expensive purchase and went on my merry way, passing out cigars to friends. It was March 10, 1954. I didn't get much work done that day. Fortunately, I didn't have a lot of work to do.

That night on his NBC sports show, Mel Allen gave Nancy's arrival a call, coast to coast, and she was acknowledged by Ed Sullivan in his column in the *Daily News.* I mused that when I had been born in the Brownlow Creek community of Giles County, Tennessee, I had hardly received such notice. I don't think the rural postman knew it for a few months.

In 1954, there were still three major league baseball teams in New York, and baseball was a big part of the sports program of that big city. The Giants were at the Polo Grounds in Harlem. Almost directly across the Harlem River were the famous New York Yankees at majestic Yankee Stadium in the Bronx. And the Dodgers were in Brooklyn at Ebbets Field. Or maybe Brooklyn was in the Dodgers. Certainly they were inseparable. Never was any baseball team more closely identified with its constituency. It was impossible to imagine Brooklyn without the Dodgers. The baseball team gave the borough its identity. They had a bridge and they had a baseball team and they had millions of loyal citizens. A lot of them found their way daily into Ebbets Field, a compact, bandbox sort of a park. But the small size did not diminish the dedication of the fans at this shrine. One does not demean the Sistine chapel because it is not as big as the Astrodome. Here came the faithful regularly to offer up their hopes and prayers for a sometimes untalented group of athletes.

Certainly Ebbets Field had incomparable and unforgettable personality. I remember the cramped clubhouse the final day of the World

Series in 1955, when the Dodgers clinched the only World Championship they ever won in Brooklyn. And Tom Gallery did a masterful job of body blocking to keep politician Averell Harriman from installing himself on camera, a very real danger in any clubhouse celebration. And I remember the opening day of the following season, when I sat in the club box with General Manager Buzzie Bavasi. After lavish ceremonies, the band marched to the flagpole in centerfield for the proper process of raising the flag. There was a delay, some confusion, and then the word that nobody had brought a flag. Only in Brooklyn.

Each of those teams had its own particular characteristics. The Giants had known the glory of John McGraw, the manager who had led them to unparalleled success, and who had been succeeded by the incomparable Bill Terry. This was the team backed by the folks on Broadway, the show-biz people, and by the Wall Streeters. Occasionally, they altered the starting time of their games to concur with the closing of the stock market.

The Polo Grounds was the home of Willie Mays and the place where, in 1951, Bobby Thomson hit the homer heard around the world, off Dodger pitcher Ralph Branca in the ninth inning of the third and deciding playoff game for the National League championship.

The Giants were owned by Horace Stoneham, who noticed that the annual receipts had shrunk greatly, but he was not all that concerned. Horace was a fan. He would watch every game and then maybe go down to Toots Shor's restaurant on Fifty-first Street and talk far into the night with another dedicated Giants fan, Toots Shor. They might do their talking and planning over a couple of bottles of brandy. More than one deal involving Giant players had its beginning and maybe its consummation in those sessions between Horace and Toots and friends.

To this day, in baseball circles there is talk of "Horace Stoneham rainouts." The stories may or may not be true. There is strong evidence, however, at least to support their probability. The offices at the Polo Grounds were in straightaway centerfield, hard against the Eighth Avenue El. Horace had an office equipped with a window through which he could watch the ball game, looking directly to the batter some four hundred feet distant. I would not wish to comment on the veracity or falsity of the charges of opposing players that there were occasions when a Giants employee armed with field glasses would pick up signs of opposing catchers from that vantage point and relay them to the home team. I would say that it seems possible.

What is almost certain is that Horace spent many an afternoon in that office, and that some of them wore on into the evening, night, early morning, and thereafter.

The story goes that Mr. Stoneham was awakened one morning by what he perceived to be the noise of a heavy rainstorm. He could hardly see through the window for the great bursts of water pouring down upon it. Since a game was scheduled for that afternoon, he picked up the phone, called the proper employee, and said, "Postpone the game because of rain." He was met with an attempted protest that got only as far as "But, but . . ." before Horace cut him off with a strong restatement of his position as boss and owner of this outfit who had just called today's game off for rain. And Horace reportedly went back to sleep.

It was said to have been one of the most beautiful, sunny days in the history of baseball in New York. It was so beautiful that the crew had decided to wash the scoreboard, and they had sent gallons of water up against that upright structure, some of it cascading down to cover the window of the boss's office.

And there were the Yankees, who were in the American League. Followers of the National League Giants and Dodgers did not willingly acknowledge the existence of any other league. The American, in their estimation, ranked in importance with the Kitty and the Epworth. Yankee Stadium was where a businessman might take his out-of-town visitors. You might take a guest to see Grant's Tomb and Yankee Stadium and maybe the Statue of Liberty. A lot of Yankee fans wore jackets and neckties. They had a lovely Stadium Club, where one could be protected from direct contact with the general population while one dined. Some were not certain that they even sold hot dogs at Yankee Stadium—maybe caviar or croissants. Oh, the Yankees won a lot of pennants and a lot of world championships. The Bronx seemed proud of them—not all of the Bronx, but a lot of it.

But the real baseball fans were out there in the backyard with their shirts off, drinking Schaeffer beer and smoking Chesterfields. Those were the fans of the Dodgers and the Giants. That's the way the baseball picture seemed to some—not all—in old New York.

The rights to televise the NCAA football games in 1954 surprisingly went to ABC, which meant that I would not be doing any college games unless my name was either Tom Harmon or Jack Drees, because they were named to the series by ABC. But as it turned out, getting that NCAA package was one of the worst things that could have happened to ABC. They were not able to sell it as strongly as they had hoped. They were unable to provide many of the promotional advantages their proposal had promised. When the season was over, director of sports Les Arries and a number of sports-department people were dismissed. The ABC–NCAA football package had not been a roaring success.

Meanwhile, in that season of 1954, Tom Gallery made a deal with the Canadian Football League for NBC to carry a Canadian game each Saturday and to top it off with the National Championship Grey Cup game. I did the play-by-play and the analyst was Jim Crowley, one of the famed Four Horsemen of Notre Dame.

When the bidding for the NCAA games came around in 1955, however, NBC was ready, and held the rights for the next five years.

It was another of those late afternoons in 1957, when I was with Tom Gallery in his car as we drove homeward toward Westchester County. As we neared the neighborhood of Yankee Stadium, I noticed that Gallery was getting a little restless. We had not forgotten that there was a championship boxing match scheduled for that evening at the stadium. It was just that we had made no specific plans to attend it.

It was apparent to me, though, that Gallery's native boxing blood was beginning to boil, and there was no way we could get by Yankee Stadium without stopping. Through his connections with the stadium personnel from his days as a Yankee executive, Gallery easily got us a place to park the car. And the first man we met was Harry Markson of the International Boxing Club, which was promoting the fight. Gallery said he would join Yankee President Dan Topping and his party in their box. Markson gave me a ticket for an aisle seat in the third row of the ringside.

First I went with Gallery to Topping's office, where he was entertaining a few friends. Among them was Yankee manager Casey Stengel. Casey and I moved off into a corner and he talked a little baseball while the others talked about the night's fight between Sugar Ray Robinson and Carmen Basilio.

I had barely settled into my seat when the occupant of the seat on my immediate left made his way down the aisle. And as he was recognized, he got a standing ovation from the adoring fight fans. By this time, he and I had become good friends and had done several television shows together. We greeted each other as Joe Louis settled into the seat next to me.

The seat behind me was still vacant, but only for a moment. Then there was an even louder ovation than that which had greeted Joe Louis, and General Douglas MacArthur strode down the aisle and took the seat directly behind me. The man who was perhaps America's greatest military hero of World War II, the man whom President Truman had referred to as "His Majesty," waved and settled into his seat.

Near the ring a couple of teenagers got into an argument and then briefly into a scuffle. The ushers rushed down to restore order. A man across the aisle said to me, "Gee, I thought for a moment that we might be getting into a free-for-all." I smiled and nodded and I thought, "Let 'em go. I will never be in better circumstances for general combat than I am right now—Joe Louis on my left and General MacArthur in the rear."

When I got home that night, Mickie was already asleep. I gently awakened her to say, "Wake up, the war is really over!"

That, of course, was not exactly news to her, and she was puzzled until I explained, "I know the war is over because at Yankee Stadium tonight General MacArthur sat *behind* me."

In the 1930s there was an agreement among the New York baseball teams that there would be no radio broadcasts of home games. It was the old fear that attendance might be adversely affected. But in other sections of the country, baseball broadcasting flourished, particularly in Chicago. And in Cincinnati, the general manager was Larry MacPhail. His broadcaster was a native of Mississippi who had grown up in Florida. His delivery ran strong to the intonations of the Old South. That was Walter (Red) Barber.

MacPhail then came to New York as general manager of the Brooklyn Dodgers, and he immediately made it plain that he intended to broadcast the Dodgers games. And he sent to Cincinnati for Barber. In 1939 baseball broadcasts inundated the New York area.

Red Barber became a star. A whole generation of Brooklyn fans tuned in daily to hear The Old Redhead punctuate his broadcasts with catchy phrases and descriptions all done with a deep flavoring of hominy grits and corn pone, delicacies generally unknown to his clientele in Brooklyn. But they loved it just the same.

And when Ted Husing of CBS turned fully toward a career as a disc jockey, Barber replaced him as director of sports there. Then when television had grown in importance, Barber returned full-time to baseball, and CBS began to build the sports department, first under the umbrella of Sig Mickelson, who was director of news, and specifically in the hands of John Derr and Judson Bailey.

But now baseball was being courted by the television folks. For years the World Series had been the big annual showpiece. Now there were moves in other directions. With an advertising agency, ABC worked out a game of the week for presentation on Saturday afternoon. There were a lot of details to be worked out, because baseball teams generally by now had their own local television deals. The teams could not afford to allow competition with these. Their value lay in their exclusivity. So the network game would not be allowed to go into any of the franchise cities. That, unfortunately, was where they would be valuable.

And then the game of the week moved to CBS, guided by the Dancer, Fitzgerald, Sample agency for their client, Falstaff beer. Jimmy Neale and Ed Scherick were handling much of the administrative work at the agency, and the announcers were Dizzy Dean and Buddy Blattner.

After his playing career had ended, Diz began a broadcasting career on the games of the St. Louis Browns. He had been an immediate hit, especially in the rural areas where baseball was understood and loved. There was nothing slick or polished about Diz's commentary. He told it like his listeners presumed it was. And Diz quickly became a folk hero.

He had a brief whirl at doing the pre and post of the Yankee games in New York, but that didn't work out. It seemed that everybody took a shot at working the Yankees pregame show including, in addition to Diz, Joe DiMaggio and movie star Joe E. Brown. The urbane New Yorkers apparently needed an interpreter for much of what Diz had to say. And the Yankee offices were not overrun with favorable fan mail. Diz was not concerned. He was playing golf most days with Dan Topping, who was the principal Yankees owner. It was said that there was considerable wagering on the outcome of the daily matches and that Diz was winning on most days by a prudent margin of one stroke, never more than two, but consistently winning nonetheless. It was surmised in some quarters that if the daily golfing competition had a long run, Dizzy Dean might very well end up as owner of the New York Yankees, having won the franchise on the links by a margin of one stroke.

In any case, Dizzy Dean did not survive in the New York broadcasting jungle, and went to the Mutual *Game of the Day* for Falstaff and then to the television game of the week.

Although Gallery was a baseball man and a baseball fan, former business manager of the New York Yankees, and in daily touch with his good friend Dan Topping, NBC had shown no great interest in getting into baseball.

I also considered myself a baseball fan and a baseball man. I had broadcast Army baseball, baseball in Knoxville, baseball for Liberty Broadcasting.

In fact, there was the afternoon back in 1953 when Mel Allen and I were doing the NCAA football games for NBC. We were on the way to the UCLA practice field in the Westwood section of Los Angeles to watch Red Sanders's Bruins work out. At the end of the 1953 baseball season, the Yankees had dropped Bill Crowley and Art Gleeson as Mel's associates, and the Yankees were reportedly looking about to recast their crew, with Mel remaining, of course, as the lead announcer.

Mel knew about my baseball broadcasting and about my interest in baseball. He was driving down Wilshire Boulevard. Mel's brother, Larry, was in the right front seat. I was in the backseat. Suddenly, Mel turned and looked at me and at the same time pulled the car to the curb and stopped. "I just had an idea," he said. "Why don't you do the Yankee games with me?"

Well, the idea certainly got my attention. I was happy at NBC and was glad to be there, but where was it written that I might not be even happier at Yankee Stadium?

Mel was enthusiastic. "When you get back to New York," he said, "dig up a tape recording of your baseball play-by-play and ship it to my agent. I'll get it to George Weiss [the Yankees general manager]," without whose approval there would be no Yankees announcers hired.

Well, when I got home I sent the tape, although I had not privately decided under what circumstances I would be willing to leave NBC. I could not do a Red Barber. The days of doubling up were over. I might work at NBC or for the Yankees, but not both.

I was surely flattered to be considered for the job by the Yankees, but on the other hand I was doing just fine at NBC.

And at about that same time, I had dinner with Al Helfer. Al was the play-by-play man on the Mutual Radio's *Game of the Day.* He and Diz had worked together on the radio series. Now Helfer was telling me that he did not plan to work baseball for more than another year. "If you want," he said, "I'll make a pitch for you to take over the *Game of the Day.*"

My cup was not only running over, it was filling up my shoetops. And about this time, I came into fortunate contact with Tom Siler, the sports editor of the Knoxville *News-Sentinel.* Tom had been in Chicago with the Associated Press and with Marshall Field's *Chicago Sun.* When he had returned to the paper after service in Europe in World War II, a mutual friend, Pulitzer Prize–winning Don Whitehead, had reported to me, "Siler is back in Chicago with his hand in Marshall Field's hip pocket." Siler and I were old hometown friends. I rushed to tell him about how things were breaking for me. Tom was not only unimpressed, he was concerned. Slowly he laid it out for me, and I have been forever grateful, because it gave me a new concept.

Tom said, "You have to be careful with those things. It's like when you are at a party and the hostess comes in with three or four different kinds of pastry on a tray. You decide that you'll take this piece, and then you change your mind. You switch to another piece. But since the tray is full, you choose yet another one. Of course, the other guests are not waiting. They are choosing, too. And in your indecision, if you are not careful, you may be left standing there in the middle of the room with nothing and the tray empty. It's often best just to make a firm choice and stick to it."

Now, that may be Jellico (Tom's Tennessee hometown) logic, but it's sound, and I continued happily on my way at NBC.

There is a brief postscript. The Yankees hired Jim Woods, who had done baseball in Atlanta for Earl Mann. Mel called from St. Petersburg where the Yanks trained to tell me that I was still being considered for the pre and the post. And then word came that they had filled that job, too. It had gone to Joe E. Brown, a headline movie star whose son would be a longtime general manager of the Pittsburgh Pirates. For Joe E. Brown, a fan, it was just a pleasant way for him to spend the day at the ball park.

And then one day the phone rang in the NBC sports department. It was a call for Tom Gallery from Niles Trammell at WCKT, the NBC affiliate in Miami.

Niles Trammell had been the president of the NBC network before he retired. Then he had hooked up in part ownership of WCKT (Cox, Knight, Trammell).

He was concerned with the baseball games on CBS.

"Here in Miami," he said, "the baseball game is getting all the audience on Saturday afternoon. I might as well go dark. The baseball gets everybody, and we have got to compete. We have got to have some baseball."

Well, it developed that Mr. Trammell was not the only one who had made that discovery. It was no problem in the franchise cities—the big cities like New York and Chicago. But there were some big cities where there was no major league team and where CBS was wiping out everything, cities like Los Angeles and San Francisco and Kansas City and Dallas and Miami.

That became project number one. And the first thing we discovered was that Jimmy Neale and Ed Scherick at Dancer Fitzgerald had pretty well tied up the supply of major league baseball games. They had not signed all of them, but they had signed enough so that it was going to be very difficult for any competitor to sign a schedule. By today's standards, the money was peanuts. But back then, it was reckoned by the ball clubs a considerable sum. The going rate for rights was about twenty-five thousand dollars per game.

We ran a quick inquiry to find out who was still loose and unsigned. The Milwaukee Braves were available, as were the Pittsburgh Pirates, the Chicago Cubs, and some American League teams, notably the Washington Senators. With the exception of the Braves, the teams available were not going to set the world on fire. But when you are doing only one game a week, that's not so important. It is today's game that counts.

As a man wise in the ways of the Madison Avenue jungle, Gallery guessed that if we made a move toward baseball we might suddenly find the remainder of the teams in the Dancer Fitzgerald package. He figured that they probably had an eye on him.

If you wanted to know what NBC Sports was doing, Gallery was the man to watch, all right. As an old promoter, he carried most of the pertinent documents in his inside coat pocket at all times. He was ready to move at a moment's notice.

I had devised a possible schedule that would consist of eleven Milwaukee games, eleven Pittsburgh games, four Cub games, and four Senator games. That would take care of us if we could arrange it. Gallery suggested that I hit the road, signing whatever teams I could as quietly as I could. He thought that Dancer would not care where I went. After all, I was an announcer.

It was not long until I had finalized all the deals we needed, and Gallery was able to announce to the NBC program board, "We are in the baseball business, and we will open with an exhibition game from Dallas, Texas—the Milwaukee Braves and the Brooklyn Dodgers." Not a bad way to open! It was 1957, and we had major league baseball on NBC.

Now that we had our schedule, what about announcers? Well, everybody knew that most of the competent baseball announcers were already employed. They were working for the teams.

But there was an interesting situation at NBC. At the close of the 1955 season, Leo Durocher had been signed to a contract at NBC for duties that were largely unspecified. He was to be a sort of goodwill ambassador among the Hollywood stars who were his cronies. Leo was married to movie star Laraine Day, and was deep into the social side of Beverly Hills.

Nobody ever said that Durocher was not interesting. Many thought he was the very best of the major league managers. Just as many could not stand the sight or mention of him. Durocher made enemies whom he never met. Some of those were his various bosses. When he had managed the Brooklyn Dodgers to victory one year, his boss, Larry MacPhail, fired him at the height of the victory celebration and rehired him the next morning. Leo seemed to inspire that sort of behavior.

Giants announcer Russ Hodges, a friend and neighbor of mine, told of the time in 1954 when he was having his annual midseason party at his home in Westchester. One of the guests was Horace Stoneham, the owner of the Giants, and during the course of the evening, Horace announced that he had every intention of firing Durocher, maybe before the night was over. Hodges interceded to put in a word in defense of the Giant manager, which prompted Horace to say, "And Hodges, if you say one more word for that no good S.O.B., I'll fire you, too."

Well, both Durocher and Hodges escaped the axe because the 1954 Giants won the pennant and swept the Cleveland Indians in the World Series in four straight. That made prospective firing of the manager ungainly, but 1955 would be just a buffer year. Bill Rigney was in the wings. Leo was not fired, at least I don't think he was. But the Giants did nothing to dissuade him from quitting and signing with NBC.

Leo had nothing to do with NBC Sports. He was in the West Coast operation. Leo told me later he had experienced the same difficulties I had in getting assigned an office. Nobody seemed to be in charge of that effort and Leo kept showing up each day and "visiting" up and down the hall. One day, he said, he had a call from Benson Ford, the auto magnate, who said he would be coming by to see Leo in his office. Leo reportedly said, "I ain't got no office. You'll have to see me in the corridor."

Well, apparently, as time wore on, not a lot of people were seeing Leo in the corridor or anywhere else, and the word was out that management was looking for some duties that might be assigned to Leo.

The company scuttlebutt we got back in New York was that Leo was drawing an annual fifty thousand dollars. And the word was that the company had sent a memo around to all the department heads asking how much of that annual nut each department would be willing to take into its budget for the services of Leo Durocher. And the word, right or wrong, was that the memo got back to its origin with the entire fifty thousand dollars unsubscribed.

When Gallery now proposed that Durocher might be employed on the baseball series as an announcer, encouragement poured in from all quarters of the company.

Gallery also said that he wanted me as one of the announcers on baseball.

Then, too, there had been a development with the Yankees. Jim Woods had surprisingly been replaced on the announcing staff by Phil Rizzuto. Mel Allen and Phil Rizzuto were not exactly bosom pals. In fact, they didn't like each other a lot. But that was the way it was, and Woods was on the street.

While Gallery as a fan did not particularly like the style and delivery of announcer Jim Woods, he did admire his professionalism, which is what we would be looking for.

So, that was our baseball announcing crew at NBC—Leo Durocher, Jim Woods, and Lindsey Nelson.

And we went away to Dallas, Texas, for our first exhibition game. We would each do three innings of play-by-play and Leo would do commentary all the time. In Dallas, Woods came to me the night before the game and said, "I need some advice. I don't know how Leo works." I said, "Well, I don't know how he works, either, but you are going to find out early because you are working the first three innings."

Our baseball presentation, produced by Perry Smith, went better than we had hoped. Gallery confided to me that Durocher had worked out better than he feared and that actually we might have too many announcers. He said that two might be enough. He said really that he had hired Woods as a backup in case Durocher didn't work out. I was never absolutely sure that was the way it was. I thought maybe Gallery had hired Woods as a backup in case I didn't work out. It occurred to me that Gallery had never heard me do a baseball game.

During the week Jim Woods came into Gallery's office with interesting news. Russ Hodges had made Woods an offer to join him on the Giants broadcasts. It would be a better baseball job than three innings once a week, and he wondered if he could be released from his commitment to NBC. He was, in about thirty seconds.

CHAPTER 18

Sports on Television

In 1957, then, I began life with Leo Durocher on the *Major League Baseball* presentations of NBC-TV. We had gone to San Antonio to watch the Milwaukee Braves and the Brooklyn Dodgers in an exhibition game because these were the two teams who would meet in that TV opener in Dallas a few days later.

As we started into the ball park in San Antonio, Durocher took me by the arm and pulled me aside. He said, "Look, I have been in the major leagues for more than thirty years and I think I know something about baseball. But I know nothing about television. You tell me what to do, and I'll do it."

That is the way we started our partnership, and I must say that Durocher carried out his part of that bargain. He was a quick study and he took direction. I know that some students of the Durocher career and temperament may find that difficult to believe, but he did. Unfortunately, there were some occasions when he also took off.

For our first telecast in Milwaukee, Leo spent the night before in Chicago and then drove up next morning. Leo appeared at the ball park with a leather briefcase and a pair of field glasses. He didn't have a scorebook because he did not know how to keep one. He didn't really need to. Leo could recap a game almost pitch by pitch, like a golfer recapping a round of golf stroke by stroke.

One Saturday night during the 1957 baseball season, when the Milwaukee Braves were on their way to a world championship, Leo Durocher and I were in Milwaukee at dinner along with Brave equipment manager Joe Taylor.

We discussed baseball, and managers, and pennant races, and women. Joe Taylor was an easy fellow who moved effortlessly through the maze of the several societies that are drawn to the baseball life. In a deep voice, he reeled off various approximations of well-known poems. That got us onto the subject of poetry, and I quoted several of my Kipling favorites plus a Justin Huntly McCarthy or two, especially passages from *If I Were King.* Leo was entranced. He said, "Damn, buddy, that's great. Say some more of that stuff."

I explained that it was neither new nor original; still Leo couldn't get enough of this new world that had been revealed to him.

So when I was leaving home for our game the following week, which would be in Washington, I took along a small bound volume of assorted poems. When we met at Washington National Airport, I offered the book to Leo. He said, "Aw, I don't want to take your book, buddy. Just tell me the title and I'll go in the bookstore here and buy a copy."

And that is how Leo Durocher happened to be in the poetry corner of the bookstore there in the Washington National Airport, searching through the titles. It was an unlikely scene.

One day we were in Washington to do a baseball game and were staying at the Shoreham Hotel. And I had discovered that one of the biggest advantages of working with Leo Durocher was the quality of my quarters. We each had a large suite.

As a manager of a major league baseball team, Leo had been accustomed to the suite that is normally accorded the manager. When he came to NBC, he insisted that he continue to occupy somewhat palatial quarters. Tom Gallery did not want to make a big deal over it one way or another, but he did announce that I would have quarters equal to whatever was arranged for Durocher. It was a step up for an announcer who had become accustomed to the single rooms normally afforded staffers.

In our third season together, Leo seemed to be having some marital difficulties with his wife, Laraine Day. Things just weren't going well. Leo seemed to be spending a lot of time outside the state of California. He went with Frank Sinatra and Dean Martin to Madison, Indiana, to shoot some scenes for *Some Came Running*. One night there was a flap with some locals about an argument concerning hamburgers, or something, and *Time* magazine, in reporting the incident, had referred to Leo as a "camp follower." The baseball players did not miss the opportunity to call this to Leo's attention when we showed up at the ball parks. He was not particularly thrilled about this.

Then there was the day that we were at Fenway Park in Boston for a Red Sox game. Leo mentioned before the game that if I didn't mind he would like to alter the rotation for the day. Usually I opened and did the first two innings. Then Leo did the next four. Then I came back and did the last three and closed. Leo said he wanted to open and do the first two, maybe three innings.

When I wondered why, Leo said he could get a plane in midafternoon that would get him down to New York's Idlewild Airport, from which he could make a connection that he wanted to make. I did not inquire of his final destination because the gossip columns were now full of little suggestions about where Leo might be spending his spare time. The columnists had an intriguing assortment of versions. I didn't know if Leo was going to all those places and seeing all of those people, mostly ladies, but if he was I wouldn't have minded going with him.

But we obviously couldn't both go. That particular day, Leo did the first three innings and then he left the rooftop perch at Fenway at a gallop. I settled in and did the rest of the ball game without mishap. And we had a quiet and uneventful week.

Next Saturday, back at Fenway, Leo revealed that he wanted to work the same rotation we had used the previous week. It had worked out just fine, he said.

But it was a case of far too much of a good thing. Leo did two innings. They had been time consuming, so he hadn't been able to make the third. I moved in and went to work alone. We never made a point of saying that Leo had left. And he must have been just landing at Idlewild in New York when we were struck with a thunderstorm that brought with it a heavy and continuing rain. The game was stopped, the camera was turned around on me, and I began the customary "rain fill." The problem was that now everybody knew I was alone. If Leo had been there, they must have reasoned, he would surely have been in this conversation. Conversation was one of Leo's big things, but here I was talking to myself. I recapped the game, and the pennant races, and the previous year's World Series, and this year's probabilities, and I threw in a little of "Casey at the Bat," and a Kipling selection or two. I had recited everything but my phone number and driver's license, and still the rain came. When we resumed, later in the day, I might just as well have opened with a poster saying, LEO AIN'T HERE. Everybody knew that Leo wasn't there.

When I got to the office on Monday morning, I was being awaited. Gallery had convened a meeting of producer Lou Kusserow, director Harry Coyle, and everybody else associated with the baseball package. "Where," Gallery wanted to know, "had Durocher gone?" Well, we didn't actually know where he had gone.

Gallery had heard further rumors. Had Durocher also disappeared the previous Saturday? Well, yes, as a matter of fact he had. Why had I not reported this to Gallery?

Well, I realized that I was on thin ice as I carefully contended that I was not in the snitching business. I was in the baseball broadcasting business, in a partnership with Leo Durocher. And presumably adjustments might have to be made during the course of a long season. And while I had not given him permission, I pointed out that he had not requested my permission. When the meeting was over, I was pleased to discover that I was still employed, but I would not have wanted to bet on Leo's continued status as a member of the NBC baseball team. He made it only until the end of that season.

In retrospect, I think it is safe to say that the surest thing about Leo Durocher is that throughout his topsy-turvy lifetime he has always been one of a kind. You can say almost anything about Durocher that you choose, supportive or derogatory, and immediately find a quorum of baseball folk to back any charge or accolade.

At the height of his managerial career with the Dodgers and the Giants, he was loud, visible, flamboyant. Frequently he ran the team from the coaching lines at third base. I recall going into Boston to do a *Game of the Week* with Leo during Mike Higgins's tenure as Red Sox manager. Higgins had sent one of his coaches up to the plate with the lineup cards and had not left the dugout himself all day. In the booth, Leo was accusative. "How can he do that?" he screamed. "The people pay to see the manager, too. He can't hide in the dugout all day." And yet, in his later days as manager at Chicago and Houston, that is precisely what Leo did.

There were sound baseball men who worshipped at the shrine of Durocher. Alvin Dark, himself an astute manager, was one of them. He has been heard to say that Leo Durocher is the only man he ever met who he thought knew everything about the game of baseball.

But there were others who were vociferous in their opposition to the life-style they supposed he led.

Durocher on the field was frequently profane, obscene, vulgar, violent, and entreating—he wouldn't hesitate to order his pitcher to "stick it in his ear." But in a mixed social gathering, if he chose, he could be the most charming man in the room, and his soft smile and gentle manner with the ladies could sweep them off their feet.

There was never a more fastidious male than Leo Durocher when he chose to be. Many have said that it was the influence of a former wife, Grace Dozier, a fashion designer, that made him the peacock fashion plate he was. When we would walk out onto the field before a game, and come back through the clubhouse before going up to the broadcast booth, Leo would invariably stop to take a clean towel and wipe the dust from his Gucci loafers.

When we were on NBC competing with Dizzy Dean on CBS, we each had a beer sponsor. Leo was usually dressed in black mohair with a light gray shirt and a hand-painted tie. Dizzy was wearing a sport shirt that looked as though he had slept in it, or perhaps had found it washed up on the beach. The advertising agency representing our beer held a high-level meeting and decided that a sport shirt was a better costume in which to sell beer than a flawless, solid-color suit. We were ordered to wear sport shirts, like Diz.

Well, we wore the sport shirts, but Durocher never looked anything like Diz. Leo always looked as though his sport shirt had been personally tailored for him by either Bill Blass or Pierre Cardin, and delivered without a wrinkle visible anywhere.

There was no doubt that Leo was an egotist and a self-promoter. But he also had fierce loyalties such as that with people like Maury Saklad, a New York dentist who had more friends among athletes, actors, and politicians than anyone I ever knew. He and Leo were close.

In almost every way, then, Leo Durocher was a paradox. Almost eighty years of age as this is written, he lives quietly in Palm Springs, California, exercises daily since his bypass surgery performed by famed surgeon Dr. Michael De Bakey, but is still capable of spellbinding a gathering of baseball fans.

I think the essence of Leo Durocher the manager might best

be illustrated by the narration of an incident, the veracity of which I cannot ensure since I was not there. But I think you will get the point. It was in Chicago one night at a popular sports gathering place called Gibbey's where arguments and discussions were known to run far into the night. These were baseball folk, knowledgeable baseball folk, and they were into a fierce session. Someone had proposed a hypothetical situation, as someone always does. These are the very best kind of problems to pursue since there is no certain solution or answer. "Suppose," said someone, "that we had two baseball teams of as nearly equal talent as you could choose. And suppose that those two, hypothetically equal, teams were going to play one game for the championship of the world. They would not play a season. They would not play a World Series of seven games. They would play only one game. And to manage your team, you could have any man, living or dead, who ever managed in the major leagues. Who would be your man?"

Well, they went around the big table with each guest choosing his man. Somebody chose John McGraw. Somebody else chose Connie Mack. There was a word for Frank Chance, Charlie Dressen, Frank Frisch, and others. And now it was time for a choice by a man who had himself managed well in the majors—Paul Richards. He thought, he pondered, and he spoke aloud, "Just one game—one game? For just one game I might want a man I can't stand—Leo Durocher."

I don't know whether that is a true story, but it is indicative of the manner in which Durocher was perceived by many. In just one big game, he might inspire his team to win it, he might pull some unorthodox strategy to win it, or he might even steal it. But not many would want to bet against him.

Tom Gallery had a number of definite ideas about what should and should not be included in the coverage of a major sports event. When it came to baseball, he had an idea that an announcer in love with statistics could drive the average fan nuts in the course of one figure-laden afternoon.

It was at the World Series, in a game involving the Yankees and the Milwaukee Braves, that Gallery decided Mel Allen had used just about enough statistics about how this game compared statistically with other World Series games in history. And Gallery was not one to keep his feelings to himself. So he said to Mel, "No more of those damned statistics. We've had enough of that. Just do the game."

Well, when a fellow has worked the baseball trick for a lot of years, as Mel had, he develops irresistible habits. When something occurs in the game, it may trigger a statistical thought in his head. And I am sure that it was an automatic reaction like that which led Mel Allen to grab *The Little Red Book,* and, holding it beneath the tabletop, to start thumbing through it. *The Little Red Book* is a standard statistical volume, and when a fellow is thumbing through it, he will not find a suspenseful plot or any glowing descriptive literary passages. All he will get out of there are numbers.

When Gallery saw what Mel was doing, he saw "red." He was furious. The closest thing that wasn't nailed down was a headset that lay near the mike. Gallery grabbed the headset and started whacking Mel Allen over the head, saying, "Didn't I tell you to leave the statistics alone?"

We had fewer statistics for the remainder of that World Series.

By the late 1950s, things seemed to be rolling for me as a television sports announcer. I was doing the game of the week in football, in baseball, and in basketball, and I was doing most of the big golf tournaments. Occasionally, I was doing the tennis at Forest Hills as well as the Davis Cup. And even a heavyweight championship fight.

I did that in 1957, when Floyd Patterson was the heavyweight champion of the world. He was matched against Hurricane Jackson in a fight to be held at the Polo Grounds in New York.

NBC was going to carry it, and Tom was working with Les Arries, who was representing the packager in putting the television presentation together.

About this time, I had arranged for Mickie and me to slip away for a short vacation to Canada. We flew up to Montreal and then we boarded a steamer for an overnight ride up the river to a point past Quebec City. We went to a lavish resort hotel named the Manoir Richelieu for a few days, and had a marvelous time. Then we took a bus through rural Canada back to Quebec City and on to Montreal, before returning to New York.

My first day back in the office I was greeted with the news that the telecast of the heavyweight championship fight would be done by Bill Corum and me.

Corum, of course, was the well-known sports columnist of the *New York Journal American* who had done fights on radio with Don Dunphy for years. Later he would succeed Colonel Matt Winn in managing the Kentucky Derby. For now, he would do the blow-by-blow of the fight and I would do the color.

I don't think I ever had an assignment that excited me quite so much as this one. It all went back to those days of sitting on the living room rug in Columbia and listening to Graham McNamee do Dempsey and Tunney.

And then it was the wonderful Louis years, listening to Sam Taub and Bill Stern. There was something so electric, so magic about a heavyweight championship to me. And now, I was going to do one myself.

I had done some fights on radio. I had done the Golden Gloves in Knoxville and I had done fights in Memphis. I was knowledgeable. But Gallery was going to back me up a little more, just in case. He had Barney Nagler working at my elbow. There was no more knowledgeable man in the field of boxing than Barney, and he would be slipping me notes if need be.

As it turned out, Bill Corum and I got one note too many that night, not from Barney but from the control truck.

To begin with, I had arrived early at the Polo Grounds. It was summertime and not yet dark. The NBC crew had apparently run into a little difficulty in trying to get the announcers' position designated and set up. The news photographers were wily old veterans who had already staked out the choice positions on the apron. And one did not get to be a veteran photographer by being kindly and yielding to requests from television announcers or networks. Roughly described, the photog's answer had been, "Why don't you guys get the hell out of here?"

Our folks, being comparatively young and inexperienced in such things, had got the hell out of there.

Now they were meeting us up the aisle to say that really the photographers were in charge. I looked toward a corner, and sure enough there was a veteran photographer who was really in charge. He was sitting on the apron and more or less daring anyone to dispute his right to be there. I was not about to dispute his right but I was about to say hello because his name was Harry Harris. He had worked for AP since roughly the beginning of time, and I had spent a good deal of time during the war in Europe in his company at the Hotel Portugal in Spa, Belgium, and other places.

Harry recognized me and smiled. We shook hands and he said, in a low voice, "Where do you want to work?" Harry was going to help an old friend and allow me a proper position, but he was not going to do it in a voice loud enough to damage his ongoing reputation as a crusty, unfeeling, unbending old pro. I wanted a seat from which I could reach out and touch the canvas of the ring.

The fight was being sponsored on home television by the Buick Division represented by the Kudner agency, and Bernie London was there as the agency rep.

We gathered in a production meeting attended by all of our production people, plus Gallery and Les Arries, Corum, and me. As we were finishing up, Bernie London said, "At the end of the fight, I want a two-minute commercial before we announce the winner." Among other things, they were doing live commercials that night. That has since proven to be not the very best way of doing that. There are too many chances for a fluff, or a missed line, or a missed cue, or a missing actor, or a run-over. But they were doing live commercials. And Bernie wanted to be sure that he got a two-minute commercial before the announcement in the ring. If it was a decision, the commercial presumably would come while the judges' cards were being collected. If it ended in a knockout, the commercial would come between the time the referee finished his count and the announcement of time in the ring.

We had not exactly anticipated a technical knockout, but that is what we got.

In the case of a TKO, there are no cards to be collected. There is no count by the referee. The referee simply stops the fight. He puts up his hand and the fight is over. That is all there is to it.

So, there we sat at ringside, Corum and I. Our stage manager was Don Ellis, an old hand. There must have been pandemonium in the truck. Don had his hand over the earpiece, straining to hear his instructions from the director. And then I saw him reach into his stack of cue cards and pull out an index card with a commercial lead-in written on it. He leaned across me to hand the card to Bill Corum. I thought I saw impending disaster on the way. Soon it arrived.

Up in the ring, they made the announcement of the time, the fighters left the ring, and the participants in the following walk-out bout were climbing in. We were into a two-minute commercial being done by a stock company in one of the upper-deck portals at the Polo Grounds. When we came back, we were pretty much in a shambles. The folks at home hadn't seen or heard the announcement of the winner from the ring or the time of the TKO. Expecting that when we came back, they got a dose of two fighters they had never heard of and weren't particularly proud to see. There was a lot of screaming and yelling. We signed off and went away home.

For several days, nobody seemed very happy with the way things had gone. The president of the Buick Division, through a national wire service, apologized to the boxing fans of the nation for the shoddy manner in which we had handled the finish of the fight. When a client issues a national apology for the presentation he paid for, he ain't happy.

There were meetings and countermeetings. Mike Kirk was the vice-president in charge of radio and television at Kudner. He kept asking Bernie, "Did you specifically ask for that last commercial?"

If I had been Bernie I would not have wanted to rush into an answer, because it was apparent that there was not a long line of volunteers about to step up there and take responsibility. And it further seemed that if and when Bernie said "yes," he might be about ready for another line of work.

It was all one great big unfortunate affair in the world of television. It was not so long before there was no longer a Kudner agency. I wouldn't say the demise can be attributed solely to that one misplaced commercial, but I will say that commercial didn't help them any.

NBC was carrying the NFL championship game, and on a cold December day of 1958 at Yankee Stadium, the New York Giants met the Baltimore Colts for the title. That is sometimes referred to as the single football game that sent the pro game on the way to the heights of popularity it has since enjoyed. It was the first sudden-death game. It was tied at the end of regulation time, and in the overtime the Colts won it.

At one point in the telecast, one of the NBC cables snapped in the bitter cold weather, and the screens across the land suddenly went dark. Well, that was a bad time for NBC. This very close and very exciting football game was, of course, about to continue, but NBC was temporarily out of business.

They wanted the referee to stop play until they could get the cable fixed. Even now, the engineers were hard at work on it. But back then, you couldn't just step out there and politely ask the referee if he would mind holding up play for a few moments. The players would not be particularly receptive to such an idea. They were freezing to death. So the Colts were back there in their huddle, ready to come up to the line. But suddenly, a drunk came out of the crowd along the sideline, stumbling out onto the field. He was inscribing a circuitous route headed for nowhere in particular. Now the game could not proceed. The referee blew his whistle and suspended play until they could get this fellow off the field. Here came the Rent-a-Cops. Most of them had been in corners trying to get next to something warm. Now they were in pursuit of this lone stumbling figure.

Meanwhile, the television engineers just about had their job done. They had worked successfully on the cable, and suddenly there was the picture again, showing the Colts just as they reconvened their huddle, the drunk having disappeared.

None of the people at home had seen the intrusion, of course, because their screens were dark at the time. And the newspaper reporters were not impressed. Fans often stumbled out onto the field.

If they had carefully examined the credentials of this particular fellow, however, they would have discovered that he was Stan Rotkiewicz, the business manager of NBC News, who doubled at sports events as a statistician. He was an old Roanoke tackle, capable of posing as an errant fan long enough to save the day for his network's nationwide telecast of a big football game.

In September 1958, Grange and I were in Birmingham to do an afternoon game between Auburn and Tennessee at Legion Field. And I was on the phone with Jim Corbett, who was the director of athletics at LSU.

Jim and I were very close friends. He had been the sports information director at LSU, then came to work in the NBC sports department in New York, then returned to LSU as director of athletics.

Sometimes Jim and I would call each other three or four times a day. When I wanted to know something about the college community, I asked Jim. And when he wanted some advice or an opinion, he asked me.

I had discovered, though, that it was dangerous for any of Jim's friends to mention that they wanted anything in particular. Because it was entirely likely that Jim would see that they got it. Nothing was too good for Jim Corbett's friends.

Ours was a big game in Birmingham, because Auburn had won the national championship the year before. But that night, LSU was to play Alabama at Ladd Memorial Stadium in Mobile. It was to be a rather special night for Alabama: A favorite son had returned home. This would be the very first game for Paul (Bear) Bryant as head coach at his alma mater, and he would lose it.

I was in my room at the Tutwiler Hotel in Birmingham on Saturday morning when Corbett called. We talked about the games. I asked about Rea Schuessler who was an old friend, former sports information director at Alabama, and at that time the general manager of Ladd Stadium as well as head honcho of the Senior Bowl. And in the conversation I said, "Golly, I'd like to see your game tonight, but there are no flights that would get me there in time." That's all I said.

During the fourth quarter, I noticed an extra fellow in our booth at Legion Field, a fellow I didn't recognize. During a commercial, I said, "Can we do something for you?"

He said quietly, "I'm your pilot."

"My pilot?"

"Yessir. Mr. Corbett sent a plane to bring you to Mobile after the game."

Well, he certainly had. And I climbed into the Cessna that Jim had sent and it was getting dark as we lifted off toward Mobile.

We landed there to be met by a sedan driven by a uniformed fellow who said, "I'm from the sheriff's office. Mr. Schuessler sent me to bring you to the stadium."

So I got into the car and away we went. It was getting pretty close to kickoff time as we made our way through the game traffic. Our car was equipped with a siren, which emitted a piercing scream from time to time. And when it did, automobiles drove off into the ditch or into somebody's front yard. We were advancing unimpeded at a rapid rate. It occurred to me that they would not have been so cooperative if they had known that the sheriff's car was bearing a passenger who was not going to broadcast or to work. I was just a spectator going to see the game.

When I got to the stadium the elevator took me rapidly up and I went into a booth on the roof to find Corbett and Schuessler waiting. Jim insisted that I sit down and rest a bit, since I had been hurrying and was a little out of breath. In a moment, he said, "Are you all right?"

I said, "I'm all right."

Then Corbett took a handkerchief out of his pocket and waved it. The referee and the officials started to the center of the field for the toss of the coin. Corbett smiled and said, "How does it feel to have them hold the game for you?"

Jim loved to do things out of the ordinary, and there was nothing ordinary about holding up a football game between coaches named Paul Dietzel and Bear Bryant and their not even being aware of it.

At the end of the game, which was won by LSU, I went with Corbett down to the Alabama locker room so he could pay his respects to Bryant, who was director of athletics as well as head football coach. Bryant said, "I didn't think either team played worth a damn."

LSU, though, led by Billy Cannon, went on to the national championship, and Bryant, though he lost that night, had begun a career as head coach at Alabama that would bring him off as one of the great legends of the game.

Years later, when Bryant was told about the events of that night, he said, "Is that what that delay was all about? I wondered about that."

I had not been oblivious to the fact that there were annual polls that selected the top performers in the various fields of radio and television. One of the most prestigious was that done by *Radio and Television Daily.* And in 1960, when the results came out for the previous season, I was listed as the number-one radio sportscaster in the nation, just ahead of Bill Stern. In the television category, I was rated in the number-two spot, just behind Mel Allen.

And then down in Salisbury, North Carolina, there was an organization that ran a national poll and prepared to hold a two-day series of events built around an awards dinner at which the nation's top sportscasters and sportswriters would be honored.

Dr. Ed McKenzie was the man in North Carolina who headed up the organization, and he came to New York to tell me that I had been selected as the top sportscaster in the country. And he went over to the *New York Herald Tribune* to tell Red Smith that he had been named the top sportswriter in the country. Red and I, with our wives, flew away to Salisbury, and that was the start of the organization that became the National Sportscasters and Sportswriters Association, and that fostered a National Sportscasters and Sportswriters Hall of Fame there. The organization has now led a thriving existence for a quarter of a century.

And if you ever wonder, in writing down the name of that outfit, which properly comes first, the "Sportscasters" or the "Sportswriters," then let me hasten to tell you that "Sportscasters" comes first. At an early meeting in North Carolina, we decided to settle the official order by a toss of a coin. Mel Durslag, a sportswriter for the *Los Angeles Herald Examiner,* and I represented our separate divisions. I won the toss, and "Sportscasters" became the leadoff division in the title.

In the matter of our personal life at that time, the numbers indicated by our annual income were not impressive, but the quality of life was. We had bought a little home of our own there on Old Scarsdale Road in Crestwood, Westchester County. We were taking occasional exotic vacation trips. I was getting calls to do high-paying commercials. And life was punctuated with all those little vignettes that one later holds so dear.

There was, for instance, the day that Nancy prepared to go to school for the first time. And the school was there on Old Scarsdale Road, maybe a quarter of a mile from our house.

There were two routes that she might pursue, following either of two parallel streets. I had decided that it would be advisable for her to stay off old Scarsdale Road because of the traffic.

The night before her first day, I took her by her tiny hand and we executed a dry run in the best traditions of the military. We walked the route from our house to the school, so that she would know precisely which way to go. This was going to be an exercise in independence and responsibility—a project to be undertaken alone.

When she had returned from her day at school, we sat down to talk it over. And she disclosed that she had gone halfway according to plan, then she said that she had made a mistake. Some of the other kids had turned at an intersection about halfway. They had gone down to Old Scarsdale Road and continued on to school that way. She also had a note from the teacher, which she handed to me. It said that children were advised to use Old Scarsdale Road as the route to school. Now I started to explain carefully that next day she was not to go the way we had planned. But Nancy beat me to it. She said, "I'll just make my mistake again."

It was the fall of 1960, and we were suddenly out of the college football business. ABC had been awarded the rights in a bizarre episode engineered by Ed Scherick, who had his bid submitted at the NCAA meeting by a low-echelon and generally unrecognized employee. It was a pivotal event in the career of Scherick, who went on to greater glory as a network executive, and is now a prominent movie and television producer.

I was in Nuremberg, Germany, with Fred Haney, doing baseball clinics for the U.S. Army in Europe, when I heard the announcement of the rights award to ABC, which meant that I would not be doing the college games. It was a shock. I wondered what we would do in the way of football.

Tom didn't care to go to Canada again. So we decided to see what we could do about getting some NFL football for Sunday presentation. There was still no league package. The Justice Department said you couldn't do that. So Gallery went out to Pittsburgh and signed Art Rooney's Steelers, and he went to Baltimore and signed Carroll Rosenbloom's Colts. We would make up a schedule of their available games.

Gallery told me immediately that I would do the pro football, and now they were casting about for an analyst. They selected Frankie Albert, the old left-hander from Stanford and the 49ers. So for the next two seasons, Frankie Albert and I teamed up on the NBC games. We had no game on Thanksgiving, and in 1961 I was assigned as a commentator on the telecast of the Macy's Thanksgiving Day Parade. It is so much a part of the New York scene that natives call it the Macy's Day Parade.

My partner was Ed Herlihy, an NBC special-events announcer who was best known as the commercial spokesman for Kraft cheese. And in that parade that day, there was a float representing a new baseball team that would be playing in New York the next season of 1962, a team called the New York Mets. Riding on the float were Casey Stengel, who would manage the team, and Gil Hodges, a former Dodger star who would be playing for that team. As that float came into view, Ed Herlihy, who was not a close friend of mine, said, "And now to describe the float, here is Leslie Nelson." The Mets were better known than I was.

This particular day, my wife and two daughters had choice seats in the knockdown bleachers across the street from the broadcast platform in Herald Square. They had got there early because the parade was being led that year by the gang from the popular television show *Bonanza.*

My family never missed an installment of *Bonanza.* The characters were absolutely real to us. We never thought of them as Lorne Greene, Dan Blocker, and Michael Landon. We thought of them as Ben Cartwright, Hoss, and Little Joe.

Well, the parade was under way and my people were absolutely thrilled to be right there on the same street with the heroes of the

Ponderosa. They came down the street on horseback early that cold morning at the head of the column. A long parade followed them with all sorts of bands and singers and floats and inflated figures. It took a couple of hours for the parade to pass. And through all of this, I was working away on the platform and my family was having a marvelous time.

Macy's department store was closed during the parade. But it had been spruced up and made ready for the Christmas season, which would be kicked off this day. Macy's had advised us that before the store was opened to the public, it would be the scene of a vast private party for the people who had been engaged in putting on the parade and telecast. After all, we'd been rehearsing out there in rural New Jersey for a week, we had been on our marks the morning of the parade at five A.M., and we deserved a party. So, when the parade was over, our family gathered and went into Macy's for the feast.

The one most excited about all of this was my daughter Sharon. One of Sharon's greatest pleasures was watching *Bonanza,* and her favorite was Hoss (Dan Blocker), the huge and kindly giant of a man. Dan played the role of this sometimes bumbling but always gentle and trusting cowboy, and Sharon adored him.

While the rest of us were intent on getting to the buffet table for the food and drink, which was there in abundance, Sharon had only one aim. She was going to visit with Hoss.

We went from one section of that mammoth store to another, from room to room, and we were saying hello to a lot of people and eating a lot of food, but Sharon was not having any of that. She was looking for Hoss, who was nowhere to be found.

In my presumed knowledge of this situation, I figured that I'd better start softening the disappointment for Sharon.

"It was a long parade," I explained carefully. "Since Hoss was at the head of the column, he was through over two hours ago. He wouldn't have waited around for two hours for the rest of the parade to finish. Especially not on Thanksgiving Day. After all, you did get to see him, and you were there on the very same street with him, but by now he's probably back in his hotel where it's warm and cozy."

"No," said Sharon, with a smile that was tolerant of my ignorance, "no, he's here. I'll see him in a minute." And off she went again, dragging her mother with her by the hand. "We're gonna see Hoss," she said.

No feeling father likes to see his children disappointed if he can help it, and I was feeling particularly disturbed by Sharon's insistent belief that she was going to find somebody who obviously wasn't there. We had searched all over that big store. And Dan Blocker just wasn't there. We had asked everybody we had met, and nobody had seen the cast of *Bonanza.* Everybody concurred that they had led the parade down Broadway, and, having finished their duties for the day, had doubtless retired to cozier quarters.

As a matter of fact, I was beginning to feel the urge for cozier quarters myself. The commentary on that parade telecast, which we hoped had sounded so ad lib, had been scripted down to the last comma, and done off cue cards and TelePrompTer with lip sync. That means a couple of hours of absolute strain and pressure, and it is fatiguing.

"Sharon," I said, patiently, "Hoss just isn't here. I'm sorry, but he has gone home and so should we."

"No," she said softly, her eyes still glistening in anticipation, "he's here. I'll find him."

I went off in another direction, and when I returned Sharon was gone. I asked, and was told that she and her mother had gone through a door into a room up near the entrance.

When I opened that door, I found a sight that I shall never, ever forget. There was little Sharon, with a contented smile as big as Santa Claus, sitting in the lap of Hoss. He was smiling, too, and gently rocking her back and forth while they talked.

"See," she said to her ignorant and unbelieving father, "I knew I'd find Hoss."

It's the story of a child's faith. Don't doubt it.

That season was also the end, for the time being, of our coverage of NFL football on NBC. The Justice Department decided that it would be all right for the league to negotiate an exclusive TV series.

The league meeting was held at the Warwick Hotel in New York. We at NBC Sports had our lunch a lot of days at a sort of super-delicatessen called Sager's, just across Sixth Avenue from the RCA building. Austin Gunsel was a former FBI agent now on the staff of the NFL. And Austin had been interim commissioner of the league between the time that Bert Bell died and Pete Rozelle was named. Austin actually lived in the Philadelphia area, but he was at the NFL meetings and often lunched at Sager's. He came in this one day to say that they were having a hell of a time getting everybody together at the meetings. That wasn't news. The NFL frequently had a hell of a time getting everybody together.

In this case, though, CBS had offered twenty-eight million dollars for a package. That was an awful lot of money. They had voted several times, but it had to be unanimous. And every time they came to the Pittsburgh Steelers, Mr. Art Rooney, clutching a cigar between his fingers, would rise and say simply that he could not vote for the deal because he still had a handshake agreement with Tom Gallery at NBC. And so the NFL and CBS were being kept apart, kept from arranging a twenty-eight-million-dollar deal by Mr. Rooney's inherent sense of honesty.

I skipped across the street to Gallery's office to tell him what was happening. He hadn't anticipated that. "I called Carroll," he said, meaning Baltimore's Rosenbloom, "and I told him he was released. I assumed that Art would know that we couldn't do anything with one team."

But Rooney knew only one way to go—a deal is a deal until it isn't a deal anymore. Gallery got him on the phone to tell him that he was released and that NBC could not combat the package.

Assured that he was now in the clear, when the next vote was called, Art Rooney voted with the rest, and CBS had twenty-eight million dollars' worth of football, including the Pittsburgh Steelers.

I also did basketball for NBC. As early as 1954, on coverage of NBA basketball, I teamed up with Marty Glickman. And then Curt Gowdy and I worked as a team for a number of years. And we sort of worked out the format as the problems arose. For instance, we discovered that we needed time-outs for the insertion of commercials at certain times when the coaches did not feel inclined to call time-outs.

There was no problem with the owners. They were perfectly willing to have time-outs called at any time. It was a matter of mechanics.

On the football field, you could get the attention of an official near the sideline between plays. But basketball was a rather continuous-action game. It would be difficult to stop the game.

It was quickly agreed that time-outs called for television would not be charged to either team, but how would this be accomplished? Well, the commissioner of the NBA at the time was Maurice Podoloff, a delightful and efficient man who was also quite practical. He was traveling to all the televised games to be sure that everything went well. He knew that the future of his sport lay in its success on the tube. He suggested that he would be available and mobile at courtside. And when television needed a time-out, the stage manager would tell Podoloff. He would then walk briskly around behind the bench, tap one coach or the other on the shoulder, and say, "Call time out." That was a direct order from the commissioner of the league, and brought no rebuttal. That's how the time-outs were handled. And most efficiently.

My partner on the basketball telecasts at one stretch was Joe Lapchick, who had coached the Knicks and St. John's, and who had been captain of the old barnstorming New York Celtics. One Saturday afternoon we were entering the old Madison Square Garden (the one on Eighth Avenue between Forty-ninth and Fiftieth). Saturday was a busy day around the Garden because the kids were out of school and they flocked by the thousands to the sports events.

Working on television makes one readily identifiable, so Joe Lapchick and I were immediately pinned to the wall by this autograph-seeking horde. There was nothing to do but sign the scraps of paper and programs that were being thrust into our faces. And the crowd was getting larger. We had been occupied for about a half hour, with no relief in sight, when Lapchick looked over to me and yelled, "When do you think we'll get out of this?"

I remembered that night years before at DuPont High School in Old Hickory, Tennessee, when the New York Celtics had played an exhibition, and I said to Joe now, "I wouldn't know. I remember one night waiting two hours to get your autograph."

He really didn't have any idea what I was talking about.

CHAPTER 19

Meet the Mets

It all happened so quickly. On New Year's Day of 1962, I was just sailing happily along. I was announcing the big sports events on television, and network organizational policy had changed my title to "Manager of Sports." (No matter what they called me, I was Gallery's assistant.) So what happened?

Well, the New York Mets happened.

After Walter O'Malley had taken the Dodgers from Brooklyn to Los Angeles and persuaded Horace Stoneham to take the Giants from the Polo Grounds to San Francisco, New York was without National League baseball. That painful deprivation went on for four years.

Then Mrs. Joan Payson was awarded a National League franchise in New York. She hired George Weiss as president. (He couldn't be general manager because the terms of his separation as general manager of the Yankees prevented his becoming GM of any other New York team for a specified period. So he wasn't the GM. He was the president. But a general manager by any other name still makes the decisions.) One of Weiss's first decisions was to hire Casey Stengel as his field manager. Casey had been fired as manager of the Yankees after the 1960 season. So he had been off the field in 1961, and that had been about as long as Casey cared to remain on the sidelines. In a few months he would reach his seventy-second birthday.

The various breweries in New York had made competitive pitches for the radio and television rights to the Met games. The award was made to Liebmann Breweries, makers of Rheingold beer. It was five years for six million dollars. Since the franchise itself and all the players had cost just a little more than three million dollars, the Mets were now firmly in the black. They always would be.

And I was being urged to take the job as the number-one broadcaster in the crew that would announce the Met games on radio and television.

There were intriguing negotiations back and forth. At one point, the agency proposed that Chris Schenkel and I take the job as a team.

At this time, though, Chris's stock as a CBS network sportscaster was really booming. He was the voice of the winning New York Giants pro football team, the toast of Manhattan. And he was doing horse racing and boxing and bowling and a little of everything. Chris had given the offer a lot of thought. He was already doing some of the Milwaukee Braves road games, but not on a regular basis. Now he decided that he did not want to make a permanent change. But there is no nicer and more considerate person in any field than Chris Schenkel, so he called and asked if I would meet him in the Cromwell drugstore on the ground floor of the RCA building. I did. Chris simply wanted to make sure that I understood his reasons for turning down the Mets job. It was a considerate gesture.

I was doing a lot of thinking about my profession. I was already aware that there were different types of sports announcers.

The network announcer has an allegiance to Nielsen and to his network. He must try to perform in a manner that will attract the highest ratings. Make no mistake about one thing. The network-television business runs on ratings. An announcer who is not aware of that will shortly be in some other line of work. He does not feel any particular elation at the identity of the winner or loser. He has no connection with the teams. He would prefer that his football games end with one team coming from behind to win on a spectacular move in the last thirty seconds of play. In that case, presumably, the audience will have stayed for the whole game.

The baseball announcer need never have the feeling of being lonely. He has thousands of friends around him everywhere he goes. He gets loads of fan mail, which sometimes get to be a pain in the neck. But he gets it. Not all of his fans approve of what he does, but they listen and watch and frequently respond and advise.

I had observed that, generally speaking, network sports announcers did not tend to live to a ripe old age. Graham McNamee had died in his fifties, absolutely burned out. Ted Husing had endured years of blindness before his death. Harry Wismer had died at age fifty-four. Bill Stern had been in an institution. Bill Slater was confined to his home during a long illness. I thought there was a reason for all this. I thought the network announcer had to strive for perfection. If he had a bad day, there was nothing he could do about it until the following weekend when he would next perform. And during that week, the concern could destroy him.

On the other hand, I had noticed that baseball announcers seemed to go right on forever. Bob Elson in Chicago had been calling balls and strikes seemingly since the beginning of time. Harry Caray must have started with Abner Doubleday, and was still going strong. Mel Allen was approaching twenty-five years in the trade. Byrum Saam had been announcing baseball in Philadelphia since 1937.

I thought there was a reason for the continuity and longevity of the baseball announcer. There is something therapeutic about being permitted to go out there and perform every day.

Baseball is broadcast like it is played. Baseball players do not try to get up, sky-high, for every game, every day. That would be impossible. There will be bad days. Maybe a player will strike out three times. But he does not allow that to destroy him. After all, he will be out there again tomorrow, maybe he'll get a couple of hits, and everything will be all right. After all, baseball is a percentage game. And that, too, is the way baseball is broadcast. There will be days when you can't get the names right, can't get the score right, can't do anything right. But not to worry. You will perform spectacularly tomorrow, and everything will be just fine.

And there seemed to me to be another valuable consideration. Consider the life of the baseball announcer. His income is sufficient to allow him to live a comfortable life. He has a month in spring training that is lived in about the most comfortable place one can imagine in the best of conditions. His season is only six months long, and you can't beat the hours. The hours aren't as short as they once were, but they aren't all that long, either. For one who likes the game, it is pleasant, exciting work. And if you don't like the game, you should be doing something else anyway.

I was beginning to be firmly convinced that the best possible life available to a sports announcer is that of the major-league-baseball announcer. It might not provide the richest financial rewards or the widest national recognition. The network announcer perhaps will achieve more fame and fortune. But it seemed to me that there was a chance for a lot of happiness and contentment and excitement in that life at the old ball park.

Then, too, there was a strong feeling for baseball in my family. My wife hadn't been nicknamed for Mickey Cochrane for nothing. And she had been to the World Series with Fette Gallery, Tom's wife. Tom had been business manager of the Yankees, and Fette still knew all the people who worked around the park, the cops, the parking-lot attendants, the ushers. Mickie had been impressed by the fact that all these people greeted Mrs. Gallery as an old friend. Mickie was beginning to realize that major league baseball in many ways was sort of a family operation. If you are part of it, you are accepted at all levels, and you can do no wrong.

Then Mickie went to a Giants game at the Polo Grounds with Maggie Hodges, the wife of Giants broadcaster Russ Hodges. Mickie and I had been through the turmoil and frustration of getting used to the traffic and parking problems of New York City. We had gone to Yankee games, with the kids, but we always had trouble, lots of trouble, in finding a place to park the car.

When Mickie came home from the Polo Grounds that day, she said to me, "Would you believe that Russ Hodges has his own private parking place at the ball park?"

It impressed us. In fact, almost everything about the baseball life was attractive to us. And I was about to change my New York job in order to get a place to park my car.

At the 1961 World Series in Cincinnati, I had spent a long and delightful evening in the company of Jack Murphy, sports editor of the *San Diego Union,* and Jesse Outler, sports editor of *The Atlanta Constitution.* We had installed ourselves in a booth of a rathskeller in the neighborhood of Fountain Square, and there we had discussed all the pertinent topics of the day—baseball, the European economy, and women. When we got to women we went into extra innings, and it was a late hour when we adjourned there on the Cincinnati sidewalk at Wiggins corner.

Jack said to me as we parted, "If you hear of any baseball broadcasting jobs, let me know. Brother Bob is looking." I promised that I would let Jack know, never dreaming that by the next season Bob and I would be partners on the Mets.

I did not know then, either, that less than twenty years later, Jack Murphy would be stricken and cut down by cancer. And that in his honor, the stadium in San Diego would be named San Diego Jack Murphy Stadium.

I was also keeping in almost hourly touch with Gallery. He thought I was getting chiseled by the Mets' offer of forty-five thousand dollars. "Nobody," he said, "sets up a budget for a new project like this at forty-five thousand dollars. It's at least fifty thousand and you are getting chiseled for the five grand." To Gallery, it was a matter of principle.

Personally, I was not all that concerned. I was still happy that baseball announcers have five months in which to do anything they want. Some worked football or basketball, and some didn't work at all. One year Ernie Harwell went with his family to Majorca in the Mediterranean.

I was more concerned about the length of the commitment than anything else. It was one of those typical deals. I had them for two years, but only for two. But with an additional three-year option, they had me for five. If for some reason the arrangement did not work out—if the team blew up, if fans weren't interested, if the sponsor's wife didn't like the color of my eyes, then I would lose it all. I knew that my departure at NBC would leave a slot that would be filled in the twinkling of an eye. If the baseball blew up, I would be back on the street. In fact, I was risking everything on the future of the New York Mets.

Of course, there had been all sorts of wild rumors in New York about who the Mets announcers would be. It seemed that the man most mentioned was Les Keiter. He had re-created National League games in New York after the Giants and Dodgers had left, and he had built up something of a following. It was said, too, that the Mets people had liked his audition tape.

Dick Young of the *Daily News* was trying to get me on the phone. He knew that Durocher and I had done the NBC *Major League Baseball* for three years, and hearing rumors that I might be interested in the Mets, Dick wanted to see if the deal included Durocher.

One Friday, Mickie and I were having breakfast at the Sheraton-West Hotel on Wilshire Boulevard in Los Angeles, when I was paged to the house phone. It was Norm Varney of the J. Walter Thompson Advertising Agency in New York. Norm had been putting the deal together and handling affairs for Rheingold and the Mets. He said it was all set, that he had approval from everyone concerned, forty-five thousand dollars per year for two years, with an additional three-year option at fifty thousand dollars a year.

I said okay and we agreed to make the announcement with a press luncheon at Mamma Leone's the following Wednesday.

When I walked back to the breakfast table, Mickie knew what had happened. She knew by the look on my face. I leaned down and gave her a kiss and said, "We're in another line of work."

It was an emotional time. It was a big move. I had risked everything in pursuit of some intangible items in the hope that they would all add up to an enrichment of our lives.

I was making a studied and calculated move from the fame and fortune of the networks to the life of a major-league-baseball announcer.

For the next seventeen seasons, the broadcasting crew of the Mets would be Lindsey Nelson, Ralph Kiner, and Bob Murphy. I would continue to do network assignments, lots of network assignments, but I would avoid a lot of the personal pressure through the simple fact that I did not make my living on network events. I felt no urge to compete with others on the staff of my network. I never felt that I had to be the headliner. I did baseball for a living, and I did network football, literally for fun, although a baseball announcer making forty-five thousand dollars does not turn down the network fee.

That afternoon, Mickie and I got into our rental car and decided just to take a long drive around Los Angeles. We wanted to talk, to soak up some of the well-advertised California sunshine, and mostly to avoid the telephones.

We stopped at a California-type drive-in for lunch, a dab of avocado and a soft drink. And we reminisced about my career, during which I had exceeded all my expectations, exceeded all the dreams I had allowed myself to dream when I was Bill Stern's student spotter. Mickie had a question.

"Is there anything," she said, "anything at all, any event that you wanted to do and have not done?"

It took me only a second to answer. I said, "Yes, there is. I always hoped that someday, somehow, I would get to do the Rose Bowl. Since that year I came out here for Bill Stern as a student at the end of the 1939 season, I dreamed about the day that I would walk into the booth and announce the Rose Bowl game myself."

I had been driving aimlessly, but now as we talked I found that I was heading for Pasadena. And when I got there, I turned off the freeway, drove down Colorado, and then turned off at the Rose Bowl.

All was quiet. There was no noise in the neighborhood. We got out of the car and walked through a tunnel into the stadium. It was before the time when our inconsiderate society would require locked doors on everything. We climbed about halfway up the stands of that magnificent saucer. We looked all about us. And I said to Mickie, "This one—this is the only event that I really wanted to do and didn't. But you can't have everything. I'm happy."

Next day at the Los Angeles Memorial Coliseum I was in the television booth getting my spotting boards checked out before the Pro Bowl game. It was a hot day. Les Keiter was doing the radio play-by-play in the adjacent booth. He had looked through the glass toward my position and then had hurried over. He stood behind me on a raised portion of the floor and said, "I just heard a rumor that you are going to take the job as broadcaster for the Mets." Well, Les had good information, and he had been in a good position to get it because if I had not taken the job, it might well have gone to him. Maybe they had told him already. But I was under bond not to say anything. All I could do was look at Les and say, "Where did you ever hear a thing like that?"

Les looked as though he had seen a ghost, perhaps the ghost of things that might have been.

In our conversations, Gallery had asked if I would mind staying through February at NBC. I would be heading for spring training in St. Petersburg on March 1. So, I was in the office on Wednesday morning when George Weiss called from his suite at the Savoy Plaza. The press conference at Leone's would be at noon. George wanted to know if I could come by his place for a moment before then.

George Weiss had the reputation in New York of being a cold fish. He was said to be an unemotional, calculating businessman. Gallery and Weiss had not exactly enjoyed a sparkling relationship during their years together at the Yankees.

Now I wondered what interesting developments might be afloat when Weiss sent for me minutes before the announcement.

In fact, it was just a courtesy call. Weiss wanted me to know how pleased he was that I was going to broadcast the Met games. He wanted me to know that he would be available at any time. It was the first in a string of events that brought me out as a fan of

George Martin Weiss, one of the shyest men I've ever known.

Just then, I had one more matter to take up with George Weiss. I said, "I want to buy a season's box of four seats."

Weiss looked a little surprised. He liked the idea of a sale, but he was painfully honest. "You don't have to buy tickets," he said. "Tickets are available to you in reasonable number."

"I know that," I said, "but I want a box that I can see from the broadcast booth. I want my family to be in the same seats every day. I want this to become a family project."

I kept a box at Mets games for eighteen years, paying the price that increased through the years. And it was the best investment I ever made. At breakfast we talked about baseball. At dinner we talked about baseball. It was the common interest of our family. Sharon developed an understanding of the game and loved it. She wrote down on her scorecard the numbers of the players in proper batting order as they were flashed up on the big scoreboard. She always had a pencil, and she kept score.

Everybody knows that the manner of keeping score, like religion, is a personal matter. Each has his own method that only he can decipher. I always liked sportswriter Henry McLemore's story of looking at his wife's scorecard and discovering that she had lettered in "HWHI." When Henry inquired about that particular symbol, his wife smilingly explained that it meant "He walked him intentionally." Well, I looked at Sharon's scorecard one day and discovered that after each player, in its proper order and inning, there was a neat zero. This seemed like an odd scoring system to me, and I inquired. Sharon patiently explained to her unlettered father, "It means that he has been here and is gone." I suppose that's as good a scoring system as any. It's important, I think, to know who has been here and is gone.

Now, since I had gone out and got a brand-new job, Mickie thought it was time that she went out and got us a brand-new house. And she began to look around.

We had discovered that for the most part people who live in the greater New York area do not know a great deal about the greater New York area except the area in which they live. To a family in Brooklyn, Westchester County is no more familiar than China. And a native of New Jersey can manipulate the tunnels and bridges with ease, but he doesn't know in which direction Long Island is.

Of course, we had no such narrow restrictions. We lived in Westchester, but we still knew where Long Island was. It was where the airports were. And we often went to the airports. We didn't go anywhere else on Long Island, but we knew it was out there.

We decided that since we had lived inland for most of our lives, it was time for us to explore the shore.

So one fine day, Mickie and I gassed up and headed without direction or specific purpose in the direction of Long Island.

We headed along the North Shore, and were surprised to find that it looked so much like New England. Of course, the only thing separating the North Shore from New England was Long Island Sound. We didn't know that.

We went through one community after another on Route 25A. And we just kept right on going. Finally, we came to Huntington. And there we found a gorgeous home under construction. It was just off Crescent Beach Drive. In fact, it was on Crescent Beach, a wide sweep of sand bordered by Lloyd's Neck and Eaton's Neck. It looked straight across to Stamford, Connecticut. And this particular house included a private beach. We couldn't have ordered anything more perfect for our purposes. So we bought it, built the house to our specifications, and lived there for years. It was a long drive from Huntington to Manhattan or to Shea Stadium. But my hours were different now. Since I was doing baseball, I wasn't in as big a hurry. And an hour on the Long Island Expressway was small price to pay for the serenity of the waterfront in Huntington.

Frequently, when one leaves one's place of employment, particularly in the flamboyant field of network television, there is a big going-away party. When I have been personally involved, I have always discouraged that sort of thing.

So on my last day at NBC, when time came for lunch we went quietly over to the Forum on Forty-eighth Street. It was a place where we sometimes lunched when we had time, and Gallery was a consistent check-grabber.

This was my going-away luncheon. In attendance were Tom Gallery, Perry Smith, Harry Coyle, and Lou Kusserow. They presented me with a black leather briefcase, and inside in silver letters was the inscription "To the world's greatest sports announcer from the NBC sports department." During lunch they had checked the case at the restaurant checkroom, and when I opened it I was surprised to see that the maître d', Andy Anderson, had slipped in a classy set of cuff links.

And that was how I left NBC after ten years of working the nation's top sports events there, and headed for full time in the wonderful world of major league baseball.

I had never had such a feeling of freedom as that I felt the day that I packed my things and started to drive south toward St. Petersburg, Florida, and the Mets spring-training camp.

As I drove down to the George Washington Bridge and crossed into New Jersey, I was almost singing. This seemed like a totally different life, and it was.

I was to learn that I was not alone in my joyous reaction to the release from daily duties that annual departure for spring training brought. I love the story that the late Red Smith once told me. Red was the sports columnist for the *New York Herald Tribune,* and he had become friends with Frank Graham, the sports columnist of the *New York Journal American.* Since they were both going to Florida for spring training, Red suggested that they go together in his car. Frank thought it was an excellent idea. On the morning they were to leave, Red left his home in Stamford, Connecticut, and picked Frank up at his home in Westchester County. Red needed to take care of a few things at the office, such as picking up a cash advance, so they drove into Manhattan. When they arrived in the crowded block where the *Trib* was located, Red said to Frank, "I'll only be a moment. If you have to move the car, just drive around the block."

With a perfectly placid expression, Graham said, "Oh, I don't drive."

Red said, "You what?"

Frank said, "I don't know how to drive an automobile. I never learned."

That meant, of course, that Red Smith was going to Florida, presumably sharing driving duties with a man who didn't drive.

Red was still a little shaken, then, as they drove across the George Washington Bridge into New Jersey. There they came upon a service station and stopped for gasoline. Since there was an adjacent restaurant and motel, they decided on a cup of coffee, and that led to lengthy conversation. In fact, they became aware that lunchtime was approaching, and they saw no reason to get on the New Jersey Turnpike immediately. Instead, they had lunch, a long lunch. And in celebration of the start of spring training, they decided on a drink. In fact, that led to more conversation, and that led to another drink. Before long it was midafternoon, and they saw no reason to advance. Instead they checked into the motel, where they had dinner, several drinks, and much more conversation. On the first day of their journey to Florida, they had made it all the way to the Jersey end of the George Washington Bridge.

Well, I made it farther than that. I got all the way down into North Carolina. I wanted to put some distance between me and Manhattan, because I was afraid that NBC might be calling.

In St. Petersburg, I located the Colonial Inn on St. Pete Beach, which housed most of the players and a lot of the Mets people, including Casey Stengel. The Mets business office had been set up in the old Soreno Hotel near Al Lang Field downtown. The Colonial Inn was a long distance from Miller Huggins Field, where daily drills were held, and Al Lang Field, where the exhibition games would be played. But there was a sound and necessary reason for its selection. In those days of almost total segregation in 1962, the Colonial Inn was the only hotel that would take the black players as well as the white.

It was a busy spring. The Mets were signing every prospect who could move. They had a stream of players coming and going. It appeared that nobody really knew who all of them were. We had a television crew on hand, and we were filming and taping and doing all sorts of commercials for Rheingold beer and features for future presentation.

When we finally broke camp and headed north, our first stop was Norfolk, Virginia. The bus scheduled to pick us up at the airport and transport us to the hotel was a no-show.

Next morning, the Met players were guests of the Norfolk Sports Club at breakfast. I was halfway through the fried eggs when I noticed that someone was tapping on my shoulder. I looked up, and discovered that it was Casey Stengel. He said, "Well, I was wondering if you'd be interested in introducing our squad to these nice people on account of they are the hosts and we should tell 'em who they are hosting and maybe you could do that."

I told Casey, in all truth, "Skipper, I would love to introduce our squad, but the fact is that I do not know all of them by sight. There are some people on our squad that I do not recognize."

Casey said, "Well, that's the problem I got—I don't know 'em either. I wonder if Mr. Hemus would like to introduce 'em."

Solly Hemus was one of Casey's coaches, and Solly made the

introductions, more or less correctly. The charm of the Mets in those beginning days, I suppose, was their informality.

The Mets then flew into New York for a one-day workout at their home park, the old Polo Grounds. The team was quartered in the plush Savoy Plaza on Fifth Avenue, where the General Motors building now stands.

When I examined the facilities available to the broadcasters, I was not all that thrilled. Originally, the press box for the print media had been suspended from the front of the upper deck, and there was one entrance, accessible by walking to the top rim, then down through the upper deck to a thin span that led over an open area into the press box. When radio came along, first the announcers had worked in the front-row boxes of the upper deck. The announcers and adjacent spectators were side by side. Finally, though, a radio booth was constructed at each end of the press box, one for home radio and one for visitors. Because the press box itself was somewhat curved, the radio boxes were situated fairly well up the first and third baselines. Now two more boxes had been tacked on for the television announcers, one on either side. The home television box was so far up the first baseline that calling pitches was extremely difficult. Squarely behind home plate a television monitor had been installed for the use of the baseball writers. It seemed to me that if an area of about two feet were made available for an announcer position behind the plate, the announcer could do his job. And it also seemed to me that if we cut a couple of holes in that tin roof at either end of the press box, there would be easier access for writers and broadcasters alike.

I was foolishly hopeful as I proposed to George Weiss that a few changes be made to give us facilities that would at least be workable.

I discussed the situation with Weiss on the plane out to St. Louis for the opening game. Knowing that Weiss was reputedly a man who did not spend money wildly, I estimated that the total expenditures would be only a few hundred dollars. Weiss said that would be no problem. He pointed out that they had already spent thousands in getting that old ball park ready.

But when we got to St. Louis and had the first game rained out, Weiss came to me and explained that my project for improving the position of the broadcasters had been killed before it got started. He had discussed it with Tom Meany, a former baseball writer who was public-relations director of the Mets. Meany had explained that the Baseball Writers Association of America was in charge of the press box. And for the next two seasons, the broadcasters sat out there on the end of the horseshoe and wondered what the pitches were. Fortunately, as it turned out, calling pitches was no big deal. The pitches served up by the Met hurlers seldom needed calling. Few of them ever got to the catcher. They were rejected by the large booming bats of the opposition.

After having been thwarted by rain once, the Mets did get the opener in against the Cardinals in St. Louis and lost. Then we came home after the game and checked into the Manhattan Hotel on Eighth Avenue. The next day was an off day, and a parade was scheduled up lower Broadway.

I realize that it seems a little odd that this baseball team had played only one game and lost it, but was now to be honored with a ticker-tape parade. But that's the way it was. National League baseball had been gone from New York for four seasons, and there were a lot of National League fans in New York. The Yankees had already discovered that those old Dodger and Giant fans were just not ever going to be Yankee fans. That first season of 1958 after the Dodgers and Giants had gone, the Yankees had anticipated that their attendance would go up. It went down.

Now those National League fans had their team—the Mets. And we were loaded into a string of open convertibles with our names on placards taped to the sides. I sat on the folded top with my feet on the backseat of a white Buick. We were the broadcasting crew and our names were there in large block letters—LINDSEY NELSON, RALPH KINER, BOB MURPHY. And here we went up confetti alley, 'midst the cheers of thousands along the curb and tons of ticker tape showering down from open office windows. This is what had been experienced by national heroes such as Lindbergh and Eisenhower. I figured it was something I would have to tell my grandchildren, about the time I was honored with a ticker-tape parade up lower Broadway in New York City, the experience and thrill of a lifetime. It was the first of a whole string of unique dividends that would derive from being associated with the Mets of New York.

From the start, though, the Mets in action looked like the Light Brigade at Balaclava. They bravely took the field each day and were systematically destroyed. Only their field marshal, Casey Stengel, remained undaunted. In an earlier life, he had acquired a continuing endurance for triumph and disaster.

The first player selected had been Hobie Landrith, a catcher. And when someone inquired of Casey why one chose a catcher first in building a new team, he patiently explained, with unassailable logic, "Because if you ain't got no catcher, you get all passed balls."

In an early game in Pittsburgh, catcher Landrith got a little overanxious and moved too far underneath the batter, who swung his bat and hit Hobie squarely in the back of the head. It was temporarily disastrous.

Preparing to do his first pregame interview as a television announcer, Ralph Kiner thought it best that he start with a question that would have an easy answer. His guest was Choo Choo Coleman. Ralph assumed that there must be an obvious story there, so he said, "Choo Choo, how did you get that nickname?"

Ralph settled down for the relation of the story that he guessed Coleman must have recounted a thousand times. Ralph was a little nonplussed when Choo Choo said, "I don't know."

And there was the day the Mets were playing the Giants at the Polo Grounds. Roger Craig was the Met pitcher, and twice Willie McCovey had pulled inside fastballs into the unoccupied grandstand seats in the right-field corner. Manager Stengel called time and went to the mound. As he faced pitcher Craig, he said, "At the end of this season they are going to tear down the Polo Grounds. And if you keep throwing inside fastballs to McCovey, they're gonna have a helluva head start down there in the right-field stands."

On a plane one day I was in conversation with Casey Stengel. Actually, to say that you have been in conversation with Casey Stengel is an inaccuracy. You did not converse with Casey Stengel, you listened. If you had anything to say, Casey couldn't care less. If you did not want to continue on those terms, take a hike. Being around Casey was therapeutic in many ways. You had to rid yourself of all ego and realize that you also had no identity. Casey not only didn't know who you were, he didn't care who you were. He had met all the new people he was interested in meeting. At his age, which was considerable, he was like the satisfied guy in the draw poker game who was just going to play it out with what he had. That was quite enough. So I listened on the plane as Casey explained about his new team.

Casey, of course, had managed those great Yankee teams, a string of world champions with superstars named DiMaggio, Berra, Ford, Reynolds, and Mantle. He was far removed from his days as manager of the Boston Braves, or Bees, or whatever they were. He had managed the Yanks to the American League pennant in 1960, and had been out of the game only the one season of 1961 before coming back with these Mets. Now he was saying, "Well, we got to work on the little finesses.

"We got to work on the pickoff of the runner at first when there's runners at first and second, and we got to work on the first baseman holding the runner in a bunt situation, breaking in a couple of steps and breaking right back to take a pickoff throw."

In the game that day, the Mets had been soundly trounced, something like 17–1. That night, Casey was beginning to see the light and suspect the worst. When he saw me, that wrinkled old face lit up in a sour smile and he said, "The little finesses ain't gonna be our problem."

The fans who gathered at the Polo Grounds to watch this new team were a conglomerate. There were old Dodger fans, old Giant fans, and young fans whose virgin allegiance was to the Metropolitans, the name chosen in a contest, although Mrs. Payson favored "Meadowlarks."

If there were some who had dreamed that this might be a competitive baseball team, they did not have long to dream. And I was one of them. I had been hopeful, but it became instantly apparent that the competitive skills on the field were a shade short.

The problem seemed more like one of survival. And yet those fans came out and seemed to have a marvelous time. And the radio and television ratings, right from the start, were better than anticipated. It has often been said that everybody loves an underdog. Well, we surely had an underdog here, and the fans of this big city loved 'em.

There were problems you wouldn't dream of, such as a language barrier. The shortstop, most days, was Elio Chacon, a Spanish-speaking ballplayer. The left fielder was Frank Thomas, sometimes referred to in baseball circles as "the big donkey." And in center field there was Richie Ashburn, a veteran who confused the issue because he still had some legitimate major-league talent left.

The issue was often confused, in fact, by a number of things. When a pop fly would go up in short left-center field, the three players would converge. Ashburn would yell, "I got it." Thomas would stop, and Chacon would run over Ashburn as the ball fell for a double.

Ashburn soon decided that in the interest of continuing good health he was going to have to take some remedial action. So he went to Joe Christopher, who also spoke Spanish, and said, "How do you say 'I got it' in Spanish?"

Joe advised him to try "Yo la tengo."

So, Ashburn went back to his position in center field, sounding like the little boy on the way to the grocery for his mother, repeating aloud, "Yo la tengo, yo la tengo, yo la tengo."

Sure enough, here came one of those pesky pop flies, and the three players converged. Ashburn yelled, "Yo la tengo, yo la tengo." And, wonder of wonders, Chacon stopped. And Thomas ran over him.

The earliest model Met, I suppose, was Marv Throneberry. As the perfect symbol for this struggling band of inept warriors, Throneberry appeared to have no talent of any kind. Baseball scouts like to catalogue the talents of players by department, pointing out that there are five general areas of performance in which one may define a player's talents. They said that Throneberry scored a clean sweep—he could not hit or hit with power. He could not field, run, or throw. The Met fans loved him.

It is perhaps worth noting that until this very day, almost a quarter of a century later, Throneberry does not see himself in that light. He had had a brief turn with the Yankees before he arrived to strain Stengel's sanity with the Mets, but he likes to recall the days when he hoped that he was on the way to becoming the next Mickey Mantle. His recollections of the Met days are strictly "laugh, clown, laugh." He has gained a modicum of late fame and income appearing in the television commercials for Miller Lite beer. But his role there, as it was with the Mets, is as a symbol of futility: "I don't know why they asked me to be in this commercial."

One afternoon against the Cubs, Marvelous Marv Throneberry lined the ball into the right-field corner, rounded first, and headed for second as the right fielder, George Altman, chased the ball. Throneberry got the sign to continue to third, and he arrived sliding safely in a great cloud of dust. The Met fans were in a state of high jubilation. And then the Cubs pulled a routine appeal play. The pitcher tossed the ball to Ernie Banks at first, and first-base umpire Tom Gorman called Throneberry out for having missed first base. Casey Stengel was off the bench in a flash, on his way out to confront the umpire. But as he passed coach Cookie Lavagetto at first base, the coach stopped him and said something. Casey slowed to a walk, approached Gorman and made a perfunctory appeal, and then retired meekly to the dugout.

When the game had ended in another Met defeat, I went by Casey's office in the clubhouse beyond center field. I said, "Skipper, it looked as though you were ready to launch a war with Umpire Gorman until you got to Lavagetto. What did he say to you?"

There was a wry smile on Stengel's face as he said, "Well, Mr. Lavagetto said, 'Don't argue too long, Skipper, he missed second, too.' "

Life with the Mets was altogether marvelous.

The All-Star game that year of 1962 was held at what was then called D.C. Stadium (now Robert F. Kennedy Memorial Stadium) in Washington. Fred Hutchinson, who had managed the Cincinnati Reds to the pennant the previous season, was manager of the National League team. And for his first-base coach, he had wisely selected Casey Stengel.

I got a call from Tom Gallery asking if I would like to be one of the announcers on the round-the-world broadcast on NBC Radio. And that is how I came to be in Washington.

I was well aware that the president of the United States, John F. Kennedy, had come out to the ball game, and he was seated in a box near the first-base dugout. At one point, he indicated that he would like to talk to the first-base coach. And I have it on no less an authority than Mr. Stengel himself that this is what happened.

The president wanted to ask the first-base coach a few questions about the game. Stengel, of course, had been in baseball since roughly the time of Abner Doubleday, or Alexander Cartwright, or whoever. And Casey knew that nobody ever talks to the first-base coach. That position is largely honorary. All the signs are flashed by the third-base coach. The first-base coach whistles, claps his hands, helps the pitcher on with his jacket if he gets on base, and slaps base runners solidly on the fanny as they fly by. Now, this very unique first-base coach was in earnest conversation with the president of the United States. He was a presidential adviser.

But, first, last, and always, Casey Stengel was a baseball man, and he knew that the leadoff batter was stepping into the batter's box, and the game was about to resume. So, without regard for presidential protocol, Casey said, "Mr. President, I'd love to stay here and talk to you, and if I was running this here team I'd do that, but I'm working for this here other fellow today, and Mr. Hutchinson, I am sure, would like for me to get back on my job at the first base, and I enjoyed visiting with you but I gotta go." And he did.

From our position in the broadcast booth, all we could see was President Kennedy bent over in laughter.

When the Mets held an Old Timers Day at the Polo Grounds and invited back some of the great stars who had played for the earlier Giants and Dodgers, one of the guests was Bill Terry. Few baseball men ever had better credentials. Terry as a player was superb and once batted .400. He had succeeded John McGraw as manager of the fabled Giants. Many thought he might have been the greatest first baseman ever. Now it was the night after the Old Timers game, and we were at a special dinner in the upstairs room at Toots Shor's restaurant. I was seated on the dais between Casey Stengel and Terry.

At one point, Terry turned to me and said, "By the way, you did a fine job of handling the introductions out there this afternoon."

I was flattered but properly modest when I said, "Well, I appreciate your saying that, but the staff did a good job of getting everything ready and Tom Meany wrote most of the introductory material."

Terry interrupted impatiently. "Oh, I understand that you had help, that the staff backed you up," he said. "But, you see, you had to *do* it."

Bill Terry reached me with that concept, which has stayed with me since. I realized that in every undertaking, despite all the preparation and all the input by others, there comes a time when somebody has to *do* it. That is the key man, the man who does it.

I came to understand, too, that all who endure for long periods in any field must have a quality of toughness and perhaps ruthlessness. If you show me a sportscaster who has been around for a lot of years, I will show you a man who from time to time has done a bit of slashing to stay there. And if he has endured for a considerable time, you can bet that he has been careful always to be ready. As Danny Kaye once remarked when we discussed this subject, "The challenger is never out of condition."

In August, we got a new catcher, a Brooklyn boy who had played for both the Dodgers and the Giants, named Joe Pignatano. And in his spare time he was also the bullpen coach.

His first night on that job, Pignatano was dutifully down in the bullpen with the relief pitchers when the phone rang in about the seventh inning. It was Mr. Stengel. In the manner of a general issuing a terse order, Stengel said, simply, "Get Nelson up."

In baseball lingo, that means that the manager wants Nelson to start warming up for possible entry into the game. Pignatano understood that. But he had made a solid study of the roster, and there was a confusing fact here. The Mets didn't have any Nelson. Pignatano knew that. But he also knew that he was not going to argue with Casey Stengel on the telephone during the game.

Of course, what Joe did not know was that all season long Casey had confused the names of Nelson and Miller. It was natural—each name had six letters. But Nelson was a broadcaster named Lindsey, and Miller was a pitcher named Bob. On the accepted premise that one who is dealing with Casey Stengel must forfeit all right to any identity, both Bob and I were aware of and accepted the switch.

Pignatano didn't know about the identity switch, but he was resourceful. In the bullpen he picked a baseball out of the bag, balanced it carefully on the pitching rubber, and said in a tone of confidence and command, "Nelson!" And Bob Miller immediately got up and started throwing. He knew who he was.

Prominent in the memory of the early Mets, there was the Sunday afternoon when a couple decided that for their entertainment they would take in a Met game at the Polo Grounds. The Mets weren't winning, but they were drawing big crowds. People came to the ball park knowing that their team wouldn't win, but some of them were determined to entertain themselves. Certainly, that's what this couple had decided.

From here on, I speak from hearsay because I was not an eyewitness. I also was not far away, but I was busy with the broadcasting business, and was behind a microphone. However, let me say that in the best journalistic traditions of responsible reporting, I have substantiated this account with more than two reports from sources that I know and consider reliable. Fairly reliable, anyway.

It seems that this Met game reached a point where it was dragging a bit, and some of the spectators were on the verge of boredom. And so this man and woman, seated in Section 22 behind home plate, drifted off into a Sunday session of oral sex.

Their neighbors there in the other seats of Section 22 were at first astounded and then intrigued. The activity of this couple was competing with the Mets for attention, and the couple was winning. Some were offended and were screaming for the policeman, but the park policemen, at least some of them, were too engrossed themselves to interfere. And they were hesitant to stop an exhibition that clearly topped anything this expansion baseball team had been able to do on the field.

At about this time, Smoky Burgess of the Pittsburgh Pirates

drilled a line drive down the right-field line. Being somewhat portly of build, Mr. Burgess was not especially speedy afoot. And so he arrived in the vicinity of second base just a step ahead of, perhaps a step behind, the throw coming in from right field. This necessitated Mr. Burgess to dip into a dust-raising slide. In order to see the play at second base more clearly, many of the fans jumped to their feet. This included the fellow in Section 22, who was at that moment more exposed than he had been before. Burgess was safe, the Pirates had a double, were threatening to score, and the fellow had a very angry lady on his hands, or wherever it was that she was by now.

When the policemen finally arrived, the couple protested that they had done nothing amiss, that they were, in fact, married.

At the end of the 1963 season the Polo Grounds was dismantled, and portions of the old park, such as the seats, were put up for public sale. Casey Stengel reportedly had met his wife there, years before. Al Moore of Rheingold beer purchased a set of four seats and presented them to Casey, who shipped them to his home in Glendale, California, and installed them in his back yard. They might have been the very seats in which Casey Stengel was introduced to Edna Lawson by Irish Meusel, the start of one of baseball's longest-running romances.

For a brief time there was a move abroad to ship the seats from Section 22 to the Baseball Hall of Fame in Cooperstown, New York. I don't think they were sent, though. The Hall of Fame didn't seem to understand. But I can tell you that it is a mark of a real student of Met history that he be able to at least identify the nature of the incident in Section 22. It became a part of Metsomania.

I continue to revel in the recollections of life with Casey Stengel that come back in ceaseless succession.

For instance, before a game one day Casey said to me, "Well, I heard ya was in Australia during the war, and I wanted to ask ya about them kangaroos. I ain't seen no kangaroos, but I wondered if they just jump around everywhere, maybe in the road, down there in Australia."

I said, "Casey, I was in Austria, not Australia—I've never seen a kangaroo, either."

My explanation failed to reach Casey. He stared at me as though I must be a moron. He was silent, but only for a moment.

"I just wanted to know, and I thought I'd ast ya, and ya don't know, huh?"

"No, sir," I said, "I don't know."

And there was the hot summer's night in 1964 when Warren Spahn was pitching for the Mets and was about to win. And if he did, that victory would put him ahead of Kid Nichols in the all-time listing of career victories. In the press box at Shea Stadium, the baseball writers were getting ready to make note of that historic achievement in their stories. But there was a problem. Nobody knew anything at all about Kid Nichols. Who the hell was Kid Nichols? Nobody had a clue. Then someone suggested that a runner be sent down to the dugout to query Casey Stengel. Surely Casey must have heard of Kid Nichols. He probably hadn't ever actually seen him, but he must have heard of him. He must have known whom he played for.

When the messenger returned, he was still in a daze. When he had put his query to Casey, the grizzled old veteran had looked at him disbelievingly as though he had said, "Did you ever hear of a fellow named Franklin Roosevelt?"

Casey said, "Hear of him? What the hell do you mean, hear of him? We lived on the same block in Kansas City and in fact he lived in the house directly across the street from where I lived."

Casey was absolutely accurate. The writers had thought that Casey might be able to tell them some vague fact about Kid Nichols, and the truth was they had grown up together.

The longer one stayed around Stengel, the less inclined one was to be surprised by anything.

There was a lot of sensitivity in Stengel, too. He had been center stage about as much as any manager in the history of the game. But now it was the final day of the 1964 season, and Casey was the manager of the Mets, who were about to finish last again. We were at old Sportsman's Park in St. Louis, and if the Cardinals won the game, they won the pennant. The Cards were managed by Johnny Keane. And now it was before the game, and all the baseball writers were crowded around Keane in the dugout, posing all sorts of questions, and the photographers were snapping pictures. Over back of home plate, near the stands, Casey stood all alone watching this scene from afar. I stopped for a moment with the old man. He was in a pensive mood, drinking in all of this. Then, very softly, he said to no one in particular, "I've been in pennant races." The fact is that there was nothing the old warrior hadn't been in.

Back in that first year of the Mets, they did not fare too well on the field, with a record of 40 wins and 120 losses. They finished

60½ games out of first place. But the attendance at the venerable Polo Grounds was almost a million.

And I was surely learning a great deal about the daily life of baseball broadcasting. I learned that a baseball broadcaster develops an automatic daily routine. Before the game he must get the starting lineups and batting orders, and he must have the identity of the umpires and their stations for that particular day. When the announcer is out there milling around before the game, his procedures are not always exactly the same from day to day. But somewhere along the way, in all that visiting and observation, he hopes to come up with the information he requires.

It may take a new man a little while to understand all of this.

A part of baseball-announcing lore is the story of the day when Mike Shannon, who had retired as a player, joined Jack Buck in the broadcasting booth for St. Louis Cardinal games. And the Cards were playing an exhibition game in St. Petersburg, Florida. It was at old Al Lang Field, where the booth was way back in the rear of the grandstand. To get to it, you had to come all the way up through the grandstand. Often it wasn't easy, because as you made your way up the crowded aisle, fans would want to talk and visit.

This particular day, Jack Buck was working on his scorebook, getting the lineups down, and he said automatically to Shannon, "Get the umpires."

Mike Shannon had been a ballplayer, and a good one. Now he was making the switch to life as an announcer. Mike was industrious and practical. Straightaway, he disappeared.

Jack Buck was busy at work on his book, but soon became vaguely aware that it was getting a little crowded in that small booth. He looked up to be greeted by a quartet of umpires, in uniform and ready to work. Jack had told Shannon to "get the umpires." He had meant, of course, to get their names and assignments for the day. But Mike had taken him literally. He had not only got the umpires, he had brought them all up through the crowd and into the booth. There they stood, four somewhat confused fellows in blue suits.

The baseball life, I learned, is rich in marvelously unusual experiences.

CHAPTER 20

Fascinating Football

About the time that Red Grange and I had started working football together, General Bob Neyland at Tennessee had retired as coach, but he still remained active as director of athletics. And he became the new chairman of the NCAA football rules committee. It is on the authority of Davey Nelson, who has been secretary and editor of the rules committee for so many years, that I relate this story.

Neyland was a staunch advocate of two-way football. He abhorred free substitution, which had insinuated itself into the game. Neyland wasn't particularly upset about the manner in which free substitution had come about. In the war years, the military academies had all the football players. That was easy to understand. A talented football player, faced with being drafted as a private or enrolled at an academy, which would bring him out an officer, was likely to end up in the academy uniform. It seemed to a lot of the coaches around the country that Red Blaik had most all of them at Army. His Mr. Outside and Mr. Inside, Glenn Davis and Doc Blanchard, won the Heisman Trophy back to back. Army was doing things like beating Notre Dame 59–0. And now, in 1945, Fritz Crisler had to field a Michigan team in opposition to Army. He decided that by playing one unit on offense and another on defense and substituting freely, he might be able to keep fresh troops on the field and provide a more even battle. It was a platoon system, which had never been seen. And it worked out well enough. Crisler didn't win, because his team was beaten by Army 28–7. But that was deemed respectable. After all, Army beat Penn that year 61–0. Since 1942, the rules had been so written that they would accommodate two-platoon football, but there had been no rush for change.

But there was a rush for change now. Just as coaches had gone snow-blind diagramming forward-pass plays on tablecloths after Gus Dorais threw those Notre Dame passes to end Knute Rockne at West Point in 1913, now they all ran for two-platoon—college and pro alike. The pros, like the colleges, had always played two-way football.

General Neyland, back from the war, had not liked it. He hadn't liked it at all, and he expressed his opinion freely. He thought it would demean the coaching profession. He thought that instead of teaching, the coaches would now start "recruiting for need." If they needed a good defensive tackle, instead of coaching him in the techniques of his position, they would simply go out and get a player who possessed that lone skill, recruit him, and forget about teaching anybody anything.

He said that the new rules would deny the individual the very rewards that the game provided. He said that the player who had never been faced with the duty of having to make a tackle in the open field would complete his career never having known the experience of one who was required to play the game both ways.

In 1953 the rules were altered to again encourage the two-way player. But a lot of coaches still favored the two-platoon. As they gathered in session, Neyland was the chairman and was rapidly running the agenda through to a conclusion. In fact, he had moved so swiftly that he was about to gavel the proceedings to a close when Coach Ray Eliot of Illinois spoke up on behalf of the coaches.

"General Neyland," said Eliot, "there are a lot of coaches in this game and a lot of people in this room, a lot of rules-committee members, who would like to move to return to two-platoon."

Maybe Neyland had anticipated that—I don't know. But Davey Nelson says that Neyland looked around and said, "I don't see any people who want to return to two-platoon." With that, he reached underneath the table and took the hand of Nelson, who, as secretary, was seated beside him. Neyland said, "All in favor of the continuation of present rules say 'aye.' "

With that, Neyland raised his own hand and Nelson's hand and roared, "Aye."

Then in a sort of burst, he said, "Opposed 'no,' the 'ayes' have it—and we won't be having any chickenshit football *this* season."

As my schedule of assignments expanded and I traveled frequently around the country, I still stayed in touch with General Neyland and I would see him now and again.

One night in New Orleans we sat and talked late into the night. Suddenly, he turned directly to me and said, "Don't call me General, call me Bob."

I said, "Not the longest day I live. If I ever called you Bob, the roof would collapse."

One night he told me, "When I came out of my hometown of Greenville, Texas, and arrived at West Point, I was devoid of all the social graces. We had to learn to pay social calls on the officers of the post, and I didn't know what to say or which knee to balance the teacup on. So I decided that if I didn't volunteer to say very much, maybe I could learn what to do without revealing myself as a complete fool."

The stern, forbidding Neyland manner, then, was a cover-up.

In the later years, though, there was still an unsolved riddle even in the mind of Bob Neyland—was he really a football coach or a soldier? He had become one of the great football coaches in the history of the game, a defensive genius. But what would his life have been like if he had pursued it to its fullest as a soldier? At West Point, as a student and as a performer, he had been clearly superior to contemporaries such as Dwight Eisenhower and Omar Bradley. No one would ever know what heights he might have achieved had he stuck to soldiering. But one could wonder. Neyland now wondered about the military life he had spurned. He had not foreseen the imminence of World War II when he retired from the Army. His wife later wrote, "He regretted that decision and so did I."

But now he discovered perhaps an even greater puzzlement. He found himself in competition with his own legend. If a man survives to become contemporary with his legend, the legend always overshadows and sometimes smothers the man. The legend is immortal, unchanging, etched forever in stone, unassailable, a source of inspiration for others, but not for him. What about the man, who is, after all, human, and still heir to human frailties? No living man has ever escaped them. The legendary Neyland discipline that had inspired and sustained so many, became unavailable to Neyland, unattainable to its creator. The lean, ramrod-straight military figure grew overweight and out of shape, which he despised and was powerless to control. The closing years were filled with frustration.

I was in spring training with the New York Mets in March of 1962 when I got word that he had died in New Orleans. He was buried at the National Cemetery in Knoxville on March 28, 1962. Coach Bowden Wyatt delivered the eulogy. "General Robert Reese Neyland now becomes a legend," he said.

And let me say here that the influence exerted on me by General Neyland has never left. At present, I live in a condominium in Knoxville, Tennessee, after twenty-seven years of living in New York and pursuing the life of a sports announcer. My townhouse is high on a bluff, and at sunset the view is spectacular. In the far distance is a mountain range. Nearer one looks out on the sprawling campus of the University of Tennessee, bathed in the setting sun and so enriched and expanded in the fifty-odd years since that young army captain reported to the ROTC department and, incidentally, to the athletic department. Workers on the way home from their day's duty drive along a broad boulevard. And they call that Neyland Drive.

Lifting one's gaze only slightly, the last towering thing one sees on the horizon is a rising silhouette of a magnificent football stadium with a capacity of more than ninety thousand. They named it Neyland Stadium.

I look at that scene and I think often of the day I first met him and he threatened me. I think of all his achievements, of the many lives he touched for the better, the man who valued loyalty seemingly above almost all other virtues.

I think of all of that. And I always smile. And, sometimes, when no one's looking, I salute.

In preparing for my new life as a baseball announcer, I had gone home and taken my football spotter's boards, wrapped them in an old army blanket, and put them away on a closet shelf. I announced a little sorrowfully to my family that I supposed my football life was over.

But then, as that summer of 1962 progressed, and I read all the football reports in the newspapers, I began to get that old feeling.

I don't suppose you can be as deeply into something as I was into football and just walk away from it.

And then one day I met Bill MacPhail of CBS on Sixth Avenue. Bill was the vice-president in charge of sports, and we had been friends for a number of years. Now he was smiling and saying, "I've been trying to get you on the phone. As you know, we have the rights to the college football games at CBS, and we'd like you to do them."

"Yeah," I said. "Yeah. I'm your man."

He was talking about the assignment as the number-one announcer on the national series, the voice of NCAA football on CBS.

I hurried home to tell my family that I was back in the football business, that I would be doing the college football games on CBS.

Mickie said, "But I thought you said you were not going to be doing any more football."

"Don't tell me what I said. I know what I said. But you just can't do that. You can't stay completely away from something you love like I love football. I'll do baseball in the spring and summer and football in the fall."

It seemed to me that life was working out extremely well.

I soon learned that the CBS interest in me as an announcer on the NCAA series had been strongly encouraged by the NCAA. When Asa Bushnell sent out the requests for bids from the various networks, that request contained a list of ground rules. And one of them was the fact that the NCAA would have final approval of announcers. The NCAA had quietly let it be known that they would approve immediately if the announcer should be Lindsey Nelson.

Now Jim Corbett, who was on that NCAA committee, was on the phone asking about the analyst. "Would you rather have Doak Walker or Terry Brennan?" he asked.

I explained that I did not know Doak Walker. Oh, I knew all about him. You couldn't live in Dallas, Texas, for five minutes and not be aware of Doak Walker. He was a legend around SMU. He had won the Heisman Trophy, and I had done some of his great games with the Detroit Lions.

On the other hand, I had met Terry Brennan several times. I had done some of the Notre Dame games when Terry was the head coach there. He was certainly a gentleman of class.

So CBS nominated Terry Brennan and the NCAA approved.

CBS also added a third announcer to handle things like the bands, halftime, and periodic reports from the field—sort of a frame around the picture. They chose the very capable Jim Simpson.

One of our games that season took us to West Point to do the game between Army and Penn State. The superintendent at the Military Academy was now Major General William C. Westmoreland. And when he had gone to the White House in Washington to get his final instructions from President Eisenhower before taking his new job, the president had said, "Westmoreland, I am giving you just one specific charge—buck up that football team."

When you have been posted by the president, you may pay attention—especially if you are a young two-star general and he is a five-star general. So, Westy went right to work. He looked over the field of young football coaches and decided that Paul Dietzel at LSU was about as good as they come. He had won a national championship in 1958. So Westmoreland hired Dietzel and installed him as head coach of the Cadets. Dietzel was not unfamiliar with the post. He had once been an assistant on the staff of Coach Red Blaik.

Our producer was Pete Molnar, who was himself a graduate of the Military Academy, so it was something like Old Home Week as the CBS crew descended on the Bear Mountain Inn the weekend following the World Series.

Pete had made his preliminary survey when he came into my room in something of a dither. "You know," he said, "I would give anything to get General Westmoreland on at halftime. You could do a great interview with him on top of the press box. But I have talked to the public-relations people, and they won't even ask him."

Pete, of course, did not know that Westy and I had been friends for a number of years. So he was a little shocked when I said, "I'll ask him."

"You'll ask him?"

"Yep," I said, and I dialed the phone.

When the secretary answered, I said, "This is Lindsey Nelson of CBS Sports. Is Westy there?"

We had an informal conversation, and he agreed to do the interview on one condition. "I'll do it if you do the interview," he said. I agreed that I would do it, and asked him to meet me at halftime on top of the press box. I hung up and said to Pete, "Okay, now you've got the interview." Pete was almost a basket case.

But a good producer, especially a former West Pointer, is not awed for long. Soon Pete was back, in even more of a dither than before. "I've just heard that General Maxwell Taylor will be here for the game Saturday. They say he will be making his first public appearance since becoming Chairman of the Joint Chiefs of Staff. Do you suppose there would be any way to get him on television?"

I said, "I don't know. Let's see." I phoned Westy again and asked if General Taylor was going to be his guest and if he thought the general would consent to the interview. Westy said he was sure he would. I hung up and said to Pete, "Okay, now you've got General Taylor."

This was a regional telecast, so we didn't have Jim Simpson. That meant that Terry Brennan and I had to do some shuttling back and forth. Terry had to cover the halftime stuff on the field and then hurry up to the booth while I was doing the interviews on top of the press box.

After I'd finished the interviews, I knew Terry had still not come back up from the field, and on my earpiece I was getting the information that no one was yet in the booth. Now I was about to dash downstairs, but General Taylor took me by the arm and started a leisurely conversation. "Westy tells me that you were with him in the Ninth Infantry Division," he said. Molnar was screaming in my earpiece for me to get the hell downstairs. But you do not just walk away from the Chairman of the Joint Chiefs of Staff, especially if you have a reserve commission and might be called to active duty at any time, like later this afternoon.

I had made my decision, and I was visiting socially with General Maxwell Taylor. Given a choice of whether I would incur the displeasure of a CBS producer or the Chairman of the Joint Chiefs of Staff, my course was clear. But as we talked, I looked down on the field at a slight commotion, and saw what had happened to our missing Coach Brennan. He had been reporting on camera from the sidelines when the West Point Drum and Bugle Corps had marched by. In one of those freak accidents that defy explanation, Terry's loose necktie had somehow become attached to a metal bracket on a bass drum. The drum, of course, was being moved down the field at a steady pace, and to avoid being choked to death Coach Brennan had very much become a marching, nonplaying, bent-over member of the West Point Drum and Bugle Corps.

Fortunately, some observing member of the military cut him loose before tragedy set in.

And then there was the time we did the 1962 Army-Navy game in Philadelphia. I had always had this thing about wanting to get a microphone down there at midfield for the toss of the coin before the game. I thought it would be especially interesting here because President John F. Kennedy was going to toss the pregame coin.

On Friday afternoon we were at what was then called Philadelphia Stadium. The name had just been changed from Municipal Stadium. The television technicians were stringing cables and wires. Various workmen were at their tasks. And the Secret Service detail was there, examining all parts of that venerable old stadium. The man in charge of the Secret Service detail was on the field.

Terry Brennan and I would be working the game in the booth and our man on the field would be Jim Simpson, as he had been all year. Jim lived in the Washington, D.C., area. In fact, he did the sports segment of the late news on the local station in Washington. He was well known in those parts, and we figured he would be the man to make our special request of the Secret Service.

Jim was on the field walking toward the Secret Service man in charge when that fellow suddenly stopped, pointed toward Jim, and said enthusiastically, "You're Jim Simpson. I see you on television every night at home. You're Jim Simpson."

Jim smiled and nodded and said, "Could we run a line out here tomorrow to pick up what the president has to say to the cadet and the midshipman who are out here for the toss of the coin?"

The fellow took no note of what Jim had said. He went right on, "You know, every night at our house there in Washington, we watch the news before we go to bed, and we see you every night. How about that!"

Jim was still smiling. He said, "Could we run a mike line out here tomorrow to pick up what the president has to say when he tosses the coin?"

The Secret Service said, "You know, I have three sons and we are all big sports fans and that's why we follow the sports news so closely, and we see you every night."

Jim's smile was fading. "Could we run a mike line out here tomorrow," he said, "to pick up the president?"

The Secret Service was still rolling. "Of course not," he said, almost casually. "You know, my wife is never going to believe that I met Jim Simpson."

We did not run the mike line out and we did not hear what President Kennedy had to say.

In the winter months now, I worked other events. NBC asked if I would be interested in doing the Bing Crosby golf tournament at Pebble Beach. My job would be to stay with Bing as we wandered the course, and when we found something interesting, I would get in touch with the director who would get us on camera. My introductory line was usually the same: "Now here's Bing Crosby!"

When we had finished, NBC thought it had gone very smoothly. They wondered if I could go down to Palm Springs and do the very same thing on the upcoming coverage of the Bob Hope Desert Classic. I explained that I probably could manage that, although it would require restructuring my part. Now I would have to say, "Now here's Bob Hope!"

During those assignments, I discovered a basic difference between these two great performers. Bing Crosby was relaxed whenever he was not working. He had a quiet sense of humor. He was easy to talk to. Bob Hope, on the other hand, was "on" all the time. He never stopped tossing the one-liners. Conversation with Bob Hope was a lot like conversation with Casey Stengel. It was one-sided. As we watched movie star Kirk Douglas plodding his way up the eighteenth fairway, Hope said, "Look at Spartacus there. Looks like he's walking in his daddy's shoes."

And there was one day when we had some time to fill on camera at the eighteenth green, and we talked with General Eisenhower and singer Frances Langford, who had been with Hope's wartime troupe. We talked of those days in North Africa during the war when we had all been there—Eisenhower, Hope, Langford, and even me.

The 1963 college football season left imprints that have endured for a lifetime. In late November I went to Yale to do THE GAME—Yale vs. Harvard. On Friday, after lunch in New Haven, we went out to watch the freshmen play. Terry and Jim Simpson and I had walked through the tunnel underneath the highway to get to the freshman game on the other side. We were along the sideline there with varsity coach John Pont when word came from some fellow who had a transistor radio in the stands—President Kennedy had been assassinated.

Everyone was stunned. No one really knew what to do or say. We didn't know how it would affect our plans. Slowly we walked back through the tunnel, and I remember Jim Simpson saying, "We will remember this walk and this moment for a long, long time."

We went back to the motel. Mickie was waiting for me there. We heard the reports and the rumors. Finally, word came that the football game would not be played. The postponement was not only out of respect for the death of the president of the United States, but in acknowledgment of the fact that John F. Kennedy had been a Harvard man.

We were packing our things and getting ready to leave when word came that I was to stay with the remote unit for a while. Technically, everything was pretty much in order for the live pickup next day. We could go live now, if need be. And CBS News thought maybe they'd want to come to New Haven for a live interview with some of the Harvard sports people who had known Kennedy as a student. I waited until well after dark, when word came that they wouldn't be needing me or the interviews.

Driving back toward New York and our home on Long Island, Mickie and I were still just crushed. As we approached Stamford, Connecticut, we decided to stop off at the home of Bill and Betty Heinz. We visited each other often. Bill and I had known each other in Europe when he had been a war correspondent for the New York *Sun,* before he became well-known author W. C. Heinz.

When we got there, Red and Kay Smith were already there. And we sat there that night in the Heinz living room talking of the improbable events of that day until in our utter despair we stopped talking about the assassination altogether, and began to talk about sports.

Our last game of the season was the Army-Navy game, which had been postponed for one week because of the death of Kennedy. When we got to Philadelphia, we were quartered at the Marriott, a little ways removed from downtown. Our producer was Bill Creasy, and our director Tony Verna. The morning of the game, Creasy had gone ahead early. Verna, Brennan, and I were in a car together headed for the stadium. During the ride, Tony Verna turned to me and said casually, "We have something that we might use today, and I want to tell you about it."

I was mildly interested. I didn't think it was going to be anything that would be of any great interest. Probably some use of an isolated camera to cover a pass route. They were doing a lot of that now that videotape had been invented. I didn't care all that much for it. A guy ran a long pass route and a few plays later you showed isolated coverage of this guy running a long pass route.

Verna went on, "We have a way now of playing back what has just been shown on the screen. We can play it right back. I don't know whether we will get to use it or not, but if we do, you will have to explain to the viewers that what they are seeing is not live, that it's a replay of what they have just seen."

I said, "Okay."

Next thing I remember is that Army, coached by Paul Dietzel, had the ball on Navy's two-yard line. Navy was coached by Wayne Hardin and starred an all-American quarterback named Roger Staubach. I had figured that we'd get some fancy scrambling maneuver of Staubach's on our gimmick, whatever it was. But Rollie Stichweh, the Army quarterback, took the ball, rolled out, and dived into the end zone for an Army touchdown. And I heard Verna saying to me, "Okay, Lindsey, here it comes again, and you've got to explain it."

Well, I started in quickly to tell the folks that what they were about to see was not live, and another touchdown, but in fact a replay of what they had just seen. I repeated my information and realized that in my urgency and excitement my voice was rising. I was practically screaming. And then came the replay. As we stared at it on the monitor in the booth, I heard Tony Verna say into my earpiece, "Hey, what do you know, it works!" We did not call it "instant replay" that day. The terminology came later. But the coverage of sports events and a good many other things changed forever that afternoon in 1963 in Philadelphia.

Toward the end of the 1963 season, I was at a college-football cocktail party in Manhattan. It was nothing unusual, just a social gathering. And then I looked across the room to see Perry Smith approaching. Perry was now essentially the executive producer of sports at NBC. He was an old friend. We had shared an office at NBC. Perry was a graduate of the Naval Academy. He had been a submariner. And he had come into television as a business manager. He was just about the best-organized fellow I had ever come across. He had joined the NBC sports department in 1953, and his talents had really been a godsend.

Now he was walking toward me across that crowded room with that little smile on his face. And what I heard him say had to be one of the highlights of my broadcasting career. Perry said, "How about doing the Rose Bowl for us?"

It had been about two years before when Mickie and I had sat in the empty Rose Bowl that afternoon and talked about the fact that the Rose Bowl football game was the one event I wanted so badly to do and had never done. The Rose Bowl was very special for all announcers. Ted Husing's mother had lived in Pasadena and Ted had spent his last years of life there. Yet, the great Ted Husing had always wanted to but had never done the Rose Bowl football game.

The Rose Bowl had been an NBC event for a long time, and Mel Allen had been the play-by-play announcer. But Mel was having some problems. For instance, he and I had done the East-West Shrine game together at Kezar Stadium in San Francisco in the early 1960s. Mel had gone through a tough afternoon. He couldn't get the ball spotted at the right place, and he couldn't get the names right. It happens to all of us at times, but a lot of mail had come in.

Then there had been the World Series in 1963. The announcers were Mel Allen and Vin Scully.

During the 1963 season, Mel had gone through some difficulty with his voice. That is not unusual for a professional announcer. At some time or another, most of us reach a point where the constant use of those vocal cords under all sorts of conditions will take its toll.

But then, during the telecast of the fourth and final game of the 1963 World Series at Dodger Stadium in Los Angeles, Mel Allen completely lost his voice. He had gone just as far as his voice would take him, and Vin Scully had to take over the play-by-play announcing, carefully explaining that Mel had simply temporarily lost his voice.

But, of course, the World Series is not your regular-season telecast from Yankee Stadium, or even the East-West Shrine game. The World Series telecast is one of the highest-rated events in the medium. And the tongues were wagging and the rumors rolling. In the poolrooms and on the street corners, they were saying that with the Dodgers sweeping his beloved Yankees in four games, the emotion had just been too much for the voice of the Yankees.

I certainly couldn't give any credence to that one. Mel had been having trouble with his voice before the Series began. He would have been more likely to lose his voice if the Yankees had been winning. I remember talking to Mel at Ebbets Field back in 1956, the day after Yankee Stadium had seen Don Larsen pitch the only perfect game ever in a World Series. Mel was hoarse—hoarse from the excitement of the previous day.

But now Perry Smith was telling me that the Rose Bowl sponsors thought that there might be some risk involved in assigning Mel again to an event like the Rose Bowl, which was just a one-afternoon spectacular. If the voice failed, they thought it would be damaging. And the sponsors had told NBC that they would be willing to accept me if I could do it. They had also said that they were appreciative of the many years of fine work that Mel Allen had done for them, and they were making this move reluctantly. In fact, when they told him about it they wanted to offer to send him on an all-expenses-paid Caribbean cruise.

When Perry mentioned that, I said, "Well, if this doesn't work out, send Mel back to the Rose Bowl and send me on the Caribbean cruise."

I mentioned that since I was doing the regular-season games for CBS, I was under an unstated obligation to do a bowl game for them if they wanted me to. So far they hadn't mentioned any assignment.

Perry asked if I would discuss it with Bill MacPhail, the sports boss at CBS, and I said I would.

We all know that the business is strange. We know that things, good and bad, happen with no notice. But can you imagine that after all these years, a fellow just walks across a room in Manhattan at a social gathering and says, "How about doing the Rose Bowl for us?" I did not waste much time in getting MacPhail on the phone. He was a good friend. We got along fine. And I got right to it.

I said, "Bill, I want to make a speech. And I don't want you to say anything during my speech. I want you to listen. And then at the end of my speech, I have a request. And I will want your answer to that."

Bill said, "Okay, let's hear your speech."

I said, "Well, to begin with, since I am doing your regular-season college football games, I feel that I should do a bowl game for you if you want me to. So, if you have sold or promised me to a sponsor on a bowl game and just haven't told me yet, then forget the rest of this speech and the request. But, if you haven't, let me tell you that the one event I have always wanted to do and haven't done is the Rose Bowl. I worked as a student spotter for Bill Stern on the NBC radio broadcast of the 1940 game. I was a junior in college, and that trip to the Rose Bowl left impressions on me that will last forever. Now, NBC has asked me to do the Rose Bowl. And that is the end of my speech and the start of my request. If you have not committed me to a conflicting game, I want your permission to do the Rose Bowl for NBC."

There was a silence. And then Bill said, "Hell, go ahead and do the Rose Bowl. I'd like to see the Rose Bowl. I've never seen it!"

That is how I came to be in Pasadena on New Year's Day, announcing the game between Illinois and Washington. But there were some trying times beforehand.

Subsequent discussions have led me to believe that, before I ever made my speech and request, CBS had already decided to send Chris Schenkel to the Cotton Bowl.

In any case, Bill MacPhail called and asked if I would do the Gator Bowl game in Jacksonville for CBS. It was North Carolina vs. the Air Force Academy and would be played several days before the Rose Bowl. Mickie said she could take care of all the family post-Christmas details while I was doing the Gator Bowl, and then meet me in Pasadena. We decided that we'd just do it up right and go on to Honolulu for a vacation after the Rose Bowl game.

But then the trouble began. During Christmas, I began coming down with all the symptoms of a terrible cold. By the time I left for Jacksonville, I was also running a pretty steady temperature. When I got to Florida, I was sick. George Olsen, the majordomo of the Gator Bowl, was an old friend, and he got me to a doctor. It seemed that what I had was the flu, and I was put to bed. I was having chills and fever. I was freezing and perspiring. At night I was climbing the walls of my room in near-delirium. Fortunately, Jim Simpson was working with me, and he was getting all the preparation done for the game and furnishing me with lineups and order-of-substitution.

I was scheduled to fly out of Jacksonville for Pasadena the morning after the Gator Bowl. But that did not now seem likely. I was going to be lucky to survive the Gator Bowl. I saw no chance that I would ever make it to Pasadena and the Rose Bowl. Mel Allen had been replaced because the sponsors were afraid to take a chance on a scratchy voice. What they had instead was an announcer who was having trouble getting all the way to the bathroom.

Then word came from Long Island that Mickie was in bed with some undiagnosed ailment and could not think of going to Pasadena, Honolulu, or anywhere else. That part of our plans had to be canceled now.

Well, the morning of the Gator Bowl, I felt pretty good. My voice was fine and my temperature was normal. And I got through the telecast of the Gator Bowl on CBS without any difficulty.

But the long flight to the West Coast took its toll, and by the time I got to the Sheraton Huntington Hotel, I was dragging again.

I sent immediately for the house doctor, who thought my problem now was mostly fatigue. He gave me a sedative and put me to bed. Before I dropped off to sleep, I put in a phone call to Tom Anderson in Knoxville. I had to call and remind him of the time I had been an unregistered guest in his hotel room twenty-two years earlier. I said, "I just wanted you to know that I am back in the Huntington Hotel in Pasadena, this time as a properly registered guest." And then I slept for about ten hours. When I awoke, I was fit for duty. I felt fine.

There was a formal cocktail party for General Dwight Eisenhower, who would be the grand marshal of the Tournament of Roses Parade. Members of the media, such as I, were told to step up to the general and by way of introduction, to state our names and affiliations. I stepped up snappily and said, "General, I'm Lindsey Nelson of CBS." He looked surprised, and said, "I thought this was an NBC event." I said, "Yes, sir, it is. I am Lindsey Nelson of NBC." What I was, I guess, was a day worker. I was like the California fruit pickers—I went where the work was.

I had now become closely identified with the NCAA series of autumn college games on television, concurrent with my summertime work with the New York Mets. After I had done the games on CBS in 1962 and 1963, the package went back to NBC for 1964 and 1965, and I had gone with it.

Jim Corbett was now a member of the NCAA television committee, so it was not exactly a surprise to me when it was announced before the 1966 season that the games would be going to ABC. The NCAA had decided not to ask for bids, but rather to negotiate a contract directly. ABC was attractive because it was the only major network not tied up in any way with professional football. The fathers at the NCAA had an abiding fear that the college game would somehow be relegated to a secondary role. ABC, of course, was delighted, and stayed absolutely clean of the taint of NFL football until their very first opportunity came along when they brought on *Monday Night Football* in 1970.

I was in spring training with the Mets in St. Petersburg when I got several calls from Roone Arledge of ABC about a role in the NCAA package. Mostly it seemed to me that he was proposing that Chris Schenkel would be the principal announcer and that I would do regional and split-network games. Although I had the strong backing of the NCAA, it was apparent to me that Roone Arledge was going to name the announcers, and that he had not signed Chris Schenkel to a lucrative ABC contract for no purpose.

In the television-network jungle, there are few secrets. Other networks knew exactly what was happening. Carl Lindemann and Chet Simmons were now running sports at NBC, and they came up with an attractive package that they presented to my agent, Ralph Mann. I would do an AFL game each Sunday, probably Buffalo, and I would also do the Rose Bowl and the East-West Shrine game, and there was a package price that would exceed any offer I had ever had. It was interesting.

Then one day as I waited in my room in the Colonial Inn at St. Petersburg Beach, I got a call from Bill MacPhail of CBS.

He got right to the point. "Are you under contract to anybody for football?"

"Nope."

"All right, I am offering you a choice of teams. You can do the games of either the Minnesota Vikings or the Chicago Bears plus some postseason games and things. We'll include a full network, prime-time game in Milwaukee to open the season, a prime-time Monday night game in October in St. Louis, and the Pro Bowl in Los Angeles."

I told him I would talk it over with Ralph Mann. And we talked it over several times. It is not often in a television career of any kind that a performer has simultaneous offers from the three networks, and I was rather enjoying it.

I had had the advantage of being on both sides of the network negotiating table, both as a junior executive on the side of management and as a performer whose talents were being bartered. I thought I had learned a few facts of that life.

The most important thing is to know precisely what your position is and where your strength lies. And right here one of General Bob Neyland's game maxims is of considerable value—"Never kid yourself."

I knew that in the battle between Arledge and the NCAA that Arledge was going to win. And if I persisted in fighting that battle to its ultimate conclusion, I might very well be left out of those other opportunities by the time a decision was reached.

Even if I won, I would lose. If I was doing Arledge's games against his wishes, it was not likely that I would be able to do them to please him. I did enjoy college football, but the simple fact was that when the NCAA had not invited bids and had not stated the previous ground rules, the choice of announcers legally and every other way was Arledge's and he knew that better than anybody.

I called Jim Corbett and I said, "I know what you have been doing on my behalf, and I know that you would continue to do it, and I appreciate the confidence of the NCAA. But this is not going to work out. I am going to bow out of this situation and sign a contract to do pro football."

As a member of the NCAA television committee, Jim was party to every phase of the negotiations. He was understanding, but was still upset. I am sure that it was at Jim's insistence that I got a letter from Walter Byers of the NCAA telling me that I was going away to the world of professional football with the blessings and personal good wishes of the NCAA.

And that seemed to take care of that little chapter. The NCAA games went to ABC and I went to CBS, where I have worked football happily for nineteen seasons. Added to the two seasons when I had previously worked college games there, that gives me a record of twenty-one years of football work for CBS-TV. I had a total of twelve seasons at NBC-TV.

Now that I had agreed to do pro football games on Sundays, it did not occur to me that there would be offers to do some forms of delayed television of college games on Saturdays. But there were. The first call came from producer Marvin Sugarman. He proposed that we do a top Eastern game, tape it, edit it, and show it on Sundays. He had permission from Penn State, Syracuse, Pittsburgh, Army, and Navy. I told him that I had plenty to do and was not interested. He asked what was the biggest fee I had ever received for doing a football game, and I told him. He said that he would match it for every game of our series. Suddenly, my interest was piqued. And I spent my Saturdays racing around the East.

Producer C. D. Chesley also called and said that he was doing a tape-delayed version of the Notre Dame games, and wanted to know if I would be interested in doing some of them. I explained that I didn't have any open dates.

But the next season, 1967, I agreed to do some of the Notre Dame games, and that began an association between Notre Dame football and me that lasted for thirteen seasons and gave me my most widespread and continuing identification in the television business.

Since we were pioneering this sort of presentation, there were no precedents. We added refinements each season. Our director was Frank Slingland of NBC Washington, who was directing the Washington end of the nightly *Huntley-Brinkley Report.* Our tape editor in Chicago was Bob Link, who had been with CBS operations in Chicago. We had a charming young lady doing some of the commercials who went on to much greater fame. Her name was Farrah Fawcett. Soon Paul Hornung was added to the crew as an analyst and later, George Connor.

Once each quarter, during a time-out, Slingland would punch up a crowd shot, and I would read a series of verbal bridges. They were things like "Now we move to further action," and "Notre Dame was unable to move the ball so they kicked to Navy." Bob Link in Chicago could then lay in a bridge and edit out whatever footage he wanted. Our aim was to get the game down to a one-hour show.

In the television trade, few knew anything about the technique we used. Most imagined that we were using the old newsreel technique, which meant that you edited the film, wrote a script, and went to a studio and read the play-by-play to fit the picture. But we didn't do that. We did the commentary live.

I learned in a hurry that there are lots of people out there, millions of them, who follow Notre Dame football one way or another. I realize that about half of them tune in hoping to see the Irish lose, but they tune in nonetheless. It has been truly said that every real college-football fan has two favorite teams each week—his own alma mater and whoever is playing against Notre Dame. But in this whole nation, there is only one college football team that has truly national appeal—and that is Notre Dame. There are other teams that have a fervent following—Alabama, Tennessee, Southern Cal, Texas, Oklahoma, Brigham Young, Nebraska, Ohio State—but the following of those teams is still largely regional. To have a truly national following, you must have the capability of really being feared and hated. And the Irish have that.

At one time we had our games on 136 stations, and the tapes were flown to Honolulu and Tokyo and shown there. I was identified with the Mets and other events in New York, but I was best known nationally as "the Notre Dame announcer."

Even after I had taken the NFL assignment at CBS, I continued to do the Rose Bowl for NBC. And one night at the Sheraton Huntington in Pasadena, when I was getting ready to do the Rose Bowl for the fourth straight year, a member of the football committee, John

Bigger, said to me, "I would think that you are going to be announcing the Rose Bowl forever."

Well, not quite.

The top announcing team for NBC now was Curt Gowdy and Paul Christman. They had started at ABC on the NCAA series in 1960–61, and then when NBC had signed the new American Football League for thirty-five million dollars, Gowdy and Christman had become their headline team of announcers. They had a backup team of Jim Simpson and Kyle Rote.

The NBC announcers, understandably, were not altogether happy with the arrangement whereby I, a CBS announcer, was doing the Rose Bowl, which was the plum of the NBC assignments.

One day Bill MacPhail called to say that CBS wanted me to do the Cotton Bowl. That would leave NBC free to make its own Rose Bowl assignment. This was a pleasant development. I had already done the Cotton Bowl a number of times for both NBC and CBS. And I was going back for a game between Bear Bryant's Alabama team and Gene Stallings's Texas Aggies. As we walked to practice one day, Bryant smiled and said, "I want you to see my left-handed quarterback, Ken Stabler." And he was worth watching.

Our producer would be Chuck Milton, our director Frank Chirkinian, and our analyst Pat Summerall. At our production meeting the night before the game, Milton explained that he had a special opening planned. Summerall and I would open on the sidelines, and then I would be broken to make a hurried trip up to the booth. There would be a pair of Texas Rangers to meet me on the sidelines and escort me up through the stands to the waiting elevator. Arrangements had been made for the elevator, the only elevator, to be held until I got there. Then I would hasten up and read a voice-over commentary to some film. When I was younger and more inexperienced, I used to get nervous over plans like these. But I got over that. Now when I hear a proposal of that sort, I am intrigued. Oh, I have no illusions that it will work. I just wonder where it will blow up.

My first real surprise came when I finished the stand-up on the sidelines and discovered that the Rangers were, in fact, waiting. Maybe this was going to work after all.

Then when we got to the elevator, it was there, with the operator holding the door open. This was too good to be true.

It wasn't true. I got in and the elevator went *down*! Nobody had explained to the operator that it was imperative for us to go rapidly *up.* When we got to the ground floor we were met by an elevator full of angry newspapermen who were not happy at having been kept waiting. When I got to the booth, the film had long since run, a completely silent film with no voice-over. I carefully fitted my headset on. All cause for haste had long since fled. The first thing I heard was producer Milton screaming at the top of his lungs. He was saying, "Nelson, Nelson—where the hell have you been?"

I said, as quietly as possible, "Me? I've been in the elevator."

When the next New Year's rolled around, 1969, I wasn't in the elevator at the Cotton Bowl or anywhere else at any bowl game. As it turned out, it was the only time in a period of thirty-five years that I did not have a New Year's bowl assignment.

Networks have a unique way of dealing with situations in which they have people that they have decided for some reason or other not to use at the moment. It is the same manner in which they deal with the problem of disposing of unwanted top executives. The weapon is silence. You just don't hear from anybody. You get no memos, few phone calls, and rare visits. There is a message in all of that. And the message is "Good-bye."

We got into December and I hadn't heard from anybody. Then I read in the trade press that the Cotton Bowl would be done by Jack Whitaker and Frank Gifford.

I did get a call saying that the Sun Bowl would be played in El Paso and carried by CBS on December 28, and I was assigned to do that with Frank Gifford as the analyst. So I went to El Paso. (In fact, I did five Sun Bowls with five different analysts—Frank Gifford, Pat Summerall, Tom Brookshier, Irv Cross, and Johnny Sauer.)

When that game was over, Gifford and a good many of our production people hurried over to the Cotton Bowl in Dallas. I hurried to Columbia, Tennessee, where Mickie and the girls were waiting. I really didn't know how to go about planning a New Year's celebration.

Mickie and I went with my sister, Mary Sue, and brother-in-law, Ed Pennington, to the Elks Club for a party one night. And on New Year's Eve we went to the home of a friend for a small party. I didn't know what to do, and I had a lousy time.

On New Year's Day I went to my parents' home. My mother had been ill for some time. She was now confined to her bed, so we sat in her room and watched the color television. Tennessee was playing Texas in the Cotton Bowl. I watched Whitaker and Gifford do their opening. My approach as a spectator was casual, but not too casual to notice that Tennessee was getting blown right out of the ball game by Texas. After a while, I quit watching altogether and left the room.

Since I did not seem to be particularly busy, Mickie and I planned a lengthy trip. It took us to Honolulu, and Tokyo and around Japan, and to Taiwan and Bangkok. We toured India from Calcutta and Benares to Agra and New Delhi. We flew across the Himalayas into Katmandu in Nepal, where we gazed spellbound at Everest. We saw the poverty and sickness in the crowded streets of Calcutta. I was entranced by the mysticism of India, the place I had wanted most to visit since I had first discovered Rudyard Kipling. We cruised down the Ganges beneath a hot Indian sun that was beating down with a fury that would make my "bloomin' eyebrows crawl."

We went to Cairo, Beirut, Istanbul, back to Cairo, and then to the shores of Tripoli. We went to Algiers, where we stayed at the Aletti Hotel, and one day I drove up to the St. George Hotel, where Eisenhower and his staff made many of the military decisions pertinent to the North African theater. And I prowled the Casbah. Then we moved to Casablanca and went one day for lunch at the Anfa Hotel out by the lighthouse, where the Casablanca Conference had been held in January of 1943. Then we went to Paris for a settling stay at the Meurice Hotel.

But that extended trip had hardly begun when we got tragic news. We had flown from Honolulu to Tokyo, and when we got to the Imperial Hotel, I was weary. As I walked across the lobby, an assistant manager came to say that there was an urgent message. My mother had died in Columbia, Tennessee.

We went to our room and I immediately started on the phone to make arrangements for a Pan Am flight back home. Mickie would wait for me in Japan.

Because my father had made our living as a traveling man, I knew the greatest influence on me had been that of my mother. I had been brought up under her careful guidance. Even during the war years, when I had been in North Africa and Europe, I had kept up a steady correspondence. I had never really been far away from my mother. And now when she had died, I was in Tokyo.

On the return trip, I had a short connection with a flight leaving Honolulu for Los Angeles. And to complicate things further, I had to clear U.S. Customs in Honolulu. I was afraid that the customs delay might cause me to miss my flight. So I approached the inspector with some dread. Fortunately, he was a sports fan. He passed me, stamped the form, slapped me on the shoulder, and said, "Welcome home."

The first loss in one's immediate family is felt the most severely, I think. I remember standing there at the funeral home, staring into that peaceful face for the last time, and fighting off the engulfing grief. Hers had not been an easy life. But there was no doubt that she had been the strong figure in our family. In fact, she was the strong figure in any company in which she found herself. In our residential block there on South Main Street, when the neighbors' children had problems they didn't want to discuss with their own parents, they discussed them with her. When there were emergencies, they turned to her. Now she was gone.

CHAPTER 21

The Rocky Road to Glory

In 1963 a resumption of the Mayor's Trophy game was arranged, with the Mets meeting the Yanks at Yankee Stadium. More than anything else, it was the clash of competing cultures. The Yankees still represented quiet and dignified efficiency. The Mets represented futility but an unwillingness to recognize or admit it.

First of all, when the Met fans showed up at the Yankee Stadium gates with their cowbells and noisemakers, they were told that such items could not be brought into the stadium. The Met fans were furious.

The Yankee players were aware that they would be the object of much loud derision from the Met fans. To get themselves into the proper mood to handle what was sure to follow, during batting practice the Yankees rehearsed on each other. Whitey Ford moved quietly up behind Elston Howard, cupped his hand around Howard's ear, and screamed, "Ah, Elston Howard, you couldn't carry Choo Choo Coleman's glove!"

It was only an exhibition game, but Casey Stengel wanted that victory. For a lot of reasons, personal and professional, he wanted to walk out of that big ball park that night on top. And he did. The Mets won. I have seldom seen such jubilation as that which engulfed the Met fans. It was as though they had won the World Series. The traffic came to a halt as the fans celebrated in the streets. It took me two hours to drive from Yankee Stadium to the Triboro Bridge, and it really isn't very far.

The Mets, meanwhile, were making progress—not rapidly, but some.

The first real Met hero, other than the retreads, was Ron Hunt, a second baseman. Before his career ended he solidly established that his greatest talent was getting hit by pitched balls. He seemed to be insensitive to pain. But in 1964 he was a starter in the All-Star game, played at Shea Stadium. In a late inning, Manager Walter Alston wanted to put up a pinch hitter for Hunt. At the home of the Met fans, Alston had to be careful not to offend. For Hunt, he put up Hank Aaron. No one objected.

The Dodgers had a first baseman named Tim Harkness, whom Manager Walter Alston would insert in the late innings of games where the Dodgers had a big lead. He was put into the lineup, it was said, "for defensive purposes." The inference was that he was a whiz with the glove but light with the bat. After the Mets acquired him, it became painfully apparent that the Dodgers actually had inserted him in the late innings of only the games that they could not possibly lose, where they led by half a dozen runs. Harkness was light with the glove and the bat both. He did win one memorable game at the Polo Grounds with a late home run, and the appreciative fans called him back out of the clubhouse to heap adoration upon him. The Met fans created easy heroes. It had to be the high point of his whole career.

Year after year, the Mets kept trying to acquire capable performers, but it was never easy. They made one deal with the Pittsburgh organization for an outfielder named Don Bosch, who came with the reputation of being in some ways similar to Willie Mays. He was in more ways similar to Eddie Gaedel, Bill Veeck's famous midget who came to bat once for the St. Louis Browns.

Even when the Mets began to show some signs of becoming a ball club, the signs were masked by unlikely circumstances. There was a good-looking left-handed pitcher named Jerry Koosman, who came up in 1967. He would become one of the all-time Met heroes, a talented performer. So where did they get him? Out of the army at Fort Bliss, Texas.

There was this usher at the Polo Grounds who had a son in

the army at Fort Bliss. The son wrote his dad that they had a pitcher on the team there who was capable. Met scout Red Murff went to San Antonio and signed Koosman for a pittance. The pitcher was wrong-handed in demeanor, too. He created a tale for every occasion. He was from rural Minnesota. And he said that he had a brother named Orville and that during the long cold Minnesota winters he and Orville would play catch in the loft of the barn. But they realized one day that Jerry was returning the ball with more velocity than Orville was delivering it. So Jerry became the pitcher. In retrospect, I don't believe I ever met anyone who had actually seen Orville Koosman.

On the banquet circuit, the great hero of the 1936 Berlin Olympics, Jesse Owens, and I had become friends. And this one night we were booked for an appearance at the Roosevelt Hotel in Manhattan. In the late afternoon I had been in the Manhattan offices of the Mets, talking to George Weiss. When I mentioned that I would be seeing Jesse Owens, Weiss said, "See if you can talk him into coming to our spring-training camp in St. Petersburg to coach our runners. I've been trying to get him on the phone but haven't been able to talk to him."

That night, as we waited to go out onto the stage, I said, "Jesse, George Weiss wants to talk to you about coaching the Met base runners. And, believe me, the Mets need all the help they can get."

When I got to the Mets' spring training a few weeks later, Jesse Owens was there, tutoring the base runners in the art of leads and starts. But after several days, Jesse himself came up on the injury list. He had pulled something in his back, and could hardly walk. Next morning I watched him make his way slowly and painfully across the lobby of the Colonial Inn. And I thought to myself, "The Mets have taken one of the world's great runners, and in three days they have brought him right down to their level. It's the great Jesse Owens and he can hardly move."

The very best day the Mets ever had was the day they signed "the franchise."

The "franchise" was Tom Seaver, who was brought up in 1967 when he was twenty-two years old. He was a baby-faced Californian who took no pleasure in the Mets' image as happy, contented failures. He was not pleased at the prospect of continued losing. More than any other performer it was Tom Seaver who gave the Mets their first semblance of quality. So, the Mets had acquired him in the normal manner—they had sent scouts to watch him, signed him, seasoned him, and brought him up, right? Well, not quite. Actually, they got him out of a hat in a sort of raffle, like you might see at the county fair.

Seaver was from Fresno, California, and had pitched at the University of Southern California. It was the Braves who drafted him and thought they had signed him. But there was an irregularity. He had been signed by Atlanta after his college team had already played an exhibition game against a service team, thus beginning their season. That was enough of an irregularity for the commissioner to declare him a free agent.

The commissioner was General Spike Eckert, formerly a somewhat obscure air-force supply officer, who had succeeded Commissioner Ford Frick in a manner that the owners who named him have never volunteered to talk much about. Suffice it to say that the owners put their game into the hands of a fellow who didn't know much about baseball and whom baseball didn't know much about. Larry Fox of the *Daily News* commented, "My God, they've named the Unknown Soldier commissioner of baseball." And they had. Current baseball historians have trouble recalling the name.

In any case, the commissioner said that any team, except Atlanta, could put up fifty thousand dollars and thus participate in a raffle for the services of Tom Seaver. Only three teams thought Seaver was worth the risk of that sum—the Philadelphia Phillies, the Cleveland Indians, and the New York Mets. That may tell you something you don't want to know about the capability of the various major league organizations in judging talent. The names of the three teams were put into a hat, and the drawing was made by an assistant to the commissioner named Lee MacPhail. That's how the Mets got the pitcher who would become their symbol of coming success and a certain Hall of Famer.

And about that time, scout Red Murff, who had signed Koosman at Fort Bliss, came up with another Texan, a right-hander from the town of Alvin, named Nolan Ryan. He came up for a brief late-season look in 1966, but was up to stay in 1968.

It was readily apparent that Ryan could throw a baseball through a brick wall. The problem was that you didn't know which brick wall. Direction and control proved to be something of a difficulty.

Ryan was a good example, though, of the old scouts' adage that "you can teach a pitcher to throw harder, but you can't teach him to throw hard." Either he can or he can't. Ryan could.

But Ryan had still another problem. He tended to rub up blisters on the fingers of his pitching hand. That can be disabling. So the Met trainer, Gus Mauch, went to work. He went to a delicatessen in the Bronx and got a small jar of pickle brine. And he instructed Ryan to soak his finger rather continuously in this pickle brine in order to toughen the skin. So Nolan Ryan started on his way to the Baseball Hall of Fame with his finger in a jar of brine. Hauling a jar of smelly fluid around can be socially restrictive, but the Mets did not seem to do anything easily.

When Yogi Berra had been fired as manager of the Yankees after winning the American League pennant, he became a Met coach. He had talked the situation over with his boyhood pal, Joe Garagiola. The Yanks had offered to keep Berra in the organization, but he had said to Joe, "I don't think the Yanks would ever give me a chance to manage again." So he went to the Mets, who, he thought, might someday make him the manager. (They did, but afterward so did the Yanks.)

But first the Mets made Gil Hodges the manager. He had been a Brooklyn and Los Angeles star, an original Met, and then manager of the Washington Senators.

A Mets front-office executive named Johnny Murphy was a former Yankee pitcher. And his roommate on the Yanks had been George Selkirk, who was now general manager of the Senators. In a phone conversation Murphy had said casually, "I don't suppose there's any point in our talking to you about the possibility of getting Hodges." And Selkirk said, surprisingly, "Oh, I don't know—let's talk about it." Washington, then, did not now consider their manager untouchable. And Hodges came back to New York.

The new manager and his staff of coaches, which consisted of Eddie Yost, Rube Walker, Joe Pignatano, and Yogi Berra, provided a professionalism at the helm that concentrated more on winning than on entertainment. The results, though, were not immediate. At the end of Hodges's first season, 1968, the Mets were a scant one game out of tenth place, just ahead of the Houston Astros. And in September in Atlanta, Hodges himself had had a heart attack. It was reminiscent of a Casey Stengel remark, "Managing that team ain't easy."

By the spring of 1969, though, several things had happened. Hodges had recovered. Bowie Kuhn was commissioner of baseball. Two new teams had been added to the National League—the Montreal Expos and the San Diego Padres. Over the past few years, the Mets had acquired some quality performers. They now had outfielders like Cleon Jones, Tommie Agee, Ron Swoboda, and Art Shamsky. They had infielders like Ed Charles, Wayne Garrett, Bud Harrelson, Al Weis, Ken Boswell, and Ed Kranepool, a native New Yorker who had now grown up. On June 15, they acquired the big bat they badly needed when Donn Clendenon joined up. Jerry Grote, J. C. Martin, and Duffy Dyer capably handled the catching. And the Mets put together a pitching staff that was simply sensational. It included Tom Seaver, Jerry Koosman, Gary Gentry, Nolan Ryan, Jim McAndrew, Don Cardwell, Cal Koonce, Tug McGraw, Danny Frisella, Jack Di-Lauro, and a few other transient personalities. The strong man in the bullpen was Ron Taylor, who was an unusual individual. He already had a degree in electrical engineering. And as an aging medical-school student, he was to become a doctor and the team physician for the Toronto Blue Jays.

My daughter Sharon returned home from school one day and came to me with a problem. Sharon struggled with the efforts of speech but she did the best she could. And we had devised a series of phrases to be used for specific purposes. If there was something that puzzled her, something about which she needed an explanation, she would come to me and say, "Daddy, I've got a problem."

So this day she was in dead earnest when she said, "Daddy, I've got a problem."

It should be pointed out that the Mets were the central point of our lives. We were proud of the Mets, even though they were inept. We went as a family to the ball park a great deal, and we talked about the Mets and the individual players a lot.

Now Sharon looked inquiringly into my face and said, "Daddy, kids at school say the Mets stink."

She looked intently for my reaction. She herself had no opinion. This was a query. She had been taunted at school, and she wanted to know the validity of the charge. She was deadly serious and this was no time for a frivolous reply.

"Well," I said, "try not to let it upset you. It is a game, and the Mets are our favorite team. Sometimes they don't play very well.

Sometimes they play terribly. But they will get better. In the meantime, do not be disturbed by what they say at school. Just smile or laugh when the kids say that. Because it is true. There are times when the Mets do stink."

That seemed to satisfy Sharon.

And then we were into the 1969 season and the Mets continued to stink. But suddenly and inexplicably in August, they were on their way to one of the great miracles in the history of the game of baseball. If the listing of miracles is alphabetical, you will find "Mets" just after "Lourdes."

For the Met faithful, it was their just reward at long last. For those in the organization, especially me, it was incomparable. When I look back now on a long career of having announced a variety of sports events around the world, people say, "What was the most exciting?"

For me, that's easy. It was the fifth game of the 1969 World Series, the most memorable sports event I ever worked. It was the day that the New York Mets became champions of the world. When I had left the national network life at NBC to take a job as the voice of the Mets, I had staked my personal and professional future on the performance of this baseball team. And they were now world champions.

But even in winning, the Mets had seemed to do it, not the hard way, but the unusual way.

Often when a team wins the pennant, they get into first place early in the season and they stay there. Or they take charge in midseason and ride in daily triumph to the pennant. The Mets didn't do that.

It was the first year of divisional play in the major leagues. The Montreal Expos and the San Diego Padres had been added to the National League to give it twelve teams, and there were now Eastern and Western divisions. At season's end, there would be a championship series to precede the World Series. This was all new.

For most of the season it looked as though the winner in the Eastern Division would be the Chicago Cubs, managed by Leo Durocher, who had given the previously listless Cubs a new life. The Mets were showing flashes of brilliance, moving up in the standings. But for the most part there was no real feeling that the Mets were on the way to a pennant.

In August they were swept by Houston in a series at the Astrodome. In fact, that pennant-winning, miraculous season of 1969 the Mets did not win a single game at the Astrodome. On August 13, the Mets were in third place, nine and a half games back of the Cubs. And as I talked to CBS about the football season, there was no reason to suspect that I wouldn't be available the day after the last game of the regular baseball season. Just the same, we had always had a verbal agreement that I would be free of any football obligations if the Mets should get into the playoffs. When we would casually mention this provision, the CBS people would usually laugh, and so would I.

But then, for no explicable reason, the Mets began to do some very unlikely things. They began to win. In St. Louis, the Mets faced Cardinal left-hander Steve Carlton. And Carlton struck out a record nineteen Mets. But he didn't beat the Mets, because Ron Swoboda hit two two-run homers and the Mets were victorious, 4–3.

In a long doubleheader at Pittsburgh, the Mets scored only two runs. And each of those was driven in by the pitcher, one by Don Cardwell and one by Jerry Koosman. And the Mets won both ends of the doubleheader by identical scores, 1–0.

The Mets won thirty-eight of their last forty-nine games. After early August, both Tom Seaver and Jerry Koosman were unbeatable. Neither lost a game the rest of the way. And on September 24, the last home game of the regular season, the Mets beat the St. Louis Cardinals to become the champions of the Eastern Division.

Sometimes it is difficult to distinguish between strongest desire and prophecy, I suppose. When Joe Torre came to bat for the Cardinals in the top of the ninth inning with a runner on first and one man out, I suddenly had the clearest and strongest feeling that Torre was about to hit into a double play. I absolutely knew it. There was not the slightest doubt. But I refrained from saying it. Years of training in proper restraint had done me in. Instead of telling this New York audience of anxious Met faithful that Joe Torre was about to hit into a double play and end the game that would make the Mets champs of the East, a fact that had certainly just now been clearly revealed to me, I chose to describe the pitch, and the swing, and the ground ball, the force at second, the relay to first, and the end of the game. I shoulda told them ahead. I knew it.

Well, I had been in victorious clubhouses. I had seen teams in full celebration. I had been in the Dodgers clubhouse at Ebbets Field the day they had won the only world championship they ever won in Brooklyn. I had been in the Milwaukee clubhouse at Yankee Stadium the day they had won the world championship in 1957. I had been in the Pittsburgh clubhouse in 1960 the day Bill Mazeroski hit the home run at Forbes Field to give the Pirates their world championship over the Yankees.

I had seen all of that. But it was nothing compared to the scene in the Mets clubhouse that night. It was incomparable because all those other times I had simply witnessed winners in high celebration. But now, I was a part of this. These were my people, and I was one of them.

Jerry Grote and I had become close friends during his years with the Mets. We talked frequently about a variety of things. I knew his wife, Sharon, his family, his dreams of someday taking the baseball money and going home to run his own ranch in San Antonio. And when I looked across that clubhouse that night at Jerry Grote, I shall never forget the look in his eyes. They were literally shining. Not a word was spoken, because that look said, "Look at us! We did it! We won the championship! What could ever be better than this?" And then he reached his arms around me and picked me up.

Ralph Kiner, Bob Murphy, and I were taking turns doing the TV interviews in the clubhouse, and we were drenched with champagne. And I discovered that when it ran into the eyes it burned, it stung. I kept a towel around my neck so that I could wipe out the champagne and keep my eyes open. In Europe during the war, I had shaved with champagne, and now we were using it for shampoo.

When I think of that scene now, and when I remember thinking, again, "What could ever be better than this?" I now have an answer.

And the answer is "Nothing." This would be the best of all. George Vecsey would write, "The honest joy in the clubhouse was one of the most absorbing studies ever seen on television." The operative word is *honest.* The television announcers were enjoying it as much as the players. It wasn't a chore, an assignment. This was all real.

There would be other clubhouse celebrations—the one after the third straight victory over Atlanta when the Mets had won the National League pennant. The scene was similar, the champagne, the squirting shave cream, the laughter. But it wasn't as pure. This time it was a little forced. It was a little rehearsed, as though all the participants had done a run-through, and of course they had. And then there was the clubhouse when the Mets had beaten the Baltimore Orioles in the World Series. This time, the celebration was seen from coast to coast on NBC-TV, and I was the announcer in the clubhouse. The commissioner of baseball, Bowie Kuhn, was there to present the trophy to General Manager Johnny Murphy, who had only about three months to live, and to M. Donald Grant, the Mets' ubiquitous chairman, and Mayor John Lindsay was there to associate himself with this band of ballplayers in a move that would make a major contribution to his reelection. But by now this sort of celebration was becoming old hat.

The one after the World Series victory was the monumental celebration to mark the Mets' place in history, of course. I can close my eyes and recall it now in exact detail.

I could hear the World Series crowd at Shea Stadium roaring on every pitch. I could hear them, but I couldn't see them. It was October 16, 1969. The Baltimore Orioles were batting in the top of the ninth. The New York Mets were leading, 5–3. I was standing now, alone, in the far corner of the washroom, beyond the Mets' locker room on the ground floor. I had been at the NBC microphone doing the television play-by-play for an audience of millions until the eighth inning when the Mets had gone ahead. Then I had run out of the booth, down the ramps, heading for what I knew would be a wild locker-room scene. For the first time, I hadn't trusted the elevators. Frantically, I envisioned the Mets celebrating the magical moment while I was stuck somewhere in an overcrowded elevator. No chance! That's why I had raced down the ramps, and now I was getting my breath, and a sobering shock at the same time. As I contemplated the moment, the realization came upon me fully. "The METS," I thought, "are about to be champions of the WORLD."

I wasn't alone in that thought. Thousands of people in Manhattan, with the same realization, were about to pour forth into the city streets—laughing, crying, dancing, tossing tons of confetti, newspapers, ticker tape, phone books into the air. Soldiers in Vietnam and Thailand were hanging on to every word of the overseas broadcast. Cab drivers all across this land pulled over to curbs to listen. Schoolchildren with smuggled transistors squealed uncontrollably in classrooms.

"There's one man out," somebody shouted to me. The network technicians had a platform ready in the center of the locker room. The camera was trained on it. The microphones were in position. There was the Telex ready to be stuck into my ear. The stage managers had the cue cards ready.

I remembered the first game the Mets ever won, an exhibition game over the Cardinals in Saint Petersburg when Manager Casey Stengel had gone to his bench for a pinch hitter named Choo Choo Coleman, and Choo Choo had hit a home run. He didn't hit many more.

I remembered the first National League game the Mets ever played. It was in St. Louis against the Cards, and Roger Craig was the Mets' pitcher. With a man on third, he committed a balk. The first run ever scored against the Mets came home on a balk.

There was Old Timers Day at the Polo Grounds that summer of 1962. And the Dodgers beat the Mets 17–3. I remembered Bill Terry that night, shaking his head and saying, "I just don't know if I could stand that."

"There are two men out," yelled a voice from the locker room. I straightened my tie and went out to the platform, where a television monitor showed the scene outside. Cautiously, I put my wristwatch into my pocket.

There was a night when I had broadcast a Met game without a monitor. I was in a cage suspended from the very top of the Astrodome in Houston, 208 feet directly over second base. I was in fair territory, but I was safe. The Mets of that year weren't hitting balls 208 feet in any direction, not even straight up. I was up there for four hours, and my only form of communication was a walkie-talkie on a wavelength that was mixed up with a local taxicab company's. The Mets lost.

I remembered Rod Kanehl in windblown Candlestick Park in San Francisco, racing from his post at third base back down the left-field line for a pop fly that fell untouched behind first base. There was Ron Swoboda racing in on a ground ball to the outfield with the bases loaded in Cincinnati and swinging his glove down in full flight like Willie Mays, only Swoboda came up empty, with three runs scoring while the ball rolled up the incline to the fence. I remembered the pain on Manager Wes Westrum's face almost any day.

Those had been painful years for the Mets, the Met fans, and the Met broadcasters. The Mets had become a symbol of ineptitude, a national joke. While they endured it, it was a role they did not relish. The Met fans survived and multiplied. They cheered and yelled and hoped and prayed—and often they laughed to keep from crying. Bad jokes were made by people who misunderstood and mistakenly thought the Met fans cherished a loser.

But this year had been so different. Manager Gil Hodges instilled quiet dignity and confidence. It was contagious. The Mets had the best pitching. They made all the plays. The defense was unbelievable. They made circus catches that no one in the game has since duplicated.

On the monitor I watched the last out being made, heard the Mets proclaimed world champions by my telecasting partner Curt Gowdy, saw fans race onto the field, digging up the turf of Shea Stadium, hurling handfuls of sod high into the air.

The locker-room door burst open, and the Mets stormed jubilantly in. It was absolute bedlam. Champagne corks popped. Somebody was pouring champagne over the head of the mayor of New York, and the mayor was pouring it on somebody else. Somebody was pouring it on me and my microphone. I felt sticky champagne in my hair, cold champagne running down my neck inside my shirt. My eyes burned with stinging champagne so that I could hardly keep them open, and I didn't care. My pockets and my watch were soaked.

But the New York Mets—*my* New York Mets—were the world champions!

They had been through seven years of famine, absolute famine. Because of those years, this year of plenty was magnified a thousand-fold.

From the day they were born, I had broadcast almost every game the Mets ever played. I used to say, not entirely facetiously, that my job was hardest—I didn't have to play the games, I had to explain them. Now all I had to do was applaud, and laugh, and soak up the magic of this rarest of moments that could never ever possibly be duplicated or forgotten.

During the clubhouse party, the Mets announced that there would be a victory party for players and their families, members of the front office, including the announcers, and their families. It would start in the Diamond Club upstairs at seven P.M., so we had several hours to kill. When I had dried off somewhat, but still smelling strongly of champagne, I loaded my family into our car, and we drove into Manhattan. It was a scene I wanted to savor, one I surely did not want to miss. The celebration was still going on, people literally dancing in the streets, throwing bits of telephone books from open windows high above the streets. I had never before known what the phrase really meant, but this was what the novelists called "pure joy unrestrained."

We drove around through the streets of Manhattan and watched this mighty metropolis for an instant become a small crossroads town.

There was nothing sophisticated about this behavior. And we were as happy as any of them.

When we got back to the party, the mood continued. The Diamond Club was crowded, a band was playing. People were still hugging each other. Jerry Koosman had been the winning pitcher of that final game. He had won two of the five games in the Series. Jerry and I were good friends. Jerry and everybody were good friends; how could you not like Koos? He and I were standing over by the big glass windows when some of the celebrants insisted that Jerry go up to the bandstand and sing "Take Me Out to the Ball Game."

Koosman turned to me and said, "I ain't going up there without you."

And so he and I went up to the bandstand and rendered a loud and not very musical version of "Take Me Out to the Ball Game." (Later that night he joined with a much better-looking songstress at the Copacabana in Manhattan for another vocal number. Koos was on a roll.)

All that had happened on Thursday, October 16. Later Al Moore of Rheingold would present me a set of cuff links, one of which was a silver calendar of the month of October 1969 with a ruby on the sixteenth. I appreciated the thought and the gift, but I would have remembered it anyway.

But there was no time for rest on these busy days. On Friday morning, I had to be off for South Bend, Indiana, and a football game on Saturday, Notre Dame vs. Southern Cal.

While I was having breakfast, Mickie was busy with the paint bucket. And when I went out to the garage to get into the car, she had written in black paint on the white garage wall, OUR METS—WORLD CHAMPS!

It was a milestone in the lives of our family. We never painted over Mickie's happy sign. It was still there when she died a few years later. It was still there when I sold the house and moved on. But when I look back and when I remember the good times and the bad, the things that didn't work out and the things that did, I remember life with the Mets as so well worthwhile for all of us.

I suspect that nothing matters much if you don't care. What's the satisfaction of the big deal in Wall Street if there is no emotion? What's the achievement if there is no one to share it with? What's the reward for a sportscaster or the value of his fortune if his work is sterile?

We had suffered, we had hoped and prayed, we had endured and taken risks that involved our future security. We felt that inner glow that comes with the success of those we care for, the action and passion. We would remember this for all the rest of our lives.

And, perhaps best of all, at school little Sharon was now a heroine. The Mets didn't stink anymore.

The game between Notre Dame and Southern Cal was a beauty. They usually are. It has been through the years perhaps the most spectacular of all the intercollegiate series. The first game had been arranged back in the 1920s, before Notre Dame Stadium was built on the campus. Coach Knute Rockne's teams were called the Ramblers because they played most of their games on the road. And now that Southern Cal was playing in the huge Los Angeles Memorial Coliseum, they wanted to get Notre Dame to come to California. Graduate manager of athletics Gwynn Wilson was dispatched with his new bride on a trip to Lincoln, Nebraska, where Rockne's Notre Dame team was playing the Cornhuskers in the season's finale, to try to talk him into a contract. Instead, Rockne insisted that the Wilsons come on back to South Bend, and so they did.

In South Bend it was cold and snowy at this time of year, and not exactly comfortable. Just the same, Knute Rockne was in no immediate mood to plan a long trip for his football team to California. So the talks had just about ground to a halt and it seemed as though there would never be any Notre Dame vs. Southern Cal series. And then one night while Wilson and Rock were in the kitchen, the two ladies, Mrs. Wilson and Mrs. Rockne, were talking in the living room. Mrs. Wilson spoke of the beauty of the weather in Los Angeles at that time of year. She spoke of the sunshine, the orange trees, the warm comfort. Mrs. Rockne, having recently wiped the snow off her boots, listened carefully. And later that night, at the first opportunity, she had a long talk with her husband. Next morning, the contract was signed for the first game between Notre Dame and Southern Cal. Football enthusiasts have spoken about how this famous series was arranged by those two great coaches, Knute Rockne and Howard Jones. It is more likely that it was arranged by Bonnie Rockne and Marian Wilson.

In any case, that afternoon in 1969, the game ended in a tie, and on the last play of the game Notre Dame tried a field goal and the ball hit the crossbar and bounced back.

The ball had hardly hit the ground and the game ended, before I was on a plane for Chicago to connect to St. Louis and another football game on Sunday for CBS—the St. Louis Cardinals and the Minnesota Vikings. In St. Louis the CBS analyst was Tom Brookshier and the color announcer was Bill Mazer. As we picked our way through the crowd at the stadium, I was greeted time and time again by enthusiastic fans. It got so funny that Brookshier started laughing. There is nothing like a few days on the tube at World Series time to increase one's national recognition factor.

But by now I had developed another problem. Throughout my lifetime I had always suffered from a bad case of overbooking. I was continuously overscheduled. In my high-school yearbook, the legend had said, "Can you imagine Lindsey Nelson with nothing to do?" Well, it had happened again.

Mayor John Lindsay had proclaimed that that Monday would be "New York Mets Day" in New York. And Harold Weissman of the Mets called to tell me that the mayor wanted me to act as master of ceremonies for the day's activities. That would be great—a ticker-tape parade up lower Broadway, a midcity celebration, a luncheon, all sorts of things. And I would be coordinating them all. The problem was that I didn't plan to be in New York on Monday.

Back in the early fall when we didn't know that the Mets were going to be playing in October, I had a request from Tom Hamilton of WNDU in South Bend to be the principal speaker at the kickoff luncheon of the United Fund drive for St. Joseph County. It would be held at the Notre Dame Convocation Center, and I had said okay.

Weissman wanted to know if I would see if I could get out of the commitment in South Bend so that he could tell Mayor Lindsay I would be in New York. It was now late Sunday afternoon, and I could not immediately get in touch with anyone in South Bend, so I went instead to Chicago. When in doubt, go to Chicago. In almost any circumstances, that is good advice. You can get help in Chicago for anything. If they can't handle it, they'll help you find it or fix it.

When I finally got the United Fund chairman in South Bend, he was kind but explicit. "We really do need you," he said. "We've built the theme of the day around your being here. A lot of people have done a lot of work and would be terribly disappointed."

That took care of that. I said, "I'll be there."

I was on North Central Airlines next morning, trying to write my speech as we bounced our way down to South Bend. I had some time to kill, so I went to the Convocation Center and sort of milled around for a few hours. Meantime, I called WOR-TV in New York, the station that carried the Mets games and would be covering the big celebration that day. I had already called Mickie the night before and suggested that she and Nancy take my place in the parade and the luncheon and anything else.

WOR-TV asked if that night I could come straight to the studios on Times Square when I got to New York and announce a two-hour television special covering all the day's activities.

So, when I finished the United Fund luncheon in South Bend, I went to the airport and got a plane that would take me to Fort Wayne and then to New York. When I got to WOR, it was early evening, and Don Criqui and I went to work getting the show together.

I loved the opportunity of seeing all that footage. It was my only way of knowing what had happened on "New York Mets Day" in New York. There were bits with Robert Merrill of the Metropolitan Opera and Pearl Bailey of Broadway, and everywhere, Mayor Lindsay.

When we finished the show, I went down to Times Square to get a taxi to take me to LaGuardia where I had left my car on Friday morning. We had ridden only a block when the cabbie turned round, and said, "Would you be Mr. Lindsey Nelson—the voice of the Mets?" I confessed. And he said, "It's such an honor to have you in the cab, and there ain't no charge."

I knew right then I had had a good day. When a New York cabbie says, "There ain't no charge," you'd better frame it.

There was one brief postscript a few months later. I got a letter from the chairman of the United Fund drive in South Bend. He said that he doubted anyone had ever told me, but he thought I should know that they had just managed to reach their full quota in funds raised and that they would be able to finance all their community obligations. St. Joseph County was grateful, he said, and he thought I should know.

That Monday had been an even better day than I'd thought.

In the wake of their world's championship, absolutely nothing was too good for the Mets. Comedian Phil Foster took one group of them out to Las Vegas, where they whipped together a nightclub act and reaped a rapid benefit of ten thousand dollars each.

A travel agent who specialized in putting together package tours announced that he had worked out a deal with Air France and Hilton Hotels, and he was prepared to invite any of the Mets and their wives on a tour, free of charge. The problem was that the Mets just hadn't counted on winning the championship of the world, and most of them had already made plans and commitments for the time just after the first of the year, when the tour was planned. Jerry Grote and his wife, Sharon, could make it. So could Bobby Pfeil and his wife, Melanie. Wayne Garrett and Rod Gaspar could go. Coach Eddie Yost and his wife, Pat, were ready. Harvey LaKind, an agent who had helped put the tour together, was ready with his wife, Blanche. And the three announcers and their wives—the Kiners (Ralph and Barbara), the Murphys (Bob and Jean), and the Nelsons (Mickie and me).

First there was a send-off party at Kennedy Airport, then an all-night flight to Orly Airport in Paris, where we were met by members of the American embassy staff and members of the Paris press.

There was a welcoming party with fancy French food and champagne, and then we piled into bed for a few hours of daytime sleep. Then we were up and off to the United States embassy on the Place de la Concorde, where we were greeted by Ambassador Sargent Shriver. He led us up to his private office on the second floor, where we gazed out onto the busy scene beyond the picture windows.

Ambassador Shriver was congratulatory, and also mentioned that as a young man he had often watched Eddie Yost playing third base for the old Washington Senators.

At one point, the ambassador said quietly to me, "What do you think they want to see?"

The problem was that we were going to be in town only that one day, and at night we would be flying on to Rabat, Morocco. I suggested that we just hit the high spots and move on. And in a very few moments, we were loaded into a bus and were driving around town. We stopped at the Eiffel Tower, where we did the tourist trick with cameras. Then we stopped at the Louvre for a fast glance at the *Vénus de Milo,* the Winged Victory of Samothrace, and the *Mona Lisa.* That's the fifteen-minute culture course. For the remainder of your life whenever you are in surroundings where the *Mona Lisa* comes up, you are able to say, proudly, "Yes, I've seen that." Admittedly, the *Mona Lisa* does not come up in many conversations at Shea Stadium. And I must confess that I have never ever heard the Winged Victory of Samothrace mentioned there. But it's a good experience to have in your verbal résumé. And now we were heading up the wide Champs-Élysées in quest of the Arc de Triomphe. You can't miss it.

Near the back of the bus, Rod Gaspar leaned across the aisle to say to Wayne Garrett, "Do you believe we're in Paris, France?"

Gaspar smiled that Huck Finn smile and said, "I don't believe this whole year."

I didn't either. I still don't.

Having been properly entertained in Paris by our gracious and smiling ambassador, we were delivered to Orly, where we boarded a plane and flew away to Rabat, the capital of Morocco.

We went on all the little side trips that had been arranged, but had to cancel the junkets to Meknes and Fez because of heavy rains. I had a distinct feeling of déjà vu. I had roamed Rabat as a soldier twenty-seven years before.

Then we made our move to Casablanca, where we boarded a cruise ship for a trip to a few Mediterranean ports before putting in at Lisbon for the flight home.

There were a few hours in Tangiers in the rain. We made a stop at Málaga on the Costa del Sol. And there was a trip to Jerez, Spain. Anybody who has a taste for sherry knows that Humbert and Williams is located in Jerez, and we made a tour of the winery and sampled the product. The order of events that day was slightly unfortunate. We went first to the distillery and then to the bullring. We should have done it the other way round.

At the ring there were some young bulls in training. And the Mets were invited to avail themselves of cape and rapier and go a few rounds with the big beasts.

Keep in mind now that these were the Mets. True, they had won the championship of the world. But just the same, these were the people who had become previously world famous in the field of ineptitude. After having made several careful and tentative moves with no permanent injuries resulting, Rod Gaspar decided that he would make his move, boldly. Unfortunately, about the same time the bull had a similar thought.

Gaspar immediately grasped the core of that situation, determining that he was at a disadvantage, outweighed by about three hundred pounds. He threw the cape and rapier skyward and headed helter-skelter for the safety of the wall. It was much closer behind him than he thought, and when he turned he hit it all at once and melted toward the ground, like Krazy Kat.

It was while we were on board ship one morning that a wire came for Coach Eddie Yost. It was from the Mets' office in New York, telling us the sad news that General Manager Johnny Murphy had suffered a heart attack and died. He had been able to savor that glorious victory for only three months. In spring training of 1972, Manager Gil Hodges would suffer a heart attack in Florida and would die instantly.

But the memory would never die. It was all once upon a marvelous time—the miracle of the Mets.

The effect of the Mets victory continued during the next baseball season. Gil Hodges was the National League manager at the All-Star game in Cincinnati, and NBC-TV assigned me to the job of "celebrity interviewer."

My duties included going into the stands and doing a live interview with the president of the United States, Richard Nixon.

In order to arrange for a little extra time, it was decided that I would make my move at the end of the third inning. And I spoke to Joe Reichler, who was on the commissioner's staff. Joe spoke to Al Barlick, who was the plate umpire, and suggested that he kill time and keep an eye on me before he allowed play to continue in the top of the fourth inning.

During play in the third inning, then, I moved down the aisle toward the commissioner's box on the first-base side, where the president was seated. I was equipped with a portable transmitter. I had a pack on my back and a large earpiece from which a high, straight antenna protruded.

When I got there, Commissioner Bowie Kuhn very graciously got up to give me his seat next to the president.

Soon the inning ended, and I heard producer Lou Kusserow saying, "Okay, Lindsey, stand by."

Lou was so calm and deliberate. I'm out there about to talk to the president of the United States before what was said later to be an audience of fifty-four million people, and Lou sounded as though he was about to introduce me at the Moose Club picnic.

Now the president moved forward. He said, "I know how this works. You have to wait until you get a cue through that earpiece before you start the interview. Isn't that right?"

I said quickly, "Yes, sir."

I was listening for the cue that would be coming at any time, and I preferred that we had a little silence around here so I could hear it. But you can't tell the president to shut up, unless, I suppose, you are Mrs. President, and she was talking to Commissioner Kuhn on my immediate left. I had introduced myself to her when I sat down. She glared at me and didn't say anything. She looked as though she might have understood me to say, "Good evening, I'm Rumpelstiltskin."

Now as I waited for a cue, the president was saying, "Lindsey, how many All-Star games for you? I think I read where Willie Mays has been in something like twenty-three."

I was about to tell him that I had maybe been to one too many when I heard Kusserow say, "You're on."

Okay, Mr. President, you ain't gonna get no answer to your question because I have one of my own. And besides, you know how this works. Since I got the cue, it's my turn.

As we proceeded with the interview, however, I kept an eye on umpire Al Barlick, and I became absolutely intrigued. Al was bending over the plate, but he was glancing up from underneath that stubby-billed cap to check on the progress of the interview.

Al brushed off the front of the plate, surveyed it, then moved around and brushed off the back of the plate. On careful inspection, that turned out to be not quite good enough. So, while batter and pitcher waited, he again brushed off the front of the plate, and now the side of the plate. There has never been a cleaner home plate in the history of this grand old game of baseball.

My reverie in admiration of Barlick's work was interrupted by the casual tones of producer Lou Kusserow in my ear saying, "Okay, wrap him up, wrap him up."

Very respectfully I said, "Thank you, Mr. President." And I left.

I marveled that my association with the Mets now had me associating with the president. The benefits of that Met victory continued for years.

CHAPTER 22

In the Booth

As a play-by-play football broadcaster, I am convinced that the fellow you should be especially nice to is the spotter. It's like in the newspaper trade where they say always be nice to the copyboy because he is going to grow up to be the editor and your boss.

The spotter is situated beside the play-by-play announcer in the booth and assists with identifications through a system of silent communications.

At Notre Dame, I had a young student as my spotter who was very industrious. We did not transport spotters, so he sometimes scrambled his own way to the cities where the road games were played. His name was Terry O'Neil. He is now the executive producer of NFL football on CBS. Among other things, he hires and assigns the announcers, and he produces the Super Bowl when it is on his network.

There was a time when I was doing the preseason games of the Chicago Bears for Channel 2 in Chicago. This bright young fellow said that he wanted to be my spotter. I explained that it was not a very remunerative job. We paid twenty-five dollars and that did not include travel expenses. He said that he would pay his own expenses. He was a marvelous spotter, and I was certainly glad to have him. He was learning the trade, and I hope that he picked up a few worthwhile tips from me. He is now one of the most visible and capable performers in sports television, and not long ago CBS and ABC waged a public battle for his services, each offering a lucrative contract. He chose to remain at CBS. His name is Brent Musburger.

I have worked with a great many others who have advanced to responsible positions in the trade, but I think you get the idea.

As a matter of personal preference, I like the method of using two spotters, one for each team, but back there ten or twelve years ago, I felt that I simply had to go to one spotter because the game and its presentation were moving so fast, and so many new techniques were being introduced and added, that I had to tighten up the operation and move along. I felt that I didn't have room for two spotters. It was more work for me, but I didn't feel that I had any choice.

In addition to the play-by-play announcer, there is the analyst. He is probably a former coach or player and he is there, as his designation indicates, to analyze the game. There was a time when there was a "color man." He was an announcer whose job it was to add color to the presentation with comments about the crowd or anything else that occurred to him. And there is a statistician who has the job of furnishing the announcers with instant statistics, such as yardage on punts, total first downs, number of passes thrown and completed, and anything else of a statistical nature that will enhance the narration. A good statistician can do wonders for the image of the announcers as bright, sharp observers.

I do not want a spotter, or anyone else, between me and the analyst. I want to be able to communicate with the analyst by holding up my hand, by putting my hand on his shoulder, or by a look.

There are play-by-play men who go further. I know one who will on occasion put his hand over the mouth of the analyst. That, I suppose, is a not-too-subtle hint that he is invited to shut up. I have worked with some analysts who might at that moment choose to belt you in the nose. I have never had the nerve to employ that method.

If only one spotter is used, he probably does the defense and the announcer does the offense himself.

Of course, there are announcers who work without spotters. They do all the identifications themselves. Most announcers could do that. After all, many of them, like me, started as spotters. If you are going to do it all yourself, though, I think you are going to miss a lot of the total presentation. A good spotter will be watching the sidelines to see what is going to happen in the way of substitutions before it happens. But if I am doing the play-by-play, I must keep my eye on the ball. I can't be watching the sidelines, and I may not be aware of the new man until he figures in a play.

A football announcer should be able to learn a lot from his analyst. Presumably, the analyst has played the game, and he should have a lot of information peculiar to himself and the position that he has played. The play-by-play man and the analyst spend a lot of time together. They travel together. They dine together. They are in constant conversation, and a good play-by-play man will soak up all of this privileged information. An average fan would give his right arm to spend time in the company of some of those great stars.

The most difficult thing, in my opinion, is to get the analyst to settle down and give opinions on the air that are based on his very special knowledge. For some reason, not many former players and coaches want to do this. Right away they want to be Graham McNamee. They want to sound like the announcers that they have heard.

The practice of using former players regularly was begun by Bert Bell when he was commissioner of a struggling National Football League. There had been former players who had worked as analysts before, but not a lot of them. Bert saw the practice as a means of extending the pension plan. He knew that there were then a lot of fellows around who had reached the end of their playing careers and now had no means of earning a living. Bert thought he could put a clause in the broadcast contract making it mandatory for a former player or coach to be teamed with a play-by-play man. And he did. That is when the practice began to spread. And almost immediately it was perceived to have considerable merchandising value.

When a regular announcer was introduced on a series, it sometimes took several years for him to become well known enough to be of "name" value. The former player had already been heavily publicized and could be merchandised immediately.

There have been some broadcast teams that have become particularly identifiable, such as Curt Gowdy and Paul Christman; Dick Enberg and Merlin Olsen; Frank Gifford, Don Meredith, and Howard Cosell; and Ray Scott and Tony Canadeo.

I have been fortunate in that I have worked with a great many analysts. I worked longer with Red Grange than with any other single analyst. And he left the greatest imprint on me. I never knew a more modest hero than Red Grange, and I hope that I learned a lot from him about how to maintain proper values in a world of mounting egos.

I worked with Jim Crowley, one of the Four Horsemen of Notre Dame. I remember Jim pointing out that some individuals were suited to be head coaches and some suited to be assistants, and the qualities were not necessarily the same. He thought that Frank Leahy, who assisted him at Fordham, was not a particularly good assistant coach but was a brilliant head coach. Being around Grange and Crowley, I always felt as though I was walking around with football history.

Benny Friedman, whom I worked one game with in Baltimore, was intense. As a former player and coach, he had definitive ideas about the game and how it should be played. He said that as a coach he always took a locker near the men's room. That way, he said, he could tell who was ready. If a player makes repeated trips to the men's room before going onto the field, he is really ready. He is anxious and can hardly wait. I suppose you might call Benny's system the "latrine system" of analysis. In his later years, Friedman, who had certainly been one of the best-known names in the game, could not understand why he could not get hired as a network analyst. He had a friend contact all three of the networks and when he didn't get so much as an interview, it puzzled him. And it also depressed him.

I thought Jim Brown was one of the best analysts ever, and I thought he was miscast by the network. Bob Stenner, a producer based in Los Angeles, was instrumental in getting Brown into the broadcasting business. And Bob asked that I work his first game with him. We did the Rams and the Packers in Milwaukee, and I thought Brown brought something to the analysis that had been missing. He gave us opinions about the manner in which the running backs performed, and who was better qualified to talk about running backs than Jim Brown?

I think it was unfortunate that the network decided to form a triumvirate, putting Vin Scully, George Allen, and Jim Brown in the booth together, mostly working games to be seen in Los Angeles, where all three lived.

To begin with, I am not a big fan of three announcers in a booth anytime, anywhere. I think that is likely to be too many, and in many cases it's two too many.

In the case of that trio, Jim Brown and George Allen ended up talking, ineffectively, to each other. I thought that Jim Brown talking to the audience, telling them what he thought about what was going on, was far more valuable. I worked a season with George Allen, who was, I thought, effective and dedicated as a single in the role of analyst.

It was back there in 1966 that the NFL was getting ideas of trying to expand coverage into the prime-time hours. Every sport wanted to do that. But these hours were jealously guarded by the entertainment divisions of the networks. Prime time was where they made their money and their reputations.

In the early years, the Friday night fights, sponsored by Gillette, had been a big hit. But the executives didn't really want sports in prime time. A lot of executives didn't want sports, period. When it became apparent that the Friday night fights would not be able to survive the network pressures for long, the NBA made a determined bid to get a foot in the prime-time door. They didn't make it.

Now the NFL was going to make a pitch with CBS. And the experimental Monday night game they chose was the Chicago Bears vs. the St. Louis Cardinals in St. Louis on Halloween Night of 1966. It was in prime time. And the announcers were Lindsey Nelson on play-by-play and Frank Gifford as analyst.

As a one-time shot, the game was attractive enough. But when the NFL offered to schedule a regular Monday night game throughout the entire season, the idea was turned down by both CBS and NBC. Their Monday night schedules were just too strongly entrenched to be upset by anything like professional football, still perceived in many of the upper administrative echelons as "fun and games."

ABC, however, was not all that strong on Monday nights, or any nights at that time. So in 1970 *Monday Night Football* began on ABC, and it proved to be a godsend.

These games got full attention because they were presented on the full network at a time when there was no sports competition. Most of the pro football telecasts were then and are now regional. They are seen by audiences of dedicated fans who are vitally interested in the outcome of the games. The Monday night games were seen by everybody, including women and children, and a lot of the viewers couldn't care less about who won. This provided a freedom of expression that was not available to those working the Sunday afternoon games. It was possible to present the game on Monday night in a less intense atmosphere.

Like performers in any field, analysts have their own peculiar characteristics. Pat Summerall, for instance, works in the low-key manner of the late Paul Christman. Pat uses the deep, rich voice to intone his comments. At first he was waiting for the day when he would make the switch to play-by-play, where he had noticed that there seemed to be more security and longevity.

Pat is a perfect partner for John Madden, who is enthusiastic, knowledgeable, and somewhat undisciplined. When Madden was breaking in, I was assigned to work a game with him in Denver. We sat down the night before to go over our game plan. John said, "Now, you want me to be finished with my comments and out by the time the ball is snapped, right?"

Somebody somewhere had obviously told him that.

I said, "No, I don't necessarily require that you be out before the snap. If you are into something pertinent, follow it to a conclusion. I will take care of the snap and what follows. But if it's pertinent, you just keep going. If it's impertinent, you shouldn't be talking anyway."

As a coach, John Madden was an excitable man in motion. He was up and down the sideline and out onto the field, waving his arms and screaming. As an analyst in the booth, he has not changed one bit.

I thought that Paul Hornung was an excellent analyst, and Paul and I worked together for a lot of years both for CBS and on the Notre Dame games. At the beginning, Paul was still into what sometimes seemed to be a frantic life-style. But that was soon gone, and he settled down in the manner of a professional. In his later years he worked as hard at the job as anybody I have ever seen, with good results. Of course, nobody in the history of the game has ever had more personal magnetism than Paul Hornung. He has a great feeling for the young people, who invariably adore him. He treats them like adults. The Golden Boy of Notre Dame and Green Bay is one of the very special individuals in the history of the game of football. It seemed to me to be a testament to his substance that he retained the respect and admiration of his stern Green Bay coach, Vince Lombardi, and of his teammates.

It was along in there during Barry Frank's tenure as boss of CBS Sports that I experienced a frightening moment in my career. We were at the Fiesta Bowl in Tempe, Arizona. Paul Hornung and I were doing the Christmas Day telecast for CBS. I did not actually know Barry Frank very well. I knew his name and reputation, but to my knowledge I had only seen him once, and that was a brief meeting at Texas Stadium in Dallas. So, along during the game a crowd shot was flashed up there on the screen and the producer, Davey Fox, said to Paul and me on the Telex in our ears, "Well, now, look who's here."

I looked at the shot and there was nobody in there that I knew. I didn't say anything. I just looked at Paul, and it was very interesting because Paul had turned a sort of Christmas purple. He was also choking a little as he leaned forward and said into his mike, "Why, there's the boss—there's Barry Frank, vice-president of CBS Sports." Son-of-a-gun! So that's who the fellow in the red vest was! Those tricky crowd shots could end your career.

Let me explain here that through the years I have been in this business I have spent most of my time at the ball park, or the stadium, or the field house, or the golf course. I have not often been in the executive corridors of the networks. For instance, I have done twenty-one seasons of football for CBS, and I have never met the real boss, Bill Paley. In fact, I have never seen Bill Paley. I don't think that this has bothered him very much.

On occasion, fans have said to me, "How well do you and the analyst know each other?" I recall a day when I worked with Emerson Boozer in Minnesota, and we had never seen each other before.

I should point out that most of my work has been done in the NFL, and Boozer had been a great running back for the New York Jets of the AFC. He was well known to the fans, particularly in New York, but he was completely unknown to me. I had never seen him. And I was not exactly well known to him. At the Marriott in Bloomington, Minnesota, we had spoken on the phone the morning of the game and agreed to meet in the lobby. I had come in late the night before from a Notre Dame game. Now when we got to the lobby, it was jammed with heavily dressed people. We wandered around quite awhile before we finally selected each other and went to the stadium to do the CBS telecast.

Over a period of more than thirty years of doing football I have worked with a lot of analysts. Listing all of them would seem to serve no purpose, but suppose we mention just the former quarterbacks with whom I've worked: Frankie Albert, Don Meredith, Eddie LeBaron, John Unitas, Bart Starr, Sonny Jurgensen, Roman Gabriel, Tom Matte, Scott Hunter, Doug Williams, Richard Todd, Steve Davis, Roger Staubach, Pat Haden, and Dennis Franklin.

I worked one full season with Don Perkins, the former great fullback for the Dallas Cowboys. Before one game, I was in the booth, carefully thumbing through the program to find the page where the queen's name and hometown were listed. Don was interested. "What are you doing?" he said. We don't have any segment to do with the queen."

"Well," I said, "I've been in this business awhile. And sometime, just out of a clear sky, the director may see this very pretty girl on camera and punch up a shot. And if I'm not able to come up with an identification immediately, I look awfully silly." It was in the third quarter of the game when things were moving a little slowly, and popping up there on the screen was this closeup of the smiling queen, whom I instantly identified, using the page I had torn out of the program and placed in front of the monitor. When I looked over at Don Perkins he was just smiling and shaking his head.

I worked four seasons with Terry Brennan after he had been head coach at Notre Dame, and I worked with Bub Wilkinson after he had retired from his legendary reign as coach of the Oklahoma Sooners. I worked with Ara Parseghian after he coached at Notre Dame. And I worked with Paul Dietzel after he had coached at LSU, Army, and South Carolina. I worked with Johnny Sauer, who had been an assistant at Army, head coach at The Citadel, and an assistant in the NFL, as well as head coach of the College All-Star team in the annual Chicago *Tribune* charity game in Chicago. I thought that Sauer did the best job of any analyst I ever saw in his fantastic ability to see everything that was happening on the field all the time. CBS director Sandy Grossman, who has done the Super Bowl a few times, put it correctly, I thought, when he said, "I can show a play, any play, on the replay, and just sit back and listen as Sauer will explain a half-dozen reasons why I ran that play again."

I worked several years with Tom Brookshier, and he was the most fun. More than anyone else I worked with, he always was intent on letting me know about the defense, whether they were playing zone or man-to-man. It was natural. He had been an All-Pro cornerback with the Eagles.

Analysts and spotters, too, will do that. They will closely watch the men playing the positions that they played.

Jerry Kramer, the great Green Bay guard, told me about the offensive line. Jack Snow, the great receiver at Notre Dame and with the Rams, told me about pass routes; Wayne Walker explained linebacking.

I worked one game with Dick Butkus, and I thought that he'd be destroyed before we ever got under way. It was in St. Louis. Dick had been working some radio in New Orleans, but this was sort of an on-the-job audition with CBS. Understandably, Dick Butkus was a little uptight. Most people are when they get into television for the first time. It isn't fear of that big audience out there, which could destroy any dramatic performer. It's fear of the whole procedure of network television. The terminology is new and different and strange. I remember producer Howard Riefsnyder running down the show, and he started by saying, "Okay, we come out of billboard to Lindsey and Butkus." And Butkus interrupted to ask, "What's the billboard?" Well, if you are new, it's a perfectly logical question. The billboard is the announcement of the sponsors. It's where this fellow is saying, ". . . brought to you by——, and by——," and so on.

Dick Butkus was appropriately attired that day, I thought, in a very fashionable leisure suit, open at the throat with the collar laid back. But when we stood up for our rehearsal and we came out of that billboard to Nelson and Butkus, there was a scream from New York. Barry Frank was the boss, and he let it be known that all of his announcers would wear jackets and neckties on camera, and that they certainly would not wear leisure suits, and put a necktie on that man, now!

Putting a necktie on Dick Butkus just ain't all that easy. To begin with, he has what I would estimate as about a size 23 neck. And next, he did not have a necktie. When you look around your average CBS booth on Sunday, you do not find a lot of loose neckties. We went next door to the press box. The visiting team was San Francisco. Now, at a home game in San Francisco you may not find a lot of neckties, either. At Candlestick you might even find a stray without shirt or shoes. But on the road it is different. The publicity director for the 49ers was George McFadden. And George was wearing a necktie. We asked if he would lend us the tie for a few moments, and George was very accommodating.

But accommodating or not, the project just didn't come out well. The collar of a leisure suit is not made to be encased in a necktie. When we got the tie around Dick's neck it looked a lot as though the whole arrangement had been devised by Rube Goldberg, and it seemed that it might explode the first time Butkus took a deep breath.

The official verdict was that Dick's performance that day was not sparkling. I was not surprised. But I have been pleased with his great success and popularity on the Miller Lite commercials in concert with another noted thespian, Bubba Smith.

There was a football announcer who was held in high regard

by the fans of the Green Bay Packers during the years when the legendary Vince Lombardi reigned supreme. His name was Ray Scott. We worked some games together, including an NFL championship and a Rose Bowl.

Ray had worked in Pittsburgh but had trouble getting headline assignments there. The Green Bay job was open, so he took it. And it proved to be a fortunate move. As the Packers began to make their move to national prominence, Ray Scott was the CBS announcer who became closely identified with them. His style was restrained. He did not bore his audience with long dissertations. A typical Ray Scott description of a scoring play was, "Starr, Dowler, touchdown."

Of course, I worked for seventeen years with Ralph Kiner, the former home-run king of the Pittsburgh Pirates. But if you are part of a team doing all the games of a particular club, it's different. Kiner worked very hard to master the details of broadcasting, and he became much more than just a former player offering opinions. Ralph and Bob Murphy and I spent an awful lot of time together. And we had very few disagreements. Like a good marriage that runs for seventeen seasons, the relationship will never be flawless. There were times when we had differences of opinion. But there was never anything serious. We went through all sorts of experiences, personal and professional, and we have continued to maintain a strong relationship. We are still very good friends. And I treasure the memory of some of the great times we had.

I worked one season with Joe Garagiola. Let me say that Joe Garagiola's early years as a broadcaster were not without difficulty. When Joe had finished his career as a catcher in the major leagues, he started to move toward broadcasting. He did a lot of the local things in St. Louis, like wrestling and anything else that would allow him to expand his experience. He worked hard at self-promotion.

And in 1957, the major league All-Star game was held in St. Louis. Well, Joe viewed this as an opportunity, with the big event being held right there in his hometown. And I do not mean for this to be in any manner unkind when I say that Joe is an opportunist. He knows when and where to make his moves. So Joe sold Gillette on the idea that he could be a valuable part of the radio and television announcing teams. He told them that he could discourse, as a former player, on "Signs—The Secret Language of Baseball." He could do an interesting commentary on the third-base coach and the catcher, and the manner in which they communicated with members of the team.

Joe knew all about signs and all about baseball. But Joe did not know anything about baseball announcers.

The television announcers were Mel Allen and Al Helfer: veterans. The radio announcers were Harry Caray and Bob Neal: veterans.

Gillette had explained to Joe that he would just sort of move loosely between the radio and television booths, and drop his expertise into the commentary.

At the production meeting, conducted by Ed Wilhelm of the Maxon Agency, representing Gillette, it sounded simple enough. Joe was glowing with anticipation. I was there in a supervisory role for NBC. I had some unexpressed reservations.

And the thing that happened was what I had feared would happen. You see, veteran announcers are not all that considerate. They are survivors. That is how they got to be veterans. And when Joe went into the TV booth, neither Mel Allen nor Al Helfer could ever seem to find just the proper spot to bring Joe in. He was on the air infrequently and briefly, and it was frustrating. "The Secret Language of Baseball," for the most part, remained secret. The radio booth was different. It was worse. Joe could not have got a lengthy spot on that mike with a writ of habeas corpus. Harry Caray and Bob Neal were the nearest thing to a never-ending sentence that had yet been invented.

Joe had gone from booth to booth and had been turned away in the manner of a volunteer from the Salvation Army who had come up with an empty tambourine. And suddenly the broadcast was over, and Joe was almost in tears.

I thought that there on that afternoon Joe Garagiola decided that that would never ever happen to him again, anywhere or anytime. And as far as I know, it never did.

Another professional player that I worked with on baseball was Willie McCovey, after he retired from the San Francisco Giants. In those late years I think McCovey was the most popular player the Giants ever had. But then he moved into a public-relations capacity and had a lot of extra time. One day as we sat in the dugout and watched batting practice, I heard the deep, mellow voice of McCovey saying, "Lindsey, I think I know something that you don't yet know. Tomorrow night in San Diego I'm going to work with you and Gary Park on the telecast."

Well, Willie was right. I did not know that, but I was not surprised. If you stay in the broadcasting business for a long while you develop an immunity to surprise.

So the next night we had three in the booth—Gary Park, Willie McCovey, and me. When we had finished, I was unable to formulate any sort of evaluation of how Willie had done because I didn't know what they had expected him to do. No one had told me that, and I am not sure that anybody had told Willie that, either.

In any case, when we set up for our next telecast, Willie was not there. I got on the line to the control truck and asked of our producer, Walt Harris, "Do we have two announcers tonight or three?"

Walt said, carefully choosing his words, "We will have only two. Management says that it is reassessing McCovey's contributions to the telecast."

One of the other things I have learned about the broadcasting business is that when management is reassessing your contributions to the telecast, you don't live there anymore. They are reassessing how to break the news to you.

My most recent partner in the booth has been Johnny Bench, maybe the best catcher ever to play the game.

CHAPTER 23

"Ball One, Strike One, First and Ten"

I don't want to be too pedantic about the way baseball announcers work. But I did games in the major leagues for more than twenty-five years, and I do have some observations to offer. For instance, the thing that I like least about baseball broadcasting is the "rain fill."

Most baseball games are played outdoors. And it is a meteorological fact that it does rain in the summertime in a lot of places. And when it rains during a baseball game, a tarp is usually spread over the infield and there is a wait of indeterminate length. Those who produce baseball broadcasts and telecasts have always had a fear of cutting away from the ball park for any other kind of entertainment, like an old movie on television or recorded music on radio. The fear is well founded. Once the audience has left the aura of baseball it may not return—not today, anyway. So the announcers are usually asked to fill the time with a variety of interviews, never straying very far from the subject of baseball.

From the announcer's point of view, the frustrating thing about all of this is that he does not know how long he will have to fill. He doesn't know how long it is going to rain or how long the umpires are going to wait before calling the game. So he is literally "backing and filling."

The producer will probably be wandering through the press box and adjacent areas in an effort to scare up subjects worthy of being interviewed. On more than one occasion, I have seen the producer push a fellow into the seat beside me as the next guest, and I have been more than slightly intrigued because I did not have the faintest idea who this fellow was. It is awkward to start an interview by saying, "Who the hell are you?"

In any baseball organization, there will be certain members of the front-office staff, in some cases the owner, who will learn about this procedure. And the moment it begins to rain, that fellow will somehow manage to be standing in the doorway to the broadcast booth ready, even eager, to go on radio, television, or both. The chances are also fairly good that he is a businesslike personality with not much programming value. But he also may be the fellow who signs your checks, which makes it advisable not to offend him too often.

Of course, there are other occasions when you can strike gold. One night at the Polo Grounds, I did a full hour of a rain fill with Danny Kaye. I once did one with Nat King Cole. If it is Old Timers Day, you are home free, because you have a number of famous ballplayers from which to draw. I remember one day at Shea Stadium watching Ralph Kiner do a rain fill with Hank Greenberg and Joe DiMaggio. It was better programming than the Met ball game that had been interrupted.

On the television side, we used to tape a variety of features early in the season, sometimes during spring training, for use during the rain. But if you get into an early-season fill of a couple of hours, you may wipe out your supply. Of course, there is no law that says you can't use them again, and you may reach a point where your regular viewers know the show better than you do.

Then there are the various World Series and All-Star highlight shows. They are tailored to about a half hour. But some of the audience is a little less than thrilled to hear the announcer say, "Now, let's look again at the highlights of the 1973 World Series."

I am equally unattracted by the pregame show. This is where you interview a player before the ball game. This can become a real mental hazard. It did for me, and contributed to my decision to retire from extensive baseball broadcasting.

When Jerry Coleman was doing the San Diego Padre games the first time around, we used to agree on the burden of the pregamer. Then, unexpectedly, Jerry was named field manager of the Padres. When I next saw him, I said, "I suppose you were willing to do almost anything to get out of doing the pregame show."

The problem with the pregame interview is that not all major league baseball players are capable of participating in a sane, communicative, baseball conversation. And another problem is that not all of them know that.

The field one may explore in these interviews is limited. In some cases it is really limited. You will learn rather early that most players have a few stock answers in mind. It doesn't matter what the question is, you are going to get one of these answers. There is nothing you can do about this. You can ask anything you wish, ranging from nuclear physics to the hit-and-run play. The answer you are going to get is, "Well, you know, I don't look for any particular pitch, you know, I just look for the baseball."

Where the announcer's mental health becomes endangered is when he starts anticipating those stock answers. He can hear them coming, long before he finishes the question. And when the ballplayer starts to reply, the announcer may have a strong urge to run somewhere far away, assume the fetal position, and mumble to himself.

Some announcers drink quite a bit in off hours. It's the pregame show that does it.

It is customary for players to be rewarded for appearances on these shows. The reward may be in cash (not much cash) or merchandise. The player may be authorized to select a gift from a catalogue of items. I remember one season when catcher Chris Cannizzaro chose a set of steak knives. When the box came, the handle on one of the knives was broken. For the rest of the season, Chris braced me about a replacement for his faulty steak knife. I didn't even know where they had come from. I wasn't in the steak-knife business. I was in charge of asking silly questions.

For a long time the favorite gift, as far as the players were concerned, was a fifty-dollar bill. The player could just put this in his pocket. It wasn't much money, but it was money that did not have to pass through the family accounting system, which might be controlled by his wife.

It is now sometimes difficult to get a player to come on the interview show because of the change that has come about in baseball economics. If a fellow is drawing a salary of eight hundred thousand dollars, he is not all that impressed with an offer of fifty bucks. And he is even less thrilled with a busted steak knife.

I think that one occupied with broadcasts and telecasts of major league baseball games must be constantly vigilant to keep the show free of garbage. And there will be those in sales, promotion, and management who will always see the long presentation of a baseball game as a place to dump all sorts of junk.

Inevitably, somebody is going to come up with the idea that the fans' birthdays be acknowledged on the air. Baseball announcers do get a lot of fan mail. And many of the fans see this as a means of competing with Hallmark. They will write, "Please say happy birthday to my Aunt Maude who will be eighty-three next Tuesday. She is a big baseball fan."

When you do that, you are pleasing that fan who wrote and possibly Aunt Maude (who may not be all that fond of remembering that she is eighty-three). But you are also boring about 99 percent of your mass audience. If you are trying to concentrate on listening to or watching a baseball game, there is hardly anything more distracting than hearing an announcer break in with a "happy birthday" to someone you never heard of.

In the world of minor league broadcasting, some years ago a practice of giveaways was devised. Fans were invited to send in cards or letters, and then in a particular inning the announcement was made that each batter was batting for a particular fan. If the batter got a hit, the fan got a prize. For that inning, there are a lot of fans out there who don't know what the hell is going on. The announcer says, "Joe Smith is batting for Susan Stone." The casual listener says to himself, "Who is Susan Stone? She's being removed for a pinch hitter, but where has she been playing?" Then old Joe hits a grand slam home run and there is screaming and yelling and word that Susan Stone has just won a hundred bucks or a hundred thousand bucks. The fact that the home team is now trailing by only 12–4 somehow makes some further explanation necessary.

This practice originated in the minors because of the economic necessity of getting one more sponsor into the show. Actually, you are selling the same inning twice. I could always endure the practice at the minor league level, but I was also convinced that it surely had no place in a major league broadcast.

Self-applause is not often attractive, but I do want to say that whenever such suggestions were made with regard to the presentations of the Met games, Bob Murphy, Ralph Kiner, and I screamed and yelled and kicked and scratched, and I believe that I do not exaggerate when I say that our broadcasts and telecasts were as clean as any in the history of the major leagues.

I do still encounter such gimmicks on the games I hear around the country, and I am always reminded of the gravel voice of the late Dan Daniel, a longtime baseball writer, who would observe some practice of which he disapproved and from the bottom of his diaphragm almost bellow, "Bush, bush, bush."

In almost every major-league-franchise city, there is a broadcaster who has established himself in the regard and affection of the fans of that team. He has become their man. And in that city he is regarded as the very best baseball broadcaster in the big leagues. He might not be so regarded by an unprejudiced panel of judges. But there is no unprejudiced panel. The man doing the games will gain the approval of most of the fans, except for those who still cling to their memories of the fellow who announced the games previously. And if you compete with memories from their youth, you lose.

The surest way to get into trouble is to start listing people, because you are going to omit some. But I cannot make the point I am trying to make without naming names, so here goes.

No one was ever more beloved in a city as a baseball broadcaster than Waite Hoyt was in Cincinnati. The fans simply adored him. When it would rain and the games were delayed, Hoyt would fill the time with marvelous stories about his days with the Ruthian Yankees.

Waite was from Erasmus Hall in Brooklyn, and Casey Stengel would claim that when Waite first came out at about age fifteen for a tryout, he was wearing a baseball uniform that had been made for him by his mother. Casey loved to tell the story. And Waite patiently endured it. Occasionally, when somebody talked about those days, Hoyt would smile and say, "That Stengel—my mother didn't make that uniform."

So don't tell those people in Cincinnati that there was ever any better broadcaster than Waite Hoyt. If you were from out of town it took a little practice listening to get the hang of it. Because Waite Hoyt was the only major league broadcaster I ever heard who did his broadcasting in the past tense with a scarcity of names. Waite might say, "He threw it in there over the plate and he hit it on the ground to shortstop and he threw him out." In more words of Stengel—and the supply is endless—"You got it?"

At his peak, Bob Prince in Pittsburgh was a stylist and a cheerleader. He made no secret of the fact that he was bending every muscle and sinew to get the Bucs a victory. But he had style.

When the Pirates would pull out a squeaker in the bottom of the ninth, Prince would scream, "We had 'em all the way." And after every victory he would intone, "How sweet it is." He claims Jackie Gleason stole it from him.

Prince was also the least little bit undisciplined, and the character he created in his personal behavior off the field was as intriguing as that of the announcer at the park. At every convention of kooks, they speak reverently of the day Prince, on a bet with Pirate player Dick Stuart, made a dive out the window of the Chase Park Plaza Hotel in St. Louis, barely clearing the concrete apron and landing in the pool. When witnesses gasped at his temerity in risking his life for twenty dollars, Prince indicated that it was really no risk. "They didn't know I was on the diving team at Harvard," he said. How's that again?

There is a Bob Prince quote that I love: "There are only two really honest sports that I know of—wrestling and maybe jai alai."

Somewhere in there Prince got fired and was away until cable brought him back. But try to tell a generation or two of Pirate fans that there was ever anybody like Bob Prince. It's nice to have him back.

I don't know why Bob got fired. I know that they put some chairs for sponsors in his booth and he didn't like the idea of working with people looking over his shoulder. And I heard there were some disagreements about that. I really don't know. I once asked Manager Danny Murtaugh why Bob got fired, and Danny said he had asked General Manager Joe Brown that very question. And Brown had told Murtaugh, "You tend to running the team on the field and we will tend to the other business." I never asked Joe Brown.

I had had a little experience with that sort of thing. One year when I was doing the Rose Bowl, sponsored by the Chrysler Corporation, I arrived to find to my surprise and horror that three chairs had been installed squarely behind my broadcast position. And the fellow sitting in the middle chair, with his breath hot on the back of my neck, was Lynn Townsend, the chairman of the board of Chrysler.

Well, like Bob Prince, I don't like to work with people looking over my shoulder, and I was tempted to be temperamental and scream and just raise hell and insist that those damned chairs be taken out of MY booth.

Fortunately, before I did that I had some further thoughts. I did believe that if I yelled a lot there probably would be fewer people in that booth. But I was not at all convinced that Lynn Townsend would be one of those leaving. I thought *I* might be one of those leaving. And I looked to my definitions. I had thought of it initially as MY booth. I now considered that Mr. Townsend might think of it as HIS booth.

In any case, I simmered down, and Mr. Townsend and I did the Rose Bowl game. And my employment continued. It was that thing about discretion and valor and all that. You know.

Harry Caray has a trademark that is universally recognized: "There's nothing like fun at the old ball park—holy cow!" Harry must have started his baseball broadcasting career in St. Louis about the time the game was invented. And I do not know of anybody who enjoys what he does like Harry.

Harry screams and hollers and yells a lot. But he develops a cult of listeners wherever he goes. There are a string of intriguing rumors about the circumstances under which Harry left his employment in St. Louis, but they are all unconfirmed by me. I do know that Harry moved for a year to Oakland before showing up in Chicago. He thoroughly reorganized the South Side as the voice of the White Sox, and then went north to Wrigley Field to take over the telecasts of the Cubbies. He is said to spend a lot of time on Rush Street, has been known to buy a beer, and his frankness has on occasion earned for him the wrath of a player here and there. But a lot of fans love Harry Caray. Don't try to tell them that there are any better baseball broadcasters.

Jack Brickhouse has retired as the voice of the Cubbies, after a long and very active career in Chicago. At one time, he did the telecasts of both the White Sox and Cub games, and did the Chicago Bears on the side.

Jack was Mr. Sunshine. He was a most happy fella on the air. It was "Hey, hey" for the Cubs, and they may be trailing by six in the bottom of the ninth, but "We're gonna get 'em." And if we don't get 'em today, we'll get 'em tomorrow. Critics from the print media would take occasional swipes at Brickhouse because he was not more critical of sloppy play when it occurred. The fans didn't seem to want any more criticism, and I certainly didn't want to hear criticism from Brickhouse. He was always such good company, never failing to brighten your day with a story, and I was always pleased with whatever time I could spend in his delightful presence.

These are just some of the giants of the industry. There are so many more. But that would take a separate book.

We cannot go, however, without a word about Vin Scully. It was the day before the Tennessee-Alabama football game in Knoxville in 1950 when I went out to the field for the warm-ups. And that was where I first met Vin Scully. He had been sent by Red Barber to do a game report next day on the CBS Radio *Football Roundup.* After practice, we walked back to town together, and that was the start of a friendship of more than thirty years.

The previous season Scully had made his debut as the number-three man on the Dodgers' baseball broadcasting crew in Brooklyn. It was Red Barber, Connie Desmond, and Vin Scully.

Scully was a graduate of Fordham University in the Bronx, which was an odd geographical position from which to effect an alliance with the Brooklyn Dodgers. But that is what he had done.

You have doubtless been apprised by your elders of the great advantage accruing to those who are somehow situated at the right place at the right time. And that is where Scully was in 1953 when Red Barber had his celebrated squabble with the Gillette company.

You see, Gillette was the sponsor of the World Series coverage and controlled the assignment of announcers. It was assumed that the World Series announcers would be the number-one announcers of the two competing teams.

Gillette was no great benefactor of announcers in general, because they had taken the attitude that any announcer should be glad to get assigned to the World Series, and that should be enough. The fee they paid was not nearly in line with what was paid for other headline events. Usually, the announcer just got a brief call telling him that he would do the Series and instructing him where to show up and when.

Red Barber had become a little sensitive about this procedure, and he determined that he was going to make a stand for at least some sort of negotiation. Walter O'Malley, who ran the Dodgers, did not seem to share Barber's concern, and before the dust had settled,

Barber had volunteered out and Scully was assigned to do the World Series with Mel Allen. It was a fortunate assignment for a young man who had not been in the baseball-broadcasting business very long. Scully was young but he was extremely bright.

When the Dodgers announced after the 1957 season that they would be going west, their broadcast crew had been Vin Scully, Al Helfer, and Jerry Doggett. And apparently all three were invited to go.

The story I heard is that Helfer decided to send O'Malley a set of conditions under which he would go to California. It was a sort of ultimatum. In retrospect, one would not have appeared to be wise in sending such a thing to O'Malley. After pennant-winning seasons in 1952 and 1953, Manager Charley Dressen had thought that he merited a multi-year contract. And he had sent a letter to O'Malley asking for or maybe demanding such a deal. In any case, the Dodgers quickly had another manager, Walter Alston, who worked out twenty-three one-year contracts on his way to the Hall of Fame.

Now Helfer was sending word that he had to be guaranteed at least equal billing with Scully, among other things. I have heard that there was never any answer to those conditions. I do know that the Dodgers went to Los Angeles with Scully and Doggett and that Helfer stayed, for the time being, in New York. He would later broadcast for Houston and Oakland.

The sprawling metropolis of Los Angeles, back there in 1958, was a gold mine in so many ways. People were arriving by the thousands every day by train, plane, and bus to make their homes in the area. But not a whole hell of a lot of sophistication had yet made its way westward. There was no doubt about where the national communications center was located. That was still New York.

Los Angeles had never had any major league baseball. They didn't know much about it. For a lot of years, the nearest team had been located in St. Louis and there were not a lot of commuters making the trip from L.A. to St. Louis.

And the Dodgers did not have a place to play. Oh, they could have played at Wrigley Field. That was the name of the minor league park in Los Angeles owned by the parent Chicago Cubs. In fact, they worked out a swap with the Cubbies of the park in Fort Worth, LaGrave Field, for the park in Los Angeles. But Walter O'Malley had bigger ideas. He was not going to allow much public television. He had fallen into what he considered that trap in Brooklyn. Once you have given the fans that free television it is not likely that you can ever take it away without incurring their wrath and possibly a boycott.

It's true that O'Malley had been holding frequent meetings with the fellows in the Gucci loafers who kept talking about untold millions to be reaped from a market like Los Angeles through a convenient arrangement known as "pay TV." He did not then know that the movie interests would be frightened of this prospect, and that they would exercise their considerable influence to get the idea placed on the ballot in California and generally disallowed.

In any case, O'Malley was going to need space for a lot of fans, because if there was to be no television, there would be need for a lot of seats at the park.

O'Malley would build his own stadium with his own capital, but that would take three or four years. He needed someplace to play now. But there wasn't anyplace.

There were suggestions that they just rope off a street, and the city council, at that time in a seemingly generous mood, might have given them that block of Rodeo Drive just off Wilshire if they had asked. Or maybe they could have had all of Pershing Square downtown if they could have moved the winos.

But they finally settled on the Los Angeles Memorial Coliseum, which had been built for track and football. It would seat almost one hundred thousand fans. That was the important thing. It didn't matter that there wasn't room there to play baseball. That was a technicality. So there was room for ninety-five thousand fans and two outfielders, who cared? The Dodgers put up a big screen in front of the stands in extremely short left field, actually just behind third base, and play began. The fans flocked to the stadium by the thousands. They didn't know anything about baseball anyway. There had been two franchises in that area in the Pacific Coast League—the Los Angeles Angels and the Hollywood Stars. But their games had been broadcast by a succession of announcers who (except for Fred Haney) didn't know any more about major league baseball than the Los Angeles fans. These fellows hadn't done much to clear up the considerable mystery about how the game was played.

And then the voices of Vin Scully and Jerry Doggett burst upon the scene. This was an absolute revelation. They knew all the basics, such as who was on base and how many were out and who was winning. This information may sound basic, but to those fans seated down near the peristyle end of the stadium it was absolutely necessary. You couldn't see the game from down there. Among other things, you couldn't see the batter. Los Angeles fans did not yet know that it is fairly important to see the batter, so they just kept paying their way in by the thousands. They did discover that if they brought along transistor radios and tuned in Scully and Doggett, they could get the information about who was winning while the game was actually going on. They didn't have to wait to ask the taxi driver, as many had been doing. And so the transistor radio as a necessary piece of equipment at the Dodger ball games was introduced, and the custom persists to this day. Visitors from out of town are sometimes amazed to see these thousands of people with radios pressed firmly against their ears, listening intently to Vin Scully's smooth description on radio of the game that they have paid to see.

Roots that last a lifetime are often begun in those first years. The phenomenon of the Los Angeles Dodgers, their fans, and their love affair with the transistor radio all began back there in those four seasons they spent at the cavernous Coliseum.

Scully and Doggett explained to them, carefully at times, all about major league baseball and how it was played. They told the fans who those players were and where they had come from.

I believe that if you can last three years as a major league broadcaster, you likely are home free in any market. By that time the manner in which you do it is the manner in which it should be done. Your way is the norm, as it was with Hoyt in Cincinnati, Caray in St. Louis, Brickhouse in Chicago, Prince in Pittsburgh, Byrum Saam in Philadelphia, Chuck Thompson in Baltimore, and so on.

Since Scully was already an accomplished baseball broadcaster by the time he got to Los Angeles, and since he had a perfect partner in Jerry Doggett, it was the start of a long-running and ardent love affair between the Dodger fans and the announcers.

In the entire history of the baseball world, we have never had an announcer held in the ecclesiastical regard with which Vin Scully is held by the citizens of Los Angeles. I do not knock or question their attitude. I suspect that there have been moments when I have been envious of it. Don't get the idea that it has always been absolutely peaches and cream. When the manner of passing out the World Series announcing assignments was altered, there were periods of friction. There was one particular World Series during which you wouldn't have wanted to invite Scully and Curt Gowdy to the same restaurant or even to the same city. And now both are in the Baseball Hall of Fame at Cooperstown, New York.

Los Angeles has always been inclined to create heroes much

larger than life. Vin Scully is surely a competent announcer. Perhaps he is the best we have ever had. That would be impossible to determine for sure. But it is doubtful that he is of the actual stature of the idolatry that has been created on his behalf by the Dodger fans. Scully is certainly the most beloved of all the Dodgers, on or off the field. To approach a similar atmosphere on the diamond the Dodgers would have to start an infield composed of Billy Graham at third, Oral Roberts at short, Norman Vincent Peale at second, and Aimee Semple McPherson at first base. (Come to think of it, that quartet could probably turn the double play better than some of the combinations who took the field for the early Mets. And they would surely surpass the Metropolitans in gross revenue earned.)

Generations that have followed have not doubted that the Scully manner is the only way. Some who have listened have performed in a like manner. You can find the Scully voice and technique in the fine work of Al Michaels and Dick Enberg. I certainly do not know of a better role model.

Scully is accomplished and talented and rich and famous, and he landed in a pot of jam when the Dodgers left Brooklyn and went to Los Angeles. And he wisely went willingly without making any demands on Walter O'Malley.

As the 1960s rolled around, there was little doubt as to who wore the mantle of the top man in the sportscasting profession. It was clearly Mel Allen.

Mel was known best as the voice of the New York Yankees. He was as popular with Yankee fans as was any Yankee player. And he was as hated by Yankee detractors as one could be. Followers of other American League teams could not stand the sound of his voice, be cause that voice meant the Yankees, and the Yankees meant supremacy.

Red Barber had become a member of the Yankee broadcasting staff, but his everlasting reputation had been made as the voice of the Dodgers in Brooklyn.

Mel Allen was winning all the top awards, he was getting the choice assignments, he was rich, popular, good-looking, single, and still in his forties. That kind of paradise would go on forever, right? Well, not quite.

For all the years since, sports fans of New York have discussed and debated what happened to Mel Allen. And there has been no definitive answer. Mel himself has told a succession of interviewers that he was then and is still now baffled in trying to define the exact cause of his dismissal by the Yanks.

I have been no less baffled in my effort to arrive at a sensible solution to what is to me a puzzlement.

I have talked to a number of people who were close to Mel and close to the situation. I have researched what has been written. Red Barber has said that he was called into the office of President Dan Topping and General Manager Ralph Houk in September of 1964 and told that they had already had Mel Allen in that day to tell him that he was through as a Yankee broadcaster. Barber has related that Topping said he had already notified the commissioner that Phil Rizzuto would be the Yankee broadcaster on the upcoming World Series.

Well, that actually was the first notice the baseball public had that the voice of the Yankees had been fired. And it burst upon the scene like a bomb. The Yankees in the World Series without Mel Allen? Unbelievable!

The day that the Series opened between the Yanks and the Cards, a New York newspaper sent a photographer to Mel's home in Bedford Village to take a picture of the famous baseball broadcaster sitting idly on his front porch.

The next year, Mel Allen went to Milwaukee. The Braves were about to move to Atlanta, and they were broadcasting their games into Atlanta to get the audience acquainted with the team. Mel, a native of Alabama, seemed like a perfect choice to broadcast the Brave games. But he did not go to Atlanta with the Braves. In a later venture, he did some of the games of the Cleveland Indians. But, essentially, Mel Allen, who may have been the greatest baseball broadcaster ever, was through.

Let me say here that I was a fan of Mel Allen, personally and professionally. We worked a season of football as a two-man team. We were in frequent contact. At one time, we joined to do the sports bits on NBC Radio's *Monitor.*

I have said, in his presence, that in my opinion Mel Allen was the best sports broadcaster of my time. But he was not only the most talented, he was also the most insecure sportscaster I ever knew. He was paranoid about his position as the top man in the field. I recall one year when he won the award as the number-one sportscaster in the country, and I went into his office to congratulate him. He thanked me and smiled faintly, then said, "But what if I don't win it again next year? People will say I'm slipping." By most definitions, *that* is insecurity.

Mel developed an urgency to talk that at times ran out of control. He became inclined toward long, rambling, time-consuming verbal dissertations on a variety of subjects. It seemed as though he might be unable to stop talking. I recall one instance when he himself broke off a sentence abruptly and said, "I'm talking too much." That seemed to indicate that he was aware of some such problem.

The late Tom Meany, a witty baseball writer, was emcee of a baseball dinner at Toots Shor's when he said, "Our next speaker was to have been Mel Allen, but we have just been notified that Mel has been held up and will be unable to appear. We are now one hour ahead of schedule."

So Mel had become a little wordy. That was no big deal. If they get around to hanging sportscasters for wordiness, I will not be alone on the scaffold.

Mel was very close to his mother, a charming lady, and she was in poor health during this period. There was no doubt, then, that Mel was under a great deal of emotional stress.

And then in 1961 there was the case of Mickey Mantle and the hip infection. Mantle, one of the big stars in the game and a very valuable property, had developed an infection that threatened to disable him. And the story making the rounds in New York was that the Yankees had come back from a road trip, arriving late at night, and that Mel had taken Mantle to his own personal physician for treatment. The same oft-repeated story was that Yankees president Dan Topping was furious and threatened to fire Allen then. A source close to the scene says that there were several occasions when Topping threatened to fire Mel, but each time relented.

It would appear, then, that a sort of accumulation of grievances led Dan Topping to a final decision to dismiss his announcer. In a flurry of temper he had once been heard to say, "The last thing I'm going to do as president of the Yankees is to fire Mel Allen."

It almost worked out that way, because the Yankees were soon sold to CBS. And two years later it was CBS who fired another of their announcers, Red Barber.

After having been away for a stretch of years, Mel Allen is back in baseball now as the voice of baseball features and shows on television.

When it was decided that baseball broadcasters would be inducted into the Baseball Hall of Fame in Cooperstown, New York, as baseball writers had been for some years, the first two to go in were Mel Allen and Red Barber. Original plans called for only one to be chosen annually, but this was an accommodation. The committee could not arrive at a choice between these two pioneers, so they went in together.

For a generation of fans who followed "The Boys of Summer" in Brooklyn, the voice of baseball would always be Red Barber, now living in Tallahassee, Florida.

When a man is spending his life as a baseball announcer, does he feel that there is any real importance to what he does?

Well, on many a hot summer's night in New York, with the mercury hovering around eighty degrees, I sat in the broadcast booth and looked around that crowded stadium. And I saw fifty thousand people in a steaming mood, screaming and yelling, giving vent to their emotions at the top of their voices.

It occurred to me that in such a state and at such a temperature, the human animal must find some way to spend that stored-up energy. And I often thought of how much better it was for this crowd to blow off steam at the ball park than to do it in the streets or at some number of dance-hall bars or other gathering places that might be explosive.

I would rather hear half a hundred thousand people screaming "Kill the umpire!" than have them killing each other, which might be the most available alternative.

Because of my association with baseball in New York, I was recognized a lot. I was recognized as Ralph Kiner, as Bob Murphy, as Chris Schenkel, as Vin Scully, and as Curt Gowdy. I usually made no corrections. They had already placed me, and it was irrevocable. If I said that I was Lindsey Nelson, they would say, "Who?" If I did not agree to be whomever they had said, then I was not permitted to be anybody.

CHAPTER 24

Shake Down the Thunder

In 1969 Notre Dame just did not go to bowl games. For most major college football teams, bowl appearances were sought-after means of making money. But Notre Dame had been to only one bowl game in the history of the school. That was the 1925 Rose Bowl game in which the Irish, featuring the Four Horsemen, defeated the Stanford team starring Ernie Nevers by a score of 27–10.

Every year since, the bowl promoters drooled and Notre Dame declined. But some alumni pressures were building. There was money to be had from bowl appearances, a lot of money. And those charged with fund-raising for the many aspects of a great university's operation were asking why the Irish insisted on passing up this enormous source of revenue. It was pointed out that Notre Dame did not propose that the bowl money be used for athletics, but instead for scholarships for underfinanced students of all sorts.

I was a little surprised, then, to get a phone call late one morning from C. D. Chesley, who produced the delayed telecasts of the Notre Dame games and was in touch. He wanted me to know that he had just finished talking to Ed (Moose) Krause, the director of athletics at Notre Dame, and Moose had advised him that there would be a noon announcement. Notre Dame would accept a bid to play Texas in the Cotton Bowl. Ches thought I might want to call CBS and nominate myself to work that game. And I did.

When noon came, so did the announcement from Notre Dame and the Cotton Bowl. And after a week or so, I got the word that I would be doing the Cotton Bowl on CBS-TV with Tom Brookshier.

It was a happy and fortunate assignment for me. Texas won that 1970 Cotton Bowl in a great game, and in a rematch the next year, Notre Dame won. It was the start of a stretch during which the aggregate ratings of the Cotton Bowl exceeded those of the Rose Bowl, and it set the Cotton Bowl up as one of the truly great sports events of the country and the showcase collegiate sports event for the CBS network.

I found a home among those football folk in Dallas, like Field and John Scovell, Wilbur Evans, Jim Brock, and J. L. Huffines and their charming wives. CBS continued to send me to the Cotton Bowl, and I liked it more and more. One New Year's Eve at the Cotton Bowl ball I was asked to crown the queen and present her court of princesses. And that soon became one of the traditions of the Cotton Bowl. The analysts working at my elbow have changed from time to time, from Tom Brookshier and George Connor, to Alex Hawkins, to John Sauer and Frank Glieber, to Paul Hornung and Don Criqui, to Roger Staubach to Pat Haden, Ara Parseghian, and Pat O'Brien. I have now worked sixteen consecutive Cotton Bowl games, and a total of twenty-five Cotton Bowls in all. It is by far the longest and closest association of any announcer with a single bowl game in football history. When this began I never dreamed that it would lead to my longest and happiest football assignment and to many of my strongest personal friendships. There have been a total of forty-nine Cotton Bowls and I have announced more than half of them.

When the milestone twenty-fifth came up last New Year's, I was presented with a fantastic sport jacket by the Cotton Bowl and a watch by veteran cameraman Herman Lang, representing the CBS crew. I got congratulatory wires from announcers who had worked as analysts with me at the Cotton Bowl, such as Pat Summerall, Tom Brookshier, and Roger Staubach. And one from competitor Keith Jackson of ABC.

I did so many games at Notre Dame through the years that I was a regular on the Friday afternoon flights from somewhere into the St. Joseph County airport. As one is inclined to do, I picked up all the little tricks of survival. For instance, I had learned it was imperative that I make an immediate move toward the short taxi line the minute the plane door opened. That meant never ever any checked luggage. It meant a carry-on bag clutched close to one's bosom, and a conscience-clear policy of running over all who interceded. You see, if you failed to get one of the few taxis out there, you might not get away from the airport until a week from next Wednesday.

It was in that attitude one afternoon that I was moving swiftly through the terminal, out toward the street and the taxi. Already, I had given the high sign to the distant vehicle to ensure my reservation. He had started to move the cab toward me, and I had started toward him, when I made a miscalculation. My eyes were so intently focused up ahead that I failed to note that there was a curb between me and the street, where I was bound. What I did was step off on the side of my ankle.

The acoustics of that particular area are excellent, and you could hear the pop all the way to Goshen. And then as I fell, I unfortunately fell across the bag I was holding clutched to my chest in the approved manner. And there I lay in a heap, all crumpled up on the asphalt pavement.

It really did hurt. And I was making no immediate progress at moving. But then I was aware there were two people bending over me, a man and a woman. The good Samaritans were right on hand and appropriately right here in St. Joseph County. I was sure they would lift me gently to my feet and steady me. However, it was going to be a pretty neat trick if they managed to pry me up with a fountain pen, and that is what the guy was holding. That's what he was holding in one hand. In the other, he held a photograph. And he was showing it to me. I really wasn't in the mood to look at possible blown-up shots of the grandchildren, but he was insisting. Thus prodded, I recognized the people in the picture. I recognized me right away. I had seen lots of pictures of me. Not particularly from that strange angle, but I would know me. And I was in a picture with this man and woman. And she was saying, "We took this picture at the Notre Dame-Southern Cal game last season. Would you please autograph it for us?" Could you believe this? I am lying out there in the road in suburban South Bend and this couple is not offering aid, they want an autograph. I said softly, "Look, I don't feel so good." And I was also trying to get up and get into that taxi, which had now arrived.

The cab is up for grabs until occupied, according to the rules of the road, and I had not yet pursued my claim to its ultimate success. But the couple didn't care about me or the cab. They wanted an autograph. The lady was saying, "Aw, don't be like that. Sign the picture." I was ready to suggest to the lady what she could do with the picture. But I didn't. Instead, I dragged myself to the backseat of the taxi and slumped in while the couple voiced their loud opinion of any guy who was too conceited to autograph a simple picture. And we drove off.

By the time I left for dinner that night with Paul Hornung and some friends, the ankle had swollen quite a bit, and there was a fierce hurting every time I laughed. I was laughing less and less, in fact. When we had had our dinner at Eddie's and started to leave, I couldn't walk without assistance.

In the middle of the night I made an interesting discovery. I had to go to the bathroom and I couldn't stand up. To get from the bed to the bathroom, I had to crawl, pulling myself along the carpet.

Next morning I couldn't get my shoe on. And by the time I got to Notre Dame Stadium it was clear that some further steps would have to be taken.

Our director, Frank Slingland, got the electric cart on which he had transported cameras, cables, and odd luggage and sent me away to the Notre Dame locker room to see the trainer.

Trainer Gene Pazkiet took a careful look and advised that they really couldn't tell definitely about the ankle without an X ray. But it was plain to see that all was not well, and he sent for a pair of crutches. He bound me up, leaving the shoe off, and sent me on my hobbling, crippled way.

And it was thus that I did the play-by-play of the Notre Dame vs. Missouri game, won by Missouri despite the unnoticed fact that the fellow who went in for the winning touchdown went in without the ball. That was not discovered until a more careful look was taken at the videotape. And sure enough, the ball carrier had divested himself of the pigskin at about the three-yard line. In fact, as the pictures showed, that particular fellow had never had the ball. He missed the hand-off. But he scored a winning touchdown with or without ball.

Paul Hornung was working the radio broadcasts of the Minnesota Vikings games in those days, and the Vikings were playing the Green Bay Packers next day in Milwaukee. I was to work the same game with Johnny Sauer for CBS-TV. Paul was going to be driven from

South Bend to Chicago to Milwaukee by some friends, and invited me to go along. Restricted by life on crutches, I didn't have too many options and graciously accepted.

Chuck Milton was the producer at Lambeau Field the next day, and he had decided that I should open with Sauer on the field. That would mean a long move from field level, back around the stadium, then up to the booth. The fact that he now had an announcer seriously incapable of movement of any kind did not alter the plans. He would send a golf cart to pick me up.

The only problem was that the golf cart blew a tire on the trip down, and now with me settled with crutches uncomfortably on the back of the cart, we bumped along the path. People every few feet were pointing and saying, "Hey, you've got a flat tire." Hell, I knew we had a flat tire! Producer Milton, who was not riding in the cart, was walking alongside, laughing as we went.

I had agreed to meet Mickie and Nancy in Knoxville on Sunday night. So now I scrambled from Green Bay to Chicago to Knoxville. When I climbed off the plane at the Knoxville airport on crutches, Mickie was considerably surprised.

Next morning she arranged for me to be taken to an orthopedic surgeon at Baptist Hospital in Knoxville. He took all sorts of X rays from this angle and from that angle. He took X rays of my ankle and of my rib cage. Every time I coughed, I felt that I was coming apart.

When he had finished studying the pictures, the doctor came back in and said earnestly, "How do you feel?"

I admitted that I didn't feel so well. I hadn't felt really well since I started for that taxi in South Bend.

He said, "Well, no wonder. You've got a chipped ankle and three cracked ribs."

Of course, I had done two football telecasts and traveled on some airplanes since that happened. Now, Mickie drove me back to Huntington, where I was attended by yet another orthopedic surgeon, before I headed for South Bend, Indiana, and the St. Joseph airport again the next Friday. By now, I had learned how to handle the crutches, so I went swinging through the terminal and got the last taxi without mishap. The mishap came the next day. When we had finished the telecast, we were making our usual dash from the booth, down a flight of half a dozen wooden stairs, to the press-box elevator. Paul Hornung was leading the way, and I was attempting to keep pace. But let me testify that Paul Hornung even then could safely outdistance an aging companion on crutches. Not by much, but he was already at the elevator when he heard a crash that sounded a lot like something that had happened in a lumber yard. I had missed the first step with the thrust of my crutch and had come tumbling down in a splintering heap 'midst crutches and stairs and adjacent folding chairs. A press-box attendant screamed for Paul. I remember the scream most of all. He was really frightened. He must have thought I was dead, because he was standing there yelling, "Paul, Paul!"

Paul thoughtfully came back to pick me out of the lumber. He could tell right away that I wasn't dead. He guessed that I might be pained, and I was.

But Paul Hornung put it all at ease, when he leaned close and whispered to me, "Lombardi says you gotta play with the small hurts."

I'll bet you thought that sports announcers spent all their time drinking champagne and chasing broads.

CHAPTER 25

Menorca in the Mediterranean

We were getting pretty well into the use of our villa on the island of Menorca in the Mediterranean by January of 1972. When I had finished with the football, Mickie and Nancy and I flew over and prepared to enjoy a vacation.

One morning we were sleeping in, still adjusting from the jet lag, when we heard an urgent rapping on the glass panes of the folding doors that opened onto the front patio. It was David and Avril Bull, a British couple who were neighbors. David had an office in Mahón, six miles away, and everybody on the island knew that we were friends. So a cable for us had been delivered to his office and he and his wife had brought it.

When we opened the door and they came in, David said immediately, "Bad news, Lindsey—Daddy is dead."

The cable was from my sister, saying, DADDY DROPPED DEAD TODAY. And that is how you get the news that your father has died. You are in a villa on a remote island in the Mediterranean, and you get a cable telling you that he has "dropped dead," meaning that he had died of a sudden heart seizure with no warning. And you hope it means with no lingering pain, as well.

Mickie and Nancy thought maybe we all should return for the funeral. But I thought it best that I hurry back immediately and that they stay.

I went to the Diplomatique Hotel in Barcelona for the night, and then flew from Barcelona to Madrid to New York to Nashville, and I drove to Columbia.

As I flew across the Atlantic, I was thinking disjointedly about my father. He was really a sports fan, and would have been more so but for the fact that he was hard pressed to stay busy in support of his family.

I remembered the time when I was still a very small boy and had never seen a college football game, and he came home one Saturday night to tell me that he had stopped in Nashville that afternoon to see Vanderbilt play at Dudley Field. I asked him about every detail. I had never had a chance to talk to anybody who had seen a college football game in person. Oh, a lot of people in Columbia went to the Vanderbilt games, but I had never talked to them about it. Now my dad was telling me in detail about the stadium, and the field, and the game. And he told me that you could tell who was carrying the ball and who made the tackle because a fellow announced all of that on a sound system that could be heard all over the area. I had never dreamed of such a thing. I thought you did what we did at the local games—run up and down the sideline and ask people who number 3 was. The lady you asked might be his mother.

I remembered the day that I got a new football for Christmas. It wasn't very heavy. The fact is that it wasn't a very good football. But my father went with me down into the lot behind our house and we passed and kicked that football between us. I think it was the only day we ever did that, but the memory was golden for me.

I remembered that he came to Knoxville for the Vanderbilt game in my freshman year. And that in my senior year he came to Nashville for the Vandy game and sat in the broadcasting booth with me. It was the only time ever that he sat with me in a booth. He had driven Mickie and Sharon to Dallas when we moved there, and he had come with me one night to the Liberty studios to watch me re-create a baseball broadcast.

Then when I had begun to do more and more things on national television, he had taken a father's pride, and I was glad. A neighbor related a story to me that was indicative.

I had won some awards by this time. I had been named the

number-one sportscaster in the nation in more than one poll. And one day my dad was in the local bank, attending to some business. A friend spotted him and came over to visit, saying, "John, I think your boy Lindsey is one of the best sports announcers in the whole country."

My dad gently corrected him, "They say he's *the* best."

Once, long after he had retired from life on the dusty road, I was talking to my dad about the discomfort of moving from hotel to hotel. I said, "The air conditioning will drive you nuts. You never know how to keep it at the right temperature so that you can sleep and not catch cold."

He smiled faintly and said, "None of my hotels was ever air conditioned."

Now he was gone.

Since her birth, there haven't been many times when Sharon has not been on my mind or near it. I have wondered about her feelings concerning her retardation. Like some handicapped individuals, does she feel unfairly deprived? Is she inwardly angry, with a why-me attitude, without being able to express it?

After her grandparents had died, she and I went once to visit their graves. And as we stood there by those mounds, I became aware of an intense pain that was showing on Sharon's face. I asked her what bothered her, and she looked at me searchingly and said, "Daddy, are we all going to die?"

It seemed to me that it was the first time that the concept had penetrated her consciousness. It was as though her own mortality had occurred to her for the very first time, and this defenseless little girl was momentarily terrified.

"Yes," I said, "we will all die sometime, but I don't think that you will die for a long, long time."

She was still not at ease. "But I don't want to die," she said. "I want to grow up and get married."

It required all the strength I had to say, with whatever reassurance, that her life had a long way to run. Because I would never know the answers to her queries. But I did know that she would never grow up and she would never get married. And it broke my heart.

Now it seemed to me that things were in just about as good shape as I could expect. Sharon was doing great in her special schooling and her work in a sheltered workshop. Nancy was a high-school cheerleader and, in the fashion of her mother, a bundle of energy, into everything that came along. Mickie and I were doing all the traveling we wanted to. We had taken a flying trip around the world and a three-continent cruise on the S.S. *United States.* We had a comfortable home on Long Island with a private beach, some property in Tennessee, and our small villa on Menorca. We had a steady income.

It seemed that we had most of the things we had worked for, many of the things we had hoped for, and that most of our material dreams had been realized.

Those are dangerous circumstances.

The year 1973 started for us like so many had started for us before. I was at the Cotton Bowl in Dallas, Texas. Mickie and Nancy and Sharon were at our home in Huntington, Long Island.

I had flown back to New York after the game, and the next day I drove Sharon back to her school while Mickie took care of some last-minute traveling plans for us. Nancy had gone back to the University of Tennessee, where she would begin the second quarter of her freshman year.

Mickie and I had decided that we wanted to get to Menorca in time to join in the traditional Christmas holiday celebrations. On January 5, the Wise Men and others bearing gifts would make their landing in the harbor and proceed in parade through the city streets of Mahón. We had always gotten there too late for this.

And then after a few weeks we would go by way of Marseilles back down to Tunis, and we had made detailed plans for a tour around the area of ancient Carthage.

I had arranged my broadcast schedule so that I would have no commitments between the Cotton Bowl and the start of the exhibition baseball season in March. That's the kind of thing I had been trying to arrange for years. Two months or so each year at the villa in Menorca. And it was so situated that I could quickly and conveniently get to any other point in Europe that I might feel the need to visit.

Because of a missed plane connection, we had to spend an entire day in Palma de Mallorca before we could get a five P.M. flight to Mahón. So we just prowled the city, and had lunch at the Mediterraneo Gran, where we had stayed so happily way back in 1956.

It had seemed idyllic then, and it was brassy Miami Beach now. But we enjoyed the revisit to a place we had liked so much.

The night of the celebration in Mahón, we drove down near the Hotel Mahón and parked our car so that we could walk on down to the docks.

It was great fun, the excitement of the crowds and the costumed travelers landing on boats at the dock. It did begin to rain slightly, so Mickie and I ducked into a small café until the weather cleared. Then we walked back to our car and drove up to the center of town where we went upstairs at the Cafe Magon to watch the parade.

Then we went out to El Serena, a favorite restaurant run by British friends in an old stone farmhouse. There we met other friends and had dinner.

The next day was gray and cold and rainy. Mickie was still feeling the effects of what we presumed to be jet lag, and was lounging around the villa. It always took a day or so to recover from the transoceanic trip. We had built a new fireplace that had not yet been tested, so I was running around trying to hustle up some wood, but I wasn't having much luck. People before me had been hustling for firewood on that island for thousands of years—Hannibal, Magon, the Moors, and untold varieties unknown to me.

We were doing a pretty good job of keeping warm with the use of the oil heater, and when darkness came we turned on the electric lights. Our electricity came on a lone line that originated somewhere back up there in the area of a villa owned by author Irving Wallace.

Mickie was still lounging and I was reading when suddenly the lights went off. That was not unusual. I lit a candle or two. And then I went in search of an electrician. I found him at the clubhouse that served the Binixica Development in which our villa was located. Together we drove back to the villa and he started working on the electric line while I held the flashlight. In the midst of this, Mickie, dressed in a bright red dressing gown, came out to see what was going on.

"We are trying to get you some light," I said.

"A likely story," she said, laughing as she went back inside.

We got the lights on again and I delivered the electrician back to his friends at the club. And I also lingered for a moment or so to partake of the hors d'oeuvres that were being offered.

And then I drove back to the villa. I parked the small Spanish car in the rear and went in the back door. I was already into the dining room and on the way to the other end of the villa when I noticed that Mickie was in the kitchen behind me. Her body was bent and she was leaning motionless against the wall. I spoke to her and when she didn't respond, I took hold of her. I shook her, but there was no response of any kind. Quickly, I fetched the neighbors next door, and they brought another neighbor, a German lady who was a retired dentist. She began administering resuscitation procedures. We got Mickie into an automobile and headed for the hospital.

I stood at the foot of a bed in the emergency room as the doctors worked over Mickie. I do not speak much Spanish, but I had no trouble understanding what they said. A British friend put his arm around my shoulders and said, "Lindsey, she's dead." I knew that already. They said it was a cerebral hemorrhage and that death had been instantaneous.

I suspected that news of Mickie's death would not be long out of the media in the United States, and my biggest concern now was Sharon and Nancy.

I would have to try to get Nancy on the phone as quickly as possible and tell her. But I couldn't get through to her, so I called my sister, who volunteered to take on the awful chore of telling this eighteen-year-old college freshman, who was barely away from home for the first time in her life, that her mother was dead.

I would get there to tell Sharon.

But before I could go, I had to stay for the coroner's inquest. There were papers to sign, statements to be sworn to, travel arrangements to be made. The consulate in Barcelona had to be notified.

Having done all of these necessary things in one day, I got the early evening plane to Palma and made a connection to Barcelona. There was a direct Mahón-to-Barcelona flight, but I could not get a seat on the plane.

I checked into the Hotel Diplomatique in Barcelona, where I had spent the night when my father had died a year before. Again, I talked to the consulate. And next day, I started the trek from Barcelona to Madrid to New York. This would be the saddest mission of my life, to tell little Sharon that her mother was dead. I kept thinking of the doctor who had said to me, "Mickie reached down and pulled Sharon up from the depths of her retardation and made her into a person." Mickie was Sharon's rock. And now she was gone.

It was early evening when we got to JFK Airport in New York. I went around to the Avis desk and got a car and started the drive to Middletown. As I progressed, I noticed that the grief and the fatigue had apparently combined to leave me in a state of physical weakness.

Then I remembered that I had not eaten all day. There had been food on the plane, but I had not been hungry. So I stopped at a roadside diner for a bowl of soup and a cup of coffee.

At her school, they had not known what hour my plane might be arriving, so they had allowed Sharon to go to bed at her regular time. Now her housemother was helping her dress. She was bright and happy. It had only been a few days since I had brought her back from her Christmas vacation, and now we were going somewhere again.

We packed a few of her necessary things and got into the car to start the drive to Huntington. We would spend the night there, and next morning Sharon and I would fly to Columbia, where Nancy had already gone. The funeral would be there.

As we drove along the Thomas E. Dewey Thruway that dark night, I would steal an occasional glance at Sharon. She was quiet but serene. I knew that sometime I would have to get to the purpose for which I had come. And so I said, "Sharon, do you remember a few years ago when your grandmother died and went to heaven?"

She thought a moment. "Yes," she said softly.

"And do you remember last year when your grandfather died and went to heaven?"

She thought again. "Yes," she said.

"Well," I said, "now your mother has died and gone to heaven."

There was a longer silence. And Sharon said, "She's not coming back?"

"No," I said, "she's not coming back. You and I are going to meet Nancy in Tennessee for the funeral. And then there will be you, and Nancy, and me—and we will take care of each other."

"We will take care of each other," said Sharon, and that was all she said. She just stared off into that black night as we continued our journey. And I felt the utter frustration I had felt so many times when I wondered at the depth of Sharon's understanding and what things she might be feeling just now—if she felt grief, loss, despair, bewilderment. I wondered if that little mind had the capacity to generate the courage that would be needed. We just drove on through the night. Our lives would never be quite the same ever again.

I thought of an evening in Montreal some years before. Rube Walker, the pitching coach of the Mets, was a close friend, and one night Rube and I had sat until a late hour in a darkened French café and talked of many things. Along the way that night, we talked of Sharon and her retardation. I explained to Rube that while her mother had molded and disciplined her, I, on the other hand, was her deliverance. She was convinced that her father could do anything. There was not the slightest doubt. And if she ever got to where she really needed something, she was sure that her father could and would provide it. She thought that no matter what the need, her father would always be there.

Rube had said, "So what do you plan to do about that?"

And I said, "Well, I suppose I plan always to be there when she needs me."

My plans have not changed.

When the girls had returned to their schools, I was living alone and feeling a great restlessness. And somehow I remembered the day when I had been a small boy and had asked my stern grandma if I could go up to the apple orchard. She did not appreciate the interruption, and announced that as far as she was concerned, I could go to Timbuktu. So I decided now to go to Timbuktu.

I had long since determined that it was a very real city. I had also discovered that in the days of Marco Polo it was a big trade center, and more than that, a university city. As the years rolled by, however, its fortunes had subsided. It was not a place that drew a lot of drop-in trade. You could come fifteen hundred tough miles inland from Dakar on the Atlantic coast of Africa, or you could start up there on the rim of the Mediterranean and come across the Sahara desert. Neither route was well marked or likely.

Several times when I had been in Casablanca, I had made further inquiry, but I was told that there just was no easy way to get to Timbuktu. It was located in the free state of Mali, and the capital of Mali was Bamako. There presumably had been a post of the French Foreign Legion in Timbuktu, but French influence had now disappeared and so had the evidence of the existence of the French Foreign Legion. It was not a happy memory for the locals.

In any case, on one Saturday night I went out to JFK Airport and boarded an Air Afrique flight to Dakar. After a wait of several days there, I got booked on a DC-3 headed for Bamako.

I had a problem there because I had not had a cholera shot, so I was sent away to the hygiene center.

The lone doctor there wore eyeglasses that looked like the bottoms of Coke bottles, but he was pleasant. He went over to the cold-water tap and gave me his version of the med-school scrub-up as he gracefully allowed the water to drain from his forearms. He explained that while the cholera serum was normally administered in two shots separated by about a week, I would have to take the whole load at once. I did not welcome the prospect.

Next day, I flew on a DC-3 into the vicinity of Timbuktu. There was not a whole hell of a lot of activity in Timbuktu. There was a place that offered bunks and food, and while it was not your latest Hilton or Holiday Inn, I was pleased to find it.

I fell in with a fellow traveler who lived in Abidjan on the Ivory Coast. He was a valuable companion, and filled me in on such things as the taste of camel, the human tendency to travel in great circles if lost in the Sahara, and the beauty of the Tuareg women. He further advised in the matter of the Tuaregs that slavery still existed in its purest form, and that if I wished I might return with a Tuareg as my companion. However, I foresaw insoluble difficulties with that proposal, and declined.

I was advised that I should be particularly careful when I put my shoes on in the morning. They said that scorpions tended to seek the moisture in the empty shoes and would crawl in during the night. They further said that they had no antidote for the scorpion's sting, which could be fatal. The very first time I removed my shoes was the day after I left Timbuktu.

When I returned to Bamako I was invited by the ambassador to a small reception at his quarters. There I met an American doctor who was on a medical mission. He said he had once gone to spring training with the Dodgers in a medical capacity. As we conversed casually, he mentioned the hygiene center in Bamako. "We heard about your visit there," he said.

I wondered how he heard. "Oh, we don't get an awful lot of casual visitors around here," he said. "You are locally famous."

Then he turned more serious. "Let me ask you something. What kind of reaction did you get from that massive cholera shot?"

"Well," I said, "it's very odd. But I didn't get any reaction at all. I expected the worst, but there was nothing."

The doctor smiled. "I'm not too surprised," he said. "I'm not sure he's ever had any cholera serum at the hygiene center. But he wouldn't want to lose face. He may have inoculated you with Seven-Up."

When I had completed my trip and come home, I went to a press luncheon at Shea Stadium, and was talking to friends about my experiences. Yogi Berra seemed unusually interested. He said to me, "Timbuktu? Is that in Indiana?"

"No, Yogi," I said. "I think you may be thinking of Kokomo."

Yogi said, "Oh."

In later years I would continue to travel. I went to Moscow again, to Kiev, Bucharest, Odessa, Papeete, and Bora-Bora. But I don't think that any of these places have held the wonder of those first few experimental journeys of my youth that took me to Murfreesboro and Hopkinsville.

Now that I was a single parent, I spent a great deal more time with both the girls, frequently taking them with me to baseball spring training and on baseball trips. There were occasions when I felt the pressure. In fact, much is made of the pressure that is endured by those who work in the mass medium of television. But let me tell you about real pressure. I was at Al Lang Field in St. Petersburg, Florida, announcing a telecast back to New York. The Mets were batting, score tied, one man out, and the bases loaded in the fourth inning. I felt a tug at my coat. But I was afraid to take my eyes off the field and the TV monitor. Here comes the pitch. And I heard a gentle little voice with a certain urgency, the voice of my little daughter Sharon, who was seated just behind me. She said, "Daddy, can I go to the bathroom?"

That is pressure.

Sharon was always gentle, and dainty, and fragile, and small. But she had an abiding interest in food. It was not good to disturb Sharon during meals. This was her principal interest. She had excellent manners, and she expected everyone else to have them. Her metabolism was such that she never gained excess weight.

When we were on this airplane once, and she was trying to have lunch, she was not happy when the fellow in the seat ahead of her reclined almost into her Roquefort dressing. Before Sharon could respond, however, the stewardess noticed what had happened and asked this fellow not to come so far back. He readjusted his seat. But after a few moments, he reclined it again all the way back, disturbing Sharon's lunch.

She was not happy. And often in such circumstances, she would voice threats that were never carried out. But they served the purpose of allowing her to express her displeasure. She said to me, "If he does that again, I'm gonna belt him."

I almost broke up. And I smiled because she did not fully understand as I said, "Please, Sharon, don't belt him."

He was Muhammad Ali.

CHAPTER 26

Mets Win Again

In the baseball season of 1973 the Mets won the pennant again. But this time it was a little different. In midseason the Mets were in last place, and there were a lot of Met fans who didn't seem to be particularly happy with Manager Yogi Berra, General Manager Bob Scheffing, or Chairman Michael Donald Grant. But the Mets were survivors, and they moved up. Right down to the last week of the season, it was anybody's pennant, and the Mets were prominent among the anybodys.

On the final weekend of the season, it rained a lot in Chicago, so the Mets went right on to the Monday past the scheduled end of play with a doubleheader against the Cubs. The way things had turned out, if the Mets could win one game they would win the pennant.

Of course, it was scheduled as a doubleheader, it was advertised as a doubleheader, and tickets were sold for a doubleheader. But the Mets promptly went to work and won the first game and with it the championship. They went into the locker room at Wrigley Field in Chicago and held a proper celebration party. Compared to the parties in 1969, it was a pink-tea party. But there was a considerable amount of champagne consumed. They had learned over the years. You don't shampoo your hair with that champagne, you drink it. But after about twenty minutes, when a lot of refreshment had been consumed, it dawned on somebody that there was another game to be played. This was a doubleheader! And if this bunch of celebrants tried to play baseball, somebody might be killed.

But you couldn't just say you weren't going to play. True, the outcome of the game didn't mean anything, but those fans out there in the stands had tickets entitling them to another game of baseball unless somebody came up with a very good reason why not.

That reason was conveniently provided by umpire Augie Donatelli.

The moment that the first game had ended, Donatelli had properly ordered the tarp spread over the infield in case of rain between games.

Now, Augie came out seemingly for the start of the scheduled second game. He walked about halfway up the third baseline and lifted the tarp a few inches off the ground with the approved two-finger grasp. He was surprised to find that the ground underneath that tarp was wet. It was too wet, in his opinion, to permit play to resume. This field was unplayable! And the season was over.

Now the Mets had to play the Cincinnati Reds for the championship series. If you examined the comparative talents of the two teams, it looked like a joke. This was the Big Red Machine—this was Bench and Rose and Perez and all those folks.

The Mets were deficient in a lot of departments. They hadn't seemed to have won the Eastern Division title as much as the other teams had successfully lost it. It really was not a very good baseball team. The Mets didn't have a lot of speed or a lot of power or a lot of defense. But they had pitchers with names like Seaver, Koosman, Jon Matlack, and Tug McGraw with his slogan "Ya gotta believe." And by now I had come to believe that pitching was at least 120 percent of the game.

Willie Mays had come back to New York from San Francisco to wear the uniform of the Mets, and this was his last active season. His marvelous talents on the field were gone, pilfered by age. Rusty Staub had been acquired from Montreal to be a key performer. But it was generally an injury-plagued season. There was John Milner, a capable hitter who suffered from a succession of temporarily disabling ailments. In his locker he kept a well-worn bathrobe. If Milner wore that robe as his teammates dressed, it meant that he had declared himself *hors de combat* for the day. Onlookers amused themselves by speculating on the exact nature of his ailment, enumerating a long list of possibilities, not all known to Medicare.

The most memorable event of the championship series was an

on-the-field fight between Cincinnati's Pete Rose and the Mets' Bud Harrelson. But the Mets won three of five to become champions of the National League.

The clinching game had been played at Shea Stadium in New York. And the Mets had a party in the terrace area on the mezzanine deck at seven o'clock that evening. But nobody had told me about the party. And I didn't particularly care.

As I walked to my car, a red Datsun 260Z in the Shea Stadium parking lot, I had the feeling that I really should do something to mark the winning of the pennant. I had no trouble finding my car. I never had any trouble. I remembered the day before Shea Stadium opened back in 1964, Jim Thomson said, "I've saved a spot for you to park your car." And I'd parked in the same spot for all those years.

Every day or night, I would get into my car after the game, jockey through the traffic out onto Roosevelt Avenue, making sure to wedge my car immediately into the right lane so that I could make the turn that would bring me out on the Grand Central Parkway, then right to the Belt Parkway and around to the Long Island Expressway, out to my home on Crescent Beach in Huntington.

But this time, when I got to the Grand Central I just kept right on driving, toward the Triboro Bridge, which would bring me into Manhattan. I didn't know where I was going or what I was going to do. But the New York Mets had won another National League pennant—*another* pennant! It would be nothing like 1969, but I would celebrate it. There was no need to hurry back to my empty, lonely home.

I parked my car in the RCA garage across the street from NBC on Forty-ninth Street. And then I started walking, and found myself at the 21 Club on Fifty-second Street.

I was not exactly a regular at 21. This was the headquarters for elegance and class. It was not a sports hangout by any means. A lot of people went there to be seen. And tonight, I guess, I wanted to see them. And the first person I saw was Bob Cochran, an old friend who was now in charge of radio and TV for the National Football League. And then, briefly, football announcer Ray Scott dropped in. Bob Considine was there with a group for dinner. Bob was an eminent writer. We were both members of the Overseas Press Club, but we weren't there much. Bob said, "Let's you and I go to the OPC sometime." I agreed it was a good idea.

Then I met some more people that I knew, and the hours passed quickly. In the group was a charming and beautiful countess who was living for the moment in Southampton, far out on Long Island. The 21 Club and Southampton went together like caviar and champagne. I was invited to join this party for dinner, and the countess and I got into a conversation. When she had been driving in that afternoon, she said, she had been listening on the car radio to my broadcast of the baseball game, and she wanted to say that I must be a poet. She had been enraptured by my baseball word-pictures.

Now, if you want to get a broadcaster's attention, just compliment something he has done. It doesn't matter what it is. It doesn't really matter if it is something that somebody else has done. He won't correct you. Anyway, I became suddenly very fond of this beautiful countess.

In fact, I got so carried away that I invited her to come to the World Series the next week when the Mets would be playing Oakland, and I assured her that I would leave good tickets.

That, by the way, is one of the penalties of life in the spotlight. When your team gets into the World Series, all of your friends and most of your acquaintances assume that you have no trouble at all getting World Series tickets, that all of the hundreds you get will be squarely behind home plate, and that they will be free. All of those assumptions are in error.

If you have maintained a close and respectful alliance with the ticket manager, he may allow you to purchase more than the normal quota of tickets. They will be located at a variety of places around the ball park, including the higher decks.

And there are no comps. You will be required to pay the full price up front.

In 1973, I bought $1,500 worth of tickets to the World Series and distributed them. For some strange reason, prospective recipients of good comp tickets are also under the impression that they are entitled to have them delivered. So I spent hours racing around the area, handing out tickets to people who showed no inclination to ask if there would be any charge.

Only my agent, Ralph Mann, insisted on paying for the tickets I got for him. And Ralph is the one person I did not want to pay me. He had done me a thousand reciprocating favors, and I was pleased to accommodate him. So in this case, I refused to allow him to pay. He was the only one who had offered, so I said, "No, you can't pay. Why should you be different?"

I had passed out the ducats, then, to my family, to my neighbors, to my associates, to people I liked and people I disliked, and to the countess.

I mention this incident just in passing to illustrate that a baseball announcer does not spend all of his time down there in the clubhouse and on the field amidst the jocks and the socks and the pine tar and the dirt. He may occasionally dine at 21 with a countess, although for me that has happened about half as often as the Mets have won pennants, which ain't too often.

In that World Series, the Mets gave it their best shot. In fact, when the series headed back to Oakland for the final two games, the Mets were ahead, three games to two. All they had to do was to split, to win one game. But they couldn't. They ran out of gas. The Oakland A's won both games and the world championship, although the Mets did take them to seven games.

More than a year later, I heard that Van Patrick had passed away while in South Bend to do a Notre Dame football game. Van was the director of sports for Mutual, he had done the Notre Dame games on radio for a lot of years, and he also did the Monday night NFL games on radio for Mutual.

I was at the Executive House in Chicago with the Mets when the operator said that it was C. Edward Little, the president of the Mutual network, calling. He wanted to know if I would do the Monday night games for Mutual. So for the next four years, I did the Monday night games, in addition to the Notre Dame games on Saturdays for C. D. Chesley, and an NFL game on Sunday for CBS. I also did a lot of postseason games, a total of 7 of those after one season when I had done 54 football games in all, in addition to more than 150 Mets games and some specials. I traveled a lot, and worked a lot, and it was a very busy time.

CHAPTER 27

End of My Life with the Mets

In New York, the Overseas Press Club of America had been holding a series of special "Old Pro" nights to honor certain of the membership. They scheduled two of them to be held in succession in 1975 at a reasonable interval. One would honor Bob Considine and one would honor me.

Mostly, these affairs were an excuse for the members to hold a night of warm memories. When Bob Considine had finished his party that night, he had gone around the town to visit some old haunts to a late hour, and then had died suddenly of a heart attack.

My party was originally scheduled in October, until somebody discovered that the date came in the middle of the World Series, so it was moved.

But nobody notified General William C. Westmoreland that the date had been moved. So at six P.M. on the appointed evening, this four-star general strode into the premises of the Overseas Press Club, on the nineteenth floor of the Biltmore, to discover no one there but the bartender and two fading newspapermen.

Several weeks later, however, when the dinner was held, Westy came back, remarking, "We of the army have a belief that if something is worth doing it is worth a dry run, and I have dry-run this exercise."

That evening was one of the most memorable nights ever for me. It was a mix of the sports and military people who had played such a big part in my life.

The master of ceremonies was Jack Whitaker, the sports essayist then of CBS, now of ABC. The Mutual network had prepared an impressive montage of recordings of my football play-by-play. It was delivered by C. Edward Little, the president of the network, who also threw in a couple of wild sport jackets.

The leadoff speaker was Met pitcher Tom Seaver, who had just received his third Cy Young Award as the top pitcher in the National league. He was speaking first so that he could continue on to a dinner at the New York Athletic Club where he was being honored as "Man of the Year."

Recorded messages had been sent by Don Whitehead, Bill Heinz, and the artist John Groth, who voiced a wartime tribute to me from Ernest Hemingway, who had worked as a war correspondent in the European theater.

Andy Rooney, whom I had known well during his days as a reporter for *Stars and Stripes* in the European war, and who had become nationally famous as a television essayist and author, was a speaker. Alluding to my habit of wearing loud jackets, Andy said, "Lindsey is the only one of my friends from those army days who was better dressed then than he is now." Rooney also said, "There have been some years when baseball had trouble getting the president to throw out the first ball. In the Nixon years, I thought baseball missed its big chance to throw out the first president."

Paul Hornung, winner of the Heisman Trophy at Notre Dame and star running back of Vince Lombardi's great Green Bay Packers, was a speaker. Paul and I were now teaming up on telecasts for Notre Dame and CBS.

Harry Harris, longtime photographer on the sports beat and in the war for the Associated Press, was a speaker. He recounted our days at the Hotel Portugal in Spa, Belgium, and the night that a public-relations officer named Stevenson from the 4th Division got carried away and fired a pistol round through the ceiling. Harry Harris was occupying "Chambre Six," the Associated Press bedroom, situated just above. "I had visions of being invalided home," he said, "and explaining to my wife that her war hero had been shot in the ass by a public-relations officer."

Joe McDonald, then general manager of the Mets, was a speaker, explaining that he had begun his employment the first year of the Mets as a statistician for the broadcast crew.

And the principal speaker was General Westmoreland, spinning some stories of the war, of my days with the Foreign Legion in Africa, and saying, "As Chief of Staff of the Division, I had to dance some pretty fancy steps to keep peace between our commanding general, Louis Craig, who was a teetotaler, and Lindsey, a junior staff officer, who was not."

There were many old friends there that night, from my army years, and from my life since as a sportscaster. I was invited to join a number of them for an assault upon the late-night city. But I quietly declined. The years, I thought, had altered my attitudes. Instead, I drove home alone, and sat for a couple of hours and pondered the series of unlikely events that had brought me along the exciting trail I had followed.

By the time I left for spring training with the Mets in 1978, I was beginning to have some thoughts about where I might set up a permanent residence for the future.

It seemed to me that a lot of people in the broadcasting business settled in Florida, California, or Arizona. And there seemed to be nothing wrong with that.

But during the four years that Nancy had spent at the University of Tennessee at Knoxville, I had managed to get sort of reacquainted. I had a lot of friends, a lot of classmates around Knoxville. I enjoyed their company. And I began to think about the prospect of buying a condominium in Knoxville. I thought about it so much that I stopped off on the way to Mets spring training, picked one out, and made a down payment.

I was not disenchanted with life in New York. I had not lost my feeling for that great city. I had so many fond memories of life there that I would always feel a part of it. But it seemed to me that the time had come in my life to move along. If he recognizes it, there usually comes a time in a man's life when he should say, "There, that's enough of that," and move on to something else.

I did not intend to play out the string to its ultimate end as a baseball announcer. I had seen others do that, and it seemed to me that it never ended well. Mel Allen and Red Barber had gone kicking and screaming. I hoped to choose my own way.

In May of that 1978 season, on a hot night in the press box at Riverfront Stadium in Cincinnati, an attendant came to tell me that I was wanted on the phone. There was plenty of time for me to take the call. The Mets and the Reds were still taking batting practice.

It was Ben Byrd, the sports editor of the Knoxville *Journal.* "It's Tom," he said. "Tom Anderson is dead, and it just occurred to me that you probably didn't know. The funeral is here in Knoxville tomorrow morning at eleven o'clock."

I said, "I'll be there."

Back at the hotel after the game, I thumbed through the airline guide. The only flight would get me to the Knoxville airport about five minutes before eleven. I could make that all right. But I also had to get back to Cincinnati in time for another broadcast that night. There was a flight through Louisville that would just make it.

When I landed in Knoxville there was not a taxi in sight. There was a fellow in a van who said he was for hire and I engaged his services. Now we were driving toward the cemetery, when it occurred to me that I was unshaven, disheveled, and late. And it also occurred to me that the one person in all my acquaintanceship who would be most understanding and tolerant of my state was the deceased. He and I had arrived jointly at a number of destinations through the years in far worse shape.

The van drove through the gates of the cemetery just as Ben Byrd was finishing the eulogy. I stayed to visit with members of the family and with friends, mostly from the University of Tennessee athletics department. Then I walked a few feet away and stood thoughtfully beneath the shelter of the leafy branches of those sturdy trees.

Tom Anderson had lived to be seventy-five years of age. He had never made a big journalistic splash, no impact on the national scene, but he had earned the professional respect of all who knew him, and for a lot of years he had entertained perhaps a quarter of a million followers on an almost daily basis. I suspect that may be enough for any man.

I thought of the day I had picked him out of the many employees in the city room of that newspaper, the trips we had taken together, the long hours spent discussing almost everything.

I remembered especially the time that I had finally made it to NBC in New York. I had made it all the way to the "big time." And at year's end, Tom had written that he took a certain vicarious personal pleasure in that. He was saying, in effect, that maybe he hadn't made it to the metropolitan scene, but I had. And that was enough for both of us.

From the cemetery, we all went to lunch and swapped stories as people do at times like that. And then I went back to the airport and flew to Cincinnati, getting there just in time to do another Met baseball telecast back to New York.

Somehow, though, all during that 1978 season, I had stronger and stronger feelings that this would be my last as the voice of the Mets. True, the Mets were not playing very well. True, they didn't have a very good team, but I had done their games when they had played worse. It wasn't that.

My relationship with the front office was fine. Mrs. Lorinda deRoulet was now in the top spot. She was Mrs. Payson's daughter. We got along fine. And Jim Thomson was still the business manager, as he had been since the start. Jim Thomson was one of the great baseball executives in the history of the game. He knew New York like Churchill knew London, probably better.

The night that the Mets played their last home game in 1978, I sat there in the booth at the end of the game and looked out at Shea Stadium and that section of Queens that twinkled beyond. I did the wrap-up and the sign-off. The crew in the booth headed for home, as they always did. Murph was gone, Artie Friedman, the statistician, was gone. Kiner would be in the press room as soon as he finished *Kiner's Korner.* I just sat there. I didn't move a muscle. I made no move to pack my scorebook and my Green Book and my pencils and my field glasses. I just sat there, all alone in that big ball park.

The field lights were extinguished, and that heightened the brilliance of the lights still burning in the press box and the broadcasting booths. And slowly I looked around the stands.

I remembered the visit Murph and I had paid to this stadium the day before it was opened back in 1964. There had been a World's Fair just across the street. Fifteen seasons had passed since then, fifteen Met seasons at Shea added to the two at the Polo Grounds.

I looked at the box of four seats just behind the Mets dugout that we had held ever since the stadium opened. I had paid for it for fifteen years now. And I had never sat in a seat in that box. Never mind, I had memories of the thousands of times I had looked down there during a game to share the excitement of Mickie, Nancy, and Sharon.

I looked out there on that field and remembered the crowd of jubilant New Yorkers who had poured out of the stands that afternoon the Mets had beaten the Baltimore Orioles in the fifth game of the 1969 World Series—October 16, 1969. I would not ever forget that date. I had an extra baseball thought in there. Baltimore had had a string of great teams, and this Baltimore team of 1969 might have been the best of them all. And the Mets had wiped them out. Don't tell me about cause and effect in baseball. We reporters ascribe much more to that than exists. You want to tell me the cause and effect of Al Weis hitting a home run to tie the score in that game, enabling the Mets to go on and win? Al Weis never hit another home run at Shea Stadium, anytime—before or since. He never had. And I had sat in the same seat all those years, and when that ball left the bat I knew it wasn't going out. I had learned to judge those things after fifteen years in the same spot. What I hadn't taken into account were the angels in the outfield, for whom there is no law of cause and effect.

I looked at this scene which, for me, had now become emotional. And at this instant I knew that I would never ever again be the Mets broadcaster for a game at this stadium or anywhere else.

I walked into the press room and visited with Ralph Kiner, and Ralph Robbins, and Louis Napoli, the bartender. I made no mention of the thoughts I had had out there in the booth just now. There was no reason to. That was my personal business and it was all settled.

When Nancy came home from California (where she was now living), I sat her down and explained that I would not be doing the New York Met games anymore. I explained my feelings and she understood. I further explained that I had a year to go on a contract with the Mets that would have been the most remunerative season I had ever had. But I anticipated no trouble in getting a release. She wanted to know if I would be doing baseball anywhere else. I said I didn't know, that I might.

The next day, I got into my car and drove from my apartment at 45 East Eighty-ninth Street to Shea Stadium, and visited with business manager Jim Thomson. I explained to Jim just how I felt. "I am not mad at anybody," I said, "and I don't think anybody is mad at me, but the time has come for me to move along."

Several days later, Mrs. deRoulet and I had a long phone conversation. Then she wrote me a very kind personal note in which she said that she was sorry that she hadn't been able to persuade me to change my mind, and that I would be missed because I had become so much a part of the Mets, but at the same time she would not oppose my wishes.

And so, after seventeen seasons, my career as the voice of the Mets, which had begun on the house phone of the Sheraton-West Hotel on Wilshire Boulevard in Los Angeles, ended on a piece of pale blue stationery in New York. I had no regrets.

The condominium in Knoxville that I had bought the spring before was now fully furnished and ready. And one snowy afternoon in January of 1979, I packed my personal things into the blue and white Cordoba (chosen to match Sharon's eyes) and drove across Manhattan to the Lincoln Tunnel.

Mickie and I had once arrived in New York via the George Washington Bridge. Now, twenty-seven years later, I was leaving via the tunnel. I was on the New Jersey Turnpike briefly, and then took up the network of interstate highways that would lead me to Knoxville.

When you have appeared on television regularly for a lot of years, people will recognize you. They may not know from where or when. Sometimes they mistake you for a former classmate, somebody with whom they served in the army, or a distant relative. When I stopped at a roadside restaurant in Pennsylvania for dinner, two waitresses were excited when they saw me. Obviously they were enlisting the aid of other colleagues, but they couldn't figure out where they had seen me before. Finally, somewhat timidly one of them said, "We're trying to figure out who you are? Are you Howard Hughes or somebody else?"

I confessed I was somebody else and knew it was time to leave town.

And when I thought of my years in New York, I regretted that I had not had the privilege of spending nearly enough time in the courtly company of the late sportswriter Grantland Rice, whose hometown was Murfreesboro, Tennessee.

What kind of a man was Grantland Rice! Well, most of those of my generation have thought that Red Smith was the greatest of the sportswriters. But here is what Red Smith had to say about Grantland Rice: "Grantland Rice was the greatest man I have known, the greatest talent, the greatest gentleman. The most treasured privilege I have had in this world was knowing him and going about with him as his friend. I shall be grateful all my life."

I saw him briefly, here and there around the town, and at sports events we both covered. And then there was one unforgettable day when we sat together at lunch at Toots Shor's restaurant, sitting side by side in one of the up-front banquettes that faced the rest of the room.

He was aware of my Tennessee roots, and so he said, "Let me ask you something. When you have done, here in New York, whatever it is that you want to do, when you have achieved whatever goals you have set for yourself, will you go back to Tennessee?"

I thought a moment, and I said, "Yes, I think I will."

He smiled that warm, wide smile and said, "Ever since we came to New York, my wife and I have told each other that. And I don't think either one of us ever believed it."

Grantland Rice died without coming home.

When I packed up to come back to Knoxville with a car full of plaques and citations and awards, one of the thoughts I had was of the day I had sat at lunch with Grantland Rice.

CHAPTER 28

Open Your Golden Gate

I think that there are a number of experiences a man should try to work into his life if the opportunity presents itself. He should see a World Series and a Super Bowl. He should see a Kentucky Derby and an Indianapolis 500. He should dabble in a little caviar and enjoy a taste of champagne. And he should spend some time in the city of San Francisco.

So, when the opportunity arose, I signed a three-year contract and headed for the City by the Bay to become, for a time, the voice of the San Francisco Giants, who played their baseball games at Candlestick Park.

Everybody who spent any time around me knew how I felt about San Francisco. But I had felt the same way about Lana Turner and nothing came of it. So my sudden move westward was unexpected, mostly by me.

I did know that the Giants had switched radio stations. They had been on KSFO for years, and Lon Simmons had done the games. And I knew the rights had been bought by KNBR. I was told that Lon Simmons would not be back, that somebody else was going to fill that job. Rumor had it that the strongest candidate was Herb

Carneal in Minnesota, formerly in Washington, who was said to be asking for a five-year contract.

When the announcement was made of my becoming the Giants broadcaster for both radio and TV, I still had the apartment in Manhattan, but I was actually already living in Knoxville. Still, I could not resist the opportunity to live for a time in that exciting city of San Francisco. As for the broadcast arrangement, I should have been a little more perceptive, but I wasn't.

A lot of the longtime Giant fans were used to Lon Simmons, and they did not like the idea of somebody (anybody) replacing him. I should have realized that, but I didn't.

I was too engrossed with the prospect of actually living in that city. Actually, my love affair with San Francisco was slow to blossom. When I first started going to that marvelous, magical, mystical City by the Bay, I couldn't understand what all the hullabaloo was about. I agreed that it was a city with great restaurants, but what did you do, I wondered, if you happened to arrive between meals, or just weren't hungry? I supposed you could spend your spare time collecting heavy coats, because you were certainly going to need them if you planned on spending any time at Candlestick Park or even Kezar Stadium. It was sort of like the day I asked Frankie Albert what was the most difficult thing about playing golf at Pebble Beach and he said, "Planning the wardrobe."

But, like a beautiful lady who works every day at a desk across the room from you, San Francisco began to grow on me.

It was difficult to define. It had something to do with attitude, and appearance, and class. I could drop into one of those Nob Hill restaurants or one of the hotels and get the feeling that this was a cut above a lot of places I had been. I felt no urge to compare San Francisco and New York. I thought there was room enough in my life for both. And I didn't feel that I had absolutely to divorce one to love the other.

Some would say, "Well, we suppose you just got fed up with living in New York." And I always said, "Oh, no. I was not unhappy in New York. That is the most exciting city on the face of the earth and I love it. But the time had simply come for me to move along."

The very best part of my situation in San Francisco was my quarters. The Giants were owned by Bob Lurie, who had inherited from his fabulous father, Lou Lurie, a good part of the buildings and real estate comprising San Francisco and other assorted cities.

Bob also owned a condominium in a building on Nob Hill, the Gramercy Towers. For the time I was there, I occupied Lurie's condo. There was a view of the Bay and the Bay Bridge. It was a short walk to anywhere. That's the charm of San Francisco. It's so compact. It took fifteen minutes to drive to Candlestick. The theaters were handy as well as the entertainment rooms of the big hotels. I usually had breakfast at the Mark Hopkins and possibly postgame supper at the Fairmont. Not far away were places like Trader Vic's, the Washington Square Bar and Grill, the Blue Fox, L'Etoile, Alexis, Le Club, and any number of other exciting spots.

On the day of the home opener, I arrived in town at three A.M. from North Carolina, where I had been inducted into the National Sportscasters and Sportswriters Hall of Fame. It was an honor in which I took considerable pride. I was the ninth sportscaster to go in, following Ted Husing, Graham McNamee, Bill Stern, Clem McCarthy, Red Barber, Mel Allen, Russ Hodges, and Dizzy Dean. Following in succeeding years would be Chris Schenkel, Curt Gowdy, Ray Scott, and Jack Brickhouse.

That night of the induction had been special for me. I had spent a couple of hours the previous night with Dr. Ed McKenzie, who had been the most prominent figure in the founding and continuing success of the project. He is a remarkable man.

The Hall had begun a special category for great Americans in other fields who had connections with sports. And I was honored to be inducted with movie star John Wayne, a former Southern Cal footballer, who was represented this night by his son, Patrick Wayne. He himself was sidelined with cancer, which would soon take his life.

Bob Hope was there to speak and lend some prestige and fun to the occasion. And General Westmoreland came to conduct my induction.

Hope and the general had become close friends during those days in Vietnam. They had been on the golf course that afternoon, and came directly to the auditorium for the program. Bob Hope was immediately surrounded by autograph-seeking fans. As I walked by in a many-colored jacket, Hope looked up and said, "Are you still getting laughs with those jackets?"

I assured him that I was.

After General Westmoreland had been given a standing ovation by the audience, I was so pleased, as an old soldier, to hear Westy say, "I am here only as a friend of Lindsey Nelson." I responded by saying truthfully, "I never knew a better soldier than William Childs Westmoreland."

I would have enjoyed staying and joining in the festivities, but there literally was a car waiting outside the stage-door entrance with the motor running. Next afternoon, I had to be in San Francisco to open the baseball season.

I got up early and had breakfast at the Mark Hopkins Hotel. Then I rented a car and started for Candlestick. I had not had time to check the mail, and it dawned on me that I did not have any credentials of any kind. For years, I hadn't worried about that. When you have been with one team for years, you don't need credentials. Everybody knows you.

But I was new. When I got to the gate of the parking lot, there was a stern attendant with a big hand stuck up there. "And who do you think you are?" he asked rather pointedly.

"I'm the Giants radio broadcaster," I said.

He said, "You don't look like Lon Simmons to me."

And for the next three baseball seasons, that was a continuing problem for me. I didn't look like Lon Simmons and I didn't sound like him, either.

A couple of weeks later, I would be in my hometown of Columbia, Tennessee, for "Lindsey Nelson Day." It was Will Rogers who pointed out that the greatest honor that can come to any man is recognition and acceptance by his own people. They know you best. And I cannot begin to describe the depth of my emotions as I sat there that night and looked out at the faces of those with whom I had gone to school and struggled through the painful and joyful years of growing up. Fred Russell of the Nashville *Banner,* who has himself received more honors than anybody I know, was the emcee. He read a number of messages, two of which I especially recall. Football coach Bear Bryant wired, I WOULD LIKE TO SELL YOU SOME HATS TO GO WITH THOSE CRAZY SPORTS JACKETS YOU WEAR. And President Jimmy Carter sent a longer message from the White House, a message of congratulations.

To sit there among those whom I had known longest and hear Fred Russell reading that message from the president of the United States was very special. So was the opportunity to introduce Sharon to that gathering. She beamed and called it "Happy Lindsey Day."

Nancy couldn't make it. She was in Cairo, Egypt, on the way around the world in a course of study that would result in a master's degree at Southern Cal. She sent a cable to Columbia from Cairo saying, WE ARE PARADING CAMELS INSTEAD OF MULES IN YOUR HONOR.

Miss Mary Virginia Graham, the teacher who had first instructed me in the basics of English grammar in high school, was there. She said, "Lindsey, did you know that this is William Shakespeare's birthday?" I admitted sheepishly to Miss Graham, ever the teacher, that it had slipped my mind, but I promised faithfully that it never would again—it's April 23rd.

With me in San Francisco and Nancy in Los Angeles, we kept in pretty close touch. One day she called to tell me that I shouldn't miss *The Mike Douglas Show* on television. It had already been taped at CBS Hollywood, and Nancy had seen it. (She worked there.)

When I tuned in, there was Mike with his cohost, Don Rickles, and Lindsay Wagner was the guest. I suppose that she gained her earliest fame on television as *The Bionic Woman,* but is now a television star of considerable magnitude.

In the course of the conversation on the talk show, Mike asked her about her name, Lindsay. "Well," she said, "my parents were big sports fans and my father had already decided that they were going to have a boy, just weren't going to have a girl at all. And he liked Lindsey Nelson, the sportscaster, so that is whom I was named for."

Can you imagine a beautiful and talented TV star named for me?

I am still working on it, but up until this writing I have never met Lindsay Wagner.

There was another day when Nancy called.

She was then living at Marina del Rey in the Los Angeles area, attending USC, where she was about to take a master's degree in broadcast journalism. She was calling to say that she was flying up for a visit, although she didn't give any reason. I guessed that perhaps we were going to celebrate her birthday.

I may have told you that Nancy is kind, considerate, and compassionate. I may not have told you that she is energetic, in motion, turned on.

She had been seated in the living room of my plush place there on Nob Hill for no more than five minutes when she got right to the heart of the matter.

"I have found the man I want to spend the rest of my life with," she said.

Well, I had known that this day would come sometime. I accepted the fact that marriage would be the natural element in the development of her ultimate happiness, and she was now telling me that he would be coming up on the next plane to meet me.

Most of all I was flattered. I was aware that in modern society not all young people feel any obligation to inform their parents about their plans in this regard. I was pleased that my daughter and my future son-in-law were slightly old-fashioned.

We talked over lunch at the Crown Room of the Fairmont, and they told me of some of the details of their plans. The marriage would be in Knoxville, Tennessee, where Nancy had a good many friends. She had taken her bachelor's degree from the University of Tennessee.

The young man's name was Andy Wyszynski, and for any man who announced a lot of Notre Dame football games, that ceaseless succession of consonants is no challenge whatsoever.

Then they told me that they wanted Sharon to be a bridesmaid. And for me that just about made things complete. After all, Sharon would never have a wedding. This would be her chance to know the happiness of such an occasion and to know, too, that she was helping her sister, Nancy, whom she adored.

On the night of the rehearsal at the church, we gathered and began to go through the motions. And the time came for Sharon to take the long walk alone up that aisle. When the cue was given for her to start, she didn't move. I was not far away, and I repeated the instructions for her to begin the walk.

And then I saw what was happening. Sharon was frightened to tears. The challenge of walking alone up that long aisle was more than she could handle. She was crying and trembling. It was a very real fear. I took her in my arms and told her not to worry—we would do it the next day when the wedding would be for real. In my own mind, I made contingency plans. If Sharon could not handle it, I would take her all the way up that aisle. And we would simply have a little stage wait while I went back for the bride.

But the father of the bride does not get enough credit. Next morning, I felt very emotional. Nancy and Sharon and I had breakfast together, just the three of us. And I realized that this would be the last time we would ever do anything just like this. Our Nancy would be married, and we were happy for her. But we were sad for ourselves—for Sharon and me—because nothing was ever going to be quite the same again.

We arrived at the church, and Nancy and Sharon went immediately to the dressing rooms downstairs where the other attendants waited. I was attending to some details with the photographer and the florist when a lady came rushing up to say, "Come quickly, Mr. Nelson, your daughter has an upset stomach."

"My daughter," I said. "Which one?"

It was Sharon. The excitement was getting to her. So I went to her room and the girls already had her settled down. She thought she would be all right, she said.

Then came the moment. The attendants had gone up. The groom and the best man were waiting at their appointed place. And it was time for little Sharon to start her long trek forward. She was holding her flowers as they had shown her, and she was all business. When the cue came, she started slowly forward, and she made it all the way to the front of the church. I have seen courage exhibited in many places by many people, soldiers, athletes, and others. But I never saw any more courage than Sharon showed that day when she made that long, lonely trip on her own.

And now it was time for Nancy and me to start. She was radiant. We laughed a little as we walked up the aisle. And when I left her at the altar, she kissed me softly on the cheek and said quietly, "I love you, Dad."

I was at that moment about as near to coming apart as I recall ever having been. I went to my place and sat. And as the wedding proceeded I noticed that Sharon was having some difficulty with her throat. She was coughing and trying to be unobtrusive. But from experience I knew that if she struggled much longer, she would be sick again.

So I left my seat and walked up to where she stood and I took her by the hand. She came with me back to the seat where the coughing, probably anxiety-induced, subsided.

Now it was almost time for the recessional, and the parade of the wedding party back down the aisle. Sharon looked at me and said, "I must get back to my place."

And so she did. And she made a proper exit.

There were the pictures, and the drive to the reception. There was food galore, and an orchestra, and fun and dancing. And then the time came when I had to leave. I had an 11:05 P.M. plane to catch. I just barely made it and connected in Atlanta for the night flight to San Francisco for a Sunday doubleheader. When I had finally quieted down, I realized that I had had nothing to eat at the reception where there had been an abundance of all sorts of exotic foods. On further reflection, I realized that I also had missed lunch. So now I had an airline snack.

As I leaned my seat back, I noticed that there was a bulge in my left jacket pocket. In my haste to get away from the reception I had been barely conscious that Nancy had slipped a piece of cloth into that pocket. Now, I pulled it out and spread it on the tray in front of me. She had been sewing it for several days, whenever she had a moment. It outlined a man between two little girls, each of whom he held by the hand. And the legend said ANY MAN CAN BE A FATHER, BUT IT TAKES SOMEONE SPECIAL TO BE A DADDY.

That's all the credit that the father of the bride needs. And I reached overhead somewhat quickly to punch the button that would extinguish the light. From somewhere, there were soft tears glistening on my cheeks.

In Knoxville, during the offseason I was getting into some activities at my old school, the University of Tennessee. We had held a seminar for the students at the Communications College with a panel of speakers that included Don Whitehead, distinguished author and two-time Pulitzer winner, Tom Siler of the Knoxville *News-Sentinel* and *The Sporting News,* Will Grimsley of the Associated Press in New York, Fred Russell of the Nashville *Banner,* George Langford, sports editor of the *Chicago Tribune,* Jay Searcy, sports editor of *The Philadelphia Inquirer,* and me.

I had been in a discussion with Dr. Don Hileman, the dean of the college, about my wish to dabble a little bit in teaching.

The dean was encouraging. What he had said, was, "Anytime you're ready, we're ready."

That was certainly one of the things I wanted to do before I got around to hanging 'em up.

In my first season with the Giants, they had the worst record on the field of any Giant team since they moved westward from New York. But in the booth my life had been enriched by an association with coannouncer Hank Greenwald, and later, David Glass. On the television side, Gary Park was a talented and enjoyable partner. And socially, there were great times with Bob Lurie and his charming wife, Connie.

But in the fall, I discovered that I was geographically a little misplaced out there on the West Coast. When I would go to South Bend for the Notre Dame games, it would take me all day to get there. And then I had the lengthy trip back from wherever I worked for CBS on Sunday. So at the end of the 1979 season, I notified Notre Dame that I would have to give up the football games. I had been there for thirteen years, and the rewards had been many. I have the deepest admiration for Notre Dame as one of our great universities. But for me that was now over.

And several years later, C. D. Chesley, who had produced the Notre Dame telecasts, passed away at his home at Grandfather Mountain, North Carolina.

From Knoxville, I drove across the mountain to the memorial service. I had many thoughts of Ches as I left I-81 and followed U.S. 23 to the intersection of Highway 321 toward Elizabethton. Then my confidence got a little shaky. There was a gas station, and inside the office I could make out one lone figure. I stopped and dashed through the rain. Inside, the custodian gave me an inquiring glance, but made no movement.

I said, "Could you tell me the way to Linville, North Carolina?"

He didn't say anything. He just jerked his thumb up over his shoulder, pointing up Highway 321.

I said, "Do I have to go through Boone to get to Linville?"

He said, "Probably."

Mountain folk don't talk much, especially to strangers. So I got back into the car and continued my journey up this rising, twisty road in a steady rain.

We used to kid Chesley about his name. I loved to introduce him at sports dinners. His name was Castleman DeTolley Chesley. Strangers always called him "Chelsey."

He had formed his own television network. He brought Atlantic Coast Conference basketball to the fore with his telecasts by an announcer he employed named Billy Packer.

Then had come the Notre Dame football games. There would always be a Friday night dinner in South Bend, or wherever, with Ches and his wife, Ruth, and probably director Frank Slingland. It was great fun. There was always singing and dancing and laughter. Ches believed in class, quality work, and good times.

When I got to Linville, North Carolina, the rain was still falling steadily. I had a good half hour to spare, so I drove around in the rain. Then I saw a little sign that said, EPISCOPAL CHURCH and I turned onto the narrow street.

We had all known that it was just a matter of time, since the doctors had said about a year before that Ches had Alzheimer's disease. His memory had faded, his ability to recognize friends had failed. His wife, Ruth, had attended him at their home.

I parked the car on the shoulder and walked through the heavy rain to the small, rustic chapel. I sat on the aisle near the back of the hall. When I felt a hand on my shoulder, I looked up to see Frank Slingland, who had come from Washington.

After the services, we drove to the big house to visit with the family and to recall the good times. There had been so many good times in the years with Ches and the Notre Dame football games.

We were still trying to keep our little three-member family together whenever we could. And in December of 1979 we decided that the three of us would take a few days together at Christmastime in New York. We all agreed on one thing. New York was the greatest place to be at Christmas.

There are various locales that seem to be made for specific times of the year. Florida is for February, the mountains are for summer, St. Moritz for winter, and New York for Christmas.

When the snow is falling softly, when the lights are glowing from the highest lighted windows of the skyscrapers, when the store windows are brilliantly decorated, when there's a Santa Claus on every corner with a Salvation Army collection pot, when there really are roasted chestnuts for sale, when people hurry by with packages piled high and smiles on their faces—that's when you want to be in New York. That's why we were there.

We had a marvelous time. We went shopping, and to the theater, and we had tea each afternoon at the Palm Court of the Plaza. We had a family tradition lasting as long as the girls could remember of having dinner once each Christmas at the English Grill of the Promenade Café at Rockefeller Plaza. We always got a window table, and had a sumptuous dinner while we watched the skaters on the ice rink outside. It was Currier and Ives.

Every family has special moments that live in the memories of the family members together. And there had been such a moment in our lives. When the girls were very small and we still lived in Crestwood, we had dutifully come into Manhattan for dinner at the Promenade Café. It was during that brief time when Sharon was still physically bigger than Nancy. She was not only the older sister, she was also the larger sister. And at the table they had soiled their hands and had asked to be excused while they went into the ladies' room to wash up. Well, Mickie and I waited and we waited, and they didn't return. A little concerned, Mickie went to see about them, and in a moment she hurried back to get me. This was too good to miss. They had discovered that the towels were too high for them to reach. So, Nancy had climbed up on the commode. And from there she had given Sharon strict orders to remain sturdily fixed while she, Nancy, would climb up on her shoulders to get to the towels. They were in midoperation, too far advanced to turn back, when Mickie had opened the door. We never forgot that night. It is of such memories that lifetimes are made.

CHAPTER 29

Commuting to Japan

During the three years I was doing the games of the Giants in San Francisco, other things were happening concurrently.

There was, for example, the time that the fellow calling on the phone was Van Gordon Sauter, in the midst of his somewhat abbreviated tenure as president of CBS Sports. His tenure was brief because he was just passing through on his way up the corporate ladder. No one seemed to be staying very long in that position. Security in that post seemed about like that on a downtown street in Beirut. Previously, though, Van and I had had a brief conversation during which I had expressed my pleasure at arrangements that had sometimes enabled me to finish my football schedule in some attractive location. This would allow me to enjoy a few days of vacation at season's end at a relatively exotic or comfortable place. I had concluded my season's work in such places as Nice on the French Riviera, and Honolulu. When I had mentioned this, Van said, "You got it."

Well, let me say here that I had been around the business long enough to observe some of the hard facts of network life. When a high network executive says to you, "You got it," sometimes you got it and at other times you ain't got it. A lot depends on intervening developments that are unpredictable. Before anything concrete develops, the fellow who has assured you that "you got it" may have got it himself. He may be in some other line of work. So I waited not too expectantly. This time, however, Van Gordon Sauter was saying, "How do you feel about doing the Japan Bowl in Yokohama, Japan, in January?"

I was delighted. I said, "I got it."

And I did get it. I went to Tokyo, where I met Charles H. Milton III, who was producing, and Bob Fishman, who was directing. It really was a great time, the kind of football game I've been looking for all my life. The Japan Bowl is laid out for fun.

The players are all-stars from colleges in the United States. Most of them have sort of played their way across the Pacific. They have already played, maybe, in the East-West Shrine game in Palo Alto, and the Hula Bowl in Honolulu, so they know each other pretty well. Their total offense consists of three or four plays, and by now they know those pretty well, too.

Dan Devine, then of Notre Dame, and Johnny Majors of Tennessee were there as coaches of one squad. Warren Powers, then of Missouri, and Ron Meyer, then of SMU, were there to coach the other. They had strict limits on the number and length of the brief workouts. This was all carefully calculated to see that preparations for the ball game did not get in the way of the social schedule. This was my kind of bowl game.

I went down to the studios of Tokyo Broadcasting to do voice tracks over some scenic tape we had shot in outlying districts of Japan. It was an intriguing mixture of the old and the new. I would do a segment in the studio, and then I would go into the control room to watch the playback. But before I could enter the control room, I had to remove my Bally boots and slip on a fragile pair of sandals. After shuffling in and out, I would put my boots on again and go back to the studio to do the next segment. I was trapped between the modern methods of television and the traditions of ancient Japan.

At the game, they had five officials, but only the referee, an American, was "hot." The referee made all the calls. Not most of them, all of them. The other four officials were not equipped with either whistles or flags. They were window dressing. When the referee called and signaled holding, the other four officials pantomimed holding. The referee, it might be noted, was not going to call holding or anything else in any circumstances less apparent than an earthquake. I don't know whether holding has ever been called in the Japan Bowl. I doubt it.

Our telecast was carried on the full CBS Television network live via satellite. The analyst was George Allen, former coach of the Rams and the Redskins. You put George around a football game in any country on the face of the globe and he sort of comes alive. The Japanese laundries probably wondered why they started getting all those tablecloths with little *x*'s and *o*'s drawn all over them. He was drawing complicated defenses for both teams.

The Japanese had built a little plywood booth for George and me. And I guess that it's true—the Japanese are generally small and they make everything small. We were crammed in there. And for the opening we had to climb out on a catwalk where we could face the camera in the booth. There was a small monitor out there on which I could see the picture for which I would ad-lib a narration. And just before we got the cue, the monitor went dark. With all the television sets manufactured in Japan, we must have been the only people in Yokohama with a set that didn't work. But there we were. My spotter was Tommy Grimes, a scout for the Oakland Raiders, who had spotted for me at the University of Miami when he was a student there.

The Japanese fans, still learning their way around the game of football, had come out early in the morning in family groups, carrying their lunch. Now the stadium was packed. Spectators were waving big, swirling banners and blowing a lot of shrill whistles. There was organized cheering that had not much to do with the antics of the cheerleaders on the sidelines. They were from the University of Southern California, and most of the Japanese would have preferred that they be from UCLA. The Bruins are popular in Japan.

Our stay was filled with surprises. One night I went to dinner with Chuck Milton, and he ordered something sensible while I ordered shrimp. That was a mistake.

I had been running with shrimp for some years, and I thought I knew shrimp when I saw it. It was curled, almost round, about the size of a half-dollar, unless you specified a size larger or smaller.

Well, the chef was there at our table, and most of our table was a grill. The chef flung some items out there on the hot grill. They were about six inches long and slender. And they broke out into the damnedest battle you ever saw. When my dinner hit that hot grill, they started dancing and expanding and contracting and moving around. The chef began hitting them with a cleaver, getting rid of a lot of the parts that were apparently considered inedible. He was failing in a valiant effort to hold them still. They were still jumping and very much alive. I said to Chuck, "Hell, hit 'em with a stick—they're not dead yet."

I had already met and sampled raw fish, but I didn't plan to eat any live fish. It was a considerable battle, and by the time I was ready for dinner we had come a long way from your quiet little shrimp cocktail with the red sauce.

I discovered, too, that the Japanese are very big for the sauna, the steam bath, that sort of thing. I learned, however, that a fellow can get into a lot of trouble with the terminology. If you are prowling around a place like, say, Kawasaki, and somebody asks if you would be interested in a "massage," you had better understand what he's talking about. It is just barely possible that you are being invited into a co-ed exercise that could get you arrested in a conservative city like Knoxville.

In the summer of 1981, the major league baseball players went on strike. There were no games. A lot of fans found themselves impatiently at leisure. And a lot of baseball announcers found themselves out of work.

My phone rang again. It was a producer asking if I would like to go to Japan and do a regular-season Japanese baseball game on a syndicated television network that would cover most of the United States.

We would be leaving right away from Los Angeles. And my visa was still in effect from my previous trip to the Japan Bowl.

So in the lobby of the Los Angeles airport, I met Jerry Coleman, a former player and manager, and presently an announcer. And we flew across the Pacific. We were greeted at Narita Airport outside Toyko by a delegation of Japanese television and sports people. And we were quickly transported to the same hotel where George Allen and I had stayed, the Takanawa Prince.

Next night, the Japanese hosts held a dinner for us at a very fashionable restaurant in midtown Tokyo. And it was interesting. There was a fellow there acting as interpreter who said he was a graduate of Southern Cal.

As we were seated, one of the network officials was on my left. And I figured I would be in for an evening of struggling with the language in an effort to keep up a rapport with this fellow. As it turned out, this was not my problem. Because on that fellow's left was Jerry Coleman's fiancée, a beautiful auburn-haired lady who had certainly come to the favored attention of this Japanese worthy. He was making the nearest thing to a pass that I had come across since leaving the permissive social climate of sunny Southern California. I mean he was already well into the saki and I feared he might be having ideas that could get us into World War III. Not only that, they were serving shrimp. And when the first one had made a leap up off that hot grill and the chef had struck it with a cleaver, that auburn-haired lady was ready to seek out the Kentucky Fried Chicken for dinner, and I was ready to go with her.

It was under such circumstances that Jerry Coleman and I made our entry into the polite circles of Japanese broadcasting.

When we started for the ball park the next afternoon, I made an interesting discovery. We were going to the Yokohama stadium, where the Japan Bowl football game had been played. I was getting to be a regular there.

I should point out here that in recent years it has been customary for an American team to make a postseason tour of Japan, playing exhibition games. In fact, the Mets had made one, but Mr. Grant had declined to include the announcers on that trip. When those tours are made by American teams, there is ample provision for information to be supplied to the representatives of the media. These are, after all, exhibition games for purposes of promotion in both countries.

But Jerry and I were just dropping in here on a warm summer's evening in Yokohama for a regular-season game between the Tokyo Yomiuri Giants and the Yokohama Taiyo Whales. And we were fortunate that Cappy Harada, a native, had been added to our crew. A fellow could use a tip now and then. For instance, when the Mets played their first game, a young Japanese lady came out to present a bouquet to Met manager Yogi Berra. When she bent low in a sweeping ceremonial bow, Yogi unfortunately bowed at the same time and cracked her in the forehead. Yogi damned near disabled his dainty hostess.

I anticipated some small trouble with the Japanese pronunciations and had been through a routine that I discovered long ago is not unusual in foreign countries. When you ask for something that they are not prepared to supply, everybody says, "Okay," and nothing happens. I had been asking for a squad list of the two teams and I had gotten nothing but smiles and "Okays." It looked as though I might have "Okay" playing all nine positions.

We got right to work on the videotaping of our opening, done on the field back of the batting cage. Through Cappy, acting as interpreter, I did an interview with Sadaharu Oh, the legendary Japanese home-run king. I wish I could tell you what he said. I was afraid he was saying that he didn't understand the questions. The best decision of that period was made by our producer, who decided not to use my taped interview with Sadaharu Oh.

I knew that each team had some players from the United States, and these imports figured to be my key people. Tokyo had Roy White, formerly with the New York Yankees, and Yokohama had Peter LaCock, formerly of the Cubs and Kansas City and the son of quiz-show host Peter Marshall.

I was getting a little more edgy about those pronunciations, so I went looking for the lineups. In the United States, you will probably find the lineup on the back of the dugout wall during batting practice. I searched. It was not on the dugout wall in Yokohama. You may find it in the pocket of one of the coaches. It was not sticking out of the pocket of any of the coaches in Yokohama. The managers didn't speak English. And I had that distinct feeling of being a bastard at a family reunion. Or a Tennessean at a Japanese baseball game.

Finally I sought out Pete LaCock and asked about the lineups. He started to laugh. "Don't you know?" he asked.

Well, obviously I didn't know much. "Know what?"

"About the lineups. They aren't posted until twenty minutes before the first pitch, and they're a secret. When they are announced on the public-address system, it's the first time the fans, or the players themselves, for that matter, know who is playing."

"Don't you know who's pitching?"

Pete said no.

So I went back up to the booth, only it wasn't so much up to the booth as it was down to the booth. We were situated behind home plate but just about at ground level.

I really did feel the strong need to ascertain the name of at least one Japanese baseball player. This telecast was going all over the United States. Admiral Husband E. Kimmel, in command of the U.S. fleet at Pearl Harbor in 1941, had more information about the Japanese than I did, and he didn't have any.

I am by nature a fairly placid fellow. But I was about to turn testy. I knew that emergency measures were usually available. Back home, I had gone out of broadcasting booths and purchased programs just to get squad lists. Now I was getting anxious. Several of the assistants in the booth spoke English, and I said, "Can't you go out and buy a program, or a scorecard or something?"

They said yes.

With a voice that was now rising in frustration, I said, "Well, for Christ's sake, go out there and do it."

The Japanese smiled politely and did not move. "They are all printed in Japanese," they said.

Yeah, well.

It is to this day to me a marvel of the broadcasting business that with the help of Cappy Harada we got the lineups down in our books, we did the game, and we had no particular trouble with identifications or pronunciations.

It was not a lucky night, though. Under such circumstances, you hope for a two-hour game with both pitchers going all the way. We didn't get that. We got three and a half hours and a total of eight pitchers.

When the first pitcher was in obvious trouble, I looked for the bullpens and the pitchers warming up. I didn't find either the bullpens or the pitchers. Cappy whispered that they warmed up underground and nobody knew who they were until they made their appearance in the game.

"I know," I said to Cappy, "it's a secret."

He smiled and said, "Right!" I was learning.

At one point, we couldn't move in our booth for the media representatives packed in there. And they all seemed to have minicams and flood lights and they were photographing Jerry and me. We were the American baseball announcers who had dropped in to Yokohama to do a regular-season baseball telecast. Cappy whispered, "You're on the eleven o'clock news of every station in Japan."

As I looked around that crowd and waited for the next cue that would resume our telecast from that scene of international sports bedlam, from somewhere deep in my subconscious I faintly heard the strains of an old soldier song, a tune from the early years of World War II: "Goodbye, Mama, I'm off to Yokohama . . ."

The next morning, I was sitting in the living room of my suite at the Takanawa Prince Hotel, picking at a room-service breakfast and scanning the front page of the English-language newspaper. And there on page 1 was an obituary and picture of Don Whitehead.

I had known that Don was in failing health, presumably bedded with lung cancer at his home in Knoxville. Now the man from Harlan, Kentucky, with the honorary doctor's degree from his alma mater, the University of Kentucky, twice the winner of the Pulitzer Prize, a great war correspondent and a distinguished author, was dead.

I had shared so many experiences in so many places with Don Whitehead. I grieved for his passing, but I was pleased that a testament to his worldwide stature was the placement of this story on page 1 of the Tokyo paper.

The last note I had received from Don was to tell me about his illness, and he mentioned that some years earlier he had gone to the Bethesda Naval Hospital for the removal of one lung. He said, "It was a lung I wasn't using much, anyway." Now Don Whitehead had passed away. As a war correspondent, he had made four assault landings on enemy-held beaches, including the one on D-Day at Omaha Beach. He had died in bed in Knoxville.

Shortly after I had taken the job as the voice of the San Francisco Giants, I was at a baseball dinner in New York and met Dodger manager Tommy Lasorda in a corridor. He said, "Hey, you and I have always been pretty good friends, but you have really done it now. You have joined up with the enemy." It was a good-natured greeting.

Then in my third season with the Giants, we were playing in San Diego one night when the Dodgers' advance scout, Ed Liberatore, came into the booth. Ed was a good friend. We had often had dinner or lunch together somewhere on the major league trail, and he had frequently given me a lift here and there when he had a car and I didn't. Now he was explaining that he had to compile an advance scouting report on the Giants because the Dodgers would be at Candlestick the following night to open a series. But Ed himself was going to have to head for Atlanta after this game. If he could get proper permission from his boss, he wondered if I would be willing to take his report and deliver it to Dodger manager Lasorda in San Francisco. I told him I would.

After the game, Liberatore came in to say that he had permission from his general manager, Al Campanis, for me to be the messenger, and he handed me his sealed scouting report.

The next late afternoon I got held up a little bit in San Francisco traffic, and when I got to Candlestick, the Dodgers were already there and Lasorda was anxiously awaiting his report.

When I handed it to him, he thanked me and went right into a session with his pitcher of the night, Jerry Reuss.

Strangely enough, in the game that followed that night, the Dodgers won. Not only did the Dodgers win, but Jerry Reuss pitched a no-hitter. When I saw Lasorda after the game, he said, "I don't think we'd better tell the press. They might not understand." I agreed.

I was drawing closer to the end of my three-season assignment in San Francisco. One day the *San Francisco Chronicle* ran a story saying that I had decided to "retire" as a major-league-baseball announcer at the end of the season. It was not a word that I had used, because I had no specific intention of retiring from sports broadcasting. But I did not intend to seek to renew the contract at season's end.

That afternoon I was in the booth at Candlestick, when the usherette said that there was someone outside who wanted to visit with me. When I asked who it was, she said, "You'll know when you see him."

About that time Danny Kaye came through the door, wearing that big grin and his eyes sparkling. He put his hands on my shoulders and said, "William Shakespeare said that anybody over forty is too old to retire."

On my last night of work at Candlestick, when we got to about the seventh inning, Ralph Nelson of the front-office staff put a big notice up on the message board saying that this was my last night there. The fans started to give me an ovation, and I responded by waving from the booth in a manner described by my partner, Hank Greenwald, as not unlike the pope dispensing a papal blessing from his balcony at St. Peter's. Then, Ralph Nelson rapped on the window to get my attention and pointed to Lasorda. He had come out of the Dodger dugout onto the warning track and, having removed his cap, was bowing deeply from the waist and saluting. I waved back in response. And I suppose that only Lasorda and I understood the full import of his salute.

In my three seasons with the Giants, they went through three field managers, two general managers, two equipment managers, two publicity directors, assorted coaches and personnel, and two player strikes. The steadiest employee was the woman who dispensed the

Polish sausages. And I was one of her best customers.

There is no need to try to overlook the fact that the San Francisco climate is a problem. It is a problem because it is treacherous and spotty. There are areas where the weather could hardly be any better. Down the peninsula around Palo Alto or across in Marin County there are times, lots of times, when it is nothing short of heavenly.

But there is just no accounting for an area like Candlestick Park. You cannot play major league baseball in Candlestick Park. They have tried. They have tried long and hard. And they have failed.

Now it was time for me to get on with the other projects I had in mind. It was time for me to wind up my experience as the voice of the Giants.

It would probably have been better all around if I had just sounded more like Lon Simmons. And if the Giants had been able to beat somebody. Life is always better for an announcer if he is doing the games of a winning team. Everybody prefers good news.

I left San Francisco feeling like a fellow who had managed to sneak in an idyll with a beautiful lady, knowing all the while that it was just an interlude. But my memories of the City by the Bay are pleasant and lasting.

Now I was ready to be off for my return to Knoxville and the University of Tennessee.

CHAPTER 30

Back in the Classroom

I looked anxiously at the watch on my wrist, and when it showed nine A.M. straight up, I opened up with what I hoped would be a booming and confident "Good morning."

I thought that I had been around too long to get seriously jittery about a performance. But I knew that my throat had tightened up a little bit, and the palms of my hands were wet with perspiration. I had opened up telecasts of the World Series, bowl games, and national golf tournaments much more calmly than this.

But the nature of this performance was different. It was my first class as an instructor in sports broadcasting in the Communications College at the University of Tennessee.

I had been working for a couple of months on the syllabus. And I had worked up my first half-dozen lectures.

I had 121 students in class, which was considerably more than I wanted. I was afraid that it was going to be difficult to get any sort of one-on-one instruction or discussion started with this big a class. It wasn't only difficult, it was impossible.

College-age people are perceptive. They knew that if they lay back and did not immediately participate, then I would be required to perform. I could always get even by throwing in a quick unannounced quiz. But that meant I had the papers to grade. I had moved into the academic world only to find that a rookie needs to take some old advice. For instance, when I gave my first quiz requiring an essay answer, I failed to put a word limit on the essay. A veteran professor, hearing what I had done, said, "That's a rookie mistake. You will discover that there are students who can't express themselves on any subject in less than three thousand words. You will be all winter getting those papers graded." He was absolutely right, and I didn't do that anymore.

I also found that discipline had changed a bit in the classroom since I was there. It would not have been difficult to employ the methods that the army used. But I thought I would have defeated the purpose. There had to be some adjusting done, and it had to be done by me. Maybe a student walking into the classroom five minutes late, eating a sweet roll and drinking a Coke, doesn't indicate lack of respect for the procedures. Maybe it means he or she hasn't had breakfast. I decided early that what it meant as far as I was concerned was nothing. I was there to offer some information about the profession of sports broadcasting. And those in class had paid a fee to be there. If they didn't want to partake, lots of luck.

I was walking to class one morning and passed a familiar sight. It was a magnolia tree, and although the buildings had been changed, old replaced by new, I remembered that this big magnolia tree had been in the front yard of the house where I had lived in the spring quarter of my freshman year. And the room where I was currently teaching a class was only about two hundred yards up the same street. In all of those years, in all that time, I had progressed only about two hundred yards.

The grades that I gave at the end of the quarter were generally high. I think they will be a little tougher next time. I gave only two F's. And I couldn't find the students to tell them that they had flunked. In fact, I didn't recall ever having seen them, all quarter. Bill Heinz suggested that perhaps they were training for careers as ghost writers.

What I am attempting to do as a teacher is convey what the profession of sports broadcasting is like right now. I realize that many courses in college are taught by people who have retired and they relate what it was like when they were still working. And I realize that other courses are taught from reference sources in the library. I try to convey what it is like today. I like the idea of working the

Cotton Bowl on television one day, and then in class next day being able to say, "This is the way that CBS did it yesterday." I also point out that I do not always agree with what CBS does, but I usually know why they do what they do.

I have not been able to keep up a continuous schedule of class instruction, as I had hoped. I have not had the time available to me to do that. As long as I continue to work at a schedule of sports broadcasts plus assorted projects, the teaching has had to be put on the back burner. But I stay in touch and it is an affiliation I intend to keep alive. I have an idea that those young people out there in class will do something toward keeping the instructor young.

I try to join in other activities also. I never miss the college baseball games. And one day a fresh-faced young manager came over to ask if I would throw out the first ball.

I went down to the corner of the dugout and properly tossed the ball the prescribed six feet to the waiting catcher. My toss just made it. I would have been embarrassed if it had bounced.

For so many years, on opening day I had always said to somebody on the press level, "Who's the old bastard throwing out the first ball?" And now, inexplicably, *I* was the old bastard throwing out the first ball.

Through a change in the NCAA television plan in 1982, CBS found itself back in the college football business. The president of CBS Sports, Neal Pilson, and executive producer Kevin O'Malley inquired if I would like to move from the NFL crew over to coverage of college football once again, with a new three-year contract. And the money had gone up since my first college assignment years before at CBS. It was about seven times as much as it had been then. (The agreement I had made with CBS to do NFL football back in 1966 when the NCAA games went to ABC had run sixteen seasons.)

Our first game would be North Carolina vs. Pittsburgh at Three Rivers Stadium in Pittsburgh. And we did a lot of preparation. This telecast, CBS's return to college football after an absence of nineteen years, would be in prime time on a Thursday night. They had not done a regular-season college game since the Army-Navy game of 1963—and I had done that one for them, too.

We had spent several days with North Carolina in their workouts at Chapel Hill, and we had been in Pittsburgh for four days, checking on the Panthers.

Now we were at Three Rivers Stadium, waiting for the start of this telecast. I remembered other telecasts on other days at this stadium, games involving the Pittsburgh Steelers, games involving the Pittsburgh Pirates. And I remembered games at Pitt Stadium and at Forbes Field. This September night was hot and humid. I remembered working on the roof at Forbes Field in the cold and snow. Yeah, that was the Philadelphia Eagles and the Pittsburgh Steelers in the final game of the 1960 regular season, and Sonny Jurgensen was at quarterback for the Eagles backing up the regular, Norm Van Brocklin. And Jurgensen's fingers were frozen and he kept dropping the snap. And on the roof, my fingers were frozen and I kept dropping my pencil. Just thoughts in Pittsburgh while I waited for a cue from producer Ric LaCivita.

I watched the monitor and saw the CBS host, Brent Musburger, come up on the screen. And I heard him in his introduction saying some nice things about this old veteran who was about to do the play-by-play. Those things Brent was saying were above and beyond the call. I remembered those nights in other booths in other cities when Brent had been learning the trade from the ground up as my spotter—"always be nice to the spotter."

And now there was the cue. Okay, pick it up and go. "Thank you very much, Brent, and hello again everybody."

It's another opening of another show.

I had gone from Tennessee to New York in 1952 to work on the series of NCAA football telecasts on NBC. Now, in 1982, I had done it again—thirty years later—this time the same trip for CBS.

Now we had been through the opening, and they had put the ball on the tee. Okay, let's see who the kicker is. You know who it should be, but you check it. A thousand things might have happened that you don't know about. Maybe the kicker got a stomachache, maybe he was called home by a family emergency, maybe the fellow getting ready to kick was added late this afternoon off the soccer squad.

And check the deep men. They had told you who they expected to have deep to receive the kickoff, but they may have changed their minds. The best returner may have stepped on a rock and turned his ankle on the walk through the gravel parking lot. The deep man may be wearing a number that identifies him as third cousin of the coach's wife, on scholarship as a favor toward family harmony. It's best if you know who those people are *before* they get the ball.

Locate the referee. He's down there near the goalposts behind the receiving team. There's some milling around up by the ball on the tee and that doesn't mean a thing. The referee is the man who will signal the kicker to start forward.

And here he comes, he kicks, and the ball is in the air. If it comes down, it's time for you to go to work. It's the start of another season, and you never felt better in your life.

You will pull together a three-hour punctuated narrative of identifications and comments. And it will be based on all the games in all the sports you ever saw, and on all the adventures in all the parts of the world you ever witnessed, and with the help of all the classes you ever took or taught, and everything you ever wrote or read.

Later in the season, I did the Army-Navy game in Philadelphia again. President Harry Truman was not there this time. Even President Ronald Reagan was not there. But the cadets and the midshipmen were. I always get such a thrill out of their march on, looking down there and seeing some of the finest young men in the nation who at this important time of decision in their lives have opted for a life of service to their country. Over director Bob Fishman's dramatic pictures of these marching units I did a restrained commentary that was strong with true emotion. As a result, I was invited by both the Naval Academy at Annapolis and the Military Academy at West Point to visit during the winter.

I went to Annapolis and stayed at the quarters of Captain Bo Coppedge, the director of athletics. I toured the facilities, was greeted by the Brigade at the noon meal, and spoke at the banquet for the football team that night. And I had a chance to visit with an old friend—Rip Miller, one of Rockne's Seven Mules, who had been around the Naval Academy for a lot of years now.

I went to West Point as the speaker for the annual formal midwinter "Dining In" of the Department of History. (It is a traditional event to which an "outside" speaker is invited. It is not a sports occasion.) The program cover had a montage of pictures of Grant, Lee, MacArthur, and Eisenhower, and the words: "At West Point, much of the history we teach was made by those that we taught."

I explained to these officers how I saw World War II, pointing out that if the great soldiers didn't have soldiers like me for comparison, they would never have known what they were better than.

As a surprise they presented me with a decoration made up of all the awards and ribbons I am entitled to wear. For me, it was a night to remember there on the plain at West Point.

After dinner we gathered there by the fire, with snow falling outside, and we talked far into the night of the Mets and of football and of war.

I have an idea that for a long, long time I will continue to recall a lot of the stories that deal with sports and the military.

CHAPTER 31

And the Beat Goes On

I have some time now to devote to thoughts of performances and to some evaluations and comments.

In baseball, pitchers are the most intriguing because they do not know from day to day just what their effective weapons will be. Frequently, up until the first pitch (and maybe after that) they are not certain whether it is the fastball, the curve ball, the slider, or the change that they will have to depend on. The great ones are the pitchers who win on the days when they don't have any of those.

His career was shortened because of injury to his arm, but on his best days I never saw a pitcher better than Sandy Koufax. I never forgot the night at Dodger Stadium in 1962 against the Mets when, in the first inning, he retired the side on nine straight strikes and continued to pitch a no-hit game.

I thought Bob Gibson of the Cardinals was superb. He might throw a shutout any time he was out there, and he might do it in about an hour and twenty minutes.

Over the long haul, I thought Warren Spahn was the most impressive, and at the finish he was doing it all with nothing much but knowledge and a screwball. But he was still doing it.

And to me the most memorable pitching performance was that turned in by Tom Seaver against the San Diego Padres at Shea Stadium in 1969 when he struck out the last ten batters in the game. He just got into a groove and it seemed to me that if batters had come up there all day and all night, he would have continued to strike them out, all of them.

I didn't see much of the American League, but in the five seasons I did the games on NBC I saw enough of Ted Williams to know that nobody ever swung the bat with more control and authority. And Henry Aaron was great. It was not particularly his home-run stroke that impressed me. At Milwaukee and Atlanta, he played in a pair of ball parks where home runs came easier than at some other places. The Henry Aaron I remember is the line-drive hitter who played for Fred Haney's great Milwaukee teams in the late fifties.

The football quarterback I best remember is John Unitas at Baltimore and those long bombs to Lenny Moore. And nothing was more beautiful than the long arc of a pass put up by Norm Van Brocklin. The most spectacular running back I saw was Gale Sayers of the Chicago Bears.

And the college quarterback most likely to bring his team from behind to a last-minute victory was Joe Montana at Notre Dame.

I fondly recall Jerry West playing basketball at West Virginia and Oscar Robertson at Cincinnati. And there was a time when Bob Cousy of the Boston Celtics was in a class by himself in the NBA. I did the game at the Boston Garden the day that Bill Russell broke in. Coming to the game, he got stuck in the traffic in Boston's Sumner tunnel and was slightly late. But when Bill Russell finally got out of that tunnel, the game of basketball changed forever. At least for the fans in Boston.

And I will never ever forget the day in 1955 that Gene Sarazen and I worked an NBC telecast of the National Open golf tournament in San Francisco and watched Jack Fleck come on to birdie the eighteenth for a tie with the great Ben Hogan. And then Fleck beat Hogan in the playoff the next day.

Those are just random things to think about on a rainy day.

Because of the many things that have happened in my life since I first left Knoxville, my present life there is immensely enriched. For all of those years that I worked baseball in the major leagues I never had any urgent reason to define my interest. I didn't really know whether I was actually an earnest baseball fan or whether I simply applied myself to earning a pleasant living. Now that I am in the role of a spectator, I can tell you that I am a dedicated baseball fan. It is such a marvelous spectator sport. And one of the joys of the game is that it can be pursued to any depth that one desires. You can watch a game superficially, enjoy it as entertainment, and carry on a conversation with a friend at the same time. Or, if you choose, you can watch in the manner of a chess match, considering the ramifications of every pitch. This great game will allow you to read every slight move of the defense, telling you perhaps what the next pitch is likely to be.

In watching games on television these days—and there are so many available on the various cable systems—I have the added pleasure of feeling that I am watching a group of old friends. And I am. It takes only an instant to conjure up memories of magic moments spent in the company of many of those whom I now watch in action.

And I have the added advantage of being able to talk back to the announcers. I do this with no malice but rather with affection. When Harry Caray says, "That pitch was low and away," I say, "Like hell it was, Harry, it was right down the pipe." I suppose it is convenient in these circumstances that I usually watch alone, so that my remarks disturb no one.

On my birthday last year, it was late afternoon and my phone rang. The operator said it was a call from Shea Stadium in New York. I knew that the Dodgers were playing the Mets. And soon I was talking to Bob Murphy and Ralph Kiner of the Mets broadcasting team, and Jerry Doggett, who has been a Dodgers broadcaster since 1956.

There are so many ways that one stays in touch, and they are a pure joy. I went to a game of the Tennessee Volunteers and discovered a number of scouts there looking at Vol outfielder Alan Cockrell. Soon I was in conversation with Vern Benson, now scouting for the Cardinals, who was a friend from many years' association in the majors. And there was Bob Fontaine of the Giants, who was once the general manager of the San Diego Padres. With him was his assistant, Bob Miller, who had a long and distinguished career as a major league pitcher, and is now pitching coach of the Giants. Miller and I stood behind home plate and reminisced about the season more than twenty years earlier when Casey Stengel confused our names for the whole year.

I went out to watch the Knoxville Blue Jays in the Southern

League and visited with Jim Marshall, managing the Nashville Sounds, a farm club of the New York Yankees. We spoke of the brief time he had spent with the original Mets when Stengel usually called him John Blanchard. Marshall had gone on to manage the Chicago Cubs and the Oakland A's, and then spent three seasons in Japan. As we stood behind the batting cage at Bill Meyer Stadium in Knoxville that night there was a special camaraderie.

And the same night, batting coach Dick Sisler was there. And we sat together in the stands and recalled so many things.

Dick is a member of a famous baseball family. His late father, George Sisler, whom I never called anything but an almost reverent "Mr. Sisler," twice batted over .400. Dick had been so imposing in the International League that Ernest Hemingway, in writing *The Old Man and the Sea,* had created a scene in which the old man proposes to the boy that they go to the ball park in Havana and perhaps see "the great Sisler." The great Sisler Hemingway referred to was not George. It was Dick.

As we sat there that night in the Knoxville ball park and talked, I remembered the day in 1950 that he had hit a tenth-inning, three-run homer against the Brooklyn Dodgers in Ebbets Field, giving the Phils the National League pennant and sending them into the World Series. And I remembered when Fred Hutchinson was dying of cancer in 1964 and turned the management of the Cincinnati Reds over to his top coach, Dick Sisler. We talked of many other days and people we had known in the major leagues. Such is the romance of the great and marvelous game of baseball.

I take great pride and pleasure now in the years I spent in major league baseball as a broadcaster. And the benefits and dividends are never-ending. Now, for instance, a visit to Manhattan and a long walk around the city is for me an exercise in nostalgia.

During one such visit, I walked up Central Park South near the Plaza Hotel, when I suddenly felt the hand of the beat policeman hard upon my shoulder, and I turned quickly to determine wherein I had run afoul of the local ordinances.

The policeman was already reaching for his book, and it seemed apparent that I was on the way to getting a ticket for something.

"Lindsey," he said, "I wonder if you would autograph my book for me. When I was growing up, I listened to the Mets every night and I will never forget you."

And then I was strolling down Sixth Avenue and there was a

police car at the curb with four cops inside. The sergeant in the right front seat said, "Hey, Lins, when are you coming back to New York? The Mets haven't won a game since you left!"

I smiled and said, "There were times when they won precious few while I was here."

Then I stopped off at the dental office of my friend Dr. Maurice Saklad and his associate Dr. Catherine Beeson on Fifty-fourth Street. As I sat in the dentist's chair, Dr. Beeson said, "There's someone out here who wants to say hello."

And at that moment, Willie Mays came in. He had that big smile on his face as he said, "Where do you live now?" I told him that I lived in Knoxville. And he brightened as he said, "You must see Bailey then." His reference was to Ed Bailey, former major league catcher. He and Willie had been teammates and friends on the San Francisco Giants. I somehow remembered the night the Giants had been shorthanded in the outfield because of injuries and they had played Bailey in right field. Willie was in center, and on anything hit in the air from center field to the right-field line, Bailey yelled "Plenty of room, Willie!" and got out of the way.

It is impossible, of course, to make a competent comparison of great players one has seen. And still from time to time, most of us do play that little game of selecting the superlatives. We like to guess who is the best. That's why we keep score of the games and season's batting averages and the number of home runs hit. For a period of twenty-five years, I saw most of the players in the major leagues, and I think that Willie Mays was the best I ever saw. I mean the best total ballplayer. He could do everything you can do in the game, and he did it with grace and style and conveyed to the fans the feeling that he was having great fun doing it. I consider one of the privileges of my life that of having been afforded the opportunity to see Willie Mays perform at the peak of his career. I never saw anything else like it.

Admittedly, it was interesting to watch the development of another characteristic of Mays. He was approached by the program chairman of every dinner, luncheon, or social gathering imaginable. He could not possibly accept all the invitations, but when he said no, the efforts to get him were doubled and intensified. As a means of survival, Willie devised a defense. He had noticed that while saying no only brought more bother, if he said yes, the calls stopped on the assumption that it was settled. So Willie started saying yes to a great many requests. Usually he didn't go to the dinners or whatever, but he had found a way to stop the pressure. If a statistical record were kept for such things, I am sure it would reveal that Willie Mays led the major leagues for years in the category of "no shows."

Of course, I never saw anything particularly wrong with the way that Joe DiMaggio played the game. And he did it with a dignity and effortlessness that was inspiring. Maybe his record of having hit safely in fifty-six consecutive games is the most imposing record in the book, the least likely to be broken. His career was shortened because of injuries, and in typical fashion he chose not to perform at less than his full capabilities. And surely I have the greatest respect for the Yankee Clipper, and what he meant to the game of baseball.

But now I was thinking of my good fortune in having come to New York from Knoxville for the briefest of visits and having had a visit with Willie Mays. Commissioner Bowie Kuhn had asked me once, after I had moved to Knoxville, if I missed New York. I told him that anyone who spends his entire lifetime in New York, or one who goes there and stays forever, misses the great thrill and satisfaction of *returning* to New York. He understood. And that is what I mean when I consider the incident of having run unexpectedly into a friend named Willie Mays.

But my adventure wasn't over. That same evening I went to a theater on Forty-fifth Street. When the show was over, I walked alone up Seventh Avenue to the area of the Sheraton Centre hotel, once the Americana. There was a fair amount of pedestrian traffic. But apart from this, a lone figure was standing across the sidewalk at the curb casually surveying the traffic jammed into the street. He was in the stance of a tourist, taking in the sights. And none of the passing people took any notice of him.

When I saw who it was, I veered in his direction and at the same time I shouted, "Clipper, what are you doing out here?"

DiMaggio turned, smiled, and said, "Hello, Lindsey. I'm just getting a breath of air. Are you living in New York now?"

He knew that I had been living in his city, San Francisco, and I explained that I now lived in neither New York nor San Francisco, but rather in Knoxville, Tennessee. Joe D. thought that called for a little further explanation, so we talked for a while. And then I bade good-bye to the great DiMaggio, and walked on up Seventh Avenue toward my room at the Essex House.

And as I walked I thought of the unlikely circumstance of a

lone tourist dropping into Manhattan from Knoxville and in the same day having unscheduled meetings with old friends named Willie Mays and Joe DiMaggio.

And I guessed that the greatest reward of all those years I spent as a sportscaster in a variety of sports is that things like that are likely to keep right on happening the rest of my life.

On a Sunday morning in September of 1984, I was climbing into the backseat of a chauffeur-driven limousine at the ramp entrance of the Grand Hyatt hotel in Manhattan. When the new hotel had been constructed on the site where the old Commodore had stood, they had been thoughtful enough to retain the entrance off the bend of Park Avenue as it comes around Grand Central Station. My daughters, Sharon and Nancy, were with me, and my son-in-law, Andy. We were on the way to Shea Stadium for a baseball game, and for pregame ceremonies during which Ralph Kiner, Bob Murphy, and I would be inducted into the New York Mets Hall of Fame.

Some weeks earlier we had sat for a sculptress who had fashioned busts of us that would be on display on the field during today's ceremonies and year-round in a glass display case in the Shea Stadium Diamond Club lobby. The night before, we had been honored at a dinner at 21.

It had been twenty-two years before, in 1962, that I had made that major career move for me and my family from life as a full-time network sportscaster to life with the New York Mets, that struggling, brand-new baseball team. Ralph, Bob, and I had worked together for seventeen seasons, and now we three were being inducted together into the Mets Hall of Fame.

As we pulled into the sunny parking lot near the Diamond Club entrance, fans were already gathering. And immediately we were into a session of autograph signing and exploding flashbulbs.

Then we went upstairs for a brunch in the directors' room with members of the Mets' official family as well as our own families.

Bob would do the radio pregame show, and he thought it would be a nice touch if Ralph and I were his guests, so we walked down to the radio booth. Next door, the Montreal Expos already had their radio position set up. Their broadcaster was Duke Snider, a Hall of Famer who had been the center fielder for the Dodgers in Brooklyn and Los Angeles as well as a one-time Met. He yelled to me, "When you finish would you come over and do a pregame show with me back to Montreal?" I said I would. Duke Snider wanted to talk about Casey Stengel, and we reminisced about some of those days.

Then we went down to the television studio beneath the stands to do a videotape of *Kiner's Korner,* the show that followed each telecast of a Met game. The three of us recalled the years that had passed. The producer of the show was Ralph Robbins, who had been there that very first day the Mets had played a home game at the Polo Grounds.

Then, we went out onto the field. The introductions were made. And in responding, I had the satisfying opportunity to introduce Sharon, Nancy, and Andy. That was the best part, having them there with me on the field, because the years with the Mets had been a big part of their lives, too.

Then came time for the throwing out of the first ball, and since Ralph and Bob had to go to work, I had the honor of performing that pleasant chore. I sat in the box on the home-plate side of the Mets dugout and tossed the ball softly to the catcher, on one hop.

We went upstairs and watched the game from a mezzanine booth, and all afternoon we had visitors coming by to say hello.

When the game ended, we went out through the Diamond Club lobby. Already the busts of Ralph, Bob, and me were installed in the display case with the light directed upon them.

When we went out into the parking lot to the limousine, there were hands to be shaken and more autographs to be signed. And then, as the big car turned toward the exit, the Met fans there applauded and waved. As the limousine moved along the service road leading out to Roosevelt Avenue, I looked through the back window at the huge stadium, casting its shadow in the late afternoon sun. And I realized that I had left a lot of my life there.

And I guess that my greatest reward now is the steady stream of middle-aged men and women who introduce themselves to me as I travel around the country on assignments. And in different words and in different ways, they say the same thing. They explain that they just want to say hello because they have such vivid memories of snuggling up close to the radio or television set in their room when they were young and listening to a voice that said, "Hello everybody, I'm Lindsey Nelson."

God bless them, every one!

Index

Aaron, Henry (Hank), 308, 416
Ali, Muhammad, 371
Allen, George, 330, 331, 401, 402
Allen, Mel, 173, 175–176, 180, 181, 206, 207, 208, 231, 237, 238, 241, 248–249, 255, 265, 296–297, 298, 337, 347, 350–353, 381
Alston, Walter, 29–30, 308, 347
American Broadcasting Company (ABC), 155, 169, 210, 233, 234, 236, 256–257, 299, 300, 311
Analysts, 328, 329, 330, 331–334
Anderson, Eddie, 67, 227
Anderson, Maxwell, 80–82
Anderson, Tom, 41, 42, 61, 65, 66, 124, 131, 135, 299, 382
Antoine, Tex, 169
Arledge, Roone, 169, 299–300, 301
Arries, Les, 234, 249, 251
Ashburn, Richie, 277–278
Associated Press (AP), 56, 97, 111, 112, 113, 124

Bailer, Judson, 236
Bailey, Ed, 419
Baltimore Colts, 252, 257
Baltimore Orioles, 384
Banghart, Kenneth, 169
Banks, Ernie, 278
Barber, Walter (Red), 136, 208, 235, 346, 350, 351, 352, 353, 381
Barnhill, John, 55
Baruch, Andre, 175
Baseball broadcasting, 339–353
Baseball Hall of Fame, 30, 282, 353
Basilio, Carmen, 234
Baugh, Sammy, 77
Bavasi, Buzzie, 232
Bell, Bert, 159, 163, 329
Bennington, Bill, 184, 185, 186, 203
Bergman, Ingrid, 108
Berra, Yogi, 311, 370, 373, 403
Bier, Zena, 173
Blackwell, Ewell, 121
Blaik, Red, 183, 285
Blair, Frank, 77
Blanchard, Felix (Doc), 173, 285
Blattner, Buddy, 236
Blocker, Dan, 257, 258, 259
Bob Hope Desert Classic, 293
Booth, Albie, 227, 228
Boozer, Emerson, 333
Bosch, Don, 308
Boston Red Sox, 245
Boyle, Hal, 111, 113–114, 139, 170
Bradley, General Omar, 16, 43, 95, 96–97, 98, 99, 287
Brandt, Fritz, 44, 75
Brave Men (Pyle), 103
Brennan, Terry, 289, 291, 292, 293, 334
Brescia, Matty, 155
Brickhouse, Jack, 345–346, 349

Index

Bridges, Tommy, 213
Brinkley, David, 172
Britt, Jim, 51, 173
Britton, Jack, 127, 138
Brooklyn Dodgers, 29, 157, 231–232, 233, 240, 243, 346–347
Brookshier, Tom, 321, 334, 336
Brown, Clarence, 61
Brown, Jim, 222, 330
Brown, Joe E., 236, 238
Brown, Lew, 159, 170
Brown, Paul, 161, 164–165
Bryant, Paul (Bear), 137, 177, 254–255, 303, 390
Bumpus, Bob, 146
Burgess, Smokey, 281–282
Bushnell, Asa, 289
Butkus, Dick, 334–335
Byers, Walter, 301
Byrd, Ben, 382

Cafego, George, 63, 131
Cahill, Joe, 149–150, 151
Campanis, Al, 406
Campbell, Archie, 139
Cannon, Billy, 255
Capa, Bob, 107, 108
Caray, Harry, 265, 337, 345, 349
Cardwell, Don, 314
Carideo, Frank, 67
Carlton, Steve, 314
Carneal, Herb, 388
Carpenter, Ken, 65
Carter, Jimmy, 390
Chacon, Elio, 277, 278
Chandler, Happy, 159
Chattanooga Times, The, 61
Chesley, C. D., 302, 355–356, 377, 395–396
Chicago Bears, 34, 153, 211, 222, 300, 301, 327
Chicago Cubs, 239, 313, 314
Chicago Daily News, 139
Chicago Tribune, 67, 68, 226
Chirkinian, Frank, 303
Christopher, Joe, 277
Churchill, Winston, 71, 86, 94–95
Cifers, Ed, 75, 78
Cincinnati Reds, 374
Cleveland Browns, 160, 161, 164–165
Cochrane, Mickey, 152
Cockrell, Alan, 417
Coleman, Choo Choo, 276, 317
Coleman, Jerry, 341, 402, 403
Coleman, Jimmy, 75
"Color man," 328
Columbia Broadcasting Company (CBS), 16, 17, 51, 118, 136, 227, 235, 236, 247, 260, 264, 294, 298, 303
NCAA football games and, 289–299, 332, 380, 411–414
Comiskey, Chuck, 154, 164
Connor, George, 301, 302
Considine, Bob, 375, 379
Coppedge, Captain Bo, 413
Corbett, Jim, 253–255, 289, 299, 301
Corum, Bill, 249–250, 251
Cotton Bowl, 138, 140, 147, 217, 298, 303, 304, 356, 364
Cousy, Bob, 416
Cowan, Howard, 112, 113
Coyle, Harry, 246, 271
Craig, Roger, 276, 317
Creasy, Bill, 118, 294
Crisler, Fritz, 285, 286
Crosby, Bing, 292–293
Crowley, Bill, 237
Crowley, Ed, 184
Crowley, Jim, 226, 227, 228, 234, 330
Cunningham, Chris, 116, 117–118

Daily Herald, The (Columbus), 26, 33, 38, 45, 72
Dann, Mike, 164
Dark, Alvin, 247
Davis, Glenn, 173, 285
Day, Laraine, 240, 244–245
Dean, Dizzy, 159, 160, 236, 237, 247
Decker, Quinn, 56
Denny, Harold, 139
DeRoulet, Mrs. Lorinda, 383, 384–385
Desmond, Connie, 346
Detroit Lions, 147, 151, 154
DeVois, Charlie, 126, 127
Dickens, Phil, 56
Dickey, Bill, 35
Dietzel, Paul, 255, 290, 295, 334
Dillon, Jack, 159, 170, 175, 176, 181, 184
DiMaggio, Joe, 236, 340, 420–421
Dodd, Bobby, 44, 56, 75
Doggett, Jerry, 138, 146, 147, 148, 154, 347, 348, 349, 417
Dolan, Jimmy, 51, 53
Doubleday, Abner, 265
Douglas, Glenn, 143
Douglas, Mike, 118, 391
Dozier, Grace, 247
Drew, Red, 218
Dumont, Dr. Allen B., 158
Dumont television network, 154, 155, 158, 169
Dunphy, Don, 249
Durocher, Leo, 240–248, 267, 313
Durslag, Mel, 256

Eckert, General Spike, 310
Eddy, General Manton S., 88, 90, 95, 101, 139

Eiges, Sid, 167–168
Eisenhower, Dwight D., 43, 94, 95, 100, 287, 290, 293, 299
Eliot, Ray, 225, 286
Elson, Bob, 265

Farris, Morgan, 28
Feathers, Beattie, 56
Fiesta Bowl, 332–333
Fisher, Charlie, 121
Fleck, Jack, 416
Fontaine, Bob, 417
Football Roundup (CBS program), 346
Ford, Whitey, 307
"Four Horsemen of Notre Dame," 226–227, 228
Fox, Davey, 333
Fox, Larry, 310
Frank, Barry, 332–333, 335
Friedman, Benny, 330
Fulton, Bob, 40

Gallery, Dan, 156
Gallery, Fette, 226, 266
Gallery, Michele, 212
Gallery, Tom S., 155–159, 166, 167–168, 169, 170, 212, 226, 232, 237, 248–249, 251, 266
  Nelson and, 155, 161, 163, 164, 165, 183, 185, 206–207, 208, 217, 244, 246, 267, 269, 271, 279
  as pioneer in televising sports events, 173, 175, 177, 234, 238–240, 241–242
Game of the Day (Mutual program), 236, 237
Garagiola, Joe, 311, 336–337
Garrett, Wayne, 323, 324
Gaspar, Rod, 323–324
Gator Bowl, 298
Gehrig, Lou, 22, 27, 35
General Motors Corporation, 175, 179, 180, 181, 182–183
Gifford, Frank, 304, 305, 311
Glass, David, 395
Glickman, Marty, 260
Gorman, Tom, 278, 279
Gowdy, Curt, 260, 303, 318, 349
Graham, Frank, 272
Graham, Mary Virginia, 391
Grange, Red, 25–26, 33, 153, 217–228, 253, 285, 329–330
Grant, M. Donald, 316, 373
Green Bay Packers, 154, 332, 336
Greenberg, Hank, 340
Greene, Tommy, 131
Greenwald, Hank, 395
Gregson, Jack, 168
Griffith, Corinne, 156–157
Grimes, Tommy, 401
Grimsley, Will, 33, 394
Grossman, Sandy, 334
Grote, Jerry, 315, 323
Gunsel, Austin, 259–260

Hackman, Buddy, 44
Halas, George, 153, 301
Harada, Cappy, 403, 404, 405
Harding, General Forrest, 74
Hargrove, Marion, 82
Harkness, Tim, 308
Harmon, Tom, 185, 233
Harriman, Averell, 232
Harris, Harry, 380
Harris, Jack, 50–51, 53, 54
Harris, Walt, 338
Harrison, Dutch, 160
Harrison, Harry, 250–251
Harwell, Ernie, 267
Hasel, Joe, 183, 214
Haverlin, Carl, 208
Heintzelman, Ken, 121
Heinz, W. C. (Bill), 116, 117–118, 128–129, 170, 221, 294, 380, 410
Helfer, Al, 237, 337, 347
Hemingway, Ernest, 140
Hemus, Solly, 273–274
Henry, Bill, 157, 175–176
Herlihy, Ed, 257
Herr, Danny, 74–75
Hickman, Herman, 56, 175
Hicks, George, 139
Hileman, Dr. Don, 394
Hitler, Adolf, 69, 112, 121
Hodges, Gil, 311, 312, 317–318, 325
Hodges, Maggie, 266
Hodges, Russ, 175, 176, 179–180, 183, 240, 242, 266
Hogan, Ben, 416
Hope, Bob, 293, 389
Hornung, Paul, 302, 332–333, 358, 359–360, 380
Houk, Ralph, 351
Howard, Elston, 307
Hoyt, Waite, 343–344, 349
Huntley, Chet, 172
Husing, Ted, 21, 51, 52, 53, 137, 148, 150–151, 169, 177, 208, 235, 265, 296
Hutchinson, Fred, 279, 418

Illinois, University of, 220, 223–225
International Boxing Club, 234
Irvin, Monte, 114

Jackson, Hurricane, 249
Jackson, Keith, 356

Index

Janowski, Gene, 227
Japan Bowl, 400, 402
Jones, James, 128, 170
Joyner, Jack, 50, 52, 53, 54–55, 60–61, 62, 63
Jurgensen, Sonny, 412

Kahn, E. J., Jr., 74–75
Kahn, Roger, 215
Kanehl, Rod, 317
Kaufman, Sid, 17
Kaye, Danny, 132, 280, 340, 407
Kazmaier, Dick, 175
Keiter, Les, 267, 269
Kennedy, John F., 77, 279, 292, 293–294
Kennedy, Joseph P., 222
Kerner, Otto, 73
Kiernan, John, 153, 167
Kiernan, John, Jr., 153, 183, 205
Kiner, Ralph, 90–91, 268, 275, 315, 323, 336, 340, 343, 383, 384, 417, 421, 422
Kiner's Korner, 383, 422
King, Billy, 59–60, 62, 66
Kinnick, Nile, 67, 227
KLIF (Dallas), 146, 148
Knickerbocker, H. R., 139
Knoxville *Journal,* 41, 46, 61, 66, 124, 382
Knoxville *News-Sentinel,* 126, 129, 238
Koosman, Jerry, 308–309, 314, 319
Koufax, Sandy, 415
Kramer, Jerry, 334
Krause, Ed (Moose), 355
Kudner Agency, 179–180, 251, 252
Kuhn, Bowie, 312, 316, 325, 420
Kusserow, Lou, 246, 271

LaCivita, Ric, 412
LaCock, Peter, 404
Lambert, Mickie, *see* Nelson, Mickie (Mrs. Lindsey)
Langford, Frances, 293
Lapchick, Joe, 33, 261
Larsen, Don, 296
Lasorda, Tommy, 406, 407, 408
Lavagetto, Cookie, 278, 279
Laval, Pierre, 121–122
Layden, Elmer, 63, 226, 227
Leahy, Frank, 330
Lebahr, Bert, 148
Lee, Clark, 98, 107
Liberatore, Ed, 406
Liberty Broadcasting System (LBS), 137, 138, 140, 141, 143, 145–154, 155
Liebling, A. J., 139, 205
Lindemann, Carl, 300
Lindsay, John, 316, 321, 322
Linebaugh, Henry, 140–141
Link, Bob, 302
Little, C. Edward, 377, 380
Lombardi, Vince, 332, 336
London, Bernie, 206, 207, 251, 252
Look, 226
Los Angeles Dodgers, 347–350
Los Angeles Rams, 16
Los Angeles Times, 157, 175
Louis, Joe, 234–235
Lurie, Bob, 388–389, 395
Lurie, Connie, 395
Lurie, Lou, 388
Lynn, Jimmy, 33

MacArthur, General Douglas, 44, 98, 235
McCovey, Willie, 276, 337–338
McEver, Gene, 44
McEwan, Colonel, 44
McGraw, John, 232
McKenzie, Dr. Ed, 255, 389
McLemore, Henry, 33, 52
McLendon, Gordon, 137, 139, 140, 143, 146, 148, 153, 154
McNamee, Graham, 21, 62, 208, 250, 265
MacPhail, Bill, 289, 297, 298, 300, 303
MacPhail, Larry, 235, 240
Macy's Thanksgiving Day Parade (1961), 257–259
Madden, John, 332
Major League Baseball (NBC program), 241–249, 267
Majors, Johnny, 400
Mann, Ralph, 300, 376
Mantle, Mickey, 352
Markson, Harry, 234
Marshall, George Preston, 77, 156–157
Mauch, Gus, 311
Mays, Willie, 232, 374, 419–420
Mazer, Bill, 321
Mazeroski, Bill, 315
Meany, Tom, 274, 280, 352
Meredith, Burgess, 102
Meyer, Dutch, 176, 177
Meyers, Ron, 400
Middleton, Drew, 95, 139
Mike Douglas Show, The, 118, 391
Miller, Bob, 281, 417
Miller, Don, 226, 227
Miller, Jack, 159, 170, 175, 176, 181
Milner, John, 374
Milton, Charles H., III, 303, 359, 400, 401, 402
Milwaukee Braves, 239, 240, 243, 244, 248, 264
Minnesota Vikings, 300, 321
Minosa, Minnie, 164
Molnar, Pete, 290, 291

Monday Night Football (ABC program), 299, 331
Monday Quarterback (NBC program), 214–215
Monitor (NBC program), 214, 351
Montana, Joe, 416
Montreal Expos, 312, 313
Moore, Al, 282, 319
Moore, Lenny, 416
Moran, Charlie, 44
Morris, Willie, 170
Morrison, Herb, 214
Munday, Bill, 208–209
Murff, Red, 309, 310
Murphy, Bob, 268, 275, 315, 323, 336, 343, 417, 421, 422
Murphy, Jack, 266, 267
Murphy, Johnny, 311, 316, 324–325
Murtaugh, Danny, 344
Musburger, Brent, 16, 17, 18, 328, 412
Musser, Tucker, 141

Nagler, Barney, 204, 250
Napoli, Louis, 384
Natalie Kalmus Company, 139
National Basketball Association (NBA), 260–261, 331
National Broadcasting Company (NBC), 51, 53, 54, 65, 66, 67, 69, 77, 79, 136, 140, 155, 158, 163, 175, 237, 303
  See also Nelson, Lindsey, NBC and
National Collegiate Athletic Association (NCAA), 161, 233–234, 285
  football package sold to television (1950s), 173–175
  Nelson's broadcasts for, 179–215, 289–299, 332, 380, 411–414
National Football League (NFL), 76, 159, 257, 259, 301–306, 331, 411
National Sportscasters and Sportswriters Association, 255
National Sportscasters and Sportswriters Hall of Fame, 255, 389–390
Neal, Roy, 185
Nelson, Davey, 285, 286
Nelson, James, 23, 24, 39, 65
Nelson, Lindsey
  Anderson (Tom) and, 41, 42, 61, 124, 131, 135, 299, 382
  on baseball broadcasting, 339–353
  boyhood of
    love of sports, 27–32
    radio broadcasting, 20–22, 32–33, 40
  football broadcasting by
    the Cotton Bowl, 217, 303, 356, 364
    NCAA games for CBS, 289–299, 332, 380, 411–414
    NCAA games for NBC, 179–215, 299
    NFL games, 257, 259, 301–306, 411
    Notre Dame, 302–303, 320, 332, 355–360, 380, 395
    the Rose Bowl, 268–269, 295–299, 303, 344–345
    the Super Bowl, 15–18
  Gallery and, 155, 161, 163, 164, 165, 183, 185, 206–207, 208, 217, 244, 246, 267, 269, 271, 279
  Heinz and, 116, 117–118, 128–129, 170, 221, 294, 380, 410
  induction into Mets Hall of Fame, 421–422
  induction into National Sportscasters and Sportswriters Hall of Fame, 389–390
  in Japan, 400–406
  at Liberty Broadcasting, 145–154
  NBC (sports announcer) and, 207–208, 271–272
    football commentator with Red Grange, 217–228, 285
    Macy's Thanksgiving Day Parade (1961), 257–259
    Major League Baseball with Durocher, 241–249, 267
    NBA basketball, 260–261
    NFL Sunday games, 257, 259
    Patterson-Jackson fight (1957), 249–252
  NBC (sports department) and, 164–208
  as New York Mets announcer, 268–284, 299, 307–313, 381–385
    1969 World Series, 313–325
    1973 World Series, 373–377
  Neyland and, 41–42, 45, 62, 136, 141–142, 146, 287–288
  Overseas Press Club "Old Pro" night for, 379–381
  parents of, 23–25, 305–306, 361–363
  Pyle and, 95, 97–105, 108
  as San Francisco Giants announcer, 387–395, 399, 407–408
  as sportswriter, 26, 27, 33–35, 38, 40
    Knoxville *Journal,* 41, 46
  Stern and, 62–66, 67, 79, 211–212, 268, 297
  at University of Tennessee, 38–70
    as instructor, 409–411
    1939 Rose Bowl game, 59–66
    as spotter for broadcasters, 50–66
  the Vol Network and, 135–136, 141–143
  Westmoreland and, 91, 109, 111, 118, 379–380, 381, 389–390
  at WHHM (Memphis), 154–162
  Whitehead and, 109, 124, 238, 380, 394, 406
  wife and
    daughters born to, 130–133, 229–231
    her death in Menorca, 366–368
    marriage, 126

Nelson, Lindsey (*Continued*)
at WKGN (Knoxville), 126–136
on working with former players in the booth, 330–338
World War II (9th Infantry Division) and, 16, 72, 73, 75
crossing the Rhine, 111–113
D-Day invasion of Europe, 99–101
encounter with Russians at the Elbe, 115–119
Fort Bragg, 73–86
Great Britain, 93–99
lasting effect of wartime experiences, 128–129, 170
Nazi slave-labor camp, 114–115
North Africa, 86–91
Paris, 109–111
at WROL (Knoxville), 136–141, 145
Nelson, Mary Sue, 23, 39, 65, 304
Nelson, Mickie (Mrs. Lindsey), 130, 146, 147, 152, 155, 160, 165, 166, 167, 168, 170–172, 205–206, 208, 211, 226, 249, 266, 268, 269, 271, 289, 293, 304–305, 319, 322, 359, 361, 362, 364–365, 397
daughters born to, 130–133, 229–231
death in Menorca of, 366–368
marriage of, 126
Nelson, Nancy Lynne, 230–231, 256, 322, 359, 361, 362, 364, 366, 381, 384, 391–394, 397, 421, 422
Nelson, Ralph, 407
Nelson, Sharon, 130–133, 135, 146, 147, 155, 160, 165, 170–172, 205, 206, 207, 258–259, 270, 312–313, 362, 363–364, 366–368, 370–371, 390, 392–393, 397, 421, 422
New York Celtics, 33
New York *Daily News,* 74, 231
New Yorker, The, 74
New York Giants, 147, 165, 231, 232, 252, 264
New York Herald Tribune, 108, 110, 151, 255, 272
New York Journal American, 249, 272
New York Mets, 257, 263–284, 307–320, 381–385
Nelson inducted into Hall of Fame, 421–422
1969 World Series, 313–325
1973 World Series, 373–377
New York Times, The, 95, 139, 153
New York Yankees, 33, 151, 152, 157, 158, 176, 231, 233, 248, 275, 307, 350
Neyland, Major Robert R., 39, 40–45, 50, 51, 52, 55–56, 60, 61, 71, 135, 136, 137, 138, 224, 285–287, 300
Nelson and, 41–42, 45, 62, 136, 141–142, 146, 287–288
Nicholas, Bill, 209, 210
9th Infantry Division, *see* Nelson, Lindsey, World War II and
Nixon, Richard, 325–326
Notre Dame, University of, 203, 302–303, 320, 332, 355–360, 380, 395

Oakes, Albert Fisher, 27
O'Donnell, Red, 33
O'Malley, Kevin, 411
O'Malley, Walter, 263, 346, 347–348, 350
Once They Heard the Cheers (Heinz), 128–129
O'Neil, Terry, 327
Orange Bowl, 51, 128
Overseas Press Club, 113–114, 375, 379–381
Owens, Jesse, 309

Parilli, Babe, 176–177
Paris, University of, 111
Parker, Dr. Roscoe E., 49–50, 55
Parks, Gary, 337–338, 395
Parseghian, Ara, 334
Patch, Colonel Alexander M., 72
Paterno, Joe, 227
Patterson, Floyd, 249
Patton, General George S., 86, 87–88, 94, 95
Payson, Mrs. Joan, 263, 277
Pearson, Fort, 69, 128
Perkins, Don, 333–334
Pfiel, Bobby, 323
Philadelphia Eagles, 75
Pignatano, Joe, 280–281, 311
Pittsburgh Pirates, 90, 239
Pittsburgh Steelers, 16, 18, 257, 260
Play-by-play announcers, 327, 328, 329
Podoloff, Maurice, 260–261
Poinsettia Bowl, 185
Pregame shows, 340–342
Price, Eddie, 165
Prince, Bob, 90–91, 344, 349
Pyle, C. C., 222
Pyle, Ernie, 90, 95–105, 108, 109, 113, 114

Quirk, Major Jim, 98–99

Radio and Television Daily, 255
"Rain fills," 245, 339–340
Ramsey, Jones, 39–40
Reagan, Ronald, 143
Reichler, Joe, 325
Reuss, Jerry, 407
Rice, Florence, 60
Rice, Grantland, 33, 52, 60, 226–227, 385–386
Riefsnyder, Howard, 335
Rizzuto, Phil, 241

Robbins, Ralph, 384, 422
Robertson, Oscar, 416
Robinson, Eddie, 164
Robinson, Jackie, 214–215
Robinson, Sugar Ray, 234
Rockne, Knute, 40, 320
Rolfe, Red, 35
Rooney, Andy, 113, 380
Rooney, Art, 257, 260
Rose, Pete, 374
Rose Bowl, 16, 51, 54, 57, 59, 128, 155, 268–269, 295–299, 303, 344–345, 355
  1939 game, 59–66
Rosenbloom, Carroll, 257
Rote, Kyle, 148, 303
Rotkiewicz, Stan, 253
Rowe, Schoolboy, 213
Russell, Bill, 416
Russell, Fred, 33, 390, 394
Ruth, Babe, 34–35
Ryan, Nolan, 310–311

Saam, Byrum, 265, 349
Sachs, Manny, 211
St. Louis Browns, 143, 236
St. Louis Cardinals, 314, 321
Saklad, Dr. Maurice, 247, 419
San Diego Padres, 312, 313
San Francisco Chronicle, 407
San Francisco Giants, 387–395, 399, 407–408
Sarazen, Gene, 416
Sarnoff, David, 158, 159, 210–211
Sauer, Johnny, 334, 358, 359
Sauter, Van Gordon, 399–400
Sayers, Gayle, 301, 416
Scheffing, Bob, 373
Schenkel, Chris, 264, 298, 299, 300
Scherick, Ed, 239, 256
Schindler, Amby, 64
Schneider, Ad, 159, 170, 175, 176
Schuessler, Rea, 52, 254
Scott, Ray, 212, 214, 336, 374
Scully, Vin, 136–137, 138, 296, 330, 346–347, 348–350
Searcy, Jay, 394
Seaver, Tom, 309–310, 314, 380, 416
Selkirk, George, 311
Shannon, Mike, 284
Shea, Ham, 164, 165
Shor, Toots, 232
Shriver, Sargent, 323
Siler, Tom, 238, 394
Simmons, Chet, 300
Simmons, Lon, 387, 388, 389
Simpson, Jim, 290, 291, 292, 293, 298, 303
Sinatra, Frank, 47, 245
Sisler, Dick, 418
Slater, Bill, 265
Slingland, Frank, 302, 396
Smith, Bubba, 335
Smith, Coy, 294
Smith, Perry, 241, 271, 295, 296–297
Smith, Red, 151, 255, 272, 385
Snelling, Major Russ, 116
Snider, Duke, 421–422
Snow, Jack, 334
Spahn, Warren, 112–113, 283, 415
Sports broadcasting
  analysts and, 328, 329, 330, 331–334
  baseball broadcasting, 339–353
  "color men" and, 328
  play-by-play announcers and, 327, 328, 329
  pregame shows and, 340–342
  "rain fills" and, 245, 339–340
  spotters and, 327–329, 334
    Nelson as, 50–66
  statisticians and, 328
  using former players in the booth, 330–338
Spotters, 327–329, 334
  Nelson as, 50–66
Stagg, Amos Alonzo, 221
Stammer, Newt, 159
Stanley, Ed, 172–173
Starr, Bart, 218
Stars and Stripes, The, 104
Statisticians, 328
Staub, Rusty, 374
Staubach, Roger, 295, 356
Stengel, Casey, 28, 164, 234, 263, 273, 275, 276–277, 278, 279, 280, 282, 283, 307, 311, 317, 343, 344, 417, 418, 422
Stenner, Bob, 330
Stern, Bill, 51, 52, 53, 54–55, 61, 128, 140, 155, 159, 160, 165, 169, 170, 183, 184, 209, 250, 255, 265
  Nelson and, 62–66, 67, 79, 210–212, 268, 297
Stoneham, Horace, 232–233, 240, 263
Stoneman, Bill, 139
Strickler, George, 226–227
Stuart, Dick, 344
Stuhldreher, Harry, 226, 227
Suffridge, Bob, 75, 76–78, 228
Sugar Bowl, 69, 128, 138
Sugarman, Marvin, 301
Sullivan, Ed, 226
Sullivan, Neal, 110, 170
Summerall, Pat, 303, 332, 356
Super Bowl (1980), 15–18
Swoboda, Ron, 314, 317

Taub, Sam, 250
Taylor, Davidson, 177, 226
Taylor, General Maxwell, 290–291

Index

Tennessee, University of, 38, 126, 394
Nelson as instructor at, 408–411
Terry, Bill, 232, 280, 317
Terway, Tys, 126
This Week in Sports (NBC program), 204
Thomas, Frank (Alabama coach), 40, 52
Thomas, Frank (Met left fielder), 277, 278
Thomas, Frank, Jr., 38, 47
Thompson, Bobby, 232
Thompson, Tommy, 77
Thomson, Jim, 374, 383, 384
Timmerman, Lieutenant Karl, 111
Tinker, Grant, 169
Toast of the Town, 226
Topping, Dan, 157, 158, 234, 236, 237, 351, 352
Torre, Joe, 314
Trafton, George, 222
Trammell, Niles, 238–239
Truman, Harry S, 183, 184
Tunney, Gene, 21
Turner, Lana, 57, 61
21 Club, 375–376, 377, 421

Unitas, John, 416
Uplinger, Hal, 118

Van Brocklin, Norm, 412, 416
Varney, Norm, 267–268
Vaughan, Les, 175
Vecsey, George, 315
Velotta, Tommy, 155
Verna, Tony, 294–295
Vol Network, 135–136, 141–143
Von Schlieben, General, 101

Wagner, Lindsay, 391
Walker, Doak, 147, 203, 289
Walker, Rube, 311, 367
Walker, Wayne, 334
Wallace, Francis, 52
Warmath, Murray, 45, 56, 69, 225
Washington *Daily News,* 97
Washington Redskins, 75
Washington Senators, 239
Washington Star, The, 124
Waskow, Captain Henry T., 97
Wayne, John, 389
Wayne, Patrick, 389
WCKT (Miami), 238
Weis, Al, 384
Weiss, George, 237, 263, 269–270, 274, 309
Weissman, Harold, 321
Wertenbaker, Charles C., 107, 108–109
Westmoreland, General William C., 73, 91, 109, 111, 118, 290, 379–380, 381, 389–390
WFAA (Dallas), 139
WHHM (Memphis), 154, 161
Whitaker, Jack, 304, 305, 380
White, Roy, 404
Whitehead, Don, 56, 97, 109, 113, 124, 139, 238, 380, 394, 406
Wilder, Roy, 139, 205
Wilkinson, Bob, 334
Williams, Ted, 416
Wilson, Gwynn, 320
WKGN (Knoxville), 126–136
WMGM (New York), 148, 151
WNOX (Knoxville), 40, 130
Woods, Jim, 238, 241, 242
World War II, *see* Nelson, Lindsey, World War II and
WROL (Knoxville), 136–141, 145
WSM (Nashville), 50, 53
WTAM (Cleveland), 160, 164, 165, 167
Wyatt, Bowden, 42, 45, 56, 288
Wyszynski, Andy, 392, 421, 422

Yost, Eddie, 311, 323, 324

Zera, Maxie, 110
Zientara, Benny, 121
Zuppke, Bob, 220, 222–224

"Events and anecdotes of the great and near-great—from Churchill and Patton to Hemingway and Pyle, from Hope and Lana Turner to Casey Stengel and Leo the Lip . . . Lindsey has woven a vivid, fast-paced and easy-reading story as comfortable as his earthy press box style and as colorful as his many-hued jackets."

—WILL GRIMSLEY
Special Correspondent, Associated Press

"Many of us tend to be a little leery of autobiographical books. We wonder how many hired pens were at work behind the scenes. But I happen to know that this is pure Lindsey Nelson talking to us. Lindsey dotted every 'i' and crossed every 't'; no ghosts hovered in the background. And what he has produced is not just a story of sports and sportscasting. It is also a story of the great Depression, of World War II, and of how a good man and his family turned the seeming tragedy of a retarded child into a triumph of the spirit."

—BEN BYRD
Sports Editor, *Knoxville Journal*

"Lindsey Nelson has succeeded where others have failed. He has brought the war back in all its phases; the heroism, the laughs and, finally, the dull horror and the sacrifice we know war to be." —DREW MIDDLETON
Columnist, The New York Times Syndicate

"I thoroughly enjoyed reading *Hello Everybody, I'm Lindsey Nelson.* The game of football has been honored by his talents as a broadcaster." —PEE WEE REESE

"Lindsey's book is excellent. I commend it."

—GENERAL WILLIAM C. WESTMORELAND

"As a youngster, I first began to follow the football fortunes of the Tennessee Volunteers through the radio broadcasts of Lindsey Nelson. They were informative and exciting. And so is *Hello Everybody, I'm Lindsey Nelson.* His intimate portrait of General Bob Neyland, one of football's all-time greatest coaches, is outstanding." —JOHNNY MAJORS
Head Football Coach, University of Tennessee

"One of the most engrossing, entertaining life stories I've ever read, written with keen perception, humor and love."

—FRED RUSSELL
Vice-President, *Nashville Banner;*
Chairman, Honors Court, National Football Hall of Fame; Member, Heisman Trophy Voting Committee